W9-CIG-443

Gramley Library
Salem Academy and College
Winston-Salem, N.C. 27108

Culture and Gender
in Nineteenth-Century Spain

Culture and Gender in Nineteenth-Century Spain

Edited by
LOU CHARNON-DEUTSCH
and
JO LABANYI

CLARENDON PRESS · OXFORD
1995

Gramley Library
Salem Academy and College
Winston-Salem, N.C. 27108

Oxford University Press, Walton Street, Oxford OX2 6DP
Oxford New York
Athens Auckland Bangkok Bombay
Calcutta Cape Town Dar es Salaam Delhi
Florence Hong Kong Istanbul Karachi
Kuala Lumpur Madras Madrid Melbourne
Mexico City Nairobi Paris Singapore
Taipei Tokyo Toronto
and associated companies in
Berlin Ibadan

Oxford is a trade mark of Oxford University Press

Published in the United States
by Oxford University Press Inc., New York

© The several contributors 1995
Introduction © Lou Charnon-Deutsch and Jo Labanyi 1995

All rights reserved. No part of this publication may be reproduced,
stored in a retrieval system, or transmitted, in any form or by any means,
without the prior permission in writing of Oxford University Press.
Within the UK, exceptions are allowed in respect of any fair dealing for the
purpose of research or private study, or criticism or review, as permitted
under the Copyright, Designs and Patents Act, 1988, or in the case of
reprographic reproduction in accordance with the terms of the licences
issued by the Copyright Licensing Agency. Enquiries concerning
reproduction outside these terms and in other countries should be
sent to the Rights Department, Oxford University Press,
at the address above

British Library Cataloguing in Publication Data
Data available

Library of Congress Cataloging in Publication Data
Culture and gender in nineteenth-century Spain / edited by Lou Charnon-
Deutsch and Jo Labanyi.
—(Oxford Hispanic studies)
Includes bibliographical references and index.
1. Spanish literature—19th century—History and criticism.
2. Spanish literature—Women authors—History and criticism. 3. Sex
role in literature. 4. Women in literature. 5. Spain—
Civilization—19th century. I. Charnon-Deutsch, Lou.
II. Labanyi, Jo. III. Series.
PQ6070.C84 1995 860.9'9287—dc20 94–43240
ISBN 0–19–815886–6

1 3 5 7 9 10 8 6 4 2

Typeset by Graphicraft Typesetters Ltd., Hong Kong
Printed in Great Britain
on acid-free paper by
Biddles Ltd, Guildford and King's Lynn

Oxford Hispanic Studies

General Editor: Paul Julian Smith

The last twenty years have seen a revolution in the humanities. On the one hand, there has been a massive influence on literary studies of other disciplines: philosophy, psychoanalysis, and anthropology. On the other, there has been a displacement of the boundaries of literary studies, an opening out on to other forms of expression: cinema, popular culture, and historical documentation.

The *Oxford Hispanic Studies* series reflects the fact that Hispanic studies are particularly well placed to take advantage of this revolution. Unlike those working in French or English studies, Hispanists have little reason to genuflect to a canon of European culture which has tended to exclude them. Historically, moreover, Hispanic societies tend to exhibit plurality and difference: thus Medieval Spain was the product of the three cultures of Jew, Moslem, and Christian; modern Spain is a federation of discrete autonomous regions; and Spanish America is a continent in which cultural identity must always be brought into question, can never be taken for granted.

The incursion of new models of critical theory into Spanish-speaking countries has been uneven. And while cultural studies in other language areas have moved through post-structuralism (Lacan, Derrida, Foucault) to create new disciplines focusing on gender, ethnicity, and homosexuality, it is only recently that Hispanists have contributed to the latest fields of enquiry. Now, however, there is an upsurge of exciting new work in both Europe and the Americas. *Oxford Hispanic Studies* is intended to provide a medium for writing engaged in and taking account of these developments. It serves both as a vehicle and a stimulus for innovative and challenging work in an important and rapidly changing field. The series aims to facilitate both the development of new approaches in Hispanic studies and the awareness of Hispanic studies in other subject areas. It embraces discussions of literary and non-literary cultural forms, and focuses on the publication of illuminating original research and theory.

Acknowledgements

The editors wish to thank the following for permission to reproduce the illustrations included in this volume: Phaidon Press (Plate 1); the Metropolitan Museum of Art, William H. Herriman Bequest (Plate 2); Oxford University Press Inc. (Plates 3 and 4); the Hemeroteca Municipal, Ayuntamiento de Madrid (Plate 5); the Frank Melville Memorial Library, State University of New York at Stony Brook (Plates 6, 8, 15); the University of Wisconsin-Madison Libraries (Plates 7, 9, 10, 11, 12, 14); and the Biblioteca Nacional, Madrid (Plate 13). The editors also thank *Dispositio* for permission to reprint substantial portions of Noel Valis's article 'La autobiografia como insulto' (1990), 1–25.

Contents

List of Plates

Contributors

MARYELLEN BIEDER is Professor of Spanish at Indiana University. She has published a book on Francisco Ayala and numerous articles on nineteenth- and twentieth-century fiction, particularly on the work of Pardo Bazán.

ALDA BLANCO is Associate Professor of Spanish at the University of Wisconsin-Madison. She has co-edited Galdós, *La de Bringas* (Madrid: Cátedra, 1983), edited two works by María Martínez Sierra, and published widely on nineteenth-century women writers. She is currently completing a book on women's fiction in mid-nineteenth-century Spain.

LOU CHARNON-DEUTSCH is Associate Professor of Spanish at the State University of New York at Stony Brook, and President of Feministas Unidas. Her books include *Gender and Representation: Women in Nineteenth-Century Spanish Realist Fiction* (Amsterdam: John Benjamins, 1990) and *Narratives of Desire: Nineteenth-Century Spanish Fiction by Women* (Penn State Press, 1994). She has published various articles on gender and nineteenth-century Spanish fiction, and is currently completing a book on illustrations of women in nineteenth-century Spanish periodicals.

STEPHEN M. HART is Associate Professor of Spanish at the University of Kentucky, and a former Lecturer in Spanish at Queen Mary and Westfield College, University of London. In addition to his wide-ranging articles on modern Spanish and Latin American literature, he is the editor of two books, including *Feminist Readings on Spanish and Latin-American Literature* (Lewiston: Edwin Mellen, 1991), and author of five others, including *White Ink: Essays on Modern Feminine Fiction in Spain and Latin America* (London: Tamesis, 1993).

CATHERINE JAGOE is Associate Professor of Spanish at Northern Illinois University. She has published various articles on gender in nineteenth-century Spanish narrative, and a book *Ambiguous Angels: Gender in the Novels of Galdós* (Berkeley, Calif.: University of California Press, 1994). She is currently co-editing *Sexualidad y género en España: una antología (1850–1900)* for publication by Siglo XXI.

SUSAN KIRKPATRICK is Professor of Spanish and Comparative Literature at the University of California, San Diego. In addition to a book on Larra and many articles on nineteenth- and twentieth- century Spanish fiction, she has published *Las Románticas: Women Writers and Subjectivity in Spain, 1835–1850* (Berkeley, Calif.: University of California Press, 1989; Spanish translation Madrid: Cátedra, 1991) and *Antología poética de escritoras del siglo XIX* (Madrid: Castalia, 1992). She is currently preparing a book on literary configurations of the seduction fantasy in late nineteenth-century Spain.

JO LABANYI is Reader in Modern Spanish and Latin American Literature at Birkbeck College, University of London. In addition to articles on nineteenth- and twentieth-century Spanish and Latin American fiction, she has published two books on contemporary Spanish fiction, edited a collective volume on Galdós, and translated Galdós's *Nazarín*. She is currently co-editing an introduction to Spanish cultural studies and completing *The Politics of the Family in the Spanish Realist Novel*, both for Oxford University Press.

ABIGAIL LEE SIX is Lecturer in Spanish at Queen Mary and Westfield College, University of London. She has published a book and several articles on Juan Goytisolo, and is preparing a book on non-verbal communication in the modern Spanish novel.

JAMES MANDRELL is Associate Professor of Spanish and Comparative Literature at Brandeis University. In addition to a wide range of articles on Spanish and Latin American literature, he is author of *Don Juan and the Point of Honour: Seduction, Patriarchal Society, and Literary Tradition* (University Park, Pa.: Pennsylvania State University Press, 1992).

GERALDINE M. SCANLON, formerly Lecturer in Spanish at King's College, University of London, is now an Honorary Research

Fellow based in Spain. Her main research areas are nineteenth-and early twentieth-century Spanish social history and literature. Her publications include articles on educational and women's history, as well as fiction. Her book *La polémica feminista en la España contemporánea (1868–1974)* (Madrid: Siglo XXI, 1976) is now in its second edition (Madrid: Akal, 1986).

ALISON SINCLAIR is Lecturer in Spanish at the University of Cambridge and Fellow of Clare College. Her books include *The Deceived Husband: A Kleinian Approach to the Literature of Infidelity* (Oxford: Oxford University Press, 1993). She has also published numerous articles on nineteenth- and twentieth-century Spanish fiction, poetry, and drama, and is currently preparing a collection of essays on *La Regenta*.

DIANE FAYE UREY is Professor of Spanish at Illinois State University. She has published numerous articles on nineteenth-century Spanish fiction, Galdós in particular; and is author of *Galdós and the Irony of Language* (Cambridge: Cambridge University Press, 1982), *The Novel Histories of Galdós* (Princeton, NJ: Princeton University Press, 1989), and a forthcoming book on Galdós's early *Episodios nacionales* and the formation of the Spanish reading public.

NOËL VALIS is Professor of Spanish at the Johns Hopkins University. She has published widely on nineteenth- and twentieth-century Spanish literature, including *The Decadent Vision in Leopoldo Alas* (Baton Rouge, La.: Louisiana State University Press, 1981) and *Leopoldo Alas (Clarín): An Annotated Bibliography* (London: Grant & Cutler, 1986). Her numerous editions include *In the Feminine Mode: Essays on Hispanic Women Writers* (London: Associated University Presses, 1990), Carolina Coronado, *Poesías* (Madrid: Castalia, 1991), and *'Malevolent Insemination' and Other Essays on Clarín* (Ann Arbor, Mich.: University of Michigan, 1990).

Introduction: Ain't I a Fluctuating Identity?

IN posing this question, a play on Sojourner Truth's 'Ain't I a woman?', Denise Riley issues a by now common plea 'for both a concentration on and a refusal of the identity of "women"' (Riley 1).[1] Questioning the category of 'women', its fictive, erratic status, has become one of the principal projects of recent feminist theory and criticism. Just as the vexing 'Woman' and the equally essentializing 'woman' have been challenged, feminists must now take care to define what we mean by 'women' and, equally important, what is meant by the 'we' that writes about categories of women. In the heady days of 1960s and 1970s liberal feminism 'we' was an unproblematic category supposedly designating all women everywhere. The determination of biological gender seemed straightforward (in the days before Judith Butler's *Gender Trouble*, Eve Sedgwick's *Epistemology of the Closet*, or Thomas Laqueur's *Making Sex*). 'Feminism' was used in the singular: whatever their differences, it was thought, oppression joined all women together into one great sorority, it was a 'pan-cultural fact' (Ortner 67). Even while femininity and masculinity were being explored and renegotiated in some academic as well as non-academic areas, studies on the images, activities, and victimization of women in various world cultures seemed to reinforce such essentializing notions as nurturing womanhood, aggressive masculinity, or innate feminine pacifism. The very fact of being a woman seemed to grant authority to speak about women in this global sense. Feminists, those feminists who had 'a room of their own', determined from that privileged space that women should 'write the body', not just be the body to somebody else. It was understood that the view from this room was framed by personal experiences, but many feminists misrecognized the contours of the frame from which such dicta could be issued, failing to understand the connection between writing the body and the body politics that had preceded this grand gesture.

Gradually it became evident (the evidence often coming from groups of women who did not choose necessarily to identify themselves in the first instance as feminists or even women) that vast categories of women were left beyond consideration in feminist discussions taking place within the academy. By not carefully historicizing the relation between the social, the political, and the sexual, by generally ignoring the connections between gender, class, and race and the equally complicated construction of male sexuality, many feminist projects had resorted to consoling goddess-worship, utopian, radical exclusionism, or its opposite, a celebration of androgyny. Others, attempting to deconstruct difference, retreated into psychoanalytic investigation that too often resulted in ahistorical, globalizing assumptions about sexual development and practice. As these retreats and consolations fail on the level of the social to theorize gender, many feminists are turning again to the local politics of gender production where there is still much work to be done on the politics of difference. There is a growing recognition, reflected in several of the following essays, that gender has to be viewed against the public spheres where political and national identities are inextricably bound together with gender ideology. Even though our categories and strategies are fraught with contradiction and difficult exclusions, there is still much to be gained by focusing not only on gender production and gender subversion as a *force majeure* in the formation of subjectivities, but on the relation between gender, race, and class.

Denise Riley (5) recommends that, to avoid deconstructive moves to transcend sex that have no political allegiances, we study the historical foundation of the instability of sexual categories, and the discursive formations that either establish or question the naturalism of sexuality. Collectively, these essays point in that direction, looking at a period in Spanish cultural history when the boundaries of gender were shifting and redefining themselves. It is of course customary to speak of gender trouble in the context of postmodern cultures and to think of nineteenth-century Spain as a vast, patriarchal landscape where configurations of gender were radically polarized and predictable. Some of the essays here examine the discursive formation of the female subject from within this patriarchal landscape. Others demonstrate that important boundaries between men and women, public and private, strong and weak, etc. were being challenged over the period covered in these essays. Just as Foucault argued that Victorian prohibitions against the subject of sex were accompanied by myriad incitements to speak everywhere and always about it, so we can see that the conspicuous gender polarizations of the nineteenth century were the effect of an increasing sexual categorization whose progress was neither smooth nor exempt from contradiction.

In *Making Sex: Body and Gender from the Greeks to Freud*, Thomas Laqueur studies how, in the eighteenth century, a single-sex model evident in medical texts beginning with Aristotle and Galen of Pergamum (second century)—according to which women were homologous to men, only with the male reproductive organs turned outside in—started to evolve into a two-sex model that we too often equate with a *natural* division of the sexes. By the nineteenth century, notions of sexual difference had become firmly established: not only were women's reproductive systems different from those of men; women were 'different in every conceivable aspect of body and soul, in every physical and moral aspect' (5). Sex became an ontological, not just a social category (8). Gender roles evolved in keeping with ever more generalized biological notions of women's physical and mental unsuitability for public roles. But Laqueur is quick to concede that the increasing legitimization of the two-sex model, with its resultant heightened gender polarity, did not mean that other, counter models simply faded away or were never produced, for 'at any given point of scientific knowledge a wide variety of contradictory cultural claims about sexual difference are possible' (175). The same is true for gender: even in nineteenth-century Spain, where gender polarization seems to be most glaring and unremitting, there are undercurrents that undermine its categorizations in many subtle ways. This is a key notion for understanding several of the essays in this collection which argue that Spain's sexual and gender polarizations were constantly problematized at the level of character development in both Romantic and realist texts. The sexual ambiguity of Julián (*Los pazos de Ulloa*) or Bonifacio (*Su único hijo*), for example, provides a platform from which to question ideal notions of gender in nineteenth-century culture. Ranging from the identity of women writers, as perceived by themselves and by male critics, to the textual construction of gender by writers of both sexes, these essays argue that there were different ways of being a woman or man, 'different densities of sexed being in operation' (Riley 6) that did not always conform to convention. Despite the debasement of the feminine seen on the manifest level of many of the texts studied here, there was a need on the part of some writers to tamper with the categories, to recognize the desirability of 'fluctuating identities' by questioning what it was and was not to be a woman or a man.

The essays that follow were written for this volume, with the exception of that by Noël Valis, an earlier version of which appeared in article form in *Dispositio* (1990) 15/40, 1–25. The 'we' that writes in this instance consists of female and male specialists in the study of Spanish culture, of American and British origin, teaching and writing in the United States, Britain, and Spain. Despite the range of approaches taken, the contributions build on a tradition of Anglo-American feminist criticism that is wary of essentialist definitions of the feminine and of women's writing. Our concern is, rather, to unsettle oppositional forms of thinking by showing how notions of sexual difference, in addition to containing a high degree of latent ambivalence, are always strategic constructions subject to contestation and renegotiation. The essays in this volume that make use of psychoanalytic theory elucidate particular historical moments in the production or interrogation of sexual difference, or show how qualities labelled as feminine and masculine pass to and fro between female and male characters in what at times comes close to a kind of competition for ownership.

The essays are arranged in chronological order of authors discussed, tracing a movement from the 1830s to the 1890s: a movement that is not one-directional but marked by hesitations, regressions, and contrary impulses. The first essay by Jo Labanyi charts the precarious construction in Romantic drama of an ideology of sexual difference that makes possible the acclimatization in Spain of liberal individualism. The next two essays discuss the problematic relation of the Romantic autobiographical genre to the gendering of subjectivity: Noël Valis shows how two provincial women poets writing in the 1840s, Carolina Coronado and Vicenta García Miranda, use autobiography to challenge contemporary male expectations of the female writer, and to break down the restricting opposition between public and private; while James Mandrell exposes the gender bias in autobiographical readings of Bécquer's work by male critics. Susan

Kirkpatrick reads the novels of Rosalía de Castro, better known for her poetry in Galician, as an extraordinary deconstruction of the fantasies of paternal seduction which lay at the heart of mid-nineteenth-century popular fiction, not to mention the later theories of Freud. The next two essays focus on the critical debates around women's writing in the mid- to late nineteenth century: Maryellen Bieder examines the cross-gendering of women's writing as masculine by male and female reviewers; Alda Blanco shows how the construction of a national literary canon by late nineteenth-century critics and their successors excluded women writers by defining them as imitators of foreign models.

The next four essays look at the treatment of gender in novels by Galdós and Alas. Diane Urey's discussion of the First Series of *Episodios nacionales* explores the notion of woman as muse and emblem, suggesting that she constitutes a shifting signifier which destabilizes fixed categories of truth; Catherine Jagoe shows how, in Galdós's late and understudied novel *Ángel Guerra*, the female muse becomes a monstrous destroyer of masculinity in a nightmarish inversion of sexual norms. A similar disturbing breakdown of sexual difference is traced in *La Regenta* by Alison Sinclair, who dissects the destructive exchange of male and female attributes by the Magistral and his mother; and in *Su único hijo* by Abigail Lee Six, who examines the use of voice and gaze to construct and subvert gender roles. The following two essays on Pardo Bazán look at fictional and non-fictional work: Stephen Hart argues that the Gothic plot of *Los pazos de Ulloa* opens up a feminine space threatening patriarchal and heterosexual norms; Geraldine Scanlon discusses Pardo Bazán's wide-ranging attention to women's issues—but not women's writing—in the cultural journal *Nuevo Teatro Crítico* that she ran, and wrote, in the 1890s. The final essay by Lou Charnon-Deutsch again focuses on journalism, commenting on the late nineteenth-century vogue for illustrations of Oriental and Andalusian women, and the anxieties about sexual difference which this construction of an exotic Other attempts to mediate.

Broadly speaking, the volume moves from early nineteenth-century concern with the need for sexual differentiation (offset by an erotic wish for fusion), through a long process of definition and negotiation of gender boundaries, to late nineteenth-century alarm (but also pleasure) at the seeming collapse of the boundaries that had been so laboriously and precariously erected. To call this a circular movement would be to impose an illusory neatness, but it is perhaps not coincidence that both the Romantic period and the *fin de siècle* posit norms of sexual difference against the counter-fantasy of an imagined Oriental eroticism. We many also note that in the 1830s the Orientalist fantasy is of the powerful woman, while in the 1890s it has become a dream of female submission. In her review of feminism in the late 1970s and early 1980s (*Around 1981*), Jane Gallop notes that theoretical work has recently moved in three new directions: away from an earlier Eurocentrism to questions of racial difference; away from the exclusive focus on women (gynocritics) to study of the wider issue of gender; and away from high literature to a less élitist, interdisciplinary cultural studies. The essays in this volume, in addition to discussing women's writing and the representation of women in canonical texts (fiction, poetry, and theatre), include discussion of race and region; of the problematic (de)construction of masculinity; and of popular fiction, criticism, journalism, and the visual arts. The approaches taken range over the disciplines of literary criticism, historiography, psychoanalysis, sociolinguistics, visual analysis, political theory, and anthropology. More work needs to be done in all the areas covered here, as well as on issues—like class—which we have only touched on. Texts—like women—are fluctuating identities that lend themselves to an endless process of interpretation and reinterpretation, not because 'anything goes', but because all readings—like the debates on gender discussed in this volume— are strategic.

NOTES

1. Sojourner Truth, the famous black abolitionist and freed slave, spoke out against the treatment of women at the 1851 Akron Convention, punctuating her speech with the refrain 'Ain't I a woman?'

WORKS CITED

FOUCAULT, MICHEL (1980). *The History of Sexuality*, i: *An Introduction*. New York: Vintage.
GALLOP, JANE (1992). *Around 1981 (Academic Feminist Literary Theory)*. New York: Routledge.
LAQUEUR, THOMAS (1990). *Making Sex. Body and Gender from the Greeks to Freud*. Cambridge, Mass.: Harvard University Press.

ORTNER, SHERRY B. (1974). 'Is Female to Male as Nature Is to Culture?', in
Michelle Z. Rosaldo and Louise Lamphere (eds.), *Woman, Culture and Society*.
Stanford, Calif.: Stanford University Press, 67–88.
RILEY, DENISE (1988). *Am I that Name? Feminism and the Category of 'Women' in
History*. Minneapolis: University of Minnesota Press.

I

Liberal Individualism and the Fear of the Feminine in Spanish Romantic Drama

Jo Labanyi

Romanticism—in Spain and elsewhere—has long been seen as the literary expression of liberalism. Even Derek Flitter, who argues that Spanish Romanticism was largely traditionalist, concedes that the works of 1834–7 were exceptional in their liberal militancy (5–49, 184). In this essay I shall examine the ways in which four major Spanish Romantic plays first staged during those years—*La conjuración de Venecia* (1834) by Martínez de la Rosa, *Don Álvaro o la fuerza del sino* (1835) by the Duque de Rivas, *El trovador* (1836) by García Gutiérrez, and *Los amantes de Teruel* (1837) by Hartzenbusch—dramatize the contradictions inherent in liberal individualism. In particular I wish to show how the latter cannot be understood without reference to gender. Martínez de la Rosa and Rivas, both prominent liberal statesmen, had firsthand knowledge of Britain and France as political *émigrés*; it was in those countries that liberal political theory was developed.[1] Hartzenbusch and García Gutiérrez were not active in liberal politics and were too young to have gone into exile in 1814–20 and 1820–34 (being born in 1806 and 1813 respectively). But their plays show an identical understanding of the construction of the individual subject, for liberal political theory was predicated on new models of the family and of sexual difference which became commonly accepted by the European bourgeoisie in the course of the eighteenth and early nineteenth centuries. I am not concerned here with the writers' personal experience of family life, but with fantasies of the family that allowed the concept of the individual subject to emerge.

In a discussion which foreshadows many of the points made

here, Stephen Hart persuasively reads the plots of Spanish Romantic plays as enactments of the Lacanian concept of the Name-of-the-Father, noting that the confrontation of the hero with his lover's father leads to the enforcement of paternal authority (11–12). Hart also notes that the father's tyranny is directed mainly against the daughter (8–9). In this essay I shall examine the four above-mentioned plays from a psychoanalytic perspective that is in disagreement with Lacanian theory: namely, the feminist critique of ego psychology outlined by Nancy Chodorow in *The Reproduction of Mothering and Feminism and Psychoanalytic Theory*, and developed by Jessica Benjamin in *The Bonds of Love*.[2] I hope to build on Hart's perception that Spanish Romantic plays dramatize the Oedipal scenario by arguing, with Chodorow and Benjamin, that any discussion of the latter must include not only father and son but also mother and daughter. The application to Romantic drama of Oedipal theory is not fortuitous for, when Freud elaborated his final version of the Oedipus complex in which the sons overthrow the Father of the Primal Horde to institute a regime based on fraternal rights, he was describing the ideals of the French Revolution: liberty, equality, fraternity. The self that emerges from the Freudian Oedipal trajectory is that of the autonomous individual posited by liberal political theory. The relevance of the Oedipus story to their own concerns did not escape Spanish Romantic playwrights and their contemporaries: Martínez de la Rosa wrote an *Edipo* during his exile in France just before writing *La conjuración de Venecia*, and Rivas's *Don Álvaro* was known to his friends as 'el *Edipo* del cristianismo'.[3]

In her book *The Sexual Contract*, Carole Pateman shows how liberal political theory arises out of the division between the public and private spheres first made by Locke in the late seventeenth century. Arguing against prevailing patriarchal theory, which maintained that both state and family were governed by paternal right transmitted by kinship, Locke claimed that this natural law applied only in the private sphere, and that the public sphere was subject to the law of contract. However, only free individuals could make legally binding contracts, and to be a free individual one had to be a property owner and thus one's own 'master'. The gender-specific term is not fortuitous, for women were legally defined as dependants and enjoyed limited property rights; as a result only men had the right to make contracts that allowed entry into the public sphere. Liberal contract theory replaces patriarchal theory, but it reinforces patriarchy by confining women to the family. This ideological shift coincides with the beginnings of capitalist development, which take away from the household its former economic function as a unit of production, creating a further split according to which production takes place in the public sphere, while the private sphere is reserved for the natural process of reproduction. The wife's role becomes limited to motherhood. The end of the household as a productive unit also means that the term 'family', which previously included all those involved in domestic output whether related by blood or not, now comes to refer to the minimum kinship unit of husband, wife, and children. In the mid-eighteenth century Rousseau modified this scheme, suggesting that the family, like the state, was governed by social contract: in this case, the marriage contract. But his notion of social contract as an improvement on nature confirmed the equation of the family with child-rearing: the difference for Rousseau was that women needed to be taught to fulfil their 'natural' duties as mothers.[4] The conceptual model of the family dominant by the end of the eighteenth century supposes that children will be brought up by one woman, their mother; and that the father's role is outside the family in the public sphere.

It is not necessary to prove that such family arrangements had become the norm in Spain by the 1830s; indeed, the greater the gap between theory and practice, the greater the insistence on the model is likely to be. Lilian Furst notes that the English Romantics laid less stress on individualism than their French counterparts, for they came from a political and religious tradition which took individualism for granted (60). Susan Kirkpatrick has suggested that the instability of the individual subject shown in *Don Álvaro* is a sign of Spain's lack of a Protestant individualist tradition (118). It seems logical to suppose that Spanish Romantic playwrights dramatize the individual's relation to the family unit so explicitly precisely because liberal values were not yet firmly established in Spain.

Raymond Williams notes that the term 'individual' (from the Latin *individuus* meaning 'indivisible') was first used to mean a single member of a species by Locke, and that it acquired the meaning of separateness from others only in the late eighteenth century; the term 'individualism' is an early nineteenth-century coinage (161–5). Liberal political theory equates selfhood with individuality in this sense of separateness. Chodorow (1989) and Benjamin argue that the modern Western concept of the individual born in the Romantic period is, in effect, that of the son who separates from the mother.[5] Such 'individuation' (to use the psychoanalytic term)is made desirable, even necessary, by the nuclear family in which the child is reared exclusively by the mother, who thus appears to the child to be all-powerful and stifling. Freudian theory posits an initial oneness of the child with the mother; Chodorow suggests that Freud was here himself responding to fantasies of maternal omnipotence encouraged by a family structure in which mothers have sole responsibility for parenting. She also notes that Lacan perpetuates such fantasies with his notion that the child's entry into the Symbolic order through the agency of language (the Name-of-the-Father) marks its exit from an initial pre-linguistic undifferentiation represented by the mother/child dyad. For both Freud and Lacan, the Oedipus complex rescues the child from this lack of differentiation through the intervention of the father, who breaks the child's primary identification with the mother. The Oedipal incest taboo declares sameness, associated with the feminine, to be a threat; and equates the self with difference in the guise of the father, whose role outside the home makes him an image of separateness. If the child is male, he will go on to assume the father's role as an individualized subject. There is, of course, a catch here, as Freud and Lacan acknowledge: by identifying with the father, the son internalizes paternal law and undermines the autonomy which identification with the father gave him in the first place. Freud and Lacan are mainly concerned with the father's role in the Oedipal scenario, and consequently with the problem of authority; female psychoanalysts have stressed the pre-Oedipal stage, where the mother's role is paramount and where the key issue is that of separation. We shall see how the two issues connect.

Chodorow's work is important for pointing out that Freudian Oedipal theory equates individuation with rejection of the mother and consequently of the feminine. The logic of Freud's notion of primary unity with the mother is that both sexes originally identify with the feminine or, as Chodorow puts it, are 'matrisexual'. Since, for Freud, individuation consists in the assumption of sexual difference, this means that the boy can define his emergent

Gramley Library
Salem Academy and College
Winston-Salem, N.C. 27108

masculinity only as not being like the mother. This turns upside down Freud's idea that both boys and girls start life as 'little men', and that the role of the Oedipus complex is to turn the girl away from this primary masculinity. It also turns on its head the accepted notion, theorized by Simone de Beauvoir in *Le Deuxième Sexe*, that woman is difined as man's Other. Chodorow's analysis suggests that it is femininity that is primary, and masculinity that is constructed as the opposite of the feminine. As she puts it: masculinity, unlike femininity, has to be learnt. The precariousness of this negatively defined masculinity, based on not being like the mother, logically leads men to devalue activities and qualities labelled as feminine, in order to assert their own insecure sense of separate identity. This, Chodorow points out, means devaluing not only women but the primary feminine part of the male self. The modern Western concept of the autonomus individual, being based on the need to differentiate from the mother, opposes selfhood to femininity, and construes the latter as a dangerous regressive force threatening to engulf the male ego.

Girls, according to Chodorow, do not have the problem of needing to repudiate their primary gender identification in order to assume a heterosexual orientation; their problem is that of over-identifying with the mother to the point of not achieving a separate sense of self at all. The problem for both men and women is that our culture privileges the masculine values of independence, separateness, and differentiation, with the result that dependence, relationship, and sameness are seen as a threat to the autonomy of the self. Chodorow notes that the genuine experience of difference involves the ability to recognize the other's subjectivity. It is only when the sense of separate selfhood is not sufficiently strong that boundaries have to be artificially erected and difference turned into an emotional, moral, or political imperative.

Benjamin takes up this last point of Chodorow, arguing that the Oedipal model needs to be reformulated so as to reconcile differentiation with recognition of the other as a subject. She stresses the dangers of Freud's view of the mother as a regressive, primitive force, pointing out that his reading of the Oedipus myth suppresses the fact that Oedipus' father tried to kill him as a child, and projects the negative qualities of the 'archaic, dangerous father' on to the mother (146). Benjamin notes that the regression to primary oneness with the feminine that is feared by the male—what Freud called 'the oceanic feeling' or sense of engulfment—is at the same time actively sought by him in the experience of love. Sexual union becomes for the male an annihilation of the self that is both terrifying and pleasurable. Benjamin quotes Bataille's contention that eroticism consists in the violation of the body's boundaries in order to plunge into the 'sea of death' represented by the loss of separateness (63–4).

Benjamin's main contribution is her analysis of the sado-masochistic tendencies inherent in male–female relations, which she sees as the inevitable outcome of our adherence to the Freudiam Oedipal scheme whereby selfhood is equated with separation from the feminine. This produces a 'fault line' in both male and female development, since the male can assert his individuality only by devaluing the feminine, and the female can achieve subject status only by rejecting her original same-gender identification and turning to the father; on being refused recognition by the father (whose masculinity depends on his repudiation of femininity), the girl is forced back to identification with the mother, now perceived through masculine eyes as a devalued object. This, Benjamin observes, gives girls a propensity to fall in love with idealized hero figures, through whom they can vicariously live out their frustrated selfhood while at the same time confirming their feminine object status. Conversely, men tend to turn the women they fall in love with into objects, by degrading them or idealizing them.

Benjamin spends some time discussing Hegel's master–slave dialectic (elaborated in 1806 at the time liberalism was consolidating itself as a political system), noting that, like Freud, Hegel assumes that relations with others are a threat to individual autonomy. As she points out, the master–slave dialectic—in which the master denies the slave's subjectivity so as to assert his own autonomy, and the slave turns herself into an object for the master so as to experience agency through him—is self-defeating because they are locked in a form of bondage that denies the freedom of both. Finally Benjamin notes that, in the Oedipal scheme, the male achieves autonomy at the expense of a 'guilty identification' with paternal domination not just because, as Freud and Lacan recognize, he limits his own freedom by internalizing paternal authority, but because he becomes a free subject by perpetuating a system that refuses recognition to women.

The use of masks and aliases in Spanish Romantic drama

makes identity problematic, as Hart notes (16–17), but at a
more fundamental level it raises the issue of recognition. In
particular, it relates identity to recognition of the other. Benjamin
(78) observes that girls, in denying their own selfhood by identifying with a mother defined as object, learn to give recognition
without receiving it. In these plays, when the hero is with the
heroine he takes his mask off, for she confers identity on him by
looking at him. He adopts a mask or alias to protect himself
from the gaze of other men, whose subjecthood makes them a
threat to his autonomy. Kirkpatrick points out that, in *Don Álvaro*,
Leonor is fleeing the gaze of others (120): when a woman is
looked at, she is reduced to object status. In *Los amantes de Teruel*,
Isabel shuns Marsilla's gaze which confirms a negative image of
her (160). In *La conjuración de Venecia*, Laura is so terrified of
being seen she feels even the statues of the dead threaten her
with their gaze (269). Manrique's gaze in *El trovador* literally
causes Leonor to lose consciousness (141). At the end of *Don
Álvaro*, Leonor's brother Alfonso sees only the degraded image of
her he has formed in his mind. The use by Romantic playwrights of the conventions of the honour code stresses the debasement of the feminine that is the other side of the liberal
concept of the autonomous individual.[6]

In a converse form of objectification, when Leonor's lover
Álvaro is reunited with her in this final scene, he sees an idealized phantom: '¡Es un espectro! . . . ¡Imagen adorada!' [It's a
ghost! . . . Adored image!] (168). When Isabel and Marsilla finally
meet in *Los amantes de Teruel*, he likewise sees an idol: '¡Prenda
adorada! . . . ¡Gloria mía!' [Adored treasure! . . . My glory!] (159).
All the heroes of these plays repeatedly use the term 'angel',
with its Victorian connotations of the 'angel of the house', when
addressing their lovers.[7] In *La conjuración de Venecia*, Rugiero
explicitly says to Laura: 'tú no eres una mujer; eres un ángel'
[you aren't a woman; you're an angel] (277). When Laura finds
Rugiero at the end of the play, her one act is to give him a
portrait of herself: an objectified image (335). It is in portrait
form that Leonor's brother Carlos will 'recognize' her in *Don
Álvaro*. The number of times the lovers see each other in these
plays is extraordinarily limited, for their love is based not on
recognition but on its lack. The recognition scenes that do take
place are between the hero and his father (or, in *El trovador*,
brother). Even in *Don Álvaro*, where the hero knows his identity

from the start, it is the episode where Alfonso provides him with new information about his father that counts as the recognition scene, rather than the final encounter with Leonor, which, far from enhancing the subjecthood of either, leads to their death.

In this play and in *Los amantes de Teruel*, where the hero's identity is also known from the start, concealed identity takes the form of the cross-dressing of a female character. In *Don Álvaro* Leonor dresses as a man first when escaping from her brother Carlos, and second when she becomes a hermit wearing the Franciscan habit. Paul Johnson reminds us that strict gender differentiation in dress, with men wearing trousers and dark colours, only became standardized in Europe in the first two decades of the nineteenth century, and that it remained common for women to dress as men when travelling (457–9, 488–9). The plays discussed here, being set in earlier periods (from the thirteenth to the mid-eighteenth centuries), require costumes that would have given their heroes a feminine appearance in the eyes of the contemporary audience. By dressing as a man, Leonor visually confirms the fact that she has fled the home for the outside world. Separation from roots does not give her the autonomy it would give a man but makes her a non-being: her penance in the hermitage is described as an entombment. The cross-dressing of the Moorish Sultana Zulima in *Los amantes de Teruel* raises different issues: as an Oriental woman, she illustrates a powerful, primitive femininity from which Marsilla must extricate himself to become a free individual. Her cross-dressing ensures that her agency is read as a usurpation (at the start of the play, she literally usurps her absent husband's power). The play begins with Zulima in control and Marsilla languishing womanlike in her bed,[8] to make the point that the hero's freedom depends on his attainment of 'proper' sexual difference by escaping Zulima's feminizing clutches and marrying Isabel, whose submission confers heroic status on him.

The medieval settings used in all these plays except *Don Álvaro* allow Islamic culture to be used as an image of threatening undifferentiated sexuality, as opposed to Christian Spain, where the roles of the sexes are clearly opposed. In addition, they offer the image of a society riven by frontier wars, whether with the Moors or Turks: this can be read as a symbolic representation of the need for boundaries to give definition to the self. In practice, both Moors and Christians move from one side of the

frontier to the other with surprising ease, suggesting that it is
largely a fiction. Part of *Don Álvaro* is set in eighteenth-century
Naples, where the Spaniards are fighting Imperial German troops.
The heroes need to assert their prowess in war and military
conquest, for their subjecthood depends on their ability to subjugate or eliminate the Other. The statutory duel scenes reduce
relationship to the violent penetration of bodily boundaries. The
duels are between men who in normal circumstances would be
friends, if not brothers or brothers-in-law: in this sense they are
linked to the internecine civil strife that also typifies these plays.
In addition to the enemy without, there is the enemy within.
The repeated motif of treachery poses the problem of the threat
of sameness: the traitor is the ally turned enemy. In *La conjuración
de Venecia*, the internecine strife is between father and son; in *El
trovador*, between brothers. The medieval Mediterranean world
and particularly medieval Spain offer the perfect scenario of
frontier war with an alien culture (Islam), plus civil war against
one's kin.[9] The self is defined in opposition to the Other, but
also by combating sameness. Identity depends on the establish-
ment, and maintenance, of difference.

The most striking common feature of these four plays is the
separation of the hero from his parents: a separation which is
felt as tragic but which allows him to assert his independence.
In *La conjuración de Venecia* and *El trovador*, the separation takes
the form of an Oedipal ignorance of origins, which leads the
hero unwittingly to take up arms against his father and brother
respectively (the brother having inherited the father's title). The
implication is that the hero would not have challenged paternal
authority had he recognized it as such. Indeed *La conjuración de
Venecia* ends with Rugiero pleading for his father's recognition,
forgetting his lover Laura in the process. The fact that his father
is the Grand Inquisitor makes it clear that final identification
with the father is achieved at the cost of insertion into a system
of domination. In this play as in *El trovador*, it is the father or
father-substitute who, unknowingly but still unjustly, orders the
son's death. This reversal of the Oedipal story (in which the son
unwittingly kills the father) suggests that the Romantic playwrights have a more negative view of paternal authority than
Freud. But they concur with Freud in seeing identification with
the father as the goal of the son's trajectory: all four plays end
with the reunion of father and son, or the son's recognition of
the father and/or the father's recognition of the son.

In *Don Álvaro* and *Los amantes de Teruel*, where separation from parents—though equally drastic—is not accompanied by ignorance of origins, there is no rebellion against the father (unless one counts as such Marsilla's refusal to obey his father's command to respect Isabel's marriage to another; the father however remains his ally). Don Álvaro's chief objective is to vindicate his father's name: before his death he learns that the latter, restored to authority and wealth, has named him his heir. In all four plays the stress is on separation from the father (or father-substitute) rather than on rebellion against his authority. And in each case, the final reconciliation is with a father (or father-substitute) whose wife is dead or never mentioned or, in *Don Álvaro*, racially alien. The paternal order is one in which women, if they exist at all, are of inferior status and at the same time idealized: Don Álvaro's mother, as an Inca princess, is a perfect example of this contradictory objectification which declares her both inferior and superior, but not a subject of equal standing. (An alternative rumour makes Álvaro the bastard of a grandee of Spain and a Moorish queen, which amounts to the same thing.) By ending with the son's *rapprochement* with the father and leaving the mother out of the picture, the plays make it clear that autonomy is achieved by final identification with the father while the primary bond with the mother remains severed.

The equation of the mother with the primitive found in *Don Álvaro* occurs even more dramatically in *El trovador* with Manrique's supposed mother Azucena, a gypsy whose mother was burnt at the stake for witchcraft and who herself is guilty of a horrendous crime. Manrique is saved—too late—from his primary identification with this monstrous mother, who has ruined his prospects by clinging to him as her son, by the revelation of his real parental origins. It does not matter that he does not live to benefit from the revelation, because the audience is liberated from this powerful incarnation of the Terrible Mother. Or is it? The play ends with Azucena's death, but her closing words 'Ya estás vengada' [You are avenged at last] suggest alarmingly that her primary loyalty is to her mother, who can be avenged only by the sacrifice of her 'son'. We are left with the primary bond of two women, mother and daughter, who represent the dissolution of the family: neither has a father or husband; as nomads they negate the concept of home; both are guilty, by imputation or fact, of infanticide. The counterpoint to the Romantic hero's struggle for selfhood is the omnipotent, devouring, archaic mother. David Punter has noted the Romantic fascination with the possibility of self-authorship, in which the male writer appropriates the mother's reproductive powers (94, 141). In the plays discussed here, it is the hero who tries to exorcize the mother's powers by separating from origins and creating himself from zero, in an act of rebirthing that writes the mother out of the story.

If the incestuous threat of primary identification with the mother is successfully overcome, it nevertheless reasserts itself in *Los amantes de Teruel* and *La conjuración de Venecia* in the form of incest with a figurative sister or first cousin. Diane Long Hoeveler suggests that, in Romantic writing, figurative incest with a sister figure functions as a deflection of the incestuous identification with the mother.[10] This is clearly the case with the first cousins in *La conjuración de Venecia*: Laura insists she was born to make Rugiero forget the loss of his mother (277). Rugiero is horrified to discover his father and Laura's are brothers, and from this moment his obsession with her is replaced by that with his father: the female lover represents an incestuous sameness that must be replaced by the father as an image of separation. In *Los amantes de Teruel*, it is the fact that Marsilla and Isabel have been brought up together from the cradle that attracts them to each other. Marsilla describes them as 'un alma en dos partida' [one soul split in two] (94). Their sameness is explicitly linked to an incestuous lack of differentiation not only between figurative brother and sister but also between infant and mother: Marsilla insists their embrace will be 'el abrazo | de un hermano dulcísimo a su hermana, | el ósculo será que tantas veces | cambió feliz en la materna falda | nuestro amor infantil' [the embrace | of a tender brother with his sister, | the kiss so many times | blissfully exchanged in the maternal lap | by our childhood love] (162). But this bond of sameness is fatal to him because he literally cannot live without her: he dies when she repudiates him. Isabel utters the fatal words of rejection when Marsilla accuses her of putting her love for her mother before her love for him: as in *El trovador*, the mother–daughter bond is implicated in the hero's death.

Perhaps the most remarkable feature of these plays is that they pay as much attention to the plight of the heroine as to that of the hero. The plot structure follows the hero's search for subjecthood, but in all four cases this is related to the heroine's reduction to object status. His proper attainment of masculinity is shown to be dependent on her proper attainment of femininity; as in the Oedipal scenario, individuation is synonymous with sexual differentiation. But in practice individuation is achieved only by the male; the heroine attains femininity by identifying with the mother as devalued object and renouncing the self. It could be argued that the plays are concerned with the heroine's selflessness simply as the precondition for the hero's autonomy. But considerable attention is given to the painful process whereby the daughter's attempt to separate is thwarted by the father's refusal of recognition, which sends her back to a negative identification with the mother.

In all the plays except *Los amantes de Teruel*, the heroine's mother is dead and therefore necessarily lacks subjecthood. In *El trovador*, where the heroine's father is also dead, this forces her into dependence on a brother who regards it as his right to dispose of her. Leonor seems to hold her mother responsible for her brother's despotism: 'que me dio mi madre en vos | en vez de amigo un tirano' [for my mother gave me in you | a tyrant instead of a friend] (118). Refusal of recognition by the brother, as father-substitute, leads her to devalue the mother who is her model of femininity. In the other three plays, the relationship between daughter and father is more complicated. In *Don Álvaro* and *La conjuración de Venecia*, the father adores the daughter. In *Don Álvaro* this does not prevent him from refusing to recognize her independence—the right to dispose of herself as she wishes—for this adoration turns her into a semi-incestuous idealized substitute for his dead wife; he himself describes his devotion to his daughter as a form of 'gallantry' (59). Leonor has internalized this attitude, identifying with an idealized image of her dead mother which the maid makes clear bears no resemblance to the haughty, ill-tempered person she actually was (63). This identification with a dead mother, coupled with her father's rejection of her as he dies, logically leads Leonor to opt for a life of entombment. A similar situation holds in *La conjuración de Venecia*, where the father adores his daughter so much that he forgives her for disposing of herself without consulting him (he was, after all, presumed dead at the time). But this does not constitute genuine recognition of her subjecthood because he persists in treating her as an objectified mirror-image (portrait) of his dead wife: 'En mi hija veía el retrato de mi pobre Constanza' [In my daughter

I saw the portrait of my poor Constanza] (296). Laura in turn
will identify with this idealized dead mother, who establishes an
equation in her mind between femininity and suffering ('my
poor Constanza'), indeed death. It is logical that she should
suggest the family pantheon to Rugiero as an amorous rendezvous. In all of these three plays the refusal (in differing degrees)
of recognition by the father and consequent identification with
a dead mother lead the heroines to subjugate their will to an
idealized man of action, who confirms their own passivity by
contrast and allows them to live out their frustrated desire for
agency by becoming his helpmeet. This idealization of the hero
verges on the idolatrous in *Don Álvaro* and *El trovador*, where the
two Leonors, on their lover's presumed death, replace him with
God, opting for the religious life. The sacrilegious rivalry between love of God and love of the hero is explicitly recognized
by Leonor in *El trovador* (150): her idolatry leads her to the
ultimate self-debasement of condemning herself to hell by committing suicide to save him.

The most interesting depiction of the heroine as daughter
occurs in *Los amantes de Teruel*, where Hartzenbusch departs from
previous versions of the legend by inventing a mother for Isabel.
Here the mother is not dead but debased by having committed
adultery.[11] This has led her to adopt a life of penance, renouncing motherhood to tend the sick, leaving the home to live in a
ruined Gothic hermitage at the bottom of the garden, and exchanging feminine dress for a penitent's habit. As when Leonor
in *Don Álvaro* takes to the roads and renounces feminine dress,
the result is not acquisition of masculine agency but simply loss
of femininity. The relationship between mother and daughter is
extremely complex. Isabel's love for Marsilla is clearly an extension of primary identification with the 'maternal lap' where both
were reared. But at the start of the play she regards her mother
as an enemy and ally of the father who refuses recognition of her
independent will. Then, when her mother gives in to her maternal sentiments and promises to support Isabel against her father, Isabel prostrates herself at her feet, declaring she had not
known such happiness since even before Marsilla left: primary
identification with the mother asserts itself over heterosexual
love. When Isabel discovers Rodrigo is threatening to publish
her mother's adulterous letters if she refuses him, she takes identification with the mother to the point of agreeing to marry a

blackmailer, in a renunciation of self which she describes as going to the 'grave' (129). What is interesting in this play is that it shows the different stages of Chodorow's and Benjamin's version of the Oedipal trajectory, as the daughter moves away from primary identification with the mother, only to be forced back into it when the father refuses her recognition, the result being the loss of subjecthood that identification with a degraded feminine image entails.

The woman's loss of self is in these plays the necessary foil to a male autonomy achieved by separating from the feminine, but all four plays end with the death of both hero and heroine (*La conjuración de Venecia* condemns Laura to mere loss of consciousness). For the male trajectory is ultimately as self-destructive as the female. The plays trace the hero's efforts to assert his independence, yet they are full of images of captivity. Favourite locations are castles, dungeons, and tombs, not to mention prison cells, monk's cells, and convent cells. In her book *Romantic Imprisonment*, Nina Auerbach notes that 'the Romantic imagination is in large part an imagination of confinement' (7).[12] Auerbach is chiefly concerned with the imprisonment of women; in Spanish Romantic drama, while the heroines may spend some time in a convent cell, it is the male heroes who are repeatedly incarcerated or taken captive. Furst notes that Romantic heroes 'condemn themselves to a life sentence within the prison of their own egocentricity' (97). A concept of the self based on separation necessarily equates autonomy with solitary confinement. The incarcerations in these plays curiously seem to be the other side of the hero's independence, for they save him from the danger of relationship with others. In the case of *Don Álvaro*, it is the hero's parents who are imprisoned, with the result that he is separated from them: despite the fact that he is born in a dungeon, their captivity gives him autonomy. In *La conjuración de Venecia*, the hero's mother is killed while being taken captive, freeing the son from primary maternal identification; as a result he is brought up in captivity, but this allows him to separate from his Grand Inquisitor father. Manrique's kidnapping by Azucena in *El trovador* and Marsilla's captivity in Moorish Valencia in *Los amantes de Teruel* put them in the power of terrible, primitive women, but also give them the opportunity to separate from family origins and prove their own worth.

Marsilla's captivity in Valencia has the additional advantage of postponing the desired union with Isabel. The plots of all four plays take the form of a succession of impediments, mostly in the form of imprisonment, placed in the way of the hero's union with the heroine, to the extent that one feels the dramatists are trying to save their heroes from fusion with the feminine. Hart notes that Spanish Romantic plays are governed by the logic of obstacle love, the obstacle being for him the Name-of-the-Father (10–11). I suggest that it is not so much that the heroes desire what is forbidden, as that they desire what they most fear: a return to the primary identification with the feminine from which they have separated to achieve subjecthood. The heroes are torn between desire to break out of the captivity of solitary confinement that is the other side of autonomy, and fear of falling captive to the feminine. Love offers the promise of a return to infantile undifferentiation, as is made explicit in *Los amantes de Teruel*, but at the cost of loss of self. To avoid engulfment, the heroes turn love into a form of conquest in which the female lover is emotionally enslaved, if not physically kidnapped as in *Don Álvaro* and *El trovador*. But, as Benjamin shows, the master–slave dialectic is self-defeating. In reducing the heroine to subservience, the hero makes her an appendage, destroying the separateness that guaranteed his autonomy. Conversely, submission to the hero allows the heroine to live through him, at the expense of having no life without him. The bonds of love place both hero and heroine in a double bind.

Auerbach notes that Romantic narrative is structured in terms of 'the double prison, in which a journey of apparent liberation from captivity leads only to more implacable arrest' (6). Here, the heroes struggle to break free of the bonds of solitary confinement, only to fall prey to the bonds of love: a form of bondage that is particularly insidious because it consists in the dissolution, rather than erection, of boundaries. Love, as a dissolving agent, is what enables the heroes to break the chains of the self; it is described via destructive images of laceration, burning, and drowning. In *Los amantes de Teruel* Marsilla, after ripping apart a succession of chains and ropes, succumbs to love in the form of a 'mortal veneno [que] rompe, rompe, me rompe las entrañas' [mortal poison [that] tears, tears, tears at my entrails] (164). *El trovador* is dominated by the fear of burning: being burnt at the stake, being consumed by passion. In *La conjuración de Venecia*, the boatman rowing Rugiero to his tryst with Laura sings of Leander drowning in the Hellespont: Rugiero and Laura appropriately embrace on a tomb. The water imagery intensifies towards the end of *Don Álvaro*: Álvaro talks of turning the river of blood that separates him from Leonor into a sea (141); before the final holocaust Hermano Melitón comments, 'Va a llover a mares. . . . Hoy estamos de marea alta' [There's going to be a deluge. . . . We're in for high water today] (161). One is reminded of Bataille's notion (quoted by Benjamin) that eroticism, in violating the body's boundaries, plunges the individual into a 'sea of death'. The hero's and heroine's statutory death (or at least unconsciousness) as the curtain falls is not yet another obstacle frustrating their union: it is the only form that love can take in an individualistic ideology which regards fusion with the feminine as loss of self. The violence of the various forms of *Liebestod* in these plays reinforces the sense of violation of bodily boundaries. (In *Los amantes de Teruel* the violence is expressed solely at the level of language: appropriately, for the message of this play is that words can kill.) The fact that a large number of these deaths are self-inflicted—something deeply shocking in a Catholic culture—shows that the heroes and heroines desire their own annihilation. The plays illustrate Benjamin's analysis of the process that creates female masochism. But the view of heterosexual union as engulfment by the feminine leads the heroes also to equate desire with a masochistic urge to self-destruction. Love does indeed feminize the hero; and feminization means, for both hero and heroine, metaphorical if not literal suicide.

These plays give a terrible view of the dangers of relations between the sexes. But they also illustrate the destructiveness of the liberal notion that selfhood depends on separation from the feminine. The attention paid to mothers and daughters as well as to fathers and sons implies a subtle awareness of the gendered nature of subject formation. It would probably be a mistake to suppose that, in their attention to the daughter–parent relationship, Spanish Romantic dramatists are criticizing the equation of femininity with selflessness. Nevertheless their depiction of the daughter's Oedipal trajectory is in many ways more perceptive than so hesitantly and unsatisfactorily attempted by Freud.

NOTES

1. Martínez de la Rosa spent 1810–11 in London negotiating arms shipments for the Spanish Independence struggle, and lived in exile in France from 1823 to 1831 (and again 1840–3). His political writings are based on the thought of Burke and Bentham; the latter, whom he met, was consulted by Spanish liberals over the drafting of the 1812 Cádiz Constitution. Martínez de la Rosa was parliamentary deputy for Granada 1812–14 and 1820–2, when he was appointed Prime Minister till exiled the following year. He was again Prime Minister 1833–5, and leader of the Moderate Party 1837–9. He subsequently served as Ambassador in Paris, Foreign Minister, Ambassador in Rome, President of Congress, and on his death in 1862 was President of the Council of State. Rivas fought in Wellington's army during the War of Independence, and lived in exile in London 1824–5, in British-controlled Malta 1825–30, and in France 1830–4. He was parliamentary deputy for Córdoba 1822–3, and in 1836 briefly served as Minister of the Interior. He would go on to serve as Senator for Córdoba, Ambassador in Naples, Prime Minister (briefly in 1854), and Ambassador in Paris. He resigned the post of President of the Council of State in 1864, a year before his death. Biographical information is given in Navas Ruiz. For Spanish liberals' contacts with Britain see Llorens, who reminds us that the word 'liberal' was first used in its political sense in Cádiz in 1811, from there passing to England and France (13).

2. Although published in 1989, Chodorow's *Feminism and Psychoanalytic Theory* consists of essays which appeared in article form before Benjamin's *The Bonds of Love*, first published in 1988. I give a general summary of both writers' ideas, with specific reference to certain points made by Benjamin.

3. See Sarrailh's introduction to Martínez de la Rosa p. xxv; and Alberto Sánchez's edition of *Don Álvaro*, 27.

4. Pateman notes that Freud writes his own version of social contract theory (12). For an excellent account of earlier concepts of the family as a unit of production, with frequent reference to Spain, see Casey.

5. Chodorow and Benjamin have been accused of giving an essentialist account of mother–child relations. Although Chodorow regards mothering of some kind as a universal phenomenon, she makes it clear that the particular model of the family she is using is historically specific (1989: 4–5, 32, 53, 57). Benjamin is less clear on this point but notes that the individualism which she finds a problem is specific to modern culture (25). It is as a description of the nuclear family which becomes dominant at the end of the 18th cent. that I read their theories. For a summary of the arguments against Chodorow and Benjamin, see McNay 92–7.

6. Kirkpatrick notes that the honour code turns Leonor in *Don Álvaro* into a 'signo degradado' (120).

7. For the use of the 'angel in the house' topos in 19th-cent. Spain, see Aldaraca.

8. Kirkpatrick notes that until 1800 Spanish women normally sat on 'Moorish' cushions while men sat on chairs, reinforcing the associations of Arab culture with a 'feminine' reclining position (65).

9. Flitter sees Spanish Romantic writers' medievalism and appeal to Golden Age drama as signs of their traditionalism. In these four plays at least, the medieval settings and use of the honour convention contribute to the dramatization of the liberal concept of the autonomous self.

10. Mellor suggests that the sister-bride motif found in Romantic writing is an attempt to turn the female lover into a mirror of the male self, thus incorporating her and denying her independence (25).
11. Iranzo notes that, in editions after the first, Hartzenbusch eliminated the actual word 'adultery'. See her edition of the play 122 n. 23.
12. See Punter for an analysis of the entrapment of the female by the male in the Gothic novel (73–83). Mellor discusses the enslavement of the female lover by the male (26).

WORKS CITED

ALDARACA, BRIDGET (1992). *'El ángel del hogar': Galdós and the Ideology of Domesticity in Spain.* Chapel Hill, NC: North Carolina University Press.
AUERBACH, NINA (1986). *Romantic Imprisonment: Women and Other Glorified Outcasts.* New York: Columbia University Press.
BENJAMIN, JESSICA (1990). *The Bonds of Love: Psychoanalysis, Feminism and the Problem of Domination* (1988). London: Virago.
CASEY, JAMES (1989). *The History of the Family.* Oxford: Blackwell.
CHODOROW, NANCY (1978). *The Reproduction of Mothering: Psychoanalysis and the Sociology of Gender.* Berkeley, Calif.: University of California Press.
—— (1989). *Feminism and Psychoanalytic Theory.* New Haven, Conn.: Yale University Press.
FLITTER, DEREK (1992). *Spanish Romantic Literary Theory and Criticism.* Cambridge University Press.
FURST, LILIAN R. (1979) (ed.). *Romanticism in Perspective.* 2nd edn. London: Macmillan.
GARCÍA GUTIÉRREZ, ANTONIO (1985). *El trovador,* ed. Carlos Ruiz Silva. Madrid: Cátedra.
HART, STEPHEN M. (1992). *The Other Scene: Psychoanalytic Readings in Modern Spanish and Latin-American Literature.* Boulder, Col.: Society of Spanish and Spanish-American Studies.
HARTZENBUSCH, JUAN EUGENIO (1989). *Los amantes de Teruel,* ed. Carmen Iranzo. Madrid: Cátedra.
HOEVELER, DIANE LONG (1990). *Romantic Androgyny: The Woman Within.* University Park, Pa.: Pennsylvania State University Press.
JOHNSON, PAUL (1991). *The Birth of the Modern: World Society 1815–1830.* London: Weidenfeld & Nicholson.
KIRKPATRICK, SUSAN (1989). *Las Románticas: escritoras y subjetividad en España, 1835–1850.* Madrid: Cátedra.
LLORENS, VICENTE (1968). *Liberales y románticos: una emigración española en Inglaterra 1823–34.* Madrid: Castalia.
MCNAY, LOIS (1992). *Foucault and Feminism: Power, Gender and the Self.* Cambridge: Polity.
MARTÍNEZ DE LA ROSA, FRANCISCO (1972). *Obras dramáticas,* ed. Jean Sarrailh. Madrid: Espasa-Calpe.
MELLOR, ANNE K. (1993). *Romanticism and Gender.* New York: Routledge.
NAVAS RUIZ, RICARDO (1982). *El romanticismo español.* 3rd edn. Madrid: Cátedra.
PATEMAN, CAROLE (1988). *The Sexual Contract.* Cambridge: Polity Press.
PUNTER, DAVID (1989). *The Romantic Unconscious: A Study in Narcissism and Patriarchy.* New York: Harvester Wheatsheaf.

RIVAS, DUQUE DE (Ángel Saavedra) (1986). *Don Álvaro o la fuerza del sino*, ed. Alberto Sánchez. Madrid: Cátedra.

WILLIAMS, RAYMOND (1990). *Keywords: A Vocabulary of Culture and Society*. 2nd rev. edn. London: Fontana.

2

Autobiography as Insult

NOËL VALIS

The autobiographical impulse begins as a way of fixing the unstable, fugitive character of human experience. Understood as an impulse, as a form of oppositional energy to ward off the entropic collapse of being, autobiography in itself is a paradoxical impossibility, whose project it attempts to define in the very act of living that project. One does not live the *aute* of a life while writing what can only become increasingly petrified in the form of testament. Autobiography as text represents the burial of being. For Paul de Man, autobiography is a form of disfigurement or mutilation: 'as soon as we understand the rhetorical function of prosopopeia as positing voice or face by means of language, we also understand that what we are deprived of is not life but the shape and the sense of a world accessible only in the privative way of understanding. Death is a displaced name for a linguistic predicament' (930).

The verbal inadequacy of the autobiographical act is undeniable. Nevertheless, this statement does not seem to me adequate as an analysis of a highly complex phenomenon like autobiographical writing, for two reasons. First, although the text attempts to fix, or immobilize, a life, it does so through a figurative movement. This same figurative movement, constituted through metaphor and metonymy, implies a linguistic space or discourse-territory in which such a process unfolds itself. Taken a step further, the text denotes a discursive context wherein that which is private defines itself in spatial counterpoint to that which is public. It is not possible to discuss autobiographical writing exclusively as if it were simply the subjective act of an individual

I would like to thank Maryellen Bieder, Cristina Enríquez, Janet Gold, Jamile Lawand, Susan Kirkpatrick, and Carolyn Richmond for their help in locating some of the 19th-cent. texts cited in this essay.

conscience. The presence of a reader—whether an anonymous, real reader or the autobiographer turned reader of self— produces a split between subject and object in the consciousness of the writer. In sum, self-consciousness as a textual process begins to function when 'the reader' is activated as an intruder into the world of the text. In this sense, the reader operates figuratively as the public sector internalized within individual consciousness.

This dialectical movement between private and public inten- sifies, shifting to a highly conflictive phase when the subject of the autobiographical act is perceived as a transgressor against normative public discourse. This is the case of the nineteenth- century woman writer who attempted to define herself as an indi- vidual, autonomous personality in a society that could neither admit nor conceive of feminine identity within the public arena. Autobiography constitutes public revelation of one's interiority. But a woman culturally defined as pure domesticity was enclosed in her own interiority. To declare oneself an autobiographical subject was tantamount to invading the verbal territory in which men operated. Speaking or writing in public exposed women writers to the terrible power of public opinion. Figured as that anonymous reader, public opinion could easily destroy a woman's reputation, that is, her generic identity as a cultural construc- tion of femininity. From this long-standing condition springs in part the dearth of letters, diaries, autobiographies, and memoirs left by Spanish women writers of the last century (Simón Palmer 594).

A significant part of the socio-moral context in which nine- teenth-century Spanish women writers moved was precisely that cultural and physical space to which Hispanic literary criticism in general has paid scant attention. I would like to focus on one particular context, the relation between poetess [*poetisa*] and village/town [*aldea/pueblo*], in order to suggest a way to read the female autobiographical act as a 'process of situation', in which the subject situates—but does not define—herself in physical and verbal spaces governed by certain linguistic and affective movements. Making use of recent anthropological research car- ried out by James Fernandez, David Gilmore, Stanley Brandes, and Carmelo Lisón Tolosana, I offer this reading as an interpre- tative experiment based on an 'anthropology of affect'.[1] In his study of the socio-moral world of small Andalusian communities,

Gilmore maintains that there exists a structure of the passions and that strong emotion is not necessarily a destabilizing factor, or a symbol of socio-affective disorder. He observes that the structure of a thing functions through a series of transformations; and that precisely what is transformed is human emotions. This transformative energy has its deepest origins in the body itself and is expressed in the complex, liminal relationship between the psychological and bodily integrity of individual and group (Gilmore ch. 9).

For Gilmore, aggression when displayed verbally serves to channel collective disorder and re-establish group norms, in small and isolated communities. But in so enthroning the ethos of public opinion, the anthropologist privileges the collective spirit (itself a mythologizing notion) and does not pay sufficient attention to the problematical situation of the marginalized individual. Fernandez points out that the catalyst for oral aggressivity in popular poetry—for example, the *loias*, *reguifas*, and *desafíos* described by Carmelo Lisón—often springs from the potentially explosive tension between the two poles of alienation and familiarization, made concrete in oppositions like *forastero/vecino* [stranger/neighbour] and *vagante/aldeano* [vagrant/villager] (468). But what happens when the 'stranger' is also a member of the community? This is the situation of the woman writer living in a village or small town in the last century, doubly marginalized by her status as a writer (a deviation from the norm) and as an inhabitant of a small community. I am suggesting that the identity of the nineteenth-century woman writer in Spain turns problematic in the very act of inserting herself within an already charged context. In this context, she is categorized as unacceptable through naming her *poetisa*. The qualifier *poetisa* in this specific context displays strongly ambivalent markings since, on the one hand, collective usage of the term disqualifies and depersonalizes in the form of an insult. Yet on the other hand, defence of the same term taken up by many women poets in this period can be interpreted as an act of personal self-definition born out of poetic sisterhood and feminine solidarity, as Susan Kirkpatrick has perceptively analysed in *Las Románticas* (79–87).

I will use as my textual point of departure a poem by Carolina Coronado, 'La poetisa en un pueblo' (1845), and two poetic compositions by Vicenta García Miranda—a friend and correspondent of Carolina's—'La poetisa de aldea' (1847) and

'Recuerdos y pensamientos' (1849). Although unknown today, García Miranda, an Extremaduran like the better-known Carolina Coronado, was part of a flourishing group of women poets, along with Josefa Massanés, Amalia Fenollosa, Gertrudis Gómez de Avellaneda, and others during the 1840s and 1850s (see Kirkpatrick ch. 2; and Manzano Garías 1957, 1962, and 1969). Strictly speaking, I am not using conventional autobiographical texts. But what is autobiographical? The very notion of the autobiographical is highly unstable, given its character as an artificial and subjective reconstruction. Moreover, as a re-creation, autobiography expresses the multiple *fictions* of the self. Hence the possibility of imagining the autobiographical in second and even third person (Smith 46–7). Finally, the autobiographical as a trope—the figurative reincarnation of an individual's face and voice (de Man 930)—reinforces precisely this identification made between *poetisa* (as rhetorical artifice) and person. An ambivalent and disturbing identification, to be sure; above all, a linguistic identification, in which a cultural construction—the idea of the *poetisa*, or poetess—is almost completely assimilated to the concrete person of the woman writer.

Poetisa, then, already marks within its function as cultural stereotype the woman writer's identity, defining her a priori and thus depersonalizing her at the same time (Gilman introd.). But what did it mean to be a *poetisa* during the last century? It depended a great deal on the way the word was used and who was using it. From a male perspective, the *poetisa*/poetess could be one of two things: either exceptional or disastrous. Examples abound throughout practically the entire nineteenth century, from the Romantic period to the turn of the century. For example, in Juan Eugenio Hartzenbusch's 1843 prologue to Carolina Coronado's *Poesías*, he says that 'sus versos son ella misma' [her poetry and her soul are one and the same] (p. ix). Or from 1869, this judgement by Emilio Castelar: 'Pero hay un ser superior al poeta, más sensible, más inteligente, más poeta, si cabe hablar así: la poetisa' [But there is a soul superior to the poet, more sensitive, more intelligent, more of a poet, if one can say such a thing: the poetess]. And '¿cuál será la poetisa más perfecta?', the celebrated orator asks. 'La que mejor conserve y refleje las cualidades de mujer en sus versos' [Who is the perfect poetess? She who best preserves and reflects a womanly character in her poetry]. Singling out Carolina Coronado as an exemplary poetess, he continues with this unconsciously damning praise: 'No le preguntéis [a Carolina] por qué canta. No lo sabe. Sería lo mismo que preguntar al arroyo por qué murmura; al astro, por qué produce la armonía en las esferas' [Do not ask Carolina why she sings. She does not know why. No more ask the brook why it murmurs, or the stars why they produce celestial harmony] (232–4).

In other words, to be a poetess was equivalent to being a woman; and the *poetisa*/female, although a superior being, is identified with Nature, that is with everything other than Culture, to use the well-known analogy critiqued by anthropologist Sherry Ortner. Thus Carolina Coronado as a poetess, by implication, lacks talent, because she is not a thinking, consciously motivated being. She is pure emotivity. She does not write, she *reproduces* unconsciously that uncultivated, wild zone in which her status as poetess has enclosed her (Showalter 1985). In sum, professional identity does not exist for the woman writer.

Much more common is the disparaging attitude of disdain toward the poetess, an attitude that lasts well into the twentieth century. Thus the comic writer Vital Aza dedicates a composition 'To a Poetess' ['A una poetisa', 1894], in which he heaps up extravagant praise for female genius while he dictates the real message as an acrostic in the heart of the poem: 'DEJESE USTED DE ESCRYBYR VACYEDADES' [Cease writing empty twaddle] (285). This two-faced poem exploits two traditional modes of poetry— the praise poem and the insult poem—but reduces the whole thing to a verbal attack.

In another example, rhymester José Gil y Campos ('A una poetisa', 1889), relying on the conventional argument of woman-as-domestic, recommends that the poetess return to the kitchen and clean her house, that she not forget the social and moral role corresponding to her sex. To clinch it all he concludes by saying, 'que para ser marido | de un *ingenio*, hay que ser muy distraído, | muy sucio, y . . . algo más de nacimiento' [to be the husband | of a *genius*, you have to be very absent-minded, | very slovenly, and . . . something else of a congenital nature]. It is evident that the occupation of poetess is a dangerous thing here, threatening to shrivel a husband's male dignity. By accusing the husband of effeminateness, the poet displaces our attention from the real problem: the act of writing as an act of self-affirmation that renders uncertain the conventional social and sexual role of a woman. A woman is defined by her sexual difference, not by her person; and once more, professional identity as a writer is denied her.

Sadly, women writers found themselves in the unenviable position of nearly always being on the defensive, as a reaction to masculine condemnation and appropriation. As Bridget Aldaraca, Susan Kirkpatrick, and Alda Blanco have shown, the notion of the *ángel del hogar* or angel in the parlour was converted into an ideology of domesticity for the woman writer, defining her through sexual difference and femininity. Similar tendencies showed up in other Western cultures at about the same time (see Armstrong, Poovey, Showalter 1977, Douglas). Evidently such an ideology suppressed the implicit contradiction between the supposed naturalness of femininity and the proliferation of conduct manuals intended to 'cultivate' the naturally feminine character of women (Poovey, Scanlon, de Diego).

Political, social, and moral institutions were inclined to mould women, thus controlling those impulses of her sexuality judged inappropriate—hence the advice of Josefa Massanés in 1841, warning the woman writer that 'una conducta extravagante o moralmente reprensible' [extravagant or morally reprehensible conduct] makes her unworthy of the title 'mujer de talento' [a woman of talent], thus appearing before the world as 'un ente original y ridículo' [a bizarre and ridiculous creature] (1841a: viii). Significantly, in the heart of the Romantic period, Massanés uses the term 'original' in its eighteenth-century sense (Babbitt 187) as a synonym for ridiculous, in order to characterize the woman who steps out of the conventional frame of things. To be 'original' in this context bordered on the monstrous.

Fear of ridicule, as Juan Nicasio Gallego observed sympathetically in the same year, was a powerful incentive to discourage any creative initiative in a woman (p. x). Nevertheless, strategies were devised to avoid the socio-sexual dilemma of having to sacrifice either one's femininity or one's talent. For some writers, the ideal of androgyny seemed like a viable alternative. This was the way the poet María Verdejo y Durán (1830–55) was described in 1855:

Parecía inverosímil, que aquella persona en la apariencia tan débil, y que aquel espíritu en realidad tan afeminado, pudieran ocultar un corazón tan varonil, mas por uno de esos escasos privilegios que Dios concede a muy reducido número de criaturas, reunía en sí todas las nobles cualidades que realzan el corazón del hombre y todos los dulces sentimientos que embellecen el corazón de la mujer.

It seemed unlikely that that individual in appearance so weak, that that spirit in reality so womanly, should hide a heart so manly, but through one of those rare privileges that God concedes to very few creatures, she united in herself all the noble qualities that elevate the heart of man and all the sweet feelings that embellish the heart of woman. (J.H. and J.M. 12)

Androgyny is proposed, irreverently, in *El caballero de las botas azules* [The Knight of the Blue Boots, 1867], by Rosalía de Castro, thus subverting the long masculine tradition that imagines creative inspiration dressed as a feminine creature. '¿Conque mi Musa era un marimacho, un ser anfibio de esos que debieran quedar para siempre en el vacío?' [So my Muse was a man-woman, an amphibious being of the sort that should remain forever in the void?], protests the Man in 'Un hombre y una musa' [A Man and a Muse], the curious prologue to this curious novel (1181). One year before, Rosalía had bitterly complained of her condition, observing that the word *poetisa* 'ya llegó a hacerme daño' [had already managed to do me harm]; to be a poetisa is 'lo peor que puede ser hoy una mujer' [the worst a woman can be nowadays] (1960*b*: 1540). Despite the ironic stance of *El caballero de las botas azules*, at heart Rosalía is seriously questioning the encasement of art and of the writer in sexually predetermined moulds.

Androgyny becomes a topos in the case of Gertrudis Gómez de Avellaneda, once the saying got about that 'es mucho hombre esta mujer' [this woman is some man] (Miller 201–2).[2] The question is still being debated at the turn of the century. Thus Concepción Gimeno de Flaquer says in 1891: 'Yo opino que [la Avellaneda] es las dos cosas a la vez: que su genio es bisexual' [I am of the opinion that Avellaneda is both things at the same time: that her genius is bisexual] (1891: 242). But she appears to have modified her opinion in 1901, writing, 'es cierto que todavía existen reaccionarios que consideran ser andrógino a la mujer que pospone la rueca y la calceta a la pluma y el pincel' [undoubtedly there still exist reactionaries who consider a woman androgynous if she prefers the pen or the brush to the spinning wheel and knitting needle] (1901: 9). But the argument she launches upon goes against a desexualizing ideology that had created a divided consciousness in the woman writer, who was anxious to justify her social and sexual transgression while proposing a double image of herself. For example, Pilar Sinués de Marco said of Faustina Sáez de Melgar in 1860: 'no la busqueis en las fiestas, pero, si penetras en su casa, la hallareis blanca, apacible y vestida con sencilla elegancia, escribiendo a la luz de su lámpara, junto a la cuna de su hija' [do not look for her at parties, but if you go inside her house, you will find her there, pale, serene, and dressed with simple elegance, writing by the light of her lamp, next to her daughter's cradle] (1860: 88).[3]

The polemic that arose over the classification and definition of Avellaneda as a poetess took another turning with Carolina Coronado's participation in 1857–8. She was astonished to hear that Avellaneda was not considered a *poetisa*, but a *poeta*: 'Los otros hombres del tiempo antiguo negaban el genio de la mujer; hoy los del moderno, ya que no pueden negar al que triunfa, la metamorfosean' [Men of antiquity denied women's talent; today men in modern times can no longer deny woman triumphant, so they simply metamorphose her]. Protesting masculine usurpation of Avellaneda's genius, she admits, nevertheless, that Gertrudis is 'tan gran poeta como vosotros' [as great a poet as you men] (1914: 482), that she is *poet* and *poetess* at the same time. But she ends up creating another category for Avellaneda when she calls her 'la amazona de nuestro Parnaso' [the amazon of our Parnassus] and, as such, 'es más fuerte, no porque es hombre-poeta, sino porque es poetisa-amazona' [she is stronger, not because she is a man-poet, but because she is an amazon-poetess] (486). Implicitly, Coronado postulates the existence of a distinct and separate universe of 'poetisas', in opposition to the world of 'poetas'. Although she defends the intrinsically feminine character of Avellaneda—analogous in method to the way other female writers declared their love of home—her creation of an extraordinary personality in Gertrudis Gómez de Avellaneda as the 'amazon-poetess' reveals a fundamental inconformity with the traditional pigeon-holing of the woman writer. In all of these cases, the hybrid character of the poetess suggested that there was something monstrous in her, that, despite her fear of ridicule, there was indeed something 'original' in her, taking the word in its double neo-classic and Romantic sense.

All these examples showing the varied semantic and ideological usage of the word *poetisa*—examples that could easily be multiplied—point to instability and confusion surrounding the term. The worst thing for a woman writer was the identification created between name and person. In this sense, *poetisa* functioned like public nicknames in small communities, that is, as a kind of verbal aggression whose effectiveness is observed in the reduction [*acto de achicar*] of self-identity and personal autonomy. In 1845, for example, Antonio Neira de Mosquera published a little book called *Las ferias de Madrid: almoneda moral, política y literaria* [Madrid Bazaar: A Moral, Political, and Literary Auction], where he attempted to ridicule Carolina Coronado as 'una mujer que se desconsuela por todo . . . Llora por la desaparición de la Primavera, por la desaparición del Estío, por la desaparición del Otoño, y por la desaparición del Invierno . . . Acompaña en su despedida a las golondrinas, a las grullas, a las alondras y a los patos' [a woman who weeps over everything . . . She cries when Spring disappears, when Summer disappears, when Autumn disappears, and when Winter disappears . . . She accompanies the departure of swallows, cranes, larks, and ducks] (132).[4]

Carolina responded drily in 1846: 'Ya Neira, despedí a la *golondrina*' [I have already said goodbye to the *swallow*, Neira]. And later, '¿Qué más da que en mi lira sean cantados | Hombres o *grullas*; si en diversos nombres | Disfrazadas las grullas van de hombres | Y los hombres de *grullas* disfrazados?' [What does it matter if my lyre sings | of men or *cranes*; if with other names | cranes go about as men | and men go about as cranes?]. 'Soldados-*grullas*' [soldier-cranes] there are, she says, and corrupt 'hombres-*patos*' [duck-men]. Why the grand attack on the poor duck, the unhappy crane? 'Cada piedra, cada ave, cada planta, | Una vida, una historia, un mundo encierra | Y muchos en el mundo, bien lo sabes, | Valen menos que piedras, plantas, aves' [Every stone, every bird, every plant, | holds a life, a story, a world | and many in the world, as you well know, | are worth less than stones, plants, or birds]. She concludes her defence by saying: 'Lo mismo dan las aves que los hombres, | Lo mismo el campo da que las ciudades | Pues componen entrambas vecindades, | Los mismos seres con distintos nombres; | *Grullas* hay en el mundo con nombres, | *Patos* bajo soberbias potestades, | Y en ciudades lo mismo que entre encinas | Sobre *grullas y patos golondrinas*' [Birds or men, what does it matter, | country or city, it matters not | if both have the same neighbours, | under different names; | *Cranes* there are with names, | *Ducks* beneath proud crowns, | And in cities or in oak trees | Over *cranes* and *ducks*, *swallows*] (1852: 134–5).

In this poem of extraordinary aggressivity, Coronado achieves two objectives: she justifies the legitimacy of her poetic project and she launches a counter-attack by rejecting the stereotypical effect of categorizing her, indirectly, as a tender-hearted, weepy poetess. There is nothing in this poem of the conventional image of Carolina Coronado as an insipid, sentimental poetess, an image of contempt that prevailed until the 1980s. Most striking for me is how Coronado exploits a long poetic tradition, both written and oral, of verbal attacks, challenges, and insults that, with very few exceptions, has been defined as a masculine tradition. Above all, oral cultures, as Spain was until modern times, flourish in a verbal setting of agonistic combativeness defined by a strong sense of territoriality. Indeed, as Father Ong has commented, until fairly recently both the academic system of debate and oral competition [*oposiciones*] and the political arena in which the orator took centre stage functioned in a moral and affective geography marked by frontiers and rivalries (Ong ch. 4). The written literary tradition frequently incorporated the same competitive sense based on orality, as seen in the classic example of the bet between Don Juan Tenorio and Don Luis Mejía in Zorrilla's Romantic drama (1844).

The strategy of counter-attack adopted by Coronado turns out to be crucial in the poem 'La poetisa en un pueblo' (1845). It is instructive to read in her letters to Hartzenbusch during the 1840s what the cultural atmosphere of Almendralejo and Badajoz was like: 'en esta población, tan vergonzosamente atrasada, fue un acontecimiento extraordinario el que una mujer hiciese versos, y el que los versos se pudiesen hacer sin *maestro*, los hombres los han graduado de copias y las mujeres, sin comprenderlos siquiera, me han consagrado por ellos todo el resentimiento de su envidia' [in this town, so shamefully backward, the fact that a woman could compose verses, and that those verses could be written without the help of a teacher, was an extraordinary event; the men say they are copied and the women, with no understanding whatsoever, have heaped upon me the full blast of their envy] (24 October 1840) (Fonseca Ruiz 176).

In another moment, she writes: 'Nada más opuesto a la educación literaria que el pueblo en donde yo recibí mi educación; nada más opuesto a la poesía que la capital en donde vivo. Mi pueblo opone una vigorosa resistencia a toda innovación en las ocupaciones de las jóvenes' [There is nothing more contrary to a literary education than the town where I received my education; nothing more contrary to poetry than the capital where I live. My townsmen oppose a vigorous resistence to any innovation in the occupation of young women]. A little later she observes:

Una mujer teme de la opinión de cada uno porque ha nacido para temer siempre: por evitar el ridículo suspendí mis lecciones y concreté mi estudio a leer las horas dedicadas al sueño. Pero eso debilitó mi salud, y mi familia, celosa de ella, me prohibió continuar. Me decidí, pues, a hacer versos solamente, a no escribirlos y a conservarlos en la memoria; pero esta *contemplación* perjudicaba al buen desempeño de mis labores y me daba un aire distraído que hacía reír a los extraños y molestaba a mis parientes . . . Me resolví a *meditar* solamente una hora cada día antes de levantarme. Pero el pensamiento no puede sufrir tanta esclavitud; el poeta no puede vivir así y mi escaso numen está ya medio sofocado.

A woman fears public opinion because she was born to fear forever: to avoid ridicule I suspended my lessons and limited my studies to reading in bed at night. But this weakened my health, and my family, ever zealous, forbade me to continue. I decided then only to make up verses in my head, not to write them, and to conserve them in my memory; but this form of *contemplation* affected the proper carrying out of my duties and gave me a distracted air that made strangers laugh and annoyed my family . . . I then resolved to *meditate* only one hour every day before arising. But thought cannot suffer so much enslavement; the poet cannot live thus and my modest well of inspiration is already half choked. (3 December 1842) (Fonseca Ruiz 178)

These personal experiences were surely incorporated into the poem 'La poetisa en un pueblo', where Carolina employs the dialogue form, not as an invitation to communication, but as the expression of the confrontational mode between poetess and town. The poem hurls its verbal challenge from the very beginning: '¡Ya viene, mírala! —¿Quién? | —Esa que saca las coplas. | — Jesús, qué mujer tan rara. | —Tiene los ojos de loca' ['Here she comes, look at her!' 'Who?' | 'The one who writes the ditties.' | 'God, what a strange woman.' | 'She has the eyes of a crazy one'] (1852: 68). These initial lines capture beautifully the provincial setting, in which a dynamic of socio-affective inclusivity-exclusivity governs. 'La que viene' in the poem quite clearly

does not belong, as we see from the contemptuous attitude of
singling her out by pointing the finger at her and marginalizing
her as an odd, even mad creature. When someone asks if she
writes poetry with a master-teacher, the answer is cutting: '¡Qué
locura! no señora' [Are you crazy? of course not]. And the proof
comes when she refuses to compose a *décima* for the wedding of
a friend, saying: 'Ustedes se han engañado. No improviso' [You
are mistaken. I don't improvise]. After this negative response
she is damned as a romantic and a liar, and advised that 'más
valía que aprendiera I a barrer que a decir coplas' [you're better
off learning I to sweep than recite poetry]. Finally they decide to
expel the poetess: 'Vamos a echarla de aquí. I —¿Cómo?—
Riéndonos todas' ['Let's throw her out of here.' I 'How?' 'Laugh
her out']. The last lines read: 'Ya mira, ya se incomoda. I Ya se
levanta y se va . . . I ¡Vaya con Dios la gran loca!' [Now she
notices, feels bad. I Now she's getting up and leaving . . . I May
the crazy one go with God!].

The insults that make up this poem work with a double perspective in mind. On the one hand, the obvious target of these
verbal assaults is the poetess herself. But by putting herself in
charge of hurling the insults, Coronado takes advantage of the
agonistic frame of the insult poem to disqualify the anonymous
and largely feminine voices representing the town's collective
judgement. The device of counter-attack is achieved by charac-
terizing the voices as gossips. Idle talk is a form of verbal
aggression, whose real message almost always is a subtext, unspoken but definitely felt (Gilmore 59).[5] The anonymous spite
heard in these voices clearly communicates a message of exclusion, a movement to isolate the individual who deviates from the
community's social and moral norms. But insults are not only
words, they are also looks [*miradas*], as the first line reveals: '¡Ya
viene, mírala!' The *mirada fuerte* or strong stare 'is the ocular
equivalent of the gossip's cutting tongue' (Gilmore 164). And
both devices—*darle a la lengua* [to gossip] and *mirar fuerte* [to
stare hard]—establish precise borders and socio-affective spaces
in exploiting the effectiveness of negative feelings like hostility,
envy, and contempt.

The worst insult in this poem by Carolina Coronado is the
fact of being a poetess. Attaching a special nickname to someone
serves in this context to humiliate, to diminish [*achicar*] the personality of one who has no real name, who is only the *poetisa*.

The nickname constitutes an attack against the person herself, something that Carolina Coronado understood only too well when she adopted ridiculing terms like 'hombres-patos' and 'soldados-grullas' in her poem 'A Neira', to turn the tables on her enemy. Both poetic compositions make evident what James Fernandez calls 'metonymic misrepresentation as movement' (469). In 'La poetisa en un pueblo' insults operate like figurative mutilations, assaulting the protagonist's bodily and psychological integrity by alluding, for example, to the bizarre character of the woman writer and to her 'ojos de loca' in the opening lines. Everything that characterizes the *poetisa* as a romantic, prevaricating, self-conscious creature has as its end the aim of ridiculing, that is, reducing her in size by attacking her weak point.

Names wound. As Gilmore observes, 'names are shorthand gossip, metonymic backbiting' (93). In this sense, the name *poetisa*—and the entire characterization given that name in the poem—is reductive, displaying a metonymic movement founded on aggressivity, on the act of diminishing the Other. Taken in this context, the words of Josefa Massanés in her poem 'La resolución' (1837) are especially revealing: '[¡¡¡] cual quedara mi persona | Mordida por tanta boca!!!' [what would remain of my person | bitten by so many mouths!!!] (196). Words devour, fragmenting and disfiguring the body of the poetess. By implication one intuits how names and insults, in attacking self identity, are intimately related to the body itself (Gilmore 84).

Seen in its entirety, Coronado's poem is structured according to a double physical and figurative movement of approach–withdrawal. The poem begins with the poetess drawing close to the town's social and moral territory. It ends with her retreat as the 'gran loca', now marginalized linguistically and spatially from the centre, that is, from the social collectivity heard in the form of voices and mocking laughter. This polarized movement between centripetal and centrifugal forces suggests a certain analogy to the alienation/familiarization opposition discussed by Fernandez. Said another way, Coronado conceives of the woman writer's condition not as something static, but as a 'process of situation' that contextualizes the poetess in her status of marginalized Other, juxtaposed to the centre, which is the town. The 'situation' of the nineteenth-century woman in general required that she be in some way invisible so as not to draw attention (Poovey 24). The poetess is too 'visible', as we see in this poem. That visibility offends the community because it contradicts the notion of a woman as an absent body. In sum, the feminine situation has ultimately to do with her reputation.

Carolina Coronado, as we see her poetically recreated here, is not only too visible, she is also too audible. When she refuses to compose *décimas* to celebrate a wedding, she gives signs of a strong, 'unfeminine' will, according to the preconceived and normative image held of a woman. Moreover, her refusal clashes with other traditional values, the sense of commensality. Offering poetry—usually improvised—at a wedding or banquet represents cultural affirmation of the group, often it must be said at the expense of an individual. According to Carmelo Lisón, an 'aggressivity in commensality' ['agresividad en comensalidad'] is produced in these situations, where the improviser—almost always male—distils village hostilities accumulated over a long time through insults and other verbal attacks directed against specific persons (see also Fernandez 459). This public discharge of aggression assumes a ritual, ceremonial character aimed toward re-establishing communal harmony. But when the poetess says, 'no improviso', she implicitly rejects the role of defender of collective values, here, by seeking out a propitiatory victim as the target of her verses.

Compare this situation with another story. In a similar vein, a dim-witted priest asked Vicenta García Miranda to make up some poetry (another *décima*) for a wedding party so that he could recite it as his own. She accepted and gave him these lines (that everyone knew were hers): 'Brindo porque siempre flores | pise el feliz matrimonio | de Mariano y Dolores; | aunque a envidiar sus amores | a mí me incite el demonio: | que es muy tentador mirar | los cariñosos mohines | de dos amantes sin par, | y después irse a rezar | vísperas, nona y maitines' [A toast, may there always be flowers | beneath the happy feet of Mariano and Dolores; | though the devil provoke me | to envy their love: | how tempting it is to see | the tender gestures | of two lovers so fine, | and then go to pray | vespers, nones, and matins] (Manzano Garías 1969: 302–3). Vicenta likewise did not improvise, but notice with what fine malice she exploits the occasion in order to pull the priest's leg. Carolina too makes use of the same oral tradition to fling verbal darts at her backbiting enemies. The fact that neither woman poet is an improviser of verses underlines the existence of two socio-poetic currents, based on certain written and oral usages. Speaking in public is part of a man's education and activities, but not of a woman's in the last century. Coronado overcomes this cultural obstacle, first, by formulating her poem in oral terms; and then by using orality itself—gossip—as a weapon against the jeering voices of public opinion.

In its guise as an autobiographical text, 'La poetisa en un pueblo' illustrates the way in which a woman writer can subvert a masculine tradition by using it as a strategy to defend the integrity of self. Against such attacks directed against her as a woman, Carolina lets loose her anger and her contempt, thus displacing the target of ridicule to the centre (the village voices) and removing it from the margins where the poet resides. It is this great storehouse of feminine energy which propels the poem, structuring it to the extent that one emotion is displaced by another, those vibrating chords of passion and protest that must be heard. The poem in itself is an affirmation of personal and professional identity when Carolina resists the accusation that she is not the author of her own poetry. Perhaps even more significant are the implications concerning the relation between the autobiographical act and the awareness of one's public identity. It would seem that the revelation of one's inner being is only possible once a notion of the public self has already been determined. The Spanish woman writer of the nineteenth century could not write about herself without having dealt previously with the thorny question of her professional identity. 'La poetisa en un pueblo' shows how problematic and difficult the relation was between woman writer and public. Such a relation was based precisely on a collective pre-judgement that denied the public self of a woman writer.[6]

As in English and American literature of the Victorian period, in Spain to speak of a vocation for the woman writer came wrapped up in its own linguistic and semantic code (Michie 62, 70). The use of certain images seemed to legitimize a woman's writing, as we have already seen, for example, in the metaphor of domesticity.[7] The language of flowers was also judged appropriate, through the analogy between flower and adornment which converted the poetess into a 'flower' (de Diego 166). These clichés and others adapted according to the circumstances and literary fashions like Romanticism tended with few exceptions to block the personal contemplation of self (Kirkpatrick 222–8). The stereotyping effects of conventional language were difficult to avoid. But the harmful consequences of such language were diluted to some extent through the ideological and lyric solidarity felt among many women writers of the period. In this very special context when one spoke of *la poetisa* one referred to all *poetisas*.

The biography of one particular poetess was often interpreted through the subjective filter of another poetess, to the point of closely identifying with the subject under study. When Pilar Sinués de Marco, for example, speaks of the cruel privations that Faustina Sáez de Melgar was forced to endure for the sake of her reading, she writes: '¿Cómo lo hacía si sus padres le quitaban los libros? se me preguntará. He aquí uno de los muchos milagros que vemos practicar a las españolas que escriben' [How did she do it if her parents took away her books?, you will ask. Here you see one of those daily miracles practised by Spanish women who write]. Later she says that the parents and siblings of Faustina 'acusábanle como de un crimen, de su afición a las letras: la mortificaban sin cesar con burlas mordaces' [accused her of practically committing a crime for her love of books: they humiliated her constantly through biting mockery] (1860: 82–3).[8] But in order to speak about Faustina, her biographer first has to set up a series of contrasts and generalizations between the Spanish woman writer and her French counterpart. That is, her way of proceeding from the general to the particular implies the construction of a paradigmatic model of the Spanish woman writer.

In a similar fashion, Carolina Coronado describes the sufferings and privations of the poet Robustiana Armiño:

Carecía de maestros, y tuvo que constituirse en maestro de sí misma, y se enseñó idiomas y se forjó versos que rompió a millares para volverlos a fundir y esto en el mayor secreto, inquieta y recelosa siempre por el temor de ver descubiertas sus pequeñas obras que, sin duda, la expondrían a la sátira de las gentes. . . . ¿Hay por ventura un solo verso, que no le haya costado una lágrima o una mortificación?. . . . [N]o se busque en el influjo de la romántica literatura, la razón de esas quejas, que un profundo sentimiento arranca a las jóvenes de nuestros días, búsquese en las circunstancias de su educación, de su estado y de su fortuna el manantial de sus lágrimas, y se hallará inagotable.

She lacked teachers, and had to become her own teacher, instructing herself in languages and composing thousands of verses she then tore up only to return to them once more, revising and revising, and all this in secrecy, uneasy and fearful always that someone would discover her little efforts and doubtless expose her to the mockery of others. . . . Is there by chance a single line of verse that has not cost her a tear or humiliation? . . . Do not look to the influence of romantic literature as an explanation for this pain torn as a deep-lying feeling out of the young women of our day; look to the circumstances of her education, of her condition, and of her fortunes to explain the fountain of tears, which you will find inexhaustible.

Then she says that Armiño 'gusta sí, de disfrazar su aflicción con la aflicción de otros seres' [prefers to cloak her affliction in the affliction of others] (Armiño 6–8).

Is there any doubt that Carolina Coronado, whose attempts at mental composition to avoid public censure have been amply documented, identifies closely with the desperation and anguish of Robustiana Armiño (and so many other women poets)? The device of masking personal affliction by alluding to that of other writers, as seen in Armiño's work, is precisely the same device Coronado uses in this introduction. Stated another way, the biography of Robustiana Armiño is also the autobiography of Carolina Coronado. This strategy of expressing the self indirectly or obliquely, a strategy that occurs equally in the Victorian writings of English and American women authors (Poovey 28, 42), ends up producing an autobiographical paradigm of the Spanish poetess, often expressed in the third person as in Coronado's 'La poetisa en un pueblo' or displaced on to another concrete figure.

This *lateralizing* contextualization of the autobiographical can also disclose itself in relational terms between one *poetisa* and another. In 'La poetisa de aldea' by Vicenta García Miranda (1847), for example, although she speaks like Carolina Coronado in the third person of the same theme (with occasional deictic shifts between the second and first persons), the context has changed. Using the Romantic cliché of the *poetisa*-as-flower, Vicenta imagines the village poetess as a 'pobre planta abandonada' [a poor abandoned flower], 'flor a quien sonora brisa | Jamás blanda acarició' [a flower that no wafting breeze | ever softly caressed]. Wounded by the thorns of the bramble bush and alone in her suffering of the ill effects of village life, the figure of the *poetisa* in García Miranda is, like that of Carolina Coronado, in the first place a Romantic construction of the divine poet or seer as a socially marginalized and alienated being.

But beyond the literary paradigm, the poetess is inseparable
from her context, from her geographically and affectively lived
experience. For García Miranda, the village poetess must be
seen in relation to the privileged figure of the poetess born into
a superior cultural environment. Establishing a poetic opposition between the poetess of the glade (that is, the village) and
the poetess of the garden, she writes that 'Jamás a las que
nacieran | En jardines conocí | Que en su círculo admitieran |
Las que de la selva fueran. . . . | Quedémonos, pues, aquí' [I
have never known those born | in gardens to admit | into their
circle | those from the glade. . . . | Let us remain here, then]. The
village poetess, according to García Miranda, is a being doubly
excluded. Within her own small community she lives isolated
and, in relation to more urban poetesses, she evidently cannot
compete. Like Coronado, the 'poetess from Campanario' does
not experience her environment from a socio-centric perspective.
Although the village of necessity represents her universe, it does
not represent her values. The poetess as outsider, paradoxically,
lives enclosed, in her 'mansión de horror | Sujeta siempre a [s]us
grillos' [mansion of horror | subject always to her chains], sur-
rounded by barricades and walls [*valla/muralla*] (1981: 12–14).
The territorial sense marks but does not define a woman's writing here.

Among these spaces of inclusion and exclusion the poetess is
situated—and not situated. In an openly autobiographical poem,
'Recuerdos y pensamientos: a Carolina', dated 1849, García
Miranda insists once more on the presence of two distinct envi-
ronments in which the poetess of her time lives, by using the
poetic figure of her own self and that of Carolina Coronado as
models. Thus she says to Carolina: 'Tú, planta cultivada en los
jardines, | Flor inodora yo de los desiertos' [You are the blossom
cultivated in gardens, | I, the scentless flower of the desert]
(154). This spatial dualism between desert/country and civiliza-
tion/garden seems to advance a feminine re-elaboration of the
long-standing literary-cultural opposition, country/city. But it is
important to stress here that, at heart, García Miranda accepts
the traditional analogy made between woman and nature.
Whether garden or desert, it hardly matters. Woman occupies
metaphorically and culturally a space apart from the dominant
order, what Elaine Showalter has labelled a 'wild zone' (1985:
262).

Most striking is *how* García Miranda finds herself by discovering the presence of another self, in this case Carolina Coronado's. One day in 1845 she happened to come across some published poems of Coronado. An accident of reading was a true awakening of her poetic impulses (Manzano Garías 1969: 300; Kirkpatrick 82). That moment she describes as an 'eco... de otra lira, | Lira de otra mujer' [echo... of another lyre, | the lyre of another woman] that 'penetró en mi alma tan sonoro, | Y se extendió vibrando por los senos | De mi fiel corazón ¡tan entusiasta!' [penetrated my soul so deeply, | and spread pulsating through the breast | of my wildly enthusiastic heart!]. The poet continues with these revealing verses: 'al choque eléctrico | Pensé que en mil pedazos se rompiera, | No cabiendo de júbilo en el pecho. | Las venas de mi frente se inyectaron, | Cruzaban mil fantasmas mi cerebro; | En tensión mis arterias no latían, | Y mi mente sufría horrible vértigo' [at this shock electric | I thought I would break into a thousand pieces, | joy bursting from my breast. | The veins of my temples were throbbing, | a thousand phantasms crossed my mind; | my stretched arteries would not beat, | and my mind suffered horrible vertigo] (152).

Undoubtedly the violent and extreme reaction Vicenta felt on reading Carolina Coronado's poetry is clothed in a markedly sexual language, rarely seen in women's writing of this period. A little later she writes that 'pasada esta crisis tan penosa, | Al ceder este estado tan violento, | Moduló mi garganta unos sonidos, | Semejantes de un niño al feble acento, | Comprensibles no más para la madre | Que adivina en su mente los conceptos' [this painful crisis having passed, | and having yielded this violent state, | my throat formed sounds, | like those of a child's feeble accents, | understandable only to a mother | who divines from within their thought] (1969: 151–3). Her poetic awakening comes, then, once the explosion of passion is spent, like a rebirth. The result is the liberation of her mind and soul, which were before 'de instintos reprimidos' [of repressed instincts] (147) and are now 'ya libre... de aquella represión del pensamiento' [now free... of that repression of thought] (153).

Vicenta García Miranda's poem sheds light on how the autobiographical process of the subject is intimately linked to the development of her poetic talents. Her life is, above all, a text, because her experience is limited to what is textually possible. In her second birth, Vicenta awakens to her life as a poet. Her rebirth is, then, textual, but it arises in part from the poetic identity of another woman writer, Carolina Coronado. Vicenta García Miranda's 'Recuerdos y pensamientos' is the very reverse of the insult poem that Coronado's 'La poetisa en un pueblo' represents. For one thing it is a poem of praise. And second, the poetic voice of 'Recuerdos y pensamientos' addresses itself to another public, with Carolina Coronado as principal listener of the poem. The apparent exclusion of the public sector as an internalized reader converts this poem into a highly private text, making it a combined form of shared experience [*convivencia*] and confession [*confesión*].

Vicenta's poem begins this way: 'Hoy que quiero aclarar mis impresiones | Y quiero analizar mis sentimientos; | Hoy que quiero bajar al pecho mío' [Now that I want to make clear my impressions | and to analyse my feelings; | Now that I want to go deep into my soul]. And a little later she writes: 'Lucharé por romper el denso velo | Que siempre me ocultó del alma mía | Las pasiones, los goces, los misterios' [I will struggle to break the dense veil | that always hid from my soul | passion, joy, mystery] (146). The tone and expression are confessional, rooted as well in the Romantic ethos of the supremacy of self. The confession is, needless to say, unorthodox, in that what is postulated is not the annulment of an imperfect self but the self's intrinsic value. Moreover, Vicenta, in confessing to herself, also speaks to Carolina, establishing a space of poetic shared experience removed from the village-territory in which she normally resides. This space is the text itself.

The problematics of professional identity do not appear to enter into this discursive space. Indeed, what interests Vicenta is the exploration of her identity as a born poet: 'La que tanto sentía fue poeta, | Fue poeta al nacer, no pudo menos' [She who felt so much was a poet, | She was a poet at birth, no less] (151). This Romantic notion of the poetic gift clashes, however, with the reality of her circumstances. Her talent lies dormant, with the early loss of her father, who was her first teacher. By the end of the poem Vicenta once more mourns the disappearance of her teacher/father, who would have showed her the road to literary fame (155). Carolina provides the catalyst for her to realize her poetic and personal identity, but by implication she cannot serve as her mentor. The role of mentor was then chiefly masculine, located in an intimate relationship with the instruments and institutions of power—something Carolina Coronado herself understood very well, as she was initially supported by Juan Eugenio Hartzenbusch (Kirkpatrick 90–2).[9] The ending to 'Recuerdos y pensamientos' alludes indirectly to this unavoidable cultural reality.

It is also evident that García Miranda vacillates in this autobiographical text between patriarchal order symbolized by paternal influence and lyric sisterhood incarnated in Carolina Coronado. The last lines degenerate into self-pity, to some extent undoing the significant poetic and personal progress she had shown in the rest of the poem. She had even imagined herself in a position of friendly rivalry with Carolina, explaining that 'la distancia que inmensa nos separa' [the immense distance separating us] was owing to 'los principios más que al genio' [more to our [different] beginnings than to genius] (153). She suggested that her own circumstances presented 'horizontes más vastos, más inmensos, | Lagos, cauces, torrentes, precipicios, | Montes, prados y limpios arroyuelos' [horizons more vast, more immense, | lakes, rivers, torrents, cliffs, | mountains, meadows, and limpid brooks] (155). Despite her vacillations and fears, García Miranda was not lacking in a clear sense of self-identity.

This is not, I would reiterate, an insult poem. Nevertheless, this composition of García Miranda has something in common with Carolina Coronado's text. Both are inserted into a libidinized verbal and social context. The offence Carolina feels so intensely on finding herself in the degrading situation of the 'poetisa en un pueblo' is directed against her very person, as we have seen in the metonymic movement to diminish in size the poet's personality by way of injurious name-calling. Verbal aggression is effective because names already come imbued with a highly affective content as symbolic bearers of the person's self (Gilmore 92). The word *poetisa* during Coronado and García Miranda's time came loaded with public censure against the too visible figure— hence too corporeal—of the woman writer. The unspoken text behind the term *poetisa* is a sexualized subtext in which, paradoxically, the real sexuality of the woman writer was not admitted, only her presumed femininity. Against this sexual encapsulation Coronado protests, unleashing her passion and contempt as weapons in 'La poetisa en un pueblo'. A great passion for breaking 'el denso velo' and the 'instintos reprimidos' also infuses the poetry of Vicenta García Miranda.

Both poets use feeling as a defence against a double anonymity. On the one hand, the anonymous force of public opinion rose up against them, as we saw in the tension created between *poetisa* and *aldea*. But on the other hand, there also emerged a subsequent anonymity of their own self, as a consequence of that same collective force. The culture in which the woman writer was immersed already disfigured her face and voice, dictating to her the kind of identity appropriate to her sex and declaring *persona non grata* the autonomous feminine personality. Against that prejudicial conception of a woman writer's autobiographical act as insult, Carolina Coronado returned insult for insult. Using another strategy, Vicenta García Miranda in her turn tried to revitalize the conventional image of the *poetisa*, by infusing it with great emotional intensity, converting the worn-out trope into the autobiographical act of 'Recuerdos y pensamientos'. The trope of course does not disappear. It is a thing inherent to language and to autobiography. In denying the woman writer individual autonomy, her culture threatened to leave her in a state of anonymity. And anonymity meant more than a woman writer's mutilation. It signified her very annulment.[10]

NOTES

1. The trend in cultural anthropology to study relationships between individual feelings and group structure has been called an 'anthropology of affect' (Gilmore 3–4). I take the term 'process of situation' from Fernandez. See also Brandes and Lisón Tolosana.

2. As late as 1900 Luis Taboada would create an anti-Romantic satire, exploiting the stereotype of the Romantic fiancée: 'Gertrudis era, en efecto, un ser impresionable y nervioso; una poetisa tierna que acababa de escribir unos versos y rompía a llorar' [Gertrude was, in effect, an impressionable and nervous creature; a tender poetess who would scribble verses and then burst out crying]. And then in an obvious parody of the Avellaneda dictum: '¡Era mucha Gertrudis aquella!' [She was some Gertrude, that one!] (116–17).

3. This double image of the woman writer, as caught between two kinds of work, or *labores*, of unequal importance, already appears in the writings of Josefa Massanés: 'Tampoco teman que la instrucción en el bello sexo redunde en contra de sus ocupaciones domésticas, ocupaciones que desempeñándose sin fijar en ellas más que una atención maquinal dejan obrar el entendimiento por reparado; no sirviendo de obstáculo en manera alguna a las labores en que se entretienen las manos, las concepciones en que al mismo tiempo se divierte la imaginación' [Do not fear either that education in the weaker sex will do injury to her domestic duties, duties that are carried out without fixing upon them more than desultory

attention, thus permitting thought to function automatically; not being an obstacle of any sort to the work with which the hands amuse themselves, or the ideas with which at the same time the imagination diverts itself] (1841*a*: p. x). See also Kirkpatrick 281–2.

4. With a honed sense of malice, this same writer begins another satire of his, 'La literata', with an epigraph from Carolina Coronado. Published in Paris and dated 1845, 'La literata' appeared in the *Semanario Pintoresco Español*, 33 (18 Aug. 1850): 258–9), a journal to which Coronado also contributed. In 1846 Carolina used the same device of heading epigraphically her poem 'A Neira' with a quotation—slightly modified—from Neira himself, 'Carolina Coronado acompaña en su despedida a las golondrinas, a las grullas y a los patos' [Carolina Coronado accompanies the departure of swallows, cranes, and ducks] (1852: 134).

5. Gilmore analyses eleven types of gossip: (1) *criticar*, (2) *rajar*, (3) *darle a la lengua*, (4) *chismorrear*, (5) *paliquear*, (6) *cortar el traje*, (7) *charlar*, (8) *hablar oculto*, (9) *contar*, (10) *cuchichear*, and (11) *murmurar* (69–74).

6. Well into the 20th cent. we find reactions like this one of Gloria Fuertes, who writes: '¡Hago versos, señores!, pero no me gusta que me llamen poetisa' [I write verses, sirs! But don't call me a poetess] (129).

7. The legitimization of women's poetry through the metaphor of domesticity is turned on its head later in the idealization of domestic work through poetry, as these comments of María del Pilar Sinués make clear: 'No es la poesía tan sólo aquel rayo que ilumina la mente del que hace versos. La poesía está en el mundo bajo diversas formas . . . La poesía es la compañera inseparable de la mujer buena y la que embellece el hogar doméstico' [Poetry is not simply that ray of light shining upon the mind of the poet. Poetry exists in the world in many forms . . . Poetry is the inseparable companion of the good woman; poetry beautifies the home] (1875: 11).

8. Josefa Massanés is already using the same terminology in 1841: '[E]l temor de que sea mirado como *un crimen* el que yo . . . entregue a la censura pública mis sencillas concepciones . . . me ha inducido a exponer las ideas que dejo vertidas en este discurso' [The fear I had that submitting to public censure my simple compositions would be regarded as *a crime* . . . has induced me to explain why I wrote this essay] (1841*a*: p. xv; emphasis added). See also Kirkpatrick 281–3.

9. The relationship between Vicenta García Miranda and her mentor, Juan Leandro Jiménez, a minor Extremaduran poet (1811–51), has been studied by Manzano Garías (1957, 1969). In the *ars poetica* that Juan Leandro wrote for Vicenta's benefit, he criticizes harshly (and with little understanding, in my view) 'Recuerdos y pensamientos' as far too lavish in its praise of Carolina Coronado. See Manzano Garías 1957: 329. Lack of space prevents me from elaborating on this very odd relationship.

10. Critics are now re-evaluating these writers of the last century. See Kirkpatrick's fine study and Valis 1990, 1991.

WORKS CITED

ALDARACA, BRIDGET (1982). ' "El ángel del hogar": The Cult of Domesticity in Nineteenth-Century Spain', in Gabriela Mora and Karen S. Van Hooft (eds.), *Theory and Practice of Feminist Literary Criticism*. Ypsilanti, Mich.: Bilingual Press/Editorial Bilingüe. 62–87.

ARMIÑO, ROBUSTIANA (1851). *Poesías*, vol. i, introd. by Carolina Coronado. Oviedo: Imprenta y Litografía de Martínez Hermanos.

ARMSTRONG, NANCY (1987). 'The Rise of the Domestic Woman', in Nancy Armstrong and Leonard Tennenhouse (eds.), *The Ideology of Conduct.* New York: Methuen. 96–141.

AZA, VITAL (1894). 'A una poetisa', *La Gran Vía* (Madrid), 2/45 (6 May): 285.

BABBITT, IRVING (1986). 'On Being Original', in *Literature and the American College: Essays on the Defense of the Humanities* (1908). Washington, DC: National Humanities Institute. 186–201.

BLANCO, ALDA (1989). 'Domesticity, Education and the Woman Writer: Spain 1850–1880', in Hernán Vidal (ed.), *Cultural and Historical Grounding for Hispanic and Luso-Brazilian Feminist Literary Criticism.* Minneapolis: Institute for the Study of Ideologies and Literature. 371–94.

BRANDES, STANLEY (1986). *Metaphors of Masculinity: Sex and Status in Andalusian Folklore* (1980). Philadelphia: University of Pennsylvania Press.

CASTELAR, EMILIO (1964). 'Doña Carolina Coronado', in J. García Mercadal (ed.), *Discursos y ensayos.* Madrid: Aguilar. 231–45.

CASTRO, ROSALÍA DE (1960a). *El caballero de las botas azules*, in *Obras completas.* 5th edn. Madrid: Aguilar.

—— (1960b). 'Las literatas (carta a Eduarda)', in *Obras completas.* Madrid: Aguilar. 1536–41.

CORONADO, CAROLINA (1852). *Poesías.* Madrid: n.p.

—— (1914). 'Galería de poetas contemporáneos: Doña Gertrudis Gómez de Avellaneda', in Gertrudis Gómez de Avellaneda, *Obras de la Avellaneda*, vol. vi. Havana: Imprenta de Aurelio Miranda. 481–7. (Orig. in *La Discusión*, 5 Aug. 1857 and 29 May 1858.)

DE DIEGO, ESTRELLA (1987). *La mujer y la pintura del XIX español.* Madrid: Cátedra.

DE MAN, PAUL (1979). 'Autobiography as De-facement', *Modern Language Notes*, 94: 919–30.

DOUGLAS, ANN (1978). *The Feminization of American Culture* (1977). New York: Avon.

FERNANDEZ, JAMES W. (1976). 'Poetry in Motion: Being Moved by Amusement, by Mockery, and by Mortality in the Asturian Countryside', *New Literary History*, 8: 459–83.

FONSECA RUIZ, ISABEL (1974). 'Cartas de Carolina Coronado a Juan Eugenio Hartzenbusch', in *Homenaje a Guillermo Guastavino.* Madrid: Asociación Nacional de Bibliotecarios, Archiveros y Arqueólogos. 171–99.

FUERTES, GLORIA (1970). '¡Hago versos, señores!', in Francisco Ynduráin (ed.), *Antología poética 1950–1969.* Barcelona: Plaza y Janés. 129.

GALLEGO, JUAN NICASIO (1869). Prologue, in Gertrudis Gómez de Avellaneda, *Obras literarias*, vol. i. Madrid: Imprenta y Estereotipia de M. Rivadeneyra. pp. vii–xiii.

GARCÍA MIRANDA. VICENTA (1855). 'Recuerdos y pensamientos: a Carolina', in *Flores del valle: poesías.* Badajoz: Imprenta y Librería de D. Gerónimo Orduña. 146–55.

—— (1981). 'La poetisa de aldea', in *Notas biográficas y breve antología poética de Vicenta García Miranda, poetisa de Campanario.* Campanario: Fondo Cultural Valeria. 12–14.

GILMAN, SANDER L. (1985). *Difference and Pathology: Stereotypes of Sexuality, Race, and Madness.* Ithaca, NY: Cornell University Press.

GILMORE, DAVID D. (1987). *Aggression and Community: Paradoxes of Andalusian Culture.* New Haven, Conn.: Yale University Press.

GIL Y CAMPOS, JOSÉ (1889). 'A una poetisa', *La Avispa* (Madrid), 6/246 (15 May): n.pag.

GIMENO DE FLAQUER, CONCEPCIÓN (1891). 'Una española insigne', *El Álbum Iberoamericano* (Madrid), 2nd series 9/21 (7 June): 242–3.

—— (1901). *La mujer intelectual*. Madrid: Imprenta del Asilo de Huérfanos.

H., J., and M., J. (1855). *Biografía de la distinguida poetisa señorita Doña María Verdejo y Durán*. Saragossa: Imprenta y depósito de libros de Antonio Gallifa.

HARTZENBUSCH, JUAN EUGENIO (1843). Introduction, in Carolina Coronado, *Poesías*. Madrid: Imprenta de Alegría y Charlain. pp. i–xii.

KIRKPATRICK, SUSAN (1989). *Las Románticas: Women Writers and Subjectivity in Spain, 1835–1850*. Berkeley, Calif.: University of California Press.

LISÓN TOLOSANA, CARMELO (1974). 'Arte verbal y estructura social en Galicia', in *Perfiles simbólico-morales de la cultura gallega* (1974). 2nd edn. Madrid: Akal. 29–60.

MANZANO GARÍAS, ANTONIO (1957). 'Historia de un manuscrito inédito (1849)', *Revista de Estudios Extremeños*, 13: 301–45.

—— (1962). 'Amalia Fenollosa', *Boletín de la Sociedad Castellonense de Cultura*, 38: 38–80.

—— (1969). 'De una década extremeña y romántica (1845–55)', *Revista de Estudios Extremeños*, 25: 281–332.

MASSANÉS, JOSEFA (1841a). 'Discurso preliminar', in *Poesías*. Barcelona: J. Rubió. pp. i–xv.

—— (1841b). 'La resolución', in *Poesías*. Barcelona: J. Rubió. 191–7.

MICHIE, HELENA (1987). *The Flesh Made Word: Female Figures and Women's Bodies*. New York: Oxford University Press.

MILLER, BETH (1983). 'Gertrude the Great: Avellaneda, Nineteenth-Century Feminist', in Beth Miller (ed.), *Women in Hispanic Literature: Icons and Fallen Idols*. Berkeley, Calif.: University of California Press. 201–14.

NEIRA DE MOSQUERA, ANTONIO (1845). *Las ferias de Madrid: almoneda moral, política y literaria*. Madrid: P. Madoz y L. Sagasti.

—— (1850). 'La literata', *Semanario Pintoresco Español* (Madrid), 33 (18 August): 258–9.

ONG, WALTER J. (1981). *Fighting for Life: Contest, Sexuality, and Consciousness*. Ithaca, NY: Cornell University Press.

ORTNER, SHERRY B. (1972). 'Is Female to Male as Nature Is to Culture?', *Feminist Studies*, 1/2 (1972): 5–31.

POOVEY, MARY (1984). *The Proper Lady and the Woman Writer*. Chicago: University of Chicago Press.

SCANLON, GERALDINE M. (1986). *La polémica feminista en la España contemporánea (1868–1974)* (1976). 2nd edn. Madrid: Akal.

SHOWALTER, ELAINE (1977). *A Literature of their Own: British Women Novelists from Brontë to Lessing*. Princeton, NJ: Princeton University Press.

—— (1985). 'Feminist Criticism in the Wilderness', in Elaine Showalter (ed.), *The New Feminist Criticism*. New York: Pantheon. 243–70.

SIMÓN PALMER, MARÍA DEL CARMEN (1986). 'La mujer y la literatura en la España del siglo XIX', in A. David Kossoff *et al.* (eds.), *Actas del VIII Congreso de la Asociación Internacional de Hispanistas*, vol. ii. Madrid: Istmo. 591–6.

SINUÉS DE MARCO, MARÍA DEL PILAR (1860). 'Biografía de la señora doña Faustina Saez de Melgar', in Faustina Saez de Melgar, *La higuera de Villaverde*. Madrid: Imprenta de D. Bernabé Fernández. 77–88.

—— (1875). 'La poesía del hogar doméstico', in *Un libro para las damas*. Madrid: A. de Carlos e Hijo, Editores. 11–18.

SMITH, SIDONIE (1987). *A Poetics of Women's Autobiography*. Bloomington, Ind.: Indiana University Press.

TABOADA, LUIS (1900). 'Cuando yo era romántico', in *Intimidades y recuerdos*. Madrid: Administración de 'El Imparcial'. 115–24.

VALIS, NOËL (1990). 'The Language of Treasure: Carolina Coronado, Casta Esteban, and Marina Romero', in Noël Valis and Carol Maier (eds.), *In the Feminine Mode: Essays on Hispanic Women Writers*. Lewisburg, Pa.: Bucknell University Press. 246–72.

—— (1991). Introduction, in Carolina Coronado, *Poesías*. Madrid: Castalia.

3
'Poesía . . . eres tú', or the Construction of Bécquer and the Sign of Woman

JAMES MANDRELL

The dictum 'Poesía . . . eres tú' [Poetry . . . is you] (59; 549)—found both in the last line of the twenty-first *rima* (*LG* 21) and in the first of the *Cartas literarias a una mujer*—sums up what has long been considered one of the more pressing questions with respect to Gustavo Adolfo Bécquer and his poetry and prose.[1] This question is nothing less than the nature of woman, as well as the identity of *the* woman, in Bécquer's work, and it has had serious implications for the study of Bécquer. With few exceptions, discussions of the poetry included in the volume known as the *Rimas* [Poems; literally, rhymes] and of the texts in prose linked to the poetry—specifically the 'Introducción sinfónica' [Symphonic Introduction], 'La mujer de piedra' [The Woman of Stone], and the *Cartas literarias a una mujer* [Literary Letters to a Woman]—tend toward an explicit or even implicit consideration of the identity of the woman or various women to have inspired or to be addressed in these works. If speculation oscillates between the real and the ideal, between Bécquer's biography and the literary texts themselves, the biographical impulse predominates.

To be sure, many of Bécquer's biographers, critics, and exegetes are following the lead of the poet himself. In the *Rimas*, Bécquer seems to speak to a specific or 'real' woman (the 'hermosa', or beautiful woman, of the first *rima* (*LG* 11) or the woman with whom the poet reads Dante's *Inferno* in the twenty-ninth (*LG* 53)), yet also to desire a woman who is intangible or 'ideal' (the 'vano fantasma de niebla y luz' [vain phantasm of mist and light] (81/573) of the eleventh poem (*LG* 51)). It therefore comes as no surprise that Francisco López Estrada suggests in his study of the *Cartas literarias* that there is most likely a particular woman to whom the letters were addressed, perhaps Julia Espín or Bécquer's future wife Casta Esteban, but that, given the nature of the publication of these works, Bécquer is directing himself to *all* women, the *ideal* woman who would read the *Cartas*:

> me parece que Bécquer (independientemente de cuanto hubiese en las *Cartas* de realidad vivida u observada) no quiso referirse en concreto a una mujer determinada, aunque todas las que tuvieron su amor puedan estar en ella, y esta mujer única de las *Cartas* se transfigure en la realidad cuantas veces sea necesario.

> it seems to me that Bécquer (independently of however much lived or observed reality there might be in the *Cartas*) refused to refer directly to a specific woman, even though all of those that he loved might be found in her. This unique woman of the *Cartas* is transfigured in reality as often as necessary. (70)

From Bécquer's poetry and prose to more recent discussions of Bécquer and his *œuvre*, then, the topic of woman has remained central and speculation endless on the identity or nature of the woman in Bécquer's poetry because we know so little for certain about the personal life of the poet that would illuminate his verse. As José Carlos de Torres remarks in the introduction to his edition of the poems—an edition that incorporates, not co-incidentally, the 'Introducción sinfónica', the 'Mujer de piedra', and the *Cartas literarias* as well as Ramón Rodríguez Correa's biographical introduction to the posthumous first and second editions of Bécquer's *Obras completas* [Complete Works]:

> Respecto a su biografía, después de la lanzada por la leyenda romántica (incluso en nuestro siglo) podemos llegar a la conclusión de que algo muy profundo de sus sentimientos, que escribió en cartas, fatalmente se ha perdido para la crítica (literaria y psicológica, aunque ya no lo sabremos nunca), al quemarlas personalmente en vísperas del fin para no comprometer su honor ... se destruyeron cartas que podían haber revelado datos claves sobre sus sentimientos y quién(es) era(n) las(s) mujer(es) inspiradora(s) de su amor. Lo que resta, puede sacarse de los mismos testimonios del poeta; las noticias que se encuentran en la prensa, ya que su profesión periodística ayuda a ello; los recuerdos de los amigos y, sobre todo, las aportaciones de una crítica objetiva interesada en la obra becqueriana por la importancia que ha supuesto para la poesía posterior española.

With respect to his biography, after the launching of the romantic legend (including in our own century), we can arrive at the conclusion that some very profound trace of his sentiments, which he included in his letters, was fatally lost to criticism (literary and psychological, even though we will never know) when he personally burned his papers on the eve of his death so as not to compromise his honour . . . letters were destroyed that might have revealed key information as to his sentiments and the identity of the woman (women) who inspired his love. All we are left with is the poet's own testimony; information found in periodicals, especially since Bécquer was a journalist; the recollections of his friends and, above all, the contributions of an objective criticism interested in Bécquer's *œuvre* because of its importance to later Spanish poetry. (11–12)

The constant return to the topic of woman indicates that there is something more of interest in the figure if not the identity of the woman in Bécquer's poetry and prose. If there can be no definitive answer to the question that is woman in Bécquer's *Rimas*, if we cannot know to whom the *Cartas literarias* were originally addressed, why are we still bothered by this issue? What itch are we trying to scratch when we once again try to read the sign of Bécquer's woman, to fit the signifier with a particular, as yet unknown, signified?

My own hunch is that interest in the woman in Bécquer's poetry and prose has less to do with the *Rimas* as poetic texts, or with the 'Introducción sinfónica', 'La mujer de piedra', and the *Cartas literarias a una mujer* as expressive poetics, than with the creation of a literary text and the patriarchal ideology often embodied in certain types of literature, particularly lyric poetry. In other words, scholars and critics have asked the wrong questions of Bécquer and his poetry, and have quite literally sought to determine the identity of the 'tú' of 'Poesía . . . eres tú' without carefully considering the various implications of the texts they are discussing. This is the case for two reasons, the first that, as Heidi Hartmann suggests, patriarchy can be defined as the 'set of social relations between men, which have a material base, and which, though hierarchical, establish or create interdependence and solidarity among men that enable them to dominate women' (14). In this guise, the itch that is scratched when discussing women in Bécquer's poetry and prose is that pertaining to furthering the hegemony of patriarchal ideologies. The furthering of this ideology brings us to the second point. As

Teresa L. Ebert explains in her Lacanian treatment of patriarchy and postmodern feminist theory, patriarchal culture tends toward concealing the ideological nature of its discourse:

ideology is the dynamic operator that organizes signifying practices and attempts to fix and to limit the representations, meaning, and subjectivities they produce according to the requirements of the symbolic order. . . . Ideology is thus misrepresentation, not in that it is a false version of some originary 'real' or that it stands in opposition to the 'truth' or an 'objective' science outside ideology (as in Althusser's theory), but in that it *represents* itself and its signifying practices as 'natural', unified—even global—totalities free of contradictions. It conceals not only its own inconsistencies but also its own construction through signification. (26–7)

Bécquer's poetry and the pertinent texts in prose are intimately implicated in patriarchal ideologies, as are most discussions of the poet and his work. And the literary texts and their explications, to say nothing of the explanations of Bécquer's life, become part and parcel of the creation of and enabling 'interdependence and solidarity among men' as well as the concealment of its 'own construction through signification'.

It is my contention, then, that discussions of Bécquer and the question of woman respond not necessarily to the poems in and of themselves, but to the thematic grouping of the poems as found in the volume entitled *Rimas*, and to the narrative given the poems by Rodríguez Correa in his biographical introduction to the posthumous *Obras completas*. Moreover, I would suggest that Bécquer's biography, especially as found in some of the more sensational and sentimental versions, furnishes an interpretative key that proves almost impossibly seductive to scholars and critics alike, whether or not these more apparently 'objective' readers realize it. Finally, the view of woman that emerges from the *Rimas*, biographies of Bécquer, and critical approaches to the question of woman in Bécquer's poetry and prose has less to do with Bécquer and much more to do with nineteenth-century attitudes toward women and artistic creation, and to the ways in which these attitudes are carried into and fostered in the twentieth century. Because any attempt to address the consequences of the question of woman in Bécquer's poetry and prose must confront prior considerations of the topic, my own argument will be elaborate, even Byzantine, since at least initially I will not be discussing the woman question in Bécquer's poetry *per se*, but the conditions that allow for this topic to appear to be so pressing and of such import. This is not intended as a slight to the topic of woman in Bécquer's poetry so much as an acknowledgment that woman as a topic is embedded in a more general literary and cultural discourse regarding Bécquer and his milieu. The question of woman remains the subtext, if not the more obvious focus, for my remarks.[2]

I also hasten to add that the topic of the text and order of the *Rimas*, and the problem of biographical interpretations, are not new to Bécquer criticism. Juan M. Díez Taboada comments in an important 1967 article that 'nos interesa penetrar ahora en el origen de esta ordenación' [it is of interest now to inquire into the origin of this ordering] (284); and he sketches out three critical paths to a consideration of the question. There is, first, biographical criticism, which deals with the literature in terms of events either real or imagined from Bécquer's life; second, the search to reproduce the chronology of the composition of the poems, which Díez Taboada deems 'very common'; and third, the search for an internal logic that would give us an idea of the 'psychological-amorous evolution that the book presents' (289). Yet these three paths—which Díez Taboada would most likely admit are not the only ones available—do not address the assumptions that such an interest in order in general and in the present order in particular supposes. In other words, the textual question has less to do with *what* order than with *why this* order.

In fact, the literary texts we are discussing are, for the most part, somewhat artificial or inauthentic, in the sense that their grouping together constitutes a critical act or act of homage, and not a creative act attributable to the author. Bécquer's *Obras completas* were first published posthumously in two volumes in 1871, following the poet's death on 22 December 1870; a second, more complete edition came out in 1877. The poetic text known as the *Rimas* is a reordering of poems found in Bécquer's 600-page manuscript volume entitled 'Libro de los gorriones: colección de proyectos, argumentos, ideas y planes de cosas diferentes que se concluirán o no según sople el viento' [Book of Sparrows: Collection of Projects, Plots, Ideas, and Plans for Different Things that Might or Might not Be Finished in Accordance with how the Wind Blows]. This bound book of blank pages and manuscript texts contains the 'Introducción sinfónica' on pages 5 to 7; the 'Mujer de piedra' on pages 9 to 19; blank sheets from page

20 to page 528; and the poems, with an index, on pages 529 to 600. The *Obras completas*, in which the *Rimas* are to be found, is therefore not Bécquer's work but the creation of a group of Bécquer's friends, principally Rodríguez Correa with the help of José Casado del Alisal, Julio Nombela, Narciso Campillo, and Augusto Ferrán. Only sixteen of the seventy-nine poems in the *Libro de los gorriones* appeared in Spanish journals during Bécquer's lifetime; of the seventy-nine poems in the *Libro de los gorriones*, only seventy-six were published in the first *Obras completas*. Neither the 'Introducción sinfónica' nor the 'Mujer de piedra' were published previous to the posthumous *Obras*. As for the *Cartas literarias a una mujer*, they are not part of the *Libro de los gorriones*. Rather, they were published anonymously in the pages of the newspaper *El Contemporáneo* on 20 December 1860, 8 January 1861, and 4 and 23 April 1861 prior to their inclusion in the second—but not the first—edition of the *Obras completas*. The Bécquer we now read is, then, the narrative constructed by his friends from his various published and unpublished works.

If the *Rimas* are not presented either in the *Obras completas* or in most subsequent editions of the poetry, including modern editions, in the order in which they appear in the *Libro de los gorriones*, and if the ordering of the *Rimas* poses a problem to which textual critics return time and again, it is nevertheless an issue for the most part easily set aside, since the individual poems now possess two numbers by which they are designated: there is a roman numeral that situates them in a posthumously created body of poetry and that usually serves to suffice as a defining mark; and an arabic number, probably overlooked by most readers, that locates the poems in the *Libro de los gorriones*. In his study of Bécquer's poetry (now in its fourth edition), José Pedro Díaz writes of the discrepancy in the order of the poems:

> Desde que las rimas fueron publicadas por primera vez, varios escritores señalaron en este orden un *sentido* y, algunos, la existencia de diversos grupos o series sucesivas. Rodríguez Correa ya insinuaba, en 1871, y otros afirmaron después concretamente, que ese ordenamiento parece descubrir las alternativas de una historia de amor que, partiendo de una primera etapa feliz y esperanzada, celebra luego francamente el amor, llora después su desengaño y canta, por último, la más angustiada soledad.

Since the poems were first published, various writers have detected in this order a *sense* and—in some cases—the existence of distinct groupings or successive series. As early as 1871, Rodríguez Correa insinuated—and others later explicitly affirmed—that this order seemed to reveal the twists and turns of a love story that, beginning with an initial happy and hopeful phase, goes on to celebrate love openly before lamenting its disillusionment and finally singing of the anguish of solitude. (370–2)

Díaz goes on to propose what is now accepted as the traditional division of the *Rimas* into four groupings. The first grouping comprises the first eleven poems and has to do with the nature of poetry itself. The second set—poems XII to XXIX—treats the topic of love in an 'affirmative and luminous tone' (374). The third series begins with poem XXX and ends with LI, and deals with disillusionment. The fourth and final group—poems LII to LXXIX—is considered the most disparate, the defining characteristic being less a topic or theme than a pervasive air of 'unfathomable pain, desperate and solitary anguish' (378). The quibbles other critics and scholars may have with Díaz's divisions and terminology, and their minor modifications to his sequence, are generally left to one side, in deference not only to Díaz but also to the overriding narrative provided by Rodríguez Correa.

By offering what is in essence a typically Romantic account of the vicissitudes of love, Rodríguez Correa pre-empts and shapes subsequent discussion. His version portrays Bécquer as a hero worthy of comparison to Goethe's Werther or many other Romantic figures, which means that the man that Rodríguez Correa identifies as Gustavo Adolfo Bécquer is not so comprehensible to us as a human of flesh and bone but as a fictional form of the tragic artist. In the end, as we shall show, Rodríguez Correa's Bécquer is not so different from Clarín's Saturnino Bermúdez of *La Regenta* (1884–5) or Benito Pérez Galdós's Horacio of *Tristana* (1892).

Rodríguez Correa's representation of the poetry also reveals Bécquer's singularity:

personalmente siente y manifiesta sus particulares sensaciones, resultando, y así debe ser, que aquéllas son comprensibles para todos, porque las experimenta ni más ni menos que como cualquier otro, si bien revela la manera de percibirlas bajo una forma poética, a fin de despertar esos mismos sentimientos en los demás. Sus pasiones, sus alegrías, sus aspiraciones, sus dolores, sus esperanzas, sus desengaños, son espontáneos e ingenuos, y semejantes a los que lleva en sí todo corazón, por insensible que sea.

he personally feels and expresses his particular sensations, so that they are comprehensible to everyone, as they should be, because his emotions are those of every man, even if he shows the ability to describe them in a poetic form so as to awaken those same feelings in the rest of us. His passions, his joys, his aspirations, his pains, his hopes, his disillusionments are spontaneous and ingenuous, and similar to those held in every heart, however insensitive. (211)

Note the way in which in this presentation Bécquer becomes the omniscient narrator of our own experiences and desires, the one who can speak of our secret lives. In generalizing from the poems that make up the *Rimas* not only the details of Bécquer's own life but also the elements of the lives of those who read the poetry, Rodríguez Correa turns Bécquer and the experiences articulated in the poetry into a master or key narrative of individual existence, a narrative that emphasizes the quintessentially Romantic character of amorous encounters as well as the quintessentially Romantic nature of the genius who speaks of them. The power of this account rests in the broad diffusion of these and similar terms for describing the surprisingly repetitive nature of love. In particular it assumes, first, the Romantic and tragic character of that love and, second, depends on a specific view of woman, both conditions that, as Susan Kirkpatrick notes, are intimately connected to the type of poetic subjectivity characteristic of Spanish Romanticism. According to Kirkpatrick, the 'self represented by the Romantic text . . . is inevitably the writing subject in the process of constructing itself' (11), as in Bécquer's poetry and as elucidated by Rodríguez Correa; but these very same texts 'tacitly acknowledge the undeniably gendered character of Romantic paradigms of selfhood by identifying them almost exclusively with male figures and coding as feminine those entities that did not represent full, conscious, independent subjects—the beloved, nature, or the poetic creation' (23).

As for the trajectory of the *Rimas*, Rodríguez Correa asserts a similarly familiar and coherent narrative, one that makes clear the nature of woman:

Todas las *Rimas* de Gustavo forman, como el *Intermezzo* de Heine, un poema, más ancho y completo que aquél, en que se encierra la vida de un poeta. Son, primero, las aspiraciones de un corazón ardiente, que busca en el arte la realización de sus deseos, dudando de su destino. . . . Siéntese poeta. . . .

No encontrando realizada su ilusión en la gloria, vuélvese espontáneamente hacia el amor, realismo del arte, y se entrega a él, y goza un momento, y sufre y llora, y desespera largos días, porque es condición humana, indiscutible, como un hecho consumado, el goce menor se paga aquí con los sufrimientos más atroces. Anúnciase esta nueva fase en la vida del poeta con la magnífica composición que, no sé por qué, me recuerda la atrevida manera de decir del Dante. . . . Sigue luego desenvolviéndose el tema de una pasión profunda, tan sentida como espontánea.

Una mujer hermosa, tan naturalmente hermosa, que . . . conmueve y fija el corazón del poeta, que se abre al amor, olvidándose de cuanto le rodea. La pasión es desde su principio inmensa, avasalladora, y con razón, puesto que se ve correspondida, o, al menos, parece satisfecha del objeto que la inspira: una mujer hermosa, aunque sin otra buena cualidad, porque es ingrata y estúpida. ¡Tarde lo conoce, cuando ya se siente engañado y descubre dentro de un pecho tan fino y suave, un corazón *nido de sierpes*, en el cual *no hay una fibra que al amor responda!* Aquí, en medio de sus dolores, llega el poeta a la desesperación; pero, cuando ésta le lleva ya al punto en que se pierde toda esperanza, él se detiene espontáneamente, medita en silencio, y aceptando por último su parte de dolor en el dolor común, prosigue su camino, triste.

All of Gustavo's *Rimas* form, like Heine's *Intermezzo*, one poem, fuller and more complete than the other, encapsulating the life of a poet. First, there are the aspirations of an ardent heart, that seeks in art the realization of its desires, doubting its own destiny. . . . He feels himself to be a poet. . . .

Failing to find his illusion realized in glory, he spontaneously turns to love, the realism of art, and he surrenders himself to it and enjoys a momentary happiness, and he suffers and cries, despairing for long days at a stretch, because it is indisputably the human condition, a consummated fact that the smallest pleasure is thus paid for with the most atrocious suffering. This new phase in the life of the poet announces itself with the magnificent composition that—for some reason—reminds me of Dante's daring manner of speaking. . . . Then the topic of a profound passion continues to unfold, as heartfelt as spontaneous.

A beautiful woman, so naturally beautiful . . . touches and fixes on the heart of the poet, who opens himself to love, forgetting everything around him. From the very beginning, the passion is immense, overwhelming, and with reason, since it is requited, or at least appears to satisfy the object inspiring it: a beautiful woman, without any other good quality, since she is ungrateful and stupid. He recognizes this all too late, feeling himself to be deceived and discovering in a breast so delicate and soft a heart like *a nest of serpents*, in which *not a single fibre responds to love!* Now in the midst of his pain, the poet plunges into despair; but when despair carries him to the point of losing all hope, he spontaneously pauses, meditates in silence, and, finally accepting his share of common pain, continues on his way, sad. (217–19)

According to Rodríguez Correa, our reading of the *Rimas* ought to uncover the tragic love story in which the personal details of Bécquer's unfortunate experience become expressive of general human truths. More to the point is the fact that it is a particular woman to whom Bécquer's downfall may be attributed, a woman who is 'naturally beautiful' but 'stupid', a woman who is associated with the eternal sin of women (since her heart is a 'nest of serpents'), the Romantic type recognized as 'la belle dame sans merci'. Bécquer's personal history as a lyric poet victimized by tragedies of love and an early death not only situates itself in the readily comprehensible narrative tradition of the tragic artist but also accuses woman as the culprit in this sad story.

What we end up with, then, is a portrait of Bécquer that is so easily understood in literary terms and in terms of the cultural discourse of the mid-nineteenth century that the prose becomes as if transparent. For those who would remark on such things, the prose is anything but neutral. But for those for whom such points of view are not only natural but givens, the description of Bécquer provided by Rodríguez Correa and perpetuated by others who spoke about Bécquer seems all too normal. As for the portrait of woman that emerges, all of the negative attributes associated with women in the nineteenth century come to mind: she is vulgar, arrogant, stupid and foolish, hopelessly earthbound in her desires and aspirations, and fully capable of plunging any man in love with her into despair, or, worse, dragging him to his death.[3] These naturalizing tendencies are, of course, similar to the ways in which Roland Barthes discusses myth in the modern world. In Barthes's Saussurian reading of myth, he shows how myth both bears and universalizes or, better, naturalizes certain parts of the world so as to make them immediately comprehensible in terms of bourgeois ideology, since, when 'practised on a national scale, bourgeois norms are experienced as the evident laws of a natural order—the further the bourgeois class propagates its representations, the more naturalized they become' (140). Thus, the temporal aspects of the world, of 'reality', are linked to the timeless discourse of myth to make things appear one way or another because that is the way they have always been and should be:

What the world supplies to myth is an historical reality, defined, even if this goes back quite a while, by the way in which men have produced or used it; and what myth gives in return is a *natural* image of this reality. And just as bourgeois ideology is defined by the abandonment of the name 'bourgeois', myth is constituted by the loss of the historical quality of things: in it, things lose the memory they once were made. (142)

Rodríguez Correa's presentation of Bécquer qualifies as an example of this type of mythical discourse. When Rodríguez Correa assumes that Bécquer's 'pasiones, sus alegrías, sus aspiraciones, sus dolores, sus esperanzas, sus desengaños, son espontáneos e ingenuos, y semejantes a los que lleva en sí todo corazón, por insensible que sea' [passions, his joys, his aspirations, his pains, his hopes, his disillusionments are spontaneous and ingenuous, and similar to those held in every heart, however insensitive], he presumes that we as readers understand those emotions as universal, that 'spontaneity' is desired and to be envied in 'every heart, however insensitive'. This is likewise the case in the discussion of the trajectory of the *Rimas*, the recurring recourse to 'spontaneity', 'the realism [and therefore naturalized comprehensibility of] art', the 'beautiful woman, so *naturally* beautiful', the italics emphasizing the 'heart like a *nest of serpents*', which harks back to the Garden of Eden and Adam and Eve. In playing on the cultural myths of love and of women, Rodríguez Correa provokes sympathy for Bécquer by creating of him the nineteenth-century Spanish version of Barthes's 'Eternal Man'; and these myths masked as cultural truths, although made, readily conceal the processes by which they have been elaborated.

We could corroborate the view that the presentation of Bécquer is all too natural in a number of different ways, including references to nineteenth-century treatises and conduct manuals, but the easiest might be to demonstrate the literary qualities of these narratives by turning to nineteenth-century novelistic texts. As points of comparison, then, consider briefly the cases of Clarín's Saturnino Bermúdez of *La Regenta* and Galdós's Horacio of *Tristana* and their relations with women, the first as a kind of parodic counterpart to the tragic poet, the second as a more sanguine version of the inspired artist. Saturnino Bermúdez is, of course, the local historian in Clarín's Vetusta, a man misunderstood by those around him, especially the single and married women to whom he devotes himself. He ends up remarking after yet another rebuff by Obdulia, a local woman of easy virtue, '¡Así eran las mujeres! ¡así era singularmente aquella mujer! ¿Para qué amarlas? ¿Para qué perseguir el ideal del amor? O mejor dicho, ¿para qué amar a las mujeres vivas, de carne y hueso? Mejor era soñar, seguir soñando' [Such was Woman! Such, in particular, was this woman! Wherefore love women? Wherefore pursue the ideal of love? Or rather, wherefore love real women, women of flesh and blood? Better far to dream—to continue dreaming] (i. 503; Eng. trans. 298). We find in Saturnino Bermúdez the pathetic reincarnation of the tragic individual who gives up on love for the inspiration afforded by the putative feminine ideal. Bermúdez becomes a virtual parody of the real yet fictionalized Bécquer, who, though supposedly not fulfilled in the same way, would never have experienced the despair attributed to him had he not opened himself up to disillusionment in love as found at the hands of heartless—and stupid—women.

In contrast, Galdós's painter Horacio is not tragic, although his affair with Tristana draws to a tragic conclusion when one of her legs is amputated. Indeed, Horacio is of interest precisely because he is not overcome and subsequently disabled by unrequited love, and because the denouement of his relationship takes place over the course of a lengthy correspondence in which the many literary references to other lovers idealize love and destroy it, much as Bécquer's affections wane in the *Cartas literarias a una mujer* as the relationship between the poet and woman recedes into the past tenses of the preterite and imperfect. In the case of Galdós's Horacio, the love that Tristana and he share is shaded ironically by the narrative presentation such that it becomes the woman who would be an artist, and not the artist himself, who bears the burden of the tragedy. When Tristana and Horacio allow their relationship to progress to include sexual congress—a development that the narrator slyly alludes to by referring to Dante's Paolo and Francesca of the *Inferno* with his mention that the two lovers rarely walked outdoors, 'Y desde aquel día ya no pasearon más' [And from that day on they walked no more] (1562)—Tristana, her ambition, and her intelligence begin to assume almost monstrous proportions and to affect Horacio in dire ways as he loses interest in painting:

Estos alientos de artista, estos arranques de mujer superior, encantaban al buen Díaz, el cual, a poco de aquellos íntimos tratos, empezó a notar que la enamorada joven se iba creciendo a los ojos de él y le empequeñecía. . . . había soñado en Tristana la mujer subordinada al hombre en inteligencia y en voluntad, la esposa que vive de la savia moral e intelectual del esposo y que con los ojos y con el corazón de él ve y siente.

Her artistic spirit, her flights of feminine intelligence, delighted young Díaz. Not long after the beginning of their intimacy he noticed that she was growing before his eyes—and diminishing him. . . . in Tristana he had dreamed of the woman subordinated to man in intellect and will, the wife who lives on the husband's moral and intellectual sap and sees and feels with his eyes and his heart. (1563)

Although Horacio laughingly allows that he will 'wear the skirts' (1566), Tristana's independence, which at times she stridently asserts, allows them to drift apart. In the end, Horacio suggests to Tristana: 'no te aferres tanto a esa aspiración, que podría resultar impracticable. Entrégate a mí sin reserva. ¡Ser mi compañera de toda la vida; ayudarme y sostenerme con tu cariño! . . . ¿Te parece que hay un oficio mejor ni arte más hermosos? Hacer feliz a un hombre que te hará feliz, ¿qué más?' [don't cling too tightly to your aspiration; it might turn out to be impractical. Give yourself to me completely, without reserve. Be my lifelong companion; help me and support me with your love! . . . Do you think there's a higher work or a more beautiful art? Make a man happy who will make you happy, what more?] (1569–70). Once Horacio escapes from Tristana, he rediscovers his pleasure in art and nature; and when one of Tristana's legs is amputated, he is free of her forever.

Tristana's personal ambition, which for Horacio represents something unnatural, finds its counterpart in Clarín's Ana Ozores, *la Regenta* of the novel of the same title. When Ana is caught writing poetry in a notebook, the world around her reacts as one. The priest Ripamilán is perhaps the most charitable when he explains, 'las mujeres deben ocuparse en más dulces tareas; las musas no escriben, inspiran' [women should occupy themselves in gentler tasks; the Muses don't write, they inspire] (i. 232; 112), but the bottom line is that 'En una mujer hermosa es imperdonable el vicio de escribir' [In a beautiful woman, writing is an unpardonable vice] (i. 234; 113). Woman becomes and is encouraged to embody in these texts the problematic yet living muse of men, and, as such, her function as an inspiration is to exist as the necessary yet secondary element in an equation involving three terms: to exist between two men (much as Ana Ozores does between Fermín de Pas and Alvaro Mesía or Tristana exists between Don Lope and Horacio), between two families (as in exchange theories), or between an author and the literary text (as women become for Saturnino Bermúdez).

The narrative created by Rodríguez Correa in his biographical introduction to the *Rimas*, as exemplified by reading the poetry as a collection of autobiographical texts, re-creates as real the standard nineteenth-century text regarding women by invoking many of the time-honoured feminine stereotypes. As Lou Charnon-Deutsch comments apropos of novelists: 'Nineteenth-century male authors, eager to explore the dilemma of individuality in their male characters, very often take short cuts and rely for their female characters on the time-worn roles women play in Western literature: wicked stepmother, femme fatale, siren, keeper of cults, virgin, goddess, fisherman's wife, and Cinderella' (17). Clearly, Rodríguez Correa would have us believe that, in the case of Bécquer, the poet deserved and in fact sought a keeper of cults, a virginal—yet sexually desirable and available—goddess, a Cinderella, but ended up time and again with some version or even combination of the wicked stepmother, *femme fatale*, siren, or fisherman's wife.

In terms of these accounts, Bécquer ought to have dealt with his desire for the all-too-real and imperfect woman by sublimating that desire in deference to the all-too-ideal yet fortunately remote woman-as-muse, as he suggests in the eleventh poem (*LG* 51). If the 'vain phantasm of mist and light' is the *ideal* for Bécquer and for those who have written sentimentally of his life, then *reality*—in the form of the hopelessly prosaic and real women he loved or his wife Casta—was terribly disappointing, and that disappointment finds expression in laments for Bécquer's unrequited loves and early death. If, on the other hand, we read the eleventh poem as exemplary of a form of discourse on women—and Rodríguez Correa's introduction as integral to that tradition—we can begin to see how the construction of Bécquer as a tragic victim of life and love both draws from and reinforces traditional views of women.

As an indication of how pervasive that tradition is as well as how eternal some would see it, we need only turn to the twenty-ninth *rima* (*LG* 53), which harks back to Dante, both in the epigraph to the poem and in the body of the poem itself. This poem is particularly resonant at this moment in our discussion, expressing the notion of the timeless quality of the experience of love—from Lancelot and Guinevere, to Paolo and Francesca, and from there to Bécquer and the nameless woman—and possibly clarifying Rodríguez Correa's remark about 'la atrevida manera de decir del Dante' [Dante's daring manner of speaking]; it also anticipates Galdós's qualified reference to the initiation of a sexual relationship between Tristana and Horacio. But the real point has to do with the fact that the view of woman found in the *Rimas* and in Rodríguez Correa's commentary presumes a remarkable constancy, at least in cultural terms, from the mythical times of Adam and Eve and the Arthurian legends into the nineteenth century.

It would be optimistic to suggest that this nineteenth-century view of woman is no longer common currency in the twentieth. Bécquer's twentieth-century exegetes, editors, and biographers almost all confirm the view of women dominant in the nineteenth century that allowed for the propagation and diffusion of the romantic legend surrounding Bécquer.

Consider two examples. The first is from Eduardo L. del Palacio's *Pasión y gloria de Gustavo Adolfo* [The Passion and Glory of Gustavo Adolfo] (1947), in which woman is seen as the divine muse. The second moves back slightly in time to Pedro Marroquín y Aguirre's *Bécquer: el poeta del amor y del dolor* [Bécquer: Poet of Love and of Pain] (2nd edition, 1938). The part played by Eduardo L. del Palacio's commentary in the trajectory being traced seems almost too easy to discern. His approach obviously develops out of Rodríguez Correa's biographical presentation of Bécquer and his poetry and pertains to traditional views of women:

Poeta . . . es quien hace, quien crea lo inmaterial, lo espiritual. . . . Por eso, los más y los mejores de los poetas cantan a Dios, que es un poco cantarse a sí mismos, o a la mujer, que es cantar a la Poesía. . . . Las mujeres son nuestras razones de ser, el eje de nuestra vida, la médula de nuestros ideales. . . . La mujer es, pues, poesía. Así la vemos . . . , o la debemos ver los varones.

The poet . . . is one who makes, who creates that which is without matter, that which is spiritual. . . . For this reason, most poets—and the best of them—sing to God, which is a bit like singing to themselves, or they sing to woman, which is to sing to Poetry. . . . Women are our *raison d'être*, the core of our lives, the marrow of our ideals. . . . Woman is, thus, poetry. And that's how we men see her . . . , or how we ought to see her. (34–5)

Woman is here seen as a kind of muse or even domestic angel, two more common types of women discussed in nineteenth-century Spain. It is but one small step from this view of woman as poetry to an invocation of the 'ideal woman' in Bécquer's poetry, the woman who is, according to del Palacio, always 'inasequible o porque en efecto no se la alcanza, o porque no se la quiere alcanzar no sea que se mancille con las impurezas de la realidad' [inaccessible either because, in effect, he cannot reach her, or because he does not wish to reach her so as not to sully her with the impurities of reality] (47–8).[4]

If the view that emerges from this discussion of Bécquer is relatively constant with respect to other considerations of the poet, we can hazard the assertion that it is absolutely consistent with respect to treatments of the woman in Bécquer's poetry in particular and of women in general. In other words, the views expressed represent nothing less than the ongoing force and reiteration of the values of patriarchal Spain. But there is an overtly political valence to the use of Bécquer and his texts that bears consideration, too. To return to Marroquín y Aguirre's thirty-eight-page appreciation of the poet, we need only look at the double dedications to observe the political cast given to texts conceived of as hospitable to traditional values.

The first dedication to Marroquín y Aguirre's essay reads:

En testimonio sencillísimo y humilde de amor a España, y como homenaje de fervorosa admiración por el bizarro Ejército de España, que por honrarla, defenderla y salvar la [*sic*], lucha con bravura ejemplar, y vitoreándola, vence y muere en los frentes, destina el autor de este librillo los productos de su venta en favor del TABACO DEL SOLDADO, colaborando modestísimamente en la obra patriótica que realiza el *Centro de Cultura Femenina*, de San Sebastián, taller elegante y coquetón, en el que manos bonitas de mujer española trabajan asidua y alegremente, poniendo en su labor cariño, entusiasmo y devoción española, porque es en pro de los bravos soldados nacionales, y para enviarles a los parapetos, a las trincheras, a los hospitales y sanatorios, el consuelo, el quita pesares [*sic*] que constituye el inocente recreo de convertir en nubes azuladas que se pierden allá arriba, el polvillo envuelto en leves papelitos blancos.

In the most simple and humble testimony of love for Spain, and as an homage of fervent admiration for the gallant Spanish Army which, as a means of honouring Spain, defending it, and saving it, fights with exemplary valour and, saluting Spain, conquers and dies at the fronts, the author of this little book destines the profits from its sale to the SOLDIER'S TOBACCO, thus collaborating modestly in the patriotic work realized by the Women's Cultural Centre at San Sebastián, an elegant and charming workshop in which the lovely hands of Spanish women work assiduously and happily, putting Spanish tenderness, enthusiasm, and devotion into their labours, which are undertaken on behalf of the brave Nationalist soldiers so as to send to them, in the parapets, trenches, hospitals, and sanatoriums, the consolation and distractions that constitute the innocent recreation of converting those fine strands wrapped in slim white papers into blue-tinged clouds that lose themselves up on high.

The second runs:

A S.E. el Generalísimo don Francisco Franco

Mi General:

¿A quién, mejor que al Jefe Supremo de los ejércitos de aire, tierra y mar, que es, en estos trágicos, pero heroicos tiempos que alcanzamos, el más glorioso representante del soldado de España, a la vez la encarnación más genuina del honor militar español, he de dedicar, obedeciendo a grato deber y a fervorosa voluntad, un librillo que tiene por finalidad llevar una agradable y hasta necesaria distracción, en sus horas de descanso, al soldado abnegado y patriota, en cuya bravura confía V.E. para realizar la excelsa tarea de reconstruir la patria?

Por esto me atrevo a rogar a V.E. que tenga a bien aceptar la humilde ofrenda, sin atender al escaso valer de tan modestas páginas, ni a la insignificancia y oscuridad de quien, doliéndole hondamente España, las escribió, fijos el pensamiento y el corazón en esta tierra inmortal que adora rendidamente; y le ruego asimismo que tan sólo vea en ella mi anhelo de servir a la causa nacional, siquiera con el pobre fruto de mi menguado ingenio, ya que el cielo no me ha concedido la ventura envidiable de dar, en fervoroso holocausto, mi vida por España.

To His Excellency Generalísimo Francisco Franco

My General:

To whom could I, obeying a welcome duty and ardent wish, better dedicate a little book that has as its end that of being an agreeable and even necessary distraction for the selfless and patriotic soldier—on whose valour Your Excellency relies for the realization of the lofty task of reconstructing the fatherland—in his hours of rest than to the Supreme Chief of the Air Force, Army, and Navy, the man who, in these tragic yet heroic times in which we find ourselves, is the most glorious representative of the Spanish soldier as well as the most genuine incarnation of Spanish military honour?

For these reasons, I venture to beg Your Excellency to be so kind as to accept this humble offering without taking note of the slight value of such modest pages or of the insignificance and obscurity of the person who, deeply afflicted by Spain, wrote them, his thoughts and heart fixed on this immortal land that he adores devotedly. And I likewise beg you only to see in them my longing to serve the National cause, even if with the poor fruits of my paltry creativity, since the heavens have not granted me the enviable fortune of offering up my life for Spain in an ardent holocaust.

To dismiss the dedications to a small, critically insignificant book on Bécquer as irrelevant to Bécquer as an author and to studies of his work would be to fail to take into account our previous discussion and the broader ideological work of which literature and its study are a part. The fact that a book on Bécquer was dedicated to Franco on the eve of his victory over the Republican forces, and, moreover, carried an additional tribute to the women working on behalf of the Nationalist forces in the Centro de Cultura Femenina at San Sebastián, implies that there is something inherent in the topic of Bécquer and woman that lends itself to such appropriation.

Such dedications help us answer the question asked earlier: 'What itch are we trying to scratch when we once again try to read the sign of Bécquer's woman?' The itch is the continuing hegemony of patriarchy; the scratch, the apparent need to reinforce its authority. The construction of Bécquer, and its relation to the sign of woman in Bécquer's works as well as in biographies and critical treatments of his poetry and prose, obeys the dynamics of patriarchal ideology and signification in the assumption of the immediate comprehensibility, essentiality, and universality of the representation of the second of the two primary players: 'woman'. As Rubén Benítez points out, Bécquer was and is a 'símbolo del alma española de su época ... [que] sufrió intensamente la nostalgia del pasado, la inseguridad del presente, el temor al futuro' [symbol of the Spanish soul of his epoch ... [who] suffered intensely from nostalgia for the past, insecurity in the present, and fear of the future] (49). Nostalgia for the past and past values is implicit in the dictum 'Poesía eres ... tú'. As the foundation on which Bécquer's poetry and interpretations of that poetry have been erected, these words relegate women to the role of muse and helpmeet, and become virtually a command, possibly a warning. The woman who is not a muse is vulgar, stupid, pathologically sexual, and therefore liable to punishment, be it in the form of dismemberment or disfigurement, as with Galdós's Tristana, or social isolation, as with Clarín's Ana Ozores.

José Carlos de Torres's 'objective criticism' aside, we must begin to read Bécquer in a much more complex manner, not only as the author of the divinely spiritual Rimas, but as someone whose life and work have become part of a hegemonic cultural discourse that reformulates and restates its aims in almost every new discussion. A more complex reading of Bécquer would take into account his involvement in the creation of the satirical/pornographic water-colours signed by the pseudonym 'SEM', as well as his writings about and visual representations of women.[5] This reconsideration of Bécquer would also have to avoid the trap of received opinion and seductive biography. In this way, we would see that the dictum 'Poesía . . . eres tú' has as much to say about us and our appropriation of Becquer as it does about Bécquer, his poetry and prose, and his cultural moment. Although such a rereading of Bécquer would represent an enormous undertaking, it would lead to a reconsideration of the nature and role of the male author in nineteenth-century Spain alongside the role relegated to women. With such a rereading, as initiated here, we may begin to understand the peculiar effect and force of the traditional lyric link between poetry and women, the peculiar effect of Bécquer's Rimas and the force of the many accounts of his poetry and life. In this new reading the words 'Poesía . . . eres tú' not only bear the mark of the construction of Bécquer and the sign of woman. The words and the ellipses that both separate and join them speak of the continuing effect and force of such classic formulations, to say nothing of the possibility of their undoing.

NOTES

1. On the few occasions necessary, I have chosen to cite the poetry from the facsimile edition, using modern orthography and accentuation but preserving the original punctuation. Page references will be given in parentheses first to the transcription in the facsimile edition and then to the original manuscript page in the Libro de los gorriones. I will, however, refer to the individual poems by the roman numerals associated with the Rimas and include parenthetical reference to the numbering in the Libro de los gorriones (LG).

2. For the most part, my argument is non-theoretical in nature, although there are a number of critical and theoretical texts and traditions that furnish the implicit framework. In addition to the essays by Ebert and Hartmann, works by the following are behind many of my ideas: in general, Nancy Armstrong, Teresa de Lauretis, Nancy C. M. Hartsock, Gayle Rubin, Eve Kosofsky Sedgwick, and Haunani-Kay Trask; with respect to Spain, see Lou Charnon-Deutsch, Susan Kirkpatrick, and Geraldine M. Scanlon.

3. For a personal turn to the discussion of woman in Bécquer, see the contemporary account of Eusebio Blasco. Blasco's assessment of Casta is cited by most of Bécquer's biographers, and is usually seconded by them. José Andrés Vázquez is perhaps more vitriolic than many, but he captures the prevailing sentiment if not the tone. Rica Brown (150–61) is more balanced than Vázquez while Gabriel Celaya attempts to restore to Bécquer's wife some measure of respectability, with mixed results (66–9).

4. Probably the most obvious expression of the role played by this 'ideal' woman in Bécquer's poetry is Díez Taboada 1965.

5. The collection of water-colours is included in Bécquer and Becquer. See also the introductory essays by Robert Pageard, Lee Fontanella, and María Dolores Cabra Loredo.

WORKS CITED

ALAS 'CLARÍN', LEOPOLDO (1981). *La Regenta* (1884–5), ed. Gonzalo Sobejano, 2 vols. Clásicos Castalia 110, 111. Madrid: Castalia. (Trans. John Rutherford. Harmondsworth: Penguin, 1984.)

ARMSTRONG, NANCY (1987). *Desire and Domestic Fiction: A Political History of the Novel*. New York: Oxford University Press.

BARTHES, ROLAND (1970). *Mythologies*, ed. and trans. Annette Lavers. New York: Hill & Wang.

BÉCQUER, GUSTAVO ADOLFO (1971). *Libro de los gorriones*. Edición facsímil, ed. Guillermo Guastavino Gallent, Rafael de Balbín, and Antonio Roldán. Madrid: Ministerio de Educación y Ciencia.

BÉCQUER, VALERIANO, and BÉCQUER, GUSTAVO ADOLFO (1991). *SEM: Los Borbones en pelota*, ed. Robert Pageard, Lee Fontanella, and María Dolores Cabra Loredo. Madrid: El Museo Universal.

BENÍTEZ, RUBÉN (1971). *Bécquer tradicionalista*. Biblioteca Románica Hispánica. Estudios y Ensayos 148. Madrid: Gredos.

BLASCO, EUSEBIO (1982). 'Gustavo Bécquer', in Russell P. Sebold (ed.), *Gustavo Adolfo Bécquer*. El Escritor y la Crítica. Persiles 155. Madrid: Taurus. 24–6.

BROWN, RICA (1963). *Bécquer*. Biblioteca Biográfica 23. Barcelona: Aedos.

CELAYA, GABRIEL (1972). 'Introducción', in *Bécquer*. Colección Los Poetas. Madrid: Júcar. 9–135.

CHARNON-DEUTSCH, LOU (1990). *Gender and Representation: Women in Spanish Realist Fiction*. Purdue University Monographs in Romance Languages 32. Amsterdam: John Benjamins.

DE LAURETIS, TERESA (1987). *Technologies of Gender: Essays on Theory, Film, and Fiction*. Theories of Representation and Difference. Bloomington, Ind.: Indiana University Press.

DEL PALACIO, EDUARDO L. (1947). *Pasión y gloria de Gustavo Adolfo*. Madrid: Libros y Revistas.

DE TORRES, JOSÉ CARLOS (1984). 'Introducción', in Gustavo Adolfo Bécquer, *Rimas*. Clásicos Castalia 74. Madrid: Castalia. 9–72.

DÍAZ, JOSÉ PEDRO (1970). *Gustavo Adolfo Bécquer: Vida y poesía*. Biblioteca Románica Hispánica. Estudios y Ensayos 39. 3rd (4th) edn. Madrid: Gredos.

DÍEZ TABOADA, JUAN MARÍA (1965). *La mujer ideal: aspectos y fuentes de las Rimas de G. A. Bécquer*. Instituto 'Miguel de Cervantes', Anejos de 'Revista de Literatura'. Madrid: Consejo Superior de Investigaciones Científicas.

——(1967). 'La ordenación de las *Rimas* de Gustavo A. Bécquer', in Jaime Sánchez Romeralo and Norbert Poulussen (eds.), *Actas del Segundo Congreso Internacional de Hispanistas*. Nijmegen: Instituto Español de la Universidad de Nimega/Asociación Internacional de Hispanistas. 283–91.

EBERT, TERESA L. (1988). 'The Romance of Patriarchy: Ideology, Subjectivity, and Postmodern Feminist Cultural Theory', *Cultural Critique*, 10: 19–57.

HARTMANN, HEIDI (1981). 'The Unhappy Marriage of Marxism and Feminism: Towards a More Progressive Union', in Lydia Sargent (ed.), *Women and Revolution: A Discussion of the Unhappy Marriage of Marxism and Feminism*. Boston: South End Press. 1–41.

HARTSOCK, NANCY C. M. (1983). *Money, Sex, and Power: Toward a Feminist Historical Materialism*. New York: Longman.

KIRKPATRICK, SUSAN (1989). *Las Románticas: Women Writers and Subjectivity in Spain, 1835–1850*. Berkeley, Calif.: University of California Press.

LÓPEZ ESTRADA, FRANCISCO (1972). *Poética para un poeta: las Cartas literarias a una mujer de Bécquer*. Biblioteca Románica Hispánica. Estudios y Ensayos 176. Madrid: Gredos.

MARROQUÍN Y AGUIRRE, PEDRO (1938). *Bécquer: el poeta del amor y del dolor*. 2nd edn. San Sebastián: Martín y Mena.

PÉREZ GALDÓS, BENITO (1970). *Obras completas*, ed. Federico Carlos Sainz de Robles, vol. v. 7th edn. Madrid: Aguilar.

RODRÍGUEZ CORREA, RAMÓN (1984). 'Gustavo Adolfo Bécquer', in By Gustavo Adolfo Bécquer, *Rimas*. Clásicos Castalia 74. Madrid: Castalia. 196–220.

RUBIN, GAYLE (1975). 'The Traffic in Women: Notes on the "Political Economy" of Sex', in Rayna R. Reiter (ed.), *Toward an Anthropology of Women*. New York: Monthly Review Press. 157–210.

SCANLON, GERALDINE M. (1976). *La polémica feminista en la España contemporánea (1868–1974)*. Madrid: Siglo XXI.

SEDGWICK, EVE KOSOFSKY (1985). *Between Men: English Literature and Male Homosocial Desire*. Gender and Culture. New York: Columbia University Press.

TRASK, HAUNANI-KAY (1986). *Eros and Power: The Promise of Feminist Theory*. Philadelphia: University of Pennsylvania Press.

VÁZQUEZ, JOSÉ ANDRÉS (1929). *Bécquer*. Los Grandes Hombres. Barcelona: Sociedad General de Publicaciones.

4
Fantasy, Seduction, and the Woman Reader: Rosalía de Castro's Novels

SUSAN KIRKPATRICK

Do you think a thriving virgin imagination can gorge itself with impunity on *Martin, the Orphan Boy*, *A Doctor's Memoirs*, and *The Man of the Three Pantaloons*? . . . Devouring *The Three Musketeers*, [the young girl learns of] Milady's evil deeds, the adulterous love of *Madame Bonacieux*, and the scandalous passion of *Mlle. Lavalliere* for the king, a passion that infiltrates young and naïve hearts the more easily when dressed in a sweetly poetic and sentimental form. . . . [T]ender female readers, when they reach thirteen, follow as best they can in the footsteps of the heroines of their novels.

(Sinués de Marco, 1859)

Nineteenth-century Spaniards defined women's relation to reading and writing as a matter of morality. Debates about women's education—that is, their access to the printed word as either consumers or producers—centred on the question of whether reading/writing would lead women astray, as the traditionalists argued, or would refine their moral sensibility, as reform-minded liberals claimed. At the heart of this debate lay the question of fantasy, of women's desire, for that was the crucial link between the printed word and feminine behaviour. In particular, the reading of novels was seen as dangerous. By the mid-nineteenth century, when the serial novel began to prove itself an effective means of expanding the market of print consumers, concerns with the genre's impact on women, a growing sector of that market, became widespread. The fear that the novelesque might contaminate the daily lives of women was exacerbated by the seductive strategies through which the serial novel secured buyers for its proliferating instalments: exalted romantic passions, melo-dramatic dilemmas, sensational plots played upon the erotic fan-tasies of its readers.

Interestingly enough, the women who now entered the ex-panding field of print culture as producers seized on the issue of fiction's contaminating influence as a means of justifying their own writing projects. Thus, Cecilia Böhl de Faber (*Fernán Ca-ballero*), defensive about putting herself forward in public as an author, claimed in 1853 that 'la tendencia de mis obritas es combatir lo novelesco, sutil veneno en la buena y llana senda de la vida real' [the tendency of my little works is to combat the novelesque, a subtle poison in the good, plain path of real life].[1] The strategy of offering one's own writing as an antidote to the poisonous effects of competing fiction became prevalent among women writers of the 1850s. It was central to the influential work cited in the epigraph, *El ángel del hogar* [The Angel in the House], Pilar Sinués's amalgam of fiction and conduct book for women. Already in a second, expanded edition in 1859, this book was re-edited many times in the nineteenth century. While admitting that reading the wrong kind of fiction (the works of Alexandre Dumas *père* are singled out as an example) can con-taminate girls' hearts with scandalous passions and overheat their imaginations (180), Sinués insists that reading works writ-ten by women committed to the domestic ideal of womanhood plays an important part in feminine moral education. She counsels mothers accordingly: 'La mujer que siente, es buena hija, buena esposa y buena madre: y para desarrollar la sensibilidad de vuestras hijas no tenéis que hacer más que enseñarlas a leer, y dirigir con tino sus lecturas' [The woman of feeling is a good daughter, a good wife, and a good mother: and to develop the sensibility of your daughters you need only teach them to read and direct their reading with judgement] (64). Sinués thus deftly transforms the concern about fiction infecting women's ima-gination into an argument for the positive effects of reading on feminine subjectivity. Women's imaginations can be nurtured and channelled in ways that protect them from the corrupting seductions of melodramatic fiction, her argument goes, if they are absorbed by 'historias dulces, llenas de sentimiento y de verdad' [agreeable stories full of feeling and truth] (188). Truth, *El ángel del hogar* makes clear, consists of women's biological mission as domestic angels, a mission significantly enhanced by certain kinds of reading and writing, that is, those capable of shaping desirable feminine subjectivity.[2] Thus, in accepting the premiss of female susceptibility to reading, Sinués makes a case justifying the moral effects of a controlled female exercise of literacy.

Sinués's adept manipulation of the ideological debate on women and literature, however, does not resolve the argument about feminine fantasy and narrative seduction. It merely proposes the replacement of one kind of fiction by another, leaving in place the restrictions on women's activity and their subordination to men. To find an intervention in nineteenth-century Spanish discourse about women's reading that confronts the subordinating effects of all types of fiction on women, we must turn to the fiction of Sinués's contemporary Rosalía de Castro. Boldly identifying herself in her epigraphs and citations as a reader of Soulié, Sand, and Dumas, novelists habitually denounced as pernicious to women, Castro sidesteps the question of morality and explores in her novels the connected issues of fiction, female fantasy, and women's oppression. What Jessica Benjamin has termed 'the intricate relationship between woman's desire and women's submission' (80) becomes the implicit problem posed in the narratives that Castro situates within or in relation to the genre of romance fiction, or popular Romantic melodrama. In this essay I will discuss at length Rosalía de Castro's engagement with this problem in her fourth novel, *El caballero de las botas azules* [The Knight of the Blue Boots], but first I want briefly to consider her treatment of seduction in her first novel, *La hija del mar* [Daughter of the Sea].

In both novels Castro was concerned with the seductive and powerful male figures that dominated popular fiction because the desire they produced had a subjugating effect on the female psyche. Moral response was not the issue: her texts suggest that, whether the woman protagonist—or reader—gives in or remains virtuous, she remains in a subordinate and disadvantaged position in this kind of narrative since her desire must be passive rather than active—the desire to be desired. Consequently, these novels can be read as attempts not only to represent but also to critique the structures that determine feminine identity in modern Western culture. One of the most basic of these structures is the one that inclines women to choose a father-figure as their love object. In featuring female characters' relationships with powerful male figures, Castro's narratives highlight the seduction scenario identified by psychoanalytic theory as the origin of heterosexual desire in the woman: the father's desire for her is perceived by the daughter as the means of her access to sexuality, to desire and power.[3] By inducing women to channel their sexuality into the wish to please the father or his substitute at all costs, the seduction fantasy subordinates women's desire to the demands of the patriarchal bourgeois family. James Mandrell has observed that the literary incarnation of this fantasy in avatars of the seducer, Don Juan, 'serves to draw the woman into the passion of patriarchy and serves as the paradigm by which desire is articulated in society, as the subtext for relations between men and women, as a literary and social text in which the latter are seduced by the former into fulfilling a specific role' (127–8). Although Castro wrote before the theoretical model of Oedipalization had been formulated, some of her narratives display the process theorized later by Freud and at the same time resist it through a critique of the woman/reader's tendency to internalize the seduction narrative as the figure of her desire.

The mid-century *folletines* that formed a literary context for Castro's novels had two main strategies for manipulating the seduction fantasy. The first was the drama of seduction and abandonment, in which the dark, Romantic hero with semi-diabolic powers occupies the position of the father in relation to the girl child who becomes his victim. The second strategy was to narrate the redemption of the seductive male by the innocent heroine, a story that was crucial to the image of *el ángel del hogar* promoted by Pilar Sinués and other writers of women's fiction. Following a pattern established by José Zorrilla in his *Don Juan Tenorio*, in these narratives the fascinating reprobate's desire for a virtuous and innocent girl transforms him into a proper bourgeois mate. For James Mandrell, the conjunction of the two scenarios—seduction and redemption—in Zorrilla's drama initiates the bourgeois domestication of the traditional figure of the seducer in nineteenth-century Spanish fiction, a process that adapts the significance of seduction to the shift in social organization from kinship structures to the nuclear family (Mandrell 265–7). The seduction and redemption fantasies coincide in identifying female sexuality with the capacity to arouse desire in the father-figure, and this feminine 'power' is clearly equated with passivity. As Alicia Andreu has shown, the Spanish fiction that incorporates this scenario insists monotonously that passivity, obedience, humility, patience, are the virtues that will arouse redemptive desire in the man (71–91). Identification with the feminine protagonists of such fiction, no matter whether they appeared in the scandalous *folletín* or in the sentimental novellas advocated by Sinués, reproduced in the woman reader a mode of sexuality and fantasy that equated femininity with being the passive object of the male desire, perpetuating in psychic life structures that support bourgeois marriage and its sexual division of labour.

Rosalía de Castro's first novel, *La hija del mar*, responds quite directly to the seduction fantasies incorporated in the popular fiction that Rosalía—only 22 when she wrote the novel—had been reading throughout her adolescence. I have argued elsewhere that while this novel acknowledges the insistent power of the seduction scenarios centred on Byronic male figures like the main male character, Albert Ansot, it also registers the extent to which such fantasies make women victims in the politics of gender relations.[4] The two female protagonists—Teresa, the passionate and powerful adult woman who finds Ansot irresistible though reprehensible, and Esperanza, the girl whom Ansot twice attempts to seduce, not realizing she is his abandoned daughter— exemplify alternative trajectories for feminine subjectivity in relation to patriarchally inscribed desire. The two women also represent two levels of female subjection—the political and the psychological. Both Teresa and Esperanza, the narrator explains, 'permanecían atadas al victorioso carro de su dueño, la una sujeta por los robustos brazos que la oprimían, la otra . . . ¡por su corazón!: cadenas que en aquellos instantes supremos no podían romperse a pesar de todas las violencias de la tierra' [were tied to the victorious chariot of their master, the one subjected by the strong arms of the man who oppressed her, the other . . . by her heart!, a chain that in those supreme moments could not be broken by all the violence on the earth] (117).[5] Teresa, whose position within the novel duplicates that of the female reader conditioned by the *folletín*, demonstrates the psychological form of subjection: despite her active resistance to Ansot's sexual power over her, that patriarchal power is continually regenerated within her—and, by implication, within the woman writer and reader—by a fantasy structured around the father's seduction. Esperanza, on the other hand, is subjected to her father only by his physical and social power, not by the psychological chains of desire. Unlike Teresa, her fantasy is not captured by the seduction scene. Staying back from the brink of seduction and sexuality, she consciously sees Ansot only as a tyrant and enslaver and learns at the end of the novel, with the revelation of her origins, that her desire is really for her mother— for the lost mother of her now unremembered earliest infancy. In Esperanza, then, Castro explores the possibility of a pre-Oedipal desire for reunion with the mother as an alternative to subjection to the sexual law of the father.

As a reading and rewriting of the fantasies projected in the popular fiction of nineteenth-century Spain, *La hija del mar* resists at a number of levels the subjecting effects of the seduction fantasy on women: it treats as tyranny both the political and the psychological power of pulp fiction's seductive father-figures; it debunks the myth of female power to redeem through passivity; and it presents the mother as an alternative object of women's desire. This struggle to transform the meanings of the given narrative materials is very clearly an unresolved process within the text. Esperanza, the 'hope' of an un-Oedipalized feminine subjectivity, can find no place in the social world and throws herself from a cliff into the sea. Her story exposes the painful dilemma of the female reader—and the feminine subject—within modern patriarchal society.

Several years after the publication of her first novel, Rosalía de Castro again addressed the issues of reading, seduction, and desire, but this time in the register of satire and self-reflexive irony rather than that of melodrama. *El caballero de las botas azules* appeared in 1867, on the eve of a revolutionary crisis of the Spanish state. In a period when the serialized novel reigned supreme, Castro's novel attacked the dominant forms of literature in her society, exposing the manipulation of desire that buttressed structures of economic exploitation and political domination. The question of women's desire is not so thematically predominant in this novel as in *La hija del mar*, yet, as I will argue, the underlying strategy of self-reflexive consciousness is directed against women's destructive habits of reading and desiring.

El caballero establishes its self-reflexive strategy by immediately implicating and satirizing its own context of production and consumption. It begins with a dialogue titled 'A Man and a Muse', in which a would-be author, only too aware that the contemporary arena of writing is a competitive market-place, seeks inspiration to create a work so original that it will triumph over all others and win him immortal fame (Castro 1977: 561–2). The ironic and unconventional Muse identifies his problem as the chaotic proliferation of print:

¿[Q]ué hacer en medio de ese desbordamiento inconmensurable en donde nadie hace justicia a nadie, y en el cual los más ignorantes y más necios, los más audaces y pequeños quieren ser los primeros? He aquí por qué me llamaste . . . por qué me buscarás siempre, pues sin mí serás '¡uno de tantos!' y nada más que esto.

What could you do in that measureless deluge in which no one does justice to anyone else, and the most ignorant and foolish, the most audacious and petty want to be number one? That is why you called me . . . why you will always seek me out, because without me you will be 'one of the crowd' and nothing more. (572–3)

This text self-consciously exposes the desire or objective motivating its own generation, as well as the generation of all works flooding the market in which it will be received, thus calling attention to the need of literature published in this context to create a singular desire in its target audience. The prefatory dialogue identifies the achievement of this aim with novelty, a degraded version of the Romantic ambition toward originality produced by the development of modern market structures as the framework of literary production.[6] The Muse reveals that her name is Novelty, and this is the key to the success she promises the Man who accepts her inspiration: 'Te haré el más popular de los hombres, y miles de corazones se estremecerán de curiosidad y emoción a tu paso' [I will make you the most popular of men, and thousands of hearts will tremble with curiosity and emotion when you go by] (579). Sired by doubt and birthed by desire (578), Novelty engenders new desires—or desire for the new—in the hearts of consumers, helping create the necessary conditions of a capitalist economy.

The story that follows this dialogue (a 'strange story' according to its own subtitle) is, to put it in the most reductive terms, the story of how the Muse, transforming the Man into the Knight of the Blue Boots, inspires him to carry out a supremely successful marketing strategy to ensure that his book, the Book of Books, is the only one read in Madrid. The incarnation of novelty with his luminescent blue boots and ambiguous cravat, which sometimes looks like a live eagle, the *Caballero* arouses and focuses on himself the unsatisfied desires of the whole city, then disappears, promising his Book in answer to their expectations. The story closes with the distribution of the Book of Books, whose contents are never revealed. As a satiric commentary on the contemporary situation of the writer, Castro's novel could not be more acerbic: the story of a successful literary inspiration has nothing to do with the textual product, but only with the strategy for marketing it.

Explicit satire on contemporary literature runs throughout the narrative. The indictment probes beneath the question of aesthetic quality in the chaotic proliferation of the printed word, and targets the economic structure of the print industry. Castro characterizes the reigning system of serial publication as exploitative when a poet laments 'la lastimosa popularidad que han llegado a adquirir esas novelas que, para explotar al pobre, se publican por entregas de a dos cuartos' [the unfortunate popularity recently acquired by those novels that, in order to exploit the poor, are published in penny instalments] (647). The exploitation of the female reading public is exposed as a particularly lucrative publishing practice by the parodically self-congratulatory remarks of a publisher commenting on women's fiction:

¡Oh! Es un éxito fabuloso el que estas novelas obtienen. Casi todos los maestros y maestras de primera enseñanza, casi todas las obreras de Madrid, se han suscrito, sin contar los directores del Hospicio, de la Inclusa y de otros colegios particulares que las compran para que las niñas, al mismo tiempo que se entretienen los días de fiesta con su amena lectura, se instruyan y aprendan en ellas a ser virtuosas.

Oh, the success these novels are having is fabulous! Almost all the primary school teachers, almost all the women workers of Madrid have subscribed, not to mention the directors of the Orphanage, of the Home for Foundlings, and of other private schools that buy them so the girls, at the same time as having enjoyable reading for holidays, are taught by them to be virtuous. (799)

The titles Castro invents to characterize this genre provide a succinct ironic summary of the ideological message of the kind of fiction Sinués advocated: *La mujer honrada* [The Honourable Woman], *El amor sacrificado* [Self-Sacrificing Love], and *La pobreza sin mancilla* [Poverty without Stain]. Indeed, the publisher uses some of Sinués's terms when he goes on to say that his novels 'además de estar llenas de escenas tiernas y conmovedoras . . .

encierran al mismo tiempo una moral que la misma Inquisición no hubiera reprobado' [besides being full of tender and moving scenes . . . contain at the same time a moral the Inquisition itself wouldn't have disapproved of]. The satiric intent of this passage is underlined by the editor's interlocutor, who remarks ironically that while this fiction may observe good morals, it does not observe good grammar, and the editor replies cynically: '¿Qué importa todo eso? ¡Aprensiones! . . . Las mujeres, que son las que realmente aman y se impresionan con esta clase de libros, no saben gramática en nuestro país' [What does that matter? Idle misgivings! . . . In our country, women, who are the ones who really love and are impressed by this kind of books, don't know anything about grammar] (799).

The conclusion of *El caballero de las botas azules* enacts Castro's condemnation of contemporary literary production as being not only aesthetically mediocre, but, even worse, shaped by economic and political interests that aim to reinforce the subordination of women and the working classes. As part of the theatrical grand finale that the *Caballero* offers to the astonished eyes of Madrid's élite before he disappears, the city's stock of current publications, which his helper has bought from the booksellers and stored in preparation for this moment, is dumped in a deep well and buried forever. With great fanfare, the *Caballero* shows the guests at his goodbye banquet the pit filled to the brim with modern literature and announces: '¡Señores, la obra está cumplida! La humanidad se ve libre de un peso inútil; . . . ya no leerá artículos distinguidos, ni historias inspiradas, ni versos insípidos, ni novelas extravagantes, ni artículos críticos cuya gracia empalagosa trasciende a necio' [Ladies and gentlemen, my mission is fulfilled! Humanity has been freed from a useless burden; . . . no longer must it read distinguished articles, or inspired stories, or insipid verses, or extravagant novels, or critical articles whose tiresome wit smells of idiocy] (825). Self-reflexive irony is not absent here, for the *Caballero* continues by observing that the field has now been cleared for his own soon-to-appear work, exposing the possibility that he is no better than the self-promoting editors and authors whose books lie buried, only a more successful strategist.

That this satiric put-down of contemporary literature has a connection with the subordination of women is suggested by another *coup de théâtre* at the book-burying. At the beginning of the banquet, the Duke of Glory (as the *Caballero* is known in Madrid) announces that the evening's festivities include the appearance of some slave-women, whom he will with his own hands set free. Indeed, just as the condemned books begin to shoot through the air on their way to the pit, another spectacle greets the eyes of the guests: tunic-clad slave-girls, their blue-painted faces hidden by the long visors of their jockey caps, come tremblingly forward to kiss the Duke's boots. A tumult of indignation arises among those present, who, recognizing the slave-girls as some of Madrid's most wealthy and beautiful noble-women, ask each other what is going on. That is a question we must ask ourselves, too, at this point. Why is this tableau of feminine subjugation, reminiscent of the image in *La hija del mar* of the two women tied to the chariot of their master, cropping up in this context? What does the Knight of the Blue Boots, Castro's instrument of satire against bad literature, have in common with the abusive and tyrannical Ansot?

To answer this question, we must go back to the activities through which the blue-booted Duke has brought all Madrid under his sway. What I have somewhat crudely characterized as a marketing strategy is, like any such strategy, a campaign to arouse and channel desires. In her perceptive Lacanian reading of this novel, Lou Charnon-Deutsch argues that the Duke's function is to teach others 'the mechanics of desire', by 'repeatedly display[ing] himself and then withdraw[ing]' (81, 85). At the most explicit level, the Duke aims to pique curiosity—the desire to know—through the novelty of his dress and behaviour; thus, his first victim, the Duke of Albuérniga, who has devoted his life to cultivating a Stoic lack of desire, is hooked when curiosity about the *Caballero's* singular appearance overcomes his anger that the other has disturbed his nap (592). What other desires may be veiled beneath Albuérniga's tormented attempts to re-press his fascination with the Duke of Glory are never made clear, but in the case of the ladies who find the Duke irresistible, his assumption of a powerfully masculine persona is a central factor, as Charnon-Deutsch argues (85). The Duke's appearance and accoutrements, along with the mystery surrounding his sudden appearance in the capital, are sufficient to arouse the interest of the *madrileñas*, who endeavour to entice him to their soirées and salons and write secretly to arrange private tête-à-têtes.

In fact, the *Caballero's* principal technique of seduction is to occupy the role of the tall, dark stranger, the magnetic male figure of the *folletín*, albeit with a disturbing ironic twist. Here is how he appears to the astonished eyes of the first persons he encounters:

Era el singularísimo y nunca bien ponderado personaje de elevada talla y arrogante apostura, de negra, crespa y un tanto revuelta, si bien perfumada, caballera. Tenía el semblante tan uniformemente blanco como si fuese hecho de un pedazo de mármol, y la expresión irónica de su mirada y de su boca era tal que turbaba al primer golpe el ánimo más sereno.

This singular and never adequately praised character was tall of stature and carried himself with arrogance. His hair was black, curly, and somewhat tousled, though well perfumed. His face was as uniformly white as if it were made of marble, and the expression of his eyes and mouth was so ironic it could instantly trouble the serenest mind. (587)

Picking up the cues concerning the fictional genre to which this character corresponds, two of the city's leading society ladies— Laura, the Countess of Pampa, and the noble Casimira—hide their identity under cloaks like countless heroines of adventure novels and roam the streets at night, hoping to encounter the mystery man. When they finally do see him in person at a ball where he confounds Madrid's assembled élite by mocking its frivolity and walking out, the snub inflames their unsatisfied longings. The next day the Duke receives billets-doux from a representative sample of Madrid's women. Each of the letters, with the exception of the one from the ignorant and innocent Mariquita, which we will take up in a moment, reveals the literary origin of the fantasy that the letter's writer wishes to enact with the Duke. Thus the letter from a Creole poetess refers to the primeval forests of 'la virgen América' [virgin America] and to the 'desgraciado e inmortal Moctezuma' [unfortunate and immortal Montezuma] (668), evoking the Romantic literature that exoticized the New World as a setting for sentimental love stories. The note from the Countess of Pampa requests an interview with the Duke because she wishes to learn from him 'cómo las mujeres de la aristocracia rusa visten de mañana' [about the morning dress of the aristocratic women of Russia] (668), thus identifying the *Caballero* with the country of Lermontov, whose novel *A Hero of our Time* obsesses her, as she has earlier confessed to Casimira. In replying to each woman, the Duke uses language corresponding to the fantasy script she has revealed and he raises the stakes by refusing the specific request made, but proposing the rendezvous secretly desired. Yet when the tête-à-tête occurs, he steps out of the role assigned, forcing the woman concerned to acknowledge the unavowed fantasy that has motivated her actions. The Duke's strategy of arousing, then thwarting, feminine desire is most fully elaborated in the subplots involving Laura and Casimira. Two significant features of these subplots—their self-conscious literariness and their sado-masochistic overtones—are connected, in my reading of the novel, and provide a key to the disturbing scene of female subjugation in the novel's finale. Confusion of life and literature occurs at several levels in this subplot. As their venture incognito into the night-time streets suggests, the two women identify themselves with the heroines of the novels they read. The influence of Romantic melodrama is particularly strong in their concept of themselves as 'las independientes', superior to other women, as free and powerful as men (639), very much along the lines of Stendhal's Mathilde. They affect Romantic ennui: 'Sólo sé que el mundo envejece rápidamente y que todo me parece usado y de mal gusto' [I only know that the world is quickly getting old and everything seems worn out and in bad taste] (639), says Laura, turning to her reading of Lermontov to imagine new thrills in the arms of a son of the Caucasus. Her projection of this fantasy on the Knight of the Blue Boots gives a comic cast to the scene of their encounter. All the Duke need do to send her into a delirium of excitement is to smile 'de la manera que se sonreía Petchorín' [in the same way as Petchorin] (742), the disillusioned hero of Lermontov's *A Hero of our Time*. Nothing will persuade her that the Duke is not the Russian poet in some form (744). Maddened in her desire to receive verification of this fantasy, Laura agrees to kiss the Duke's boots in exchange for learning who he is. Her awakening will occur when the concluding scene demonstrates to what extent her literary fantasies of love have enslaved her.

Casimira seems to seek her thrills in fantasies of domination and surrender. In her note, she offers the Duke a role similar to that of Albert Ansot: '¿Sin duda es [el duque] un tirano que se digna regir a los suyos con mano de hierro? De cualquier modo, yo seré siempre su fiel amiga, seré su sierva, su esclava seré si él lo desea' [Doubtless [the Duke] is a tyrant who deigns to rule his subjects with an iron hand? At any rate, I will always be his faithful friend, I will be his handmaiden, his slave, if he so desires] (677). It is she, then, who has introduced the sado-masochistic script that the Duke develops, both in his reply, which he addresses 'Señora y esclava mía' [My lady and slave] (678), and in his subsequent interview with her. In this encounter, he ironically calls attention to the melodramatic language of her note, letting her know that, far from engaging in the gallant badinage she expects, he intends to play out the metaphor on a more literal level: 'Pero cuando se trata de una sierva . . . de una esclava . . . ¡oh! entonces mi severidad no tiene límites: me vuelvo analítico, meticuloso' [But when dealing with a handmaiden . . . a slave . . . oh, then my severity has no limits: I become analytical, meticulous] (699–700). Playing on Casimira's wish to emulate audacious novelistic heroines who will stop at nothing, the Duke ultimately induces her to promise to play his slave in the public tableau he is planning.

What Casimira hopes to obtain from accepting the subjugated role becomes clear when she states what she expects in return if she does as the Duke demands:

(ya he dicho que no pretendo ser la amante ni la esposa del señor duque), lo que sí pretendo es que en tal caso me haga su confidenta, la depositaria de sus secretos . . . la fuerte y fiel guardadora de los misterios que nadie sino yo entienda. Sí, señor duque: quiero saber su historia; quiero saber qué significan esa corbata y esas botas.

(I've already said I don't want to be your lover or wife), what I do want in such a case is for you to make me your confidante, the depository of your secrets . . . your strong and faithful guardian of the mysteries no one understands but me. Yes, Duke, I want to know your story; I want to know what that cravat and those boots signify. (708)

Castro has here revealingly rewritten the seduction scenario that figured so prominently in her first novel. In *La hija del mar* the woman's seduction into heterosexual sexuality was linked directly to a power relationship that subjugated her; here the power relationship of master and slave presents more analytically the underlying exchange operating in the sexual economy of gender difference. Casimira is willing to occupy the subordinated position in the belief that thus she will gain access to the secret source of male power, tantalizingly symbolized in the Duke's

cravat and boots. If we find that this revised representation of
the seduction scene seems to prefigure the terms in which psychoanalytic theory would later theorize the feminine relationship
to phallic desire, then it should not surprise us that the Duke
seems to behave very much like a psychoanalyst in relation to
Casimira and the other women he 'treats'. He attracts upon
himself the projection of their repressed or barely conscious
desires, then, by refusing to play the role assigned him, forces
them both to acknowledge their fantasies and to recognize the
impossibility or undesirability of satisfying them. The therapeutic intent of the final tableau now becomes clear. In appearing
as slave-girls and kissing the Duke's boots, Casimira and Laura
act out on a very different level from the one they anticipated
their fantasies of seduction in relation to the Duke;[7] they take
part in the tableau with full awareness that there is no pleasure
for them in the scenario, only humiliation. And the knowledge—
that is, the possession of the 'secret'—they expected to obtain
eludes them. But they have learnt something about themselves.
Once they have performed their part of the bargain, the Duke
pronounces them free, declaring 'Esas pobres hijas de la esclavitud
aman la libertad como el mayor bien de la vida, pero no han
comprendido todavía la manera de alcanzarla' [These poor
daughters of slavery love freedom as life's greatest good, but
they have not yet understood how to achieve it] (823).

In playing a therapeutic role, a consciousness-raising role, in
relation to women, the Duke functions like a text that demands
a different kind of reading from the one the female characters
are used to. Like an enticing novel, he engages their fantasies,
insinuating that his story will provide mysterious satisfactions
while repeatedly deferring the desired outcomes and disclosures.
Yet, unlike the popular fiction that traded on mysteries and
revelations (Eugène Sue's *The Mysteries of Paris* had initiated a
whole subgenre of translations and imitations in Spain), the
Caballero baffles his readers' desire to know his story. Instead of
playing out the expectations his feminine admirers have internalized from their reading, he turns these expectations back on
themselves to produce uncomfortable self-consciousness rather
than satisfaction. This, then, is what unites the two spectacles
with which the blue-booted Duke concludes his sojourn in
Madrid. His staging of the liberation of the slave-girls while
having modern literature cast into the pit implies a connection

between the sexual enslavement of women and the reading habits through which women seek pleasure in fiction. The Duke attempts to teach women to be resistant readers, to read critically the fantasies scripted for them.[8]

The idea of the Duke's function as a text that invites women's fantasy projection and then promotes a critical evaluation of that fantasy casts light on the other important subplot of the novel as well, the story of his interaction with Mariquita, an innocent girl of the lower middle class who lives in a village— satirically named Dog Run—outside Madrid. Mariquita has been kept as ignorant as possible, having been brought up in the way considered exemplary for Spanish girls of her class. Castro's indignation is palpable in the description of the systematic deprivation of any form of self-expression or pleasure to which Mariquita is subject; so deprived is she that solitary strolls through the nearby cemetery constitute her only enjoyment. Unfortunately for the matchmaking plans of her aunt and father, they have kept her so rigorously isolated from images and analogues of sexuality that, when presented with the young man intended to be her husband, Mariquita finds him utterly ridiculous and repellent. Following the pattern Castro is exploring in these novels, her desire is instead awakened by a seductive stand-in for the father, when Mariquita observes the Duke one day in the graveyard (like any Romantic ironist worth his salt, he is conversing with the grave-digger). The experience is analogous to that of reading: not only is everything about the *Caballero* as distant from her daily life as pulp fiction, but she is also hooked as passionately as if she had picked up a forbidden novel: 'pudo Mariquita contemplarle a su gusto, desde los pies a la cabeza y desde la cabeza a los pies, sin pestañear siquiera y sin tomar apenas aliento. Sucedíale a la niña que cuanto más le miraba mayor placer y encanto le causaba verle' [Mariquita was able to gaze at him as much as she liked, from head to toe and back again, without even blinking and hardly drawing breath. What was happening to the child was that the more she looked at him, the more pleasure and enchantment she felt from seeing him] (621). Desiring more of this enchanting experience, she dreams obsessively of the *Caballero* and ends up doing exactly what the worldly society ladies do—she writes to him. Unlike the ladies, however, she is direct about her desires: she wishes to be near him again and states that if her father decided to marry her to the Duke, she would be very happy (669). In response to her directness and innocence, the Duke is gentler in teaching her to understand the impossibility of realizing her desire. He makes her see that union with a character like him—powerful and dominating—would bring pain and not pleasure. Essentially, he shows her that a sado-masochistic fantasy is not love, and leaves her grieving for the loss of her dreams, but now emotionally prepared to find another kind of relationship with her intended— an authentic artistic genius whose creations, significantly, have not yet been commercialized.

The gentler treatment accorded to Mariquita and her intended distinguishes them from Madrid's élite, the members of the aristocracy and the urban bourgeoisie relentlessly mocked by the Duke. Castro's critique of women's 'enslavement' does not fail to make it clear that the class structure of society enslaves some women more than others. Indeed, some of the novel's most biting scenes show the aristocratic women's imperious and il-logical treatment of their maids, who as feminine subjects also feel the Duke's seductive power but have not their mistresses' freedom to try to enact their fantasies.

There is more to be said about the process the Duke sets in motion within the narrative, however. In eliciting seduction fantasies and then subjecting them to critique, he also registers the instability of the gendered positions within them. Castro develops the possibilities of treating gender as a position or a role rather than a stable identity in a number of ways. Let us return for a moment to the episode involving Casimira, whose interaction with the Duke highlights the reversibility of roles in the sado-masochistic schema that structures their relationship. The Duke interprets the text of her note, which ostensibly offers to be his slave, as a subtextual desire to dominate him, to be the seducer rather than the seduced. 'Historia de José' [Joseph's story], he exclaims after reading her letter and gazing at the portrait sent with it, 'ven a mi pensamiento y sé para mis deseos lo que son los diques para las hirvientes olas del mar.... Y tú, Musa o demonio, no te burles de mi flaqueza ni me abandones cuando la serpiente tentadora, atraída por mis botas azules, se me acerca presentándome la dorada manzana para hacerme perder mi paraíso' [come into my thoughts and be to my desires as dykes to the boiling waters of the sea.... And you, Muse or demon, don't mock my weakness nor abandon me when the tempting serpent, attracted by my blue boots, approaches, offering me the golden apple to make me lose my Paradise] (677–8). The *Caballero* is here projecting a fantasy of his own—the counter-transference, to extend our earlier analogy with psychoanalysis—in which Casimira becomes Potiphar's wife, the agent rather than object of seduction, or, alternatively, occupies the masculine position as Tempter with the Duke playing the feminine part of Eve.[9] That he does not cast himself as Adam to Casimira's Eve suggests that gender ambiguity is implied in the play with role reversal here. For her part, Casimira clearly seeks the advantageous, active position in her verbal fencing match with the Duke; as we have seen, she is willing to enact servitude only because she believes it will give her access to the secret of the Duke's power.

Just as the narrative shows instability in the positions that the Duke and Casimira occupy in the sado-masochistic fantasy, so too it explores reversals of the active and passive roles related to the textual communication situation. Women, who are generally positioned as readers in this novel—readers of novels and Romantic poetry, readers of the Duke as text—become writers once the Duke has elicited their desires. In a complex and ambiguous passage, Castro introduces the transition from one gendered role to another by the women who write notes to the Duke. Playing on the conservative Spanish assumption that the ability to write leads women into sin, which would be one way of interpreting this episode, the narrator describes this and other hazards women face in writing, not least of which is the danger of revealing their ignorance and lack of education.[10] The narrator then goes on to beg indulgence for real women's imperfections in relation to their literary models, and the critical bite in these comments makes itself felt:

no debe culpárselas a fe porque cumplan debidamente su misión, haciendo hasta la muerte su papel de mujeres. Cosa es esta digna de la mayor alabanza, cuando hay tantos hombres que ejecutan el suyo de la peor manera . . . puesto que nacieron para vivir modesta y honradamente, haciendo compás, con el martillo o el azadón, al huso con que hilan el blanco lino sus buenas esposas.

they should not be blamed, surely, for fulfilling their mission as expected, for playing their part as women until they die. This is something worthy of the highest praise, when there are so many men who play their part in the worst way . . . given that they were born to live modestly and honourably, keeping time with their hammer or spade to the wheel on which their good wives spin white linen thread. (667)

Aside from the irony with which Castro suggests that women are scorned for an ignorance that is prescribed as necessary to their social function, what I want to emphasize in this passage is the treatment of gender positions, represented here through highly traditional images, as assigned roles. The Spanish term she uses— 'papel' meaning both 'part' and 'paper'—intensifies the theatricality implied by the concept of part as something scripted and assigned by society rather than by nature. And although, tragically, those assigned the part of women seem to have little choice but to play it 'until they die', this narrative suggests that the parts are to some degree transferable, interchangeable, for women can imagine writing their own script, as Casimira seems to do, and men can find themselves slipping into the feminine position, as the Duke does momentarily.

Sliding out of his privileged male position is not the only slippage that threatens the Knight of the Blue Boots in a narrative that shifts playfully among frames without confirming any point of origin or fixed reference. In the key episode we have already examined, as the Duke peruses Casimira's note and portrait, he begins to slip into the character of another story, presumably prior to the story he is tracing with the help of the Muse in the main body of the narrative. He has known Casimira in another time and under another identity: '¡El duque conocía demasiado aquel rostro que en otro tiempo había adorado en vano!' [The duke knew only too well that face, which he had once adored in vain!] (677). The Duke's earlier life, mentioned only in scattered references, cannot be read as his 'real' life, however. The vocabulary and punctuation of these references give this other life the status of pulp fiction, suggesting that the Duke played the same part as victim of *folletín*-inspired fantasies that his female admirers play in the story he is currently developing. The ironic stance he maintains, not without some struggle, is what permits him to free himself from the seductions of fiction and to teach the women of Madrid to do the same, just as the self-reflexivity of Castro's text transcends her earlier novel's reproduction of the seduction fantasy.

The Duke's mysterious power is not, in fact, the power of phallic privilege, which is elusive and precarious in this novel, but of self-knowledge and self-criticism. He eludes both seduction and attack by laughing at himself, indicting himself as he indicts others: 'Lo conozco: yo merecería el primero ser arrojado en el pozo de la moderna ciencia en compañía de las "historias inspiradas", de los malos versos, de las zarzuelas sublimes y de las novelas que se publican por entrega de a dos cuartos' [I know it: I deserve to be the first one thrown into the pit of modern knowledge along with the 'inspired stories', the bad verses, the sublime *zarzuelas*, and the novels sold by penny instalments] (788). Addressing these words to the Muse, the *Caballero* refers to yet another frame to the main story: the dialogue of the Man and the Muse, the interaction that transformed him into the Duke by teaching him the advantages of irony and ambiguity.

Here the roles, later duplicated in the relation of the Duke and the women, are reversed: the Man seeks from the Muse fulfilment of his 'más ferviente deseo' [most fervent desire] (561), but she does not conform to his expectations, and instead teases and provokes him into jettisoning his fantasies and self-deceptions about writing, fame, and genius. As in the implied story of his previous relations with Casimira, he occupies the position of desirer, but at this level the object is literary glory. The question of gender is foregrounded almost as soon as the Man invokes the Muse: when she refuses to step out of the cloud that veils her, he counters with a misogynist commonplace about women, '¡Hasta las Musas son coquetas!' [Even the Muses are coquettes!], to which she replies, 'Considera que soy Musa pero no dama, y que no debemos perder el tiempo en devaneos' [Bear in mind that I am a Muse but not a lady, and that we shouldn't waste time on idle flirtation] (561).[11] In bringing to the surface of the text and then mocking traditional assumptions about the gendered relation of muse to writer, Castro prepares for the destabilizing ambiguity of the Muse's appearance when she does reveal herself visually: 'Su rostro es largo, ovalado y de una expresión ambigua; tiene los ojos pardos, verdes y azules, y parecen igualmente dispuestos a hacer guiños picarescamente o languidecer de amor. Un fino bozo sombrea el labio superior de su boca, algo abultada' [Her face is long, oval, and has an ambiguous expression; her eyes are grey, green, and blue, and seem equally likely to wink roguishly or to languish with love. A fine moustache shadows the upper lip of her rather thick mouth] (577). The Man reacts emphatically to the gender indeterminacy of a being whom he, along with literary tradition, had cast firmly in the feminine part: 'Conque mi Musa era un marimacho, un ser anfibio de esos que debieran quedar para siempre en el vacío? ¡Qué abominación!' [So my Muse was a man-woman, an amphibious being of the sort that should remain forever in the void? What an abomination!] (577). It is this attitude the Muse must change to make the Man into the Knight of the Blue Boots. It is necessary, she tells him, 'que concluyas por apreciarme en lo que valgo' [that you end up appreciating what I'm worth] (577). And when he finally understands the advantage of ironic double vision and can take pleasure in ambiguity, he is ready to sally forth, a new kind of Quijote, to defeat fantasies through critical self-consciousness.[12]

The indeterminacy of meaning in this text, which has been analysed in semiotic terms by Antonio Risco, was noted by the person who was presumably its first reader, Castro's husband Manuel Murguía.[13] The novel is constructed, he said, in such a way 'que al final se pregunte [el lector], entre dudoso y confiado, si es verdad que lo ha comprendido' [that at the end [the reader] asks himself, hesitating between doubt and confidence, if it is true that he has understood it] (Risco 1982: 193). This uncertainty is intensified by the novel's self-reflexive satire, which uses the technique of *mise en abyme* to subject its own procedure to ridicule. In the final banquet scene, for instance, a critic mocked by the Duke declares that he is reading a novel called *El caballero de las botas azules*: 'Solo puede decirse de tal novela que le falta todo para serlo: argumento, pensamiento, moral . . . en fin, es una simple monstruosidad, lo peor entre lo peor' [All that can be said about it is that it has nothing that makes a novel a novel—plot, ideas, moral judgement . . . in short, it's simply a monstrosity, the worst of the worst] (801). The novel's destabilization of even its own ground of narration, I would argue, is closely connected with its treatment of gender categories. Just as the protagonist, in learning to appreciate the Muse's gender ambiguity, frees himself from the literalness of fixed positions, so too the text teaches its readers to break out of an economy of desire that reinforces women's subordination.

Rosalía de Castro's novels situate themselves in a troubled relationship to the fiction of her time, particularly in regard to how the narratives elicited the reading pleasure of women. Mandrell comments that, as a prototype of women reading seductive texts, Ana Ozores's response to *Don Juan Tenorio* in *La Regenta* shows how 'reading and interpretation, even if loosely construed in terms of watching a drama, draw women more deeply into the web of patriarchy' (149). To combat the effects of texts that acted the role of seducing fathers, leading women's desire along the path that would subject them to patriarchy, Castro attempted to replay the fantasies in new and liberating ways. In *La hija del mar* she exposed as violently oppressive the effects of the seduction fantasy and experimented with attaching women's desire to the maternal object. Later, in *El caballero de las botas azules*, she turned to an attack on the conventional erotics of reading. Peter Brooks has argued that the reader's desire in nineteenth-century narratives follows a pattern of arousal, expectation, and discharge that seems clearly masculine and Oedipal (61, 107–12).[14] Castro's novel certainly does not follow this trajectory. The Duke, functioning as a text within the text, refuses to permit the desire he arouses to follow the phallic pattern described by Brooks, but instead turns his audience's attention to the structure of desire itself. In the same way, this novel, by refusing to resolve its ambiguities into stable meaning, will not allow the reader a satisfactory identification with the subject positions fixed by such resolution. Formally as well as thematically, Castro calls for a new narrative paradigm, and, by implication, a new social organization.[15]

The Muse of Novelty who presides over *El caballero de las botas azules* is the Muse of Mutability, and, as the Muse observes of herself, she has 'su contra y su pro' [her pros and cons] (577). Although Castro seems to symbolize in her the stimulus to capitalism's commodification of culture, this same figure also suggests the possibility of change and transformation. At the end of the novel, on the morning after the Duke's spectacular demonstration of the absurdity of current literature and the oppressiveness of current social forms, Madrid awakes to a sense of agitation and expectancy. ' "¿Hay revolución?" preguntaban algunos con sobresalto' ['Has a revolution started?' asked some with consternation] (829). One passer-by, explaining that no one is sure what is happening, but that all are waiting for the arrival of the Book of Books, adds that he is ready for another kind of fiction: 'Por mi nombre, como ya me canso de tan estupendas mentiras como por ahí se escriben para engañarnos . . . Dicen que va a aparecer ahora un libro cual no se ha visto otro todavía . . . Por ese, por ese aguardo yo' [Upon my honour, I'm getting tired of such stupendous lies as the ones they write around here to deceive us . . . They say that now there's about to appear a book like no other that has yet been seen . . . That's the one I'm waiting for]

(830). In 1868, a year after the novel's publication, the long-expected Glorious Revolution occurred and, in its aftermath, a new national novelistic tradition arose. But neither the revolution nor the realist canon incorporated the radical openness of structure that Castro's Muse sought to inspire.

Receiving more critical attention now than in Castro's own time, her novels elicit the desirous readings of late twentieth-century feminist critics, who can find in their complex ambiguities corroboration of their own interest in understanding gender identity as discursively constructed and inherently unstable. Yet at the same time, the fate of the liberatory project these texts embody offers us a salutary warning about the intractable embeddedness of discursive systems in the material relations of human society: it reminds us that too many individuals did, and still do, play their part as women 'until they die'.

NOTES

1. This defence of Böhl's work was published in *La Ilustración* (quoted in Montesinos 35).
2. Blanco makes a similar point.
3. See Laplanche and Pontalis 5–34. Jane Gallop discusses the treatment of the father–daughter seduction scenario in the psychoanalytic tradition, along with Luce Irigaray's critique of it: Gallop 70–9.
4. See Kirkpatrick.
5. All translations of Castro's texts are mine.
6. Francisco Rodríguez argues that this and other novels by Castro show the influence of utopian socialism in a subtextual critique of developing capitalist forms (Rodríguez 169–79).
7. Casimira alludes to these fantasies early in the novel, when she recognizes that Laura harbours the same hopes as she in relation to the Duke: 'Te veo y te comprendo . . . Caminamos a un mismo paso y por un mismo sendero; falta ahora saber quién llegará la primera' [I see what you're up to . . . We're going at the same pace down the same path; we'll see who gets there first] (639).
8. The foregoing reading of the Duke's relation to the women characters coincides in many respects with that of Charnon-Deutsch. It differs in so far as I am concerned with women as reading subjects, while Charnon-Deutsch is interested in suggesting that the underlying desire the Duke's shenanigans reveal in women is the desire to be a writing or speaking subject: 'What their impossible demands finally reveal is that beyond sexual desire lies the will to know and understand things, that is, to be in possession of the words that would make the unknown familiar' (88). She argues that the freedom mentioned by the Duke as what women regard as the greatest good 'is clearly related to women imagining themselves as writing subjects' (94).

9. It might be noted here that the psychoanalytical account of primal fantasies like the seduction fantasy implies that the subject is not fixed in any one position. Laplanche and Pontalis stress this in their article.

10. This is Castro's tactic also in other pronouncements on women writing: she focuses on the negative experiences of women who write, leaving the tacit indictment of the injustice of this situation for the reader to infer. Shelley Stevens analyses this rhetorical strategy in her discussion of 'Las literatas' (1866) and the prologue to *Follas novas* (1880) (Stevens 79–85).

11. Castro plays simultaneously with gender difference and class difference here: the Muse in effect says, 'I'm not a woman and I'm not an aristocrat.' The Muse's democratic tendencies are suggested in a number of ways throughout the dialogue: her citation of the popular French poet Béranger, for example (573).

12. Don Quijote comes up once or twice in the dialogue. When the Man asks the Muse if she wants to make a rascal or a Quijote out of him, she replies that he already is a little of each (580). Several critics have noted the Cervantine references and textual strategies in the novel, among them Germán Gullón (490) and Enrique Miralles (459). It should be pointed out that the *Caballero*, in attacking the fantasies elicited by the serial novel, acts not so much like Don Quijote the character, as like *Don Quijote* the text.

13. See Risco 1982: 184–97. Risco cites Murguía's commentary on the novel. These comments were, according to F. Rodríguez (206), first published in Murguía's essay 'Rosalía de Castro', *La Voz de Galicia* (La Coruña), 17 July 1885.

14. Susan Winnett questions the universalization of paradigms of male sexual pleasure to all narratives and representation (505–18).

15. Many critics consider the demand for a new kind of novel to be a central theme. See articles by Enrique Miralles, Carme Fernández-Pérez Sanjulian, Antonio Risco (1982). Risco (1986), Miralles, and F. Rodríguez (176–9) link Castro's critique of literature with her critique of society.

WORKS CITED

Actas do Congreso internacional de estudios sobre Rosalía de Castro e o seu tempo (1986), 3 vols. Santiago de Compostela: Consello de Cultura Galega.

ANDREU, ALICIA G. (1974). *Galdós y la literatura popular*. Madrid: SGEL.

BENJAMIN, JESSICA (1986). 'A Desire of one's Own: Psychoanalytic Feminism and Intersubjective Space', in Teresa de Lauretis (ed.), *Feminist Studies/Critical Studies*. Bloomington, Ind.: Indiana University Press. 78–101.

BLANCO, ALDA (1989). 'Domesticity, Education and the Woman Writer: Spain 1850–1880', in Hernán Vidal (ed.), *Cultural and Historical Grounding for Hispanic and Luso-Brazilian Feminist Literary Criticism*. Minneapolis: Institute for the Study of Ideologies and Literature. 371–94.

BROOKS, PETER (1984). 'Freud's Masterplot', in *Reading for the Plot: Design and Intention in Narrative*. New York: Knopf.

CASTRO, ROSALÍA DE (1977). *Obras completas*, vol. ii, ed. Victoriano García Martí. 2nd edn. Madrid: Aguilar.

—— (1986). *La hija del mar*. Madrid: Akal.

CHARNON-DEUTSCH, LOU (1992). 'Desire in Rosalía de Castro's *El caballero de las botas azules*', in Lou Charnon-Deutsch (ed.), *Estudios sobre escritoras hispánicas en honor de Georgina Sabat-Rivers*. Madrid: Castalia. 79–96.

FERNÁNDEZ-PÉREZ SANJULIAN, CARME (1986). 'O prólogo de *El caballero de las botas azules* ou o ensaio dunha poética nova', in *Actas* i. 475–82.

GALLOP, JANE (1982). *The Daughter's Seduction: Feminism and Psychoanalysis*. Ithaca, NY: Cornell University Press.

GULLÓN, GERMÁN (1986). '*El caballero de las botas azules*: farsa de las letras decimonónicas', in *Actas* i. 483–91.

KIRKPATRICK, SUSAN (1990). 'La narrativa de la seducción en la novela española del siglo XIX', in Giulia Colaizzi (ed.), *Feminismo y teoría del discurso*. Madrid: Cátedra. 153–67.

LAPLANCHE, JEAN, and PONTALIS, JEAN-BERTRAND (1986). 'Fantasy and the Origins of Sexuality', in Victor Burgin, James Donald, and Cora Kaplan (eds.), *Formations of Fantasy*. London: Methuen. 5–34.

MANDRELL, JAMES (1992). *Don Juan and the Point of Honor: Seduction, Patriarchal Society and Literary Tradition*. University Park, Pa.: Pennsylvania State University Press.

MIRALLES, ENRIQUE (1986). '*El caballero de las botas azules*, un manifiesto anti-anovelado', in *Actas* i. 457–63.

MONTESINOS, JOSÉ F. (1961). *Fernán Caballero: ensayo de justificación*. Berkeley, Calif.: University of California Press.

MUNDI PEDRET, FRANCISCO (1986). '*El caballero de las botas azules*: la nueva estética de Rosalía', in *Actas* i. 465–74.

RISCO, ANTONIO (1982). *Literatura y figuración*. Madrid: Gredos.

—— (1986). 'Unha novela fantástica de Rosalía: *El caballero de las botas azules*', in *Actas* i. 449–55.

RODRÍGUEZ, FRANCISCO (1988). *Analise sociolóxica da obra de Rosalía de Castro*. Vigo: AS-PG.

SINUÉS DE MARCO, MARÍA DEL PILAR (1859). *El ángel del hogar*. 2nd edn. Madrid: Nieto y Ca.

STEVENS, SHELLEY (1986). *Rosalía de Castro and the Galician Revival*. London: Tamesis.

WINNETT, SUSAN (1990). 'Women, Men, Narrative, and Principles of Pleasure', *PMLA* 105: 505–18.

5
Gender and Language:
The Womanly Woman and
Manly Writing

MARYELLEN BIEDER

In the nineteenth century, male and female literary figures move
in separate spheres, and the labels used to designate their activities meld the author's gender with the written product. The
most common gendered pairs of words in the Spanish language
to identify authors are *poeta/poetisa* [poet/poetess], *literato/literata*
[man of letters/literary woman], and, less frequently, *escritor/
escritora* [writer/woman writer]. This binary division displays the
gender of the writer but also implicates writing itself. Since masculine cultural forms constitute the norm, the work of a female
literata or *poetisa* represents that-which-is-not-the-norm, the
otherness of non-male writing. In short, the perceived insepara-
bility of biology and language: writing 'like a woman'. Catharine
Stimpson states the case cogently: 'Scholars have shown that
Western culture has propagated an ideology of creativity that
says men produce art, women children; that literary texts both
reflect and reinforce sex/gender systems' (55). Men's writing is
in effect considered gender neutral, and thus is not generally
marked as writing 'like a man'. With the assumption that the
author's gender and writing are consonant, 'women's writing' is
coded as implicitly inferior to that of their male counterparts,
and the usage of the female terms (except at times by women)
is frequently derogatory. In her landmark study of Spanish
Romantic female poets, Susan Kirkpatrick characterizes the
image Spanish culture held out to women writers in the 1840s
as, if not 'psychological monsters, immoral to boot', then 'highly
conditioned by the ideology of female difference' (1989*b*: 92).
When a woman authors a text that breaks with these gendered

expectations and renegotiates the boundaries of women's writing, she crosses into territory already staked out as male. The only category available to define writing that moves beyond the confines of the feminine is *varonil* [masculine]. Thus 'manly writing' conveys not only the trespass on to male plots and tropes, but an inherently biological invasion of male space (*varonil*, as opposed to the culturally masculine *masculino*). For a woman, writing 'like a man' is read as a double-edged gesture: negative because it breaches the (devalued) space assigned to women, but at the same time potentially positive in that a woman can position herself within the (valued) territory of male writing. It is a commonplace of nineteenth-century critics, for example, that Carolina Coronado's poetry is 'feminine', whereas Gertrudis Gómez de Avellaneda's writing is 'masculine', with all the ambiguity this boundary violation carries with it.[1] Lyric poetry offers a case in point. Its strong and assertive 'I' breaks with cultural assumptions about women's writing, as Sandra Gilbert and Susan Gubar have observed (1979: p. xxii). Terry Eagleton elaborates on this point:

nineteenth-century criticism continued to quibble at any lyrical introspection that appeared too self-absorbed. A commitment by the female lyricist to herself or her art could be interpreted as dangerously assertive or egotistical, to focus on Nature, God, or a loved one offered safer material. (quoted in Hanson 57)

Thus lyricism, while inherently 'feminine' in its invocation of 'Nature, God, or a loved one', carried within it the danger for the woman poet of transgressing the bounds of the permissible and straying on to the 'dangerously assertive or egotistical' terrain of the 'masculine'.

The tidy gendering of writing—men's language and writings are masculine, women's feminine—grows more complex across the century, especially in the social conservatism of the last decades. Cultural strictures rigidify and what are seen as deviations from the codified norms, such as those carried out in the realist and naturalist novels of Emilia Pardo Bazán, often generate great opprobrium. Women who do not write 'like a woman' breach the conventions of genre and language and are therefore suspected of not conforming to their proper biological role. To stray from the strict allegiance between socio-sexual gender and writing is to open oneself up to public exposure as not-a-woman.

In attempting to account for such anomalous texts, some critics seek to redefine women's writing within the polarized parameters. In reviewing texts by women, these critics, both male and female, give the adjective *varonil* a positive charge and at the same time overtly acknowledge the author's 'womanliness' by invoking her domesticity and beauty, in order to offset the danger inherent in this cross-gendering of her writing. In effect, to denote a woman's writings as 'manly' breaks the convention that posits an innate bond between the author's biological self and her language.

This study proposes to explore the repositioning of women's writing within the gendered boundaries of language in the last decades of the nineteenth century. It centers on the strategies employed by both male and female reviewers which effectively cross-gender women's writing by labelling it as masculine. What is of interest here is not the works themselves but their reception, the way in which they are read as conforming to or violating the contemporary construction of gender. The reclassification of women's writing from an implicitly inferior 'not-male' to an androgynous 'manlike' reaches beyond the obvious examples of the mid-century Avellaneda and the late-century Pardo Bazán to other women as well. I shall also examine attempts by Pardo Bazán, Concepción Gimeno de Flaquer, and other women to renegotiate the separate spheres of gendered writing and claim for some women the neutral status of *poeta*. Poetry is the only form of creative authorship that can be designated with a neutral term in Spanish, since the single word conflates the two genders and can thus serve to name either a female or a male poet. The use of the article marks the difference between *la poeta* [the female poet] and *el poeta* [the male poet]. Because of its linguistic cross-coding (as a noun it is masculine in gender while its ending appears to be feminine), it leaves room for dual-gendering. In contrast to the marked female forms *poetisa*, *literata*, and even *escritora* or *autora*, *poeta* can function as an unmarked category. This opening up of *poeta* to women poets is not a manœuvre exclusive to the end of the century. Kirkpatrick gives an example from the mid-1840s of a male critic, Gustave Deville, admitting women to the unmarked status of 'poeta, artista; pero nunca sabia' [poet, artist, but certainly not a wise woman] (1989*b*: 93). And women poets themselves, such as Coronado in her 1846 poem 'Último canto' [Last Song], invoke the irresolvable tension between their social and their writing selves: 'mi espíritu de poeta' [my poet's spirit] and 'mis plantas de mujer' [my woman's feet] (Kirkpatrick, 1992: 117–19).

No such inclusive term as *poeta* is available for women prose writers. Both *escritora* and *autora* are still marked for gender, although they are culturally less derogatory than *literata*. Indeed, the latter is so bound to feminine writing that it implies communication within a female circle of readers. Pardo Bazán seems to be the one woman of her generation in the last decades of the century to break free of the mould and not only gain but retain public recognition as an *escritora*. From the early 1880s, with the publication of her first novels and especially her first volume of literary criticism, *La cuestión palpitante* [The Burning Question], it becomes impossible for male critics to continue to dismiss her as a *literata*. Whereas a *poetisa* or *literata* is always an inferior imitation of an unattainable male model (the *poeta* or *literato*), an *escritora* is a female *escritor*. Unlike the feminine form, the masculine *literato* carries no sanction. An all-encompassing category, it embraces without distinction or judgement all men of letters whatever their pretensions or achievements. As such, it is employed routinely by and in reference to such major literary figures as Benito Pérez Galdós and Juan Valera. The cultural usage that prevails in the twentieth century is the paired terms *escritor/escritora*, which replace the outmoded *literato* and its devalued counterpart, *literata*.

Before looking at the ways in which women writers in nineteenth-century Spain manœuvre within the gendered space of writing, it is important to recall that the coding of literary language as masculine or feminine is not unique either to the nineteenth century or to Spanish literature, although clearly the cultural configuration shifts across time and perhaps more significantly between cultures. Nevertheless, the unmarked status of men's language and the devaluation of women's writing as a deviation from it appear to be constant at least in Western cultures. A recent study of *Grammar and Gender* begins by citing the 'common though mistaken notion that, as women derive from men in the biblical story of creation, women's words, or anything linguistically associated with women, can be seen as derivative of, and by implication inferior to, the masculine equivalent' (Baron 1). The correlation of linguistic control with sexual identity, again according to this study, is grounded in a primary negative assumption: 'that women know fewer words than men and are less creative linguistically' (80). In a recent essay that brings together gender, language, and sexuality, Gilbert and Gubar remind us that 'there is a long masculine tradition that identifies female anatomy with a degrading linguistic destiny' (1989: 82). Thus this tradition that fuses language with anatomy shapes the way literary texts are read and makes especially problematic the critical response to female-authored texts. The nineteenth-century 'gendering of poetics', to borrow Naomi Schor's felicitous phrase (59), has its roots in earlier centuries and in the inherited construction of gender. The premisses that Nancy K. Miller has identified as underlying critical practice in late eighteenth-century France accord with those of Spanish critics in the next century. She observes of the author and literary critic Choderlos de Laclos that he 'reads women's writing through a set of clichés of femininity that leave the category of novelist masculine and originary: for Laclos the class of novelists is male' (46). From this Miller draws two important conclusions: first, that 'the category of the writer remains the male-universal against which the woman as writer is judged', and secondly, that the male writer assumes 'the self-appointed role . . . *as critic*' (47). After surveying examples from the past two centuries, she concludes that 'the protocol that regulates the social relations between the sexes takes the place of—at the very least displaces—literary criteria' (47). That is, as I will attempt to show, contemporary critics extrapolate gendered social relations on to the dynamics that govern their reading of texts. In her study of the changing reception accorded George Sand's novels throughout the nineteenth century, Schor has traced the shifting weave of what is considered gender appropriate. Her conclusion, and one of the premisses on which the present essay rests as well, is that writing is not—cannot be—inherently gender coded; the attributing of maleness or femaleness to writing is always a critical manœuvre.

It should come as no surprise that the link between manliness, womanliness, and writing continues to be drawn in our own century. Catharine Stimpson cites Lionel Trilling's 1941 characterization of the style of Ernest Hemingway, frequently held to be the most 'masculine' of American writers, as 'oddly "feminine"' (69). A curious example from a 1964 treatise on style makes explicit this distinction between sexual identity and the perception of gender in writing: 'Underlining is generally described as "feminine", by which it is to be inferred that no real man would make use of it, for fear of being thought womanly, while no real woman would use it either, because it is unmanly' (quoted in Baron 65). This perceived desire on the part of a 'real woman' to break free from her prescribed confines and strive for 'manly writing' that 'bear[s] no trace of the feminine or the effeminate' echoes a long-standing preoccupation of male critics. A frequently cited 1852 essay on 'The Lady Novelists' by G. H. Lewes offers an example that addresses not only language but characterization and plotting. 'To write as men write', he asserts, 'is the aim and besetting sin of women; to write as women is the real office they have to perform' (quoted in Showalter 3). Returning to the present day, Brad Epps has perceptively argued that critics continue to read such contemporary Spanish novels as Carmen Martín Gaite's *El cuarto de atrás* [The Back Room] as 'in one form or another an illustration of feminine writing' (76).

Women's writing that is perceived to deviate from the conventions of the feminine provokes a cross-gendered reading. In his discussion of George Sand, Henry James identifies in her genius something 'very masculine', and yet he is constrained to recognize in the last analysis that 'our final impression of her always is that she is a woman and a Frenchwoman' (155). Despite the seeming dominance of the womanly in James's view of Sand, he continues to struggle with her doubleness in order to account for her genius: 'What was feminine in her was the quality of her genius; the *quantity* of it—its force, and mass, and energy—was masculine, and masculine were her temperament and character' (161). James ultimately merges Sand's social transgressions and her writing; for him, the masculine in a woman is the violation of limits in both writing and the social sphere.

Turning now to Spanish literature, the most frequently cited pronouncement on Gertrudis Gómez de Avellaneda's writing is the oxymoronic outburst of one of her male contemporaries: 'es mucho hombre esta mujer' [this woman is some man] (quoted in Beth Miller 201–2). Similarly, Zorrilla's evaluation of Avellaneda's poetry as 'pensamientos varoniles, algo viril y fuerte' [manly thoughts, somewhat masculine and strong] evinces the confusion of his expectations for women's verse (quoted in Gómez de Avellaneda 22). Avellaneda herself expresses the incompatibility between her sense of self as writer and normative gender expectations when she writes of her two natures, 'la de una mujer y la de un poeta' [that of a woman and that of a poet], leaving poet in its masculine form (quoted in Beth Miller 204). Any deviation from the strict middle-class sphere of action for the female seems to provoke the need to explain this breach in terms of a crossing of prescribed boundaries. In short, a woman who does not conform to the restrictive pattern for the female is defined in terms of male qualities. This move repositions the female in cultural, not biological, terms, although the spectre of the cross-coded *marimacho* [masculine woman], who embodies the collapse of biological differentiation, looms in the background of the more violent of these cultural dislocations.

Several manœuvres take shape in nineteenth-century Spanish criticism to open up the rigid inscription of writing within these recognized conventions and counter the devaluation of feminine writing as the inferior 'Other' of male writing. While most critics still reveal their anxiety at the encroachment of women into the implicitly male spheres of poetry and prose fiction, others, especially a small number of women, seek to find a way within this dichotomy to revalorize women's writing to equal that of men. Pardo Bazán, as already stated, effects this shift in valuation in her own career from the *literata* of her early years to the established *escritora* (Bieder, 1993: 23). Carmen de Burgos, a generation younger than the Galician writer, could still recall in her 1913 autobiographical sketch the significance of this move out of gendered writing into gender-neutral writing: '[l]a primera vez que me llamaron *escritora* volví la cara a ver si se lo decía a otro; y me ofendí cuando me dijeron *literata* . . . ¡Casi me sigo ofendiendo!' [the first time anyone called me a *writer* I turned around to see whether they were addressing someone else; and I was offended when they called me a *literary lady* . . . I still find it almost offensive!] (p. xi).

The relationship of women writers to this renegotiation of male/female territory is problematic at best. One of the most visible spokeswomen for the *literata*, Gimeno uses the language of battle to record women's jockeying for position as writers. In her sketch of the literary woman, she condemns those who 'careciendo de valor para sostener perpetua lucha con el hombre, abandonan la pluma y matan su inspiración, guardando un mutismo eterno' [lacking the valour to sustain a continued struggle with men, abandon the pen and kill their inspiration, keeping forever silent] (1877: 211; see Bieder 1990). If here Gimeno perceives that in order to write a woman must accept the consequence of the challenge she poses to society, later in the same sketch she defends the writing woman from ridicule by making her embody the traditional feminine virtues of domesticity. Gimeno seems to distinguish between the culturally problematic *literata* and the more neutral *escritora*, but she then erases any difference by rewriting the *escritora* as 'siempre mujer; pues se ocupa del costurero, el tocador y la cocina' [always a woman, since she busies herself at the sewing table, the dressing table, and in the kitchen] (1877: 225). Addressing this insistence by both male and female writers on women's domesticity, Kirkpatrick concludes that, 'by stressing women's difference from men' the image acquires 'a certain empowering effect for women', since it 'granted them a degree of authority and even superiority in their designated sphere' (1989a: 367). Whenever Gimeno moves her defence of the woman as writer too far away from its centre in this domestic sphere, she returns to home territory and reinscribes her in the cultural construction of femininity.

A prime manœuvre in this shifting of women's writing out of the confines of prescriptive gendering is the revalorization of unconventional, 'masculine' writing as positive, rather than 'unfeminine.' In the discussion of women's writing in nineteenth-century Spain, the poetry of Avellaneda and Coronado became the polarized touchstones of masculine and feminine language. Kirkpatrick cogently observes that, in contrast to Avellaneda, 'Coronado's lyrical voice is coded much more explicitly as feminine according to cultural gender conventions' (1989b: 209). The way in which critics continue throughout the century to invoke these poets to code the reading of women's writing is evident in the example of an 1890 biographical sketch of Gimeno by the *literato* Teodoro Guerrero:

Su lira es a veces tan viril, que no se ve a la mujer; y a veces es tan dulce, que parece que los sonidos de sus cuerdas salen de la enramada. Concha no se arrulla con las tempestades, como Gertrudis Avellaneda; no se inspira con las flores silvestres, como Carolina Coronado; no moja su pluma en el fango del naturalismo para buscar efectos, como otras escritoras que se dejan arrastrar por las fatales corrientes de la época.

Her lyre is at times so masculine that one cannot see the woman; and at other times it is so sweet that the sounds from its strings seem to come from the branches themselves. Concha is not swept away by storms, like Gertrudis Avellaneda; she does not find her inspiration in wildflowers, like Carolina Coronado; she does not seek to achieve effects by dipping her pen into the slime of naturalism, like other women writers who let themselves be dragged along by the fatal currents of the day.

One can see here how the gendering of the poetry of the two renowned women of the previous generation (at this time Coronado was, of course, still alive but no longer a public presence) has hardened into an unnuanced polarity of masculine and feminine, while Pardo Bazán's association with naturalism has created a new deviation from the feminine norm against which to define acceptable writing by women. Guerrero opens by evaluating Gimeno's prose in masculine terms—the obliteration of the woman by male qualities is necessarily a negative criticism—but then balances his condemnation with its opposite. In fact, he rejects equally an excess of masculine or feminine language in women's writing; nevertheless, he seems to accord virility, balanced by the feminine, a positive charge. His reading of Gimeno's language remains prescriptive, but he reserves his praise for writing that can embrace with moderation some element of the masculine. In short, he is trying to inscribe Gimeno into the ranks of the daring writers who break free from the confines of the feminine, yet he is still unable to imagine writing in any terms other than those of gender.

Pardo Bazán enacts a similar manœuvre of disengaging writing from the author's biological identity in her reading of Coronado. She affirms the feminine nature of Coronado's writing while erasing the difference between the female *poetisa* and the male *poeta* by designating her, in an oxymoron, 'el tierno poeta Carolina Coronado' [the tender poet Carolina Coronado] (1889: 174).[2] Noël Valis has argued that for some women writers 'el ideal andrógino parecía una alternativa viable' [the androgynous ideal seemed to be a viable alternative] (1991a: 37). As she reads it, Coronado's strategy in asserting to her male contemporaries that Avellaneda was 'tan gran poeta como vosotros' [as great a poet as you men] generates a new category for the woman poet, one in which 'la amazona de nuestro Parnaso . . . es más fuerte, no porque es hombre-poeta sino porque es poetisa-amazona' [the amazon of our Parnassus . . . is stronger, not because she is a man-poet, but because she is an amazon-poetess] (37). The result is, in Valis's words, to situate Avellaneda within a female tradition of strength and visibility that 'revela una disconformidad fundamental con el encasillamiento tradicional de la mujer escritora' [reveals a fundamental rejection of the traditional pigeon-holing of the woman writer] (37). Despite Pardo Bazán's repeated use of similar strategies, she does not eschew simple polarities as a shorthand in her criticism. For example, she gallantly gives precedence to reviewing books by 'las poetisas' over those of 'los poetas', and, in a similar shorthand gesture, she rejects the practice of comparing women's verse 'a las viriles estrofas de la Avellaneda, o a las ardientes y tiernas confesiones de la Coronado' [either to Avellaneda's virile stanzas, or to Coronado's fervent and tender confessions] (1893*b*: 139). There is surely something of a parody, however, in her use of these well-worn phrases.

In contrast to Pardo Bazán or Coronado, Gimeno, writing within the often contradictory discourses of a moderate Spanish feminism, reiterates the commonplace that Avellaneda's poetry is masculine, but she treats it as an attempt by the dominant literary community to claim for itself an important female precursor. She therefore resists their move to 'usurpárnosla para el Parnaso masculino bajo el pretexto de que no es poetisa sino poeta' [steal her away from us for inclusion in the male Parnassus on the pretext that she is not a poetess but a poet] (Gimeno 1885). She concludes that Avellaneda is both 'poetisa' and 'poeta,' that 'su genio es bisexual' [her genius is bisexual]:

Si como poeta asombra su pujanza, como poetisa encanta su ternura. . . . Nos admira en ello el brío, la concisión, la entereza y el desenfado del gran poeta, y nos encanta la flexibilidad, la dulzura, la gracia, la sensibilidad de la escritora eminente.

If as a poet her force surprises us, as a poetess her tenderness enchants us. . . . We admire in it the spirit, the concision, the strength of character, and the self-assurance of the great poet, and we find enchanting the flexibility, the sweetness, the grace, the feeling of the eminent writer.

Her fusion of feminine and masculine in Avellaneda's poetry thus reinscribes, rather than contesting, established categories. In a sense, she wants to have it both ways, valorizing the poet, which implicitly situates her within the masculine tradition, without releasing her from the female literary tradition. But if, for Gimeno, Avellaneda's verses 'tienen la robustez del numen masculino' [have the robustness of masculine poetic inspiration], she points to the parallel case of (French) men, Lamartine and Michelet, whose writings 'llevan impreso el sello de una delicadeza femenina' [carry the seal of a feminine refinement]. Thus, while Pardo Bazán moves to collapse the distinction between poet and poetess, Gimeno naturalizes the cross-gendering of writing.

Since virility is the hallmark of men's writing, it necessarily comes to encode literary merit. Men write 'like a man' in a masculine language that produces virile texts. To read a woman poet as exclusively feminine is not a sign of admiration for her but of her exclusion from literary value. To find that her writing verges into the territory of the masculine becomes a sign of her approximation to value. When Pardo Bazán speaks of her sister Galician poet, Rosalía de Castro, she praises her as a true poet, a *poeta*, not a *poetisa* (1973: 671). She defines Rosalía's poetry as the representation of female experience in masculine language (682). In a contrasting and more petulant manœuvre, Rosalía's husband Manuel Murguía situates his wife among the 'poetisas españolas' and queries rhetorically: '¿Acaso no es Rosalía en sus versos tan varonil como la Avellaneda, sin sus grandes incorrecciones y prosaismos, y tan correcta como la Coronado sin su flojedad?' [Is Rosalía not, in fact, every bit as masculine in her verse as Avellaneda, but without her many flaws and banalities, and just as correct as Coronado, but without her limpness?] (quoted in Davies 612). This rhetorical ploy represents an attempt to wrest his wife's poetry away from exclusive association with feminine writing, on the model of Coronado, and to dispute Avellaneda's right to be the sole representative of masculine writing from a female pen. But implicit in Murguía's attempt to revalorize his wife's position within the field of *poetisas* is his inability to imagine her outside the circle of women poets. Nevertheless, his insistence that she is as masculine a poet as Avellaneda, as well as a better one, transforms the latter from a negative to a positive model for women, and at the same time underscores the shift in value of *viril*, once an inherently negative denunciation of women's poetry, to an index of positive value.

Pardo Bazán's most significant manœuvre in this debate over the language of literary creation is to resist the dominant critical practice of assigning gender to writing. From her earliest forays into the world of letters, her own writing does not respect the division between male genres and female ones. As we have seen, one of her prime manœuvres is to redefine women poets like Rosalía de Castro out of the devalued category of *poetisa* and into a gender-neutral designation of *poeta*. In a like manner, in her evocation of Carmen Silva, the Queen of Romania, she addresses the 'poeta' with her 'bella alma de poeta' [beautiful poet's soul], a phrase that fuses the feminine into the unmarked (1902: 8). Pardo Bazán was not the only woman of her generation to call for a reading of women's writing without reference to gender, although doubtless her position in the literary world gave her an edge not every other woman enjoyed. Her contemporary Rosario Acuña, one of the most iconoclastic women of the last decades of the century, suggests a different tack when she sets to verse her opposition to this practice in '¡Poetisa . . . !': 'Si han de ponerme nombre tan feo, I todos mis versos he de romper: I no me cuadra tal palabra, I no la quiero' [If they are going to call me by such an ugly name, I I am going to tear up all my verses: I such a word I doesn't suit me, I I don't want it] (Kirkpatrick 1992: 289–90). In contrast to Acuña's self-silencing gesture, Pardo Bazán holds to her premiss that neither the writer nor writing is bound by gender, arguing that '[d]entro del terreno literario no hay varones ni hembras' [in literary terrain there are neither males nor females] (quoted in Scanlon 144). Geraldine Scanlon considers this Pardo Bazán's declaration of a theoretical position, not a pragmatic one, arguing that 'she was aware that this ideal of literary androgyny was wish-fulfillment rather than actuality' (144). But Pardo Bazán's realignment of the gendered spheres of writing in her criticism and the distance she maintains from the community of writing women tend to confirm her desire to be read—and to read others—outside the framework that imposed gendered assumptions on authors and their writing.

It is in her prologue to a volume of verse by a woman poet that Pardo Bazán gives clearest expression to her understanding of the relationship between gender and women's writing. Her introduction's 'Dos palabras' [A few Words] about Carolina Valencia's *Poesías* [Poems] address directly the question of how a woman manages to write when writing itself is perceived as gendered. These few pages are unique among her writings in a number of important ways. This is her only prologue to a volume written by a living, Spanish woman, and it constitutes the only occasion on which she speaks directly and publicly to a woman about her writing.[3] It is also the first time she engages in the discourse of mentor to a younger woman writer. Although only a decade apart in age, the two women differ markedly in their experience of authorship; the older woman published her first poem at 15 and her first novel at 18, while the younger is publishing her first book at 30. What is of greatest significance in the present context, however, is the way the prologue projects a successful woman author dealing with the relationship between gender and writing.

In her prologue Pardo Bazán, at the petition of another woman, writes to and about that woman as poet. Her first manœuvre is to remove her words from the familiar discourse of literary friendship by declaring that she knew nothing of Valencia prior to her request for a prologue. Further, she explicitly distances herself from the female literary community and women's writing by asserting that she has done very little to cultivate 'el terreno de las simpatías femeniles' [the field of female friendships] (1890: p. viii). She makes clear from the outset the unequal positions that the two women occupy by specifying, in gender-neutral language, that she, 'veterano ya en guerras literarias' [already a veteran in literary warfare], is responding to 'el principiante' [the beginner] (p. viii). Thus she begins by writing both herself and Valencia out of feminine writing, and in so doing moves the question of gender off-centre. To bolster this move she stakes out her position that readers comprise a gender-neutral whole—'el público debe ser, como la humanidad, un todo andrógino, indivisible' [the reading public should be, like humanity, an indivisible, androgynous whole]—thus arguing against women writing a marginalized literature in 'feminine' language for a female readership. Much as Gimeno does in 'La literata', she argues that the strongest opposition to this erasure of gender difference will come from other women: 'los que prescindimos de la arbitraria división . . . corremos el peligro de enajenarnos, más aún que la aprobación del sexo fuerte, la del sexo paria' [those of us who avoid the arbitrary division . . . run the risk of alienating ourselves, not only from the approval of the stronger sex, but from that of the outcast sex] (p. viii). One result of her rejection of this 'arbitraria división' is that, rather than making common cause with the marginalized status of other women writers, she positions herself outside gender difference and, in a parody of masculine language, refers to women as 'el sexo paria' [pariahs]. From this premiss of unmarked writing and unmarked readers, she states her criterion for women whose writing interests her: 'si tienen suficiente vocación para creer, desde el primer instante, que en el reino de las letras no hay, como en las iglesias protestantes, *lado de las mujeres y lado de los hombres*' [whether they have a strong enough vocation to believe that in the world of letters there is not, as there is in Protestant churches, *a women's side and a men's side*] (pp. ix–x). That is, in reading the works of other women she looks for the confirmation of her premiss that writing should be gender-neutral writing.

Underscoring her affirmation that women's writing should be gender free is Pardo Bazán's reliance in addressing Valencia on the unmarked 'principiante', the value-neutral 'autora', and the social marker 'señora'. Only when she engages directly the nature of the poetry itself does she designate Valencia a 'poetisa', and she does so precisely because of the poet's absence, in Pardo Bazán's reading, from her own verse: 'Sus poesías . . . me dan poca luz para representarme a la poetisa' [Her poems . . . give me very little insight for projecting an image of the poetess] (p. x). She intuits that Valencia writes a feminine language precisely to absent herself from the public arena into which the act of publication inserts her, as though she could make herself invisible within generically feminine verse: 'Versos [que pecan] de excesivamente genéricos; por encerrarse (creo que de propósito) en un círculo de temas y de pensamientos que ni asusta ni sorprende, ni se presta a ningún comentario malévolo en pluma femenil' [Verses [that suffer from] being excessively general, because they close themselves up (I believe on purpose) in a circle of themes and ideas, that, coming from the pen of a woman, do not startle or surprise, or lend themselves to any malicious comments] (p. x). This conformity to gendered writing is precisely what Pardo Bazán sets out to reform in her prologue.

In reading Pardo Bazán's words to Valencia it is essential to keep in mind that the poet, like Carolina Coronado a half-century earlier, and indeed like most women poets of the century, writes from a small, provincial town. Valis makes explicit the tension between the woman poet's private self and the public act of publication, a tension exacerbated in the close confines of middle-class provincial life:

Hablar o escribir en público exponía a la mujer escritora a la terrible fuerza de la opinión pública, ese lector anónimo que podía destruir fácilmente la reputación de una mujer, su identidad genérica como construcción cultural de la feminidad.

Speaking or writing in public exposed the woman writer to the terrible force of public opinion, that anonymous reader who could easily destroy a woman's reputation, her gender identity as the cultural construction of femininity. (Valis 1991*a*: 36)

What in Valencia is an attempt not to attract public attention, by submerging her difference into the common language of women poets while paradoxically claiming the attention of a reading public, is to Pardo Bazán a useless repetition of conventional themes and language that constitutes a form of self-censorship. Although strictly speaking she is not asking Valencia for auto-biographical verse, the thrust of her prologue is specifically to recommend that the poet write from her own experience and put herself into her poetry. This is what would move her from 'el rango de dulce y amable *poetisa*' [the ranks of a sweet and pleasing *poetess*] to the category of '*poeta* sin sexo' [gender-neutral *poet*] (1890: p. xi). Pardo Bazán here defines 'poeta' not as masculine but as neutral ['poeta sin sexo'] and therefore equally open to the men and women who share her definition of a poetry infused with the poet's own voice. In her strongest praise of Valencia, the critic affirms her potential to move beyond the confines of feminine writing and become a 'poeta': 'yo estoy persuadida de que la señora vive, siente, piensa y dice más que sus versos; que el campo de sus ideas propias es extenso y digno de traducirse en los acordes de su bien templada lira' [I am persuaded that this woman lives, feels, thinks, and says more than her poems; that the range of her own ideas is broad and worthy of being translated into chords from her well-tempered lyre] (p. x). These are words that correspond rather clearly to Pardo Bazán's perception of her own writing project. In short, she is asking Carolina Valencia, a conventionally proper married lady from the provincial market town of Medina de Rioseco, to break the mould of feminine writing and join female precursors such as Avellaneda, Coronado, and the Galician author herself in the public eye. Despite the evasive manœuvres of her poetry, there is something in Valencia that Pardo Bazán seems to recognize; after all, she herself began as a young girl by writing poetry in provincial La Coruña. Her recommendation is premissed on a writer's implicit desire for recognition: 'si aspira a crearse un nombre (aspiración muy noble y muy natural)', to which she adds her encouragement: 'Cobre ánimo y revélese sin timidez alguna en sus cantos futuros' [Pluck up your courage and express yourself without timidity in your future poems] (pp. x–xi). But this underlying assumption is itself gendered (she would argue that it is neutral), and cultural norms dictate a public display of 'timidity' as an essential quality of women's writing.

The gendering of this desire for public recognition and its writing into language is precisely what separates a Carolina Valencia from Emilia Pardo Bazán. The former's relationship to the public nature of this step of launching her first book of poetry is the opposite of the older writer's. Valencia wants to preserve her status as a private lady within the public sphere, while enhancing her reputation as a cultured lady with a volume of verse. The ambivalence of this ploy is clearly what Pardo Bazán cannot understand and what she seeks to dispel by citing examples of women who wrote themselves out of the feminine sphere into public space:

Y sobre todo recuerde la señora Valencia que las excelsas mujeres que dejaron huella de sí, nunca tuvieron presente al escribir, como cortapisa, la especialidad de su función dentro del plan trazado por el Autor de la naturaleza para la reproducción de las especies.

And above all let Mrs Valencia remember that the sublime women who left behind a record of themselves were never conscious, when writing, as of an obstacle, of the specialized nature of their function within the plan drawn up by the Author of the natural world for the propagation of the species. (p. xi)

This is indeed a remarkably forthright statement, and one of Pardo Bazán's strongest, against the dictum that biology is destiny. Here she succeeds in shifting the question of value from gender on to writing: the woman who writes well does not write as a woman but as a writer. She counters the convention of gendered writing by asserting that each writer, male or female, must give expression to the inner, individual voice. If the primary recipient of these words is Valencia herself, it seems clear that the Galician literary critic is addressing as well a larger public of women and men writers. The prologue gives her the opening to set forth her own 'poetics of gender'.

In hindsight the incompatibility between these two women's understanding of gender and writing seems obvious, and the intriguing question remains as to why Valencia solicited the prologue and why Pardo Bazán accepted. The petition suggests the provincial poet's perceived need for the protection of an established author to cover or legitimize her transgression. The Galician critic reads Valencia's invitation as a flattering gesture; she calls it an honour, 'un testimonio de respetuosa estimación' [an affirmation of respectful esteem] (p. viii), that allows her to demonstrate her solidarity with other writing women. The nature of her advice, however, undercuts this potential female solidarity. Or perhaps she merely seizes an unremarkable opportunity to set forth her own ideas on gendered writing for a woman author and her readers. In any event, Pardo Bazán's generous—to her own mind—affirmation that behind Valencia's conventional sentiments and language lie real emotional and intellectual experiences does not conform to the superficial commonplaces and empty praise that are the standard rhetoric of such prologues. Not surprisingly, the prologue seems to have eclipsed the poetry, although this was surely the opposite of what Valencia had in mind when she contacted Pardo Bazán. At the same time, it served to put the poet more strongly in the public eye, rather than obscuring her in the shadow of a woman with both a well-earned literary reputation and an enviable social position.[4]

In any event, Valencia certainly does not heed Pardo Bazán's words. She publishes a further book of poetry in each of the next two years, but both are extended occasional poems to mark the anniversary of important (male) historical figures, Columbus and San Juan de la Cruz. As if to negate Pardo Bazán's advice, her *Oda a San Juan de la Cruz* [Ode to St John of the Cross] receives the prize in a contest sponsored by the Spanish Royal Academy of Language. Each work enhances somewhat her public visibility at the same time that it erases her individuality more effectively from public view beneath her conventional evocation of a consecrated hero. It could be argued that it is precisely the lack of individuality that makes this poetry acceptable to the poet, the Academy, and to her public.[5]

The discomfort Valencia feels at reading Pardo Bazán's 'Dos palabras' is recorded in an exchange of letters between herself, her husband, and the influential, conservative bachelor critic

Marcelino Menéndez Pelayo.[6] Again, this appears to be a unique set of documents on the negotiation of gender and writing at the end of the century. Following the publication of her poems, Valencia solicits the opinion of Menéndez, alleging that the book 'ha dado que murmurar a algunos escritores sectarios' [has given rise to criticism of her from some biased writers] (Menéndez Pelayo 24 June 1890). Her husband follows up with a letter of his own, requesting the critic's 'juicio imparcial' [impartial judgement] in order to counter Pardo Bazán's assertions (Menéndez Pelayo 3 August 1890). This, of course, constitutes a reversal of Valencia's initial strategy, as she, joined by her husband, now solicits protection from a prominent male critic to escape the effect of the woman writer's 'Dos palabras'. Pardo Bazán's gesture of writing Valencia out of the gendered sphere of women's writing produces the opposite response from what she proposes: Valencia takes refuge in the gendered sphere of feminine writing and the subordination to male authority. In his reply, addressed to the husband, Menéndez Pelayo acknowledges 'cierta desconfianza respecto de los versos femeninos' [his misgivings about verses by women], but gallantly offers to include Valencia among 'las poetisas que exceptúo . . . desde hoy en adelante' [the lady poets that from now on . . . I will exempt from this judgement] (Menéndez Pelayo 23 September 1890). His judgement of her poems rests not only on their recognized feminine qualities of 'pureza y elevación de ideas' [purity and loftiness of ideas], but also on detecting in them 'una firmeza y seguridad de ejecución que son muy raros en versos de mujer, y que para sí quisieran muchos de nuestros actuales poetas' [a strength and sureness of execution that are very rare in poems written by women, and that many of our present-day [male] poets would like to have at their command]. Having clearly inscribed Valencia's verse into feminine writing, he suggests the contrary manœuvre of making it extraordinary within both female and (average) male writing.

This is precisely the gesture of praise that Pardo Bazán refuses to make, either to Valencia in her prologue or, as discussed earlier, in her assessment of Rosalía de Castro. The nature of the male critic's encomium establishes the dynamics of the expected response to women's verse at the end of the nineteenth century. While certainly not collapsing, as Pardo Bazán does, the boundaries of male and female writing, in an empty gesture Menéndez Pelayo does give Valencia's poetry precedence over that of the

many male poets, thus ostensibly inverting the absolute hierarchy of male and female verse. But his is a backhanded com-
pliment, and his gentlemanly but duplicitous rhetoric leaves
the hierarchy of value essentially unaltered. His letter also specifies the flaws in her verse and concludes by reinscibing her as
a 'poetisa' in 'aquella esfera de lirismo suave, abundante y
cadencioso que parece su región poética propia' [that sphere of
smooth, bountiful, and melodious lyricism that seems to be her
proper poetic realm]. The tempest in the teapot generated by
Pardo Bazán's 'Dos palabras' has subsided, and Valencia is
safely returned by the voice of the leading male critic to the fold
of the feminine.[7]

It comes as no surprise that Pardo Bazán is one of the few
women writing at the end of the century who tries to collapse
the gendered boundaries of writing and reading, although many
contradictions remain within her own critical practice. It is she
who envisions the possibility that a woman write from her own
experience, following her own inner voice, and not in conformity
to socially imposed gender identity. That is, she attempts to
move writing outside a rigid dichotomy, as illustrated by her use
of gender-neutral terms for the woman writer and her attempts
to present writing as neither exclusively feminine nor masculine.
Her attempts to manœuvre critical discourse on to neutral ground
notwithstanding, the reading of language as already gendered
does not yield its essential binarism easily. The example of her
own critical essays and her fiction cannot dislodge the perception of separate masculine and feminine spheres of language.[8]

NOTES

1. See Kirkpatrick 1989*b* for an excellent analysis of the gendered reception of
   Avellaneda's and Coronado's poetry. My study will not consider the gender
   confusion that occurs when a man writes 'like a woman', except to observe
   that, on the one hand, it holds out certain advantages in terms of sidestep-
   ping the 'anxiety' of influence, and, on the other, it has the potential to
   attract a female readership. See also Morgan's comments (8).
2. For Coronado as *poetisa*, see Valis's nuanced analysis of the poet's 'La
   poetisa en un pueblo' [The Small-Town Poetess]; see also her reading of
   Vicenta García Miranda's attempt to infuse new life into 'el tropo desgastado'
   [worn-out trope] of the *poetisa* (Valis 1990: 15; a revised version of this
   article is printed in this book).
3. A frequent prologuist for books by younger male writers, she penned intro-
   ductions to the few works by women, all of earlier centuries, in her series for

women readers, Biblioteca de la Mujer [The Woman's Library]. The only other time she ostensibly addresses a woman author is her letters to the deceased Avellaneda ('Cartas a Tula' [Letters to Tula]), a rhetorical flourish that allows her to dramatize the two women's shared experience of rejection by the Spanish Royal Academy.

4. Two very brief reviews of Valencia's *Poesías* consist almost entirely of a quotation from Pardo Bazán's prologue.

5. I am currently pursuing this question in a study of the dynamics of gender underlying the reception accorded Carolina Valencia's poetry.

6. DeCoster summarizes, albeit unsympathetically, Pardo Bazán's literary relations with Menéndez Pelayo. The latter wavers, but is ultimately uncharitable, in his opinion of the woman who in her early years had enthusiastically, if naïvely, presented herself to him as an admiring disciple: 126–7.

7. The last letter in the exchange is Valencia's relieved and satisfied 'thank you' for Menéndez Pelayo's 'halagüeñas frases' [flattering phrases] (Menéndez Pelayo 14 Oct. 1890).

8. In her introduction to her *Antología poética*, Kirkpatrick also discusses Pardo Bazán's prologue. She concludes that the key lies not in negating or essentializing gender difference but, as Pardo Bazán is, in being 'conscientes de sus efectos' [conscious of its effects] (63).

WORKS CITED

ALAS, LEOPOLDO (1883). Prologue to Emilia Pardo Bazán, *La cuestión palpitante* 2nd edn. Madrid: Imprenta central a cargo de Víctor Saiz.

BARON, DENNIS (1986). *Grammar and Gender*. New Haven, Conn.: Yale University Press.

BIEDER, MARYELLEN (1990). 'Feminine Discourse/Feminist Discourse: Concepción Gimeno de Flaquer', *Romance Quarterly*, 37: 459–77.

—— (1993). 'Emilia Pardo Bazán and Literary Women: Women Reading Women's Writing in Late 19th-Century Spain', *Revista Hispánica Moderna*, 46 (June): 19–33.

BURGOS, CARMEN DE (1913?). 'Autobiografía', in *Al balcón*. Valencia: Sempere. pp. vii–xiv.

CORONADO, CAROLINA (1850). 'Contestación a Madame Amelie Richard', *Semanario Pintoresco Español*, 25: 194–5.

DAVIES, CATHERINE (1984). 'Rosalía de Castro's Later Poetry and Anti-Regionalism in Spain', *Modern Language Review*, 79: 609–19.

DECOSTER, CYRUS C. (1984). 'Emilia Pardo Bazán and her Contemporaries', *Anales Galdosianos*, 19: 121–31.

EPPS, BRAD (1991). 'The Space of Sexual History: Reading Positions in *El cuarto de atrás* and *Reivindicación del conde don Julián*', in Luis T. González-del-Valle and Julio Baena (eds.), *Critical Essays on the Literatures of Spain and Spanish America*. Supplement to *Anales de la Literatura Española Contemporánea*. 75–85.

GILBERT, SANDRA M., and GUBAR, SUSAN (1979) (eds.). *Shakespeare's Sisters: Feminist Essays on Women Poets*. Bloomington, Ind.: Indiana University Press.

—— —— (1989). 'Sexual Linguistics: Gender, Language, Sexuality', in Catherine Belsey and Jane Moore (eds.), *The Feminist Reader: Essays in Gender and the Politics of Literary Criticism*. New York: Basil Blackwell. 81–99.

GIMENO DE FLAQUER, CONCEPCIÓN (1877). 'La literata', in *La mujer española: estudios acerca de su educación y sus facultades intelectuales*. Madrid: n.p. 211–26.

—— (1885). 'Una española ilustre', *El Album de la Mujer*, 3/4: 132.

GÓMEZ DE AVELLANEDA, GERTRUDIS (1989). *Poesía y epistolario de amor y de amistad*, ed. Elena Catena. Biblioteca de Escritoras 9. Madrid: Castalia/Instituto de la Mujer.

GUERRERO, TEODORO (1890). 'Concepción Gimeno de Flaquer', *La Ilustración Española y Americana*, 34/36 (30 Nov.).

HANSON, CLARE (1989) (ed.). *Re-reading the Short Story*. New York: St Martin's Press.

JAMES, HENRY (1964). 'George Sand' (1877), in Leon Edel (ed.), *French Poets and Novelists*. New York: Grosset & Dunlap. 149–85.

KIRKPATRICK, SUSAN (1989a). 'The Female Tradition in Nineteenth-Century Spanish Literature', in Hernán Vidal (ed.), *Cultural and Historical Grounding for Hispanic and Luso-Brazilian Feminist Literary Criticism*. Minneapolis: Institute for the Study of Ideologies and Literature. 343–70.

—— (1989b). *Las Románticas: Women Writers and Subjectivity in Spain, 1835–1850*. Berkeley, Calif.: University of California Press.

—— (1992). 'Introducción', in *Antología poética de escritoras del siglo XIX*. Biblioteca de Escritoras 34. Madrid: Castalia/Instituto de la Mujer. 7–67.

MENÉNDEZ PELAYO, MARCELINO (1986). *Epistolario*, ed. Manuel Revuelta Sañudo, vol. x. Madrid: Fundación Universitaria Española.

MILLER, BETH (1983). 'Gertrude the Great: Avellaneda, Nineteenth-Century Feminist', in Beth Miller (ed.), *Women in Hispanic Literature: Icons and Fallen Idols*. Berkeley, Calif.: University of California Press. 201–14.

MILLER, NANCY K. (1991). 'Men's Reading, Women's Writing: Gender and the Rise of the Novel', in Joan DeJean and Nancy K. Miller (eds.), *Displacements: Women, Tradition, Literature in French*. Baltimore: Johns Hopkins University Press. 37–54.

MORGAN, SUSAN (1989). *Sisters in Time: Imagining Gender in Nineteenth-Century British Fiction*. Oxford: Oxford University Press.

PARDO BAZÁN, EMILIA (1889). 'La cuestión académica: cartas a Gertrudis Gómez de Avellaneda', *La España Moderna*, 1: 173–84.

—— (1890). 'Dos palabras', in Carolina Valencia, *Poesías*. Palencia: Imp. y Lit. de Alonso y Z. Menéndez. pp. vii–xi.

—— (1893a). 'Cuatro españolas', *Blanco y Negro*, 3: 344–5.

—— (1893b). 'Libros nuevos', *Nuevo Teatro Crítico*, 3/29 (Nov.): 137–58.

—— (1902). 'La tregua de Dios', in *Cuentos de Navidad y Reyes*. 3rd edn., in *Obras completas*, vol. xxv. Madrid: Administración de las Obras de E. Pardo Bazán. 7–8.

—— (1973). 'La poesía regional gallega' (1885), in *Obras completas*, vol. iii. Madrid: Aguilar. 671–89.

PUJOL DE COLLADO, JOSEFA (1885). 'Concepción Gimeno de Flaquer', *La Ilustración de la Mujer*, 3/38 (1 Mar.): 107.

—— (1890a). Review of Carolina Valencia, *Poesías*, 'Boletín bibliográfico', *Revista Contemporánea* (30 June): 667.

—— (1890b). 'Noticias', *La España Moderna*, 2/7 (July): 223.

SCANLON, GERALDINE M. (1990). 'Class and Gender in Pardo Bazán's *La tribuna*', *Bulletin of Hispanic Studies*, 67: 137–50.

SCHOR, NAOMI (1991). 'Idealism in the Novel: Recanonizing Sand', in Joan DeJean and Nancy K. Miller (eds.), *Displacements: Women, Tradition, Literature in French*. Baltimore: Johns Hopkins University Press. 55–73.

SHOWALTER, ELAINE (1977). *A Literature of their Own: British Women Novelists from Brontë to Lessing.* Princeton, NJ: Princeton University Press.

STIMPSON, CATHARINE R. (1979). 'The Power to Name: Some Reflections on the Avant-Garde', in Julia A. Sherman and Evelyn Torton Beck (eds.), *The Prism of Sex: Essays in the Sociology of Knowledge.* Madison, Wis.: University of Wisconsin Press. 55–77.

VALIS, NOËL M. (1988). 'The Female Figure and Writing in Fin de siglo Spain', *Romance Quarterly,* 35: 369–81.

—— (1990) 'La autobiografía como insulto', *Dispositio,* 15/40: 1–25 (revised version printed in this volume).

—— (1991*a*). 'La autobiografía como insulto', *Anthropos,* 125 (Oct.): 36–40 (revised version printed in this volume).

—— (1991*b*). Introduction to Carolina Coronado, *Poesías.* Biblioteca de Escritoras 19. Madrid: Castalia/Instituto de la Mujer. 7–41.

6

Gender and National Identity: The Novel in Nineteenth-Century Spanish Literary History

ALDA BLANCO

The adjective 'castizo' is most frequently used of language and style. In Spain, to describe a writer as 'castizo' is to imply that one deems him more Spanish than others.[1]

(Miguel de Unamuno)

José Montesinos in his *Introducción a una historia de la novela* (1955), one of the standard texts for the study of the history of the nineteenth-century novel in Spain, states that:

Estas almas [de mujeres] contaminadas de la pasión literaria, que las afecta como un morbo, son las que más van a contribuir al triunfo de lo extranjero. . . . Pero atendiéndonos sólo a lo que la historia de la novela interesa, insistiremos en que ese modo [el bovarismo] de comprender y de gustar la fabulación novelesca hizo imposible por mucho tiempo una novela española.

It was these women's souls, contaminated and infected by their passion for literature, which were to contribute above all to the triumph of foreign influence. . . . As regards the history of the novel, which is what interests us here, we will insist that that way of interiorizing and savouring novelistic narration [bovarism] was to rule out for a long time the development of a Spanish novel. (162–3)

For the contemporary critic steeped in the literary histories of the nineteenth-century novel which include, at the most, two or three women novelists, Montesinos's indictment of women as writers and readers is indeed an intriguing proposition. Montesinos's significant premiss in this fragment is that women as reading and writing subjects were responsible for arresting the development of the 'Spanish' novel. While clearly positioning them as powerful subjects, Montesinos's critical move of privileging the 'Spanish' over the 'foreign' transforms women into the objects to be blamed for having impeded the autochthonous. His need to construct an Other, in this case women, as the bearer of the responsibility of a perceived short-coming, is paradigmatic of the Spanish critical tradition about the novel. Montesinos's text, when read in conjunction with the rest of the Spanish critical tradition, is, in fact, merely a rearticulation of certain notions about this genre and its relationship to women which, by 1955, were firmly entrenched within the domain of critical common sense. It is a new version of an old narrative. Although this essay will focus primarily on the period in which the emergent discourse of literary criticism constructs the novelistic canon based on the criterion of Spanishness, pivotal to which, as we shall see, is the exclusion of a majority of the women novelists of the period, I have introduced Montesinos's contemporary text in order to point out the modern inheritance of this tradition.

The object of this paper is to chart the critical tradition's transformation of women as subjects of writing and reading into objects of blame and their subsequent exclusion from the text of literary history. That woman should be the one to bear the burden of blame should come as no surprise. This figure is, after all, as old as Eve herself. But to invoke misogyny alone as an explanation of Montesinos's indictment of the woman reader is not enough. For misogyny cannot explain a critical tradition which, from the outset, relentlessly, and maybe even obsessively, inscribed the figure of woman into its discourse as its object of blame. Rather, I would like to suggest that by mapping out the discursive underpinnings of the ideological project of Spanish literary scholarship with relationship to gender we can begin to elucidate the original nexus that forged its construction. When they were first being made, these linkages were often the subject of controversy and debate; yet now they have become commonsensical to our study of literary history. Hence the project of this essay, which is to trace the changing contours and articulations of this critical tradition in an effort to explain the reasons for its historic grip on literary studies about the novel.

'Lo castizo' *and the shaping of the Spanish novel*

Literary scholarship, in Terry Eagleton's words, 'was for the most part born in the service of an urgent ideological project: the construction and refurbishing, in nineteenth-century Europe, of the various "national" cultures and lineages' (125). Indeed, the same can be argued about Spanish literary criticism, which began to take shape after the Glorious Revolution of 1868. In contrast to prescriptive essays about the novel, which had been the norm until that time, literary scholarship as a field of inquiry emerged simultaneously with a new way of novel writing.[2] The new novelists and critics—some of whom were both—quickly heralded this new novel as the truly 'Spanish' one and agreed that the watershed period for its emergence was 1868–70. Before then, in Menéndez Pelayo's words, 'entre ñoñeces y mon-struosidades dormitaba la novela española por los años de 1870, fecha del primer libro del señor P. Galdós' [until around the year of 1870, the publication date of Mr P. Galdós's first novel, the Spanish novel dozed amidst inanities and monstrosities] (Baquero Goyanes 211). Although it is important to point out the simultaneity of these new ways of reading and writing, what is significant for my argument here is that literary scholarship about this genre takes the new novel as its critical reference point and anchors itself within it. The immediate identification between the new novel and Spanishness served to begin con-struction of a national culture from which the shaping of the Spanish novelistic canon would begin to take place.

Many critics and literary historians shared in this endeavour. Some, like Marcelino Menéndez Pelayo and his school, dedi-cated their life's work to the rewriting of literary history from the 'origins' of what they called 'Spanish' literature. Others, like Leopoldo Alas ('Clarín') and Juan Valera, as practising literary journalists, concentrated their attention on the contemporary period. Although the literary critics during this period were politi-cally and ideologically disparate—Menéndez Pelayo, for exam-ple, was a well-known Catholic conservative whereas Valera and Clarín were self-proclaimed liberals—their literary criticism was uniformly shaped by the discourse and language of nationalism.[3]

Writing, after 1870, from a seemingly stable and identifiable national identity and culture, literary critics undertook the pro-ject of making sense of Spain's previous novelistic production.

Generally, the point of departure in their thinking and writing about the *Spanish* novel was the need to understand a felt difference with regard to the appearance and development of the novel in other European national literatures. Because of this and from the outset, Spanish literary criticism of the novel not only took as the object of study its own national production, but also inscribed into it the perceived relationship to other European literatures. Often, this discussion was expanded to include a discussion of the cultural relationship between Spain and Europe. Although each critic envisioned and articulated Spain's relationship to Europe, especially France, in a different way, common to all was the idea that the sovereignty of Spanish culture and literature had been lost prior to the emergence of what was being heralded as the national novel. The imperative of literary scholarship, then, became to interpret and theorize the mechanisms and reasons for this perceived loss in order that it might not recur.

Haunted by the not-so-distant Napoleonic incursion as well as the memory of the 'Frenchification' of Spain begun in the eighteenth-century, the copious amounts of translated literature, and the growing presence of foreign capital and culture, Spain was imagined as a boundaryless nation subject to invasion and subjugation. For the literary criticism of the period, this sense of a lack of firm boundaries translated into an obsessive fear of cultural invasion which resulted in what 'Clarín' calls 'intellectual patriotism' (Beser 163). The literary criticism of Valera, for example, shows a characteristic slippage between discursive levels in the literary scholarship of this period in which politics and culture are seen as naturally intertwined. In a letter to his friend Menéndez Pelayo Valera writes:

Ya es tiempo, después de dos siglos de vasallaje y de sumisión recompensada con que nos califican siempre de bárbaros y de beocios, de que sacudamos el yugo intelectual en que los franceses nos tienen. Y yo quiero hacer algo de esto.

After two centuries of servitude and submission, whose reward has only been to be continually called barbarians and ignoramuses, it is high time that we shook off the intellectual yoke under which the French have us. And I want to do something towards this. (1946: 309)

It is by situating himself as speaking from the position of the oppressed Other that Valera can conflate the political and the cultural. 'Servitude' and 'submission' function in this fragment as totalizing descriptions of the dialectic of oppression. The ambiguity of these two terms also serves to blur the lines between the specific areas and aspects of domination. While he sees this dialectic as abstractly taking place between peoples and cultures, his proposal that the Spanish concretely shake off the intellectual 'yoke' suggests that resistance in one specific arena will generate resistance in the others. Valera interprets Spain's *otherness* from the French point of view and argues that the 'payoff' for the long period of submission has been the labelling of Spaniards as 'barbarians' and 'ignoramuses'. Through his novel-writing he intends to resist cultural oppression and empower an autochthonous Spanish writing.

Like Valera, Menéndez Pelayo also theorized the mechanisms of cultural dependency. Yet significantly absent from his argument is Valera's pivotal notion of imposition and oppression. Instead, Menéndez Pelayo articulates Spain's cultural dependence on France as a question of collusion, that is to say, the willing consent, acceptance, and, finally, the internalization of another culture's perceived superiority:

[E]l servil afán de parodiar y remedar sin discernimiento lo último que nos cae en las manos, como si temiésemos quedarnos rezagados en el movimiento progresivo de la humanidad (propio e instintivo temor de todos los pueblos que están realmente abatidos, y que han perdido su conciencia nacional), el embebecimiento, como de bárbaros de Oceanía, con que recibimos todo libro o todo artículo que nos llega de Francia, sin distinguir nunca las obras fundamentales de las miserables rapsodias, no lo que es bello y bueno de lo que nace de deleznable antojo de la moda.

The servile eagerness to ape and imitate, without any trace of discrimination, every new thing that comes along, as if we were afraid of being left behind in humanity's march of progress (the natural and instinctive fear of all truly demoralized peoples, whose national consciousness has been lost), the rapturous amazement with which, like South Sea savages, we receive every book and article that comes from France, never distinguishing the profound works from paltry rhapsodies, nor the beautiful and good from what is born of the ephemeral whim of fashion. (479)

Menéndez Pelayo casts Spaniards—a group in which he clearly includes himself—as 'servile' imitators and metaphorically depicts them as 'savages of the South Seas', in order to appeal to their inherent sense of European superiority. By suggesting that the behaviour of Spaniards matches that of supposedly inferior peoples, he hopes to rouse their nationalist emotions out of a complacency which manifests itself through imitation. Imitation, he argues, is an attribute of a dejected and spiritless people who have lost their 'national consciousness' and, therefore, their capacity to create. The sense of amazement and astonishment shown by Spaniards regarding any French literature has resulted in the loss of the fundamental ability to distinguish between what is 'beautiful' and 'good' and what is 'fashionable'. In this way, then, Menéndez Pelayo introduces the concepts and draws the lines which will configure the paradigm for a national novel. The key words for literary criticism during this period are imitation, fashion, barbarism, and a lost national consciousness which are used in opposition to originality, the timelessness of beauty and goodness, civilization, and a 'Spanish' consciousness. In other words, 'lo castizo'.

By recycling the concept of 'lo castizo', a notion which had historically denoted Spanish purity—racial, linguistic, and cultural—literary criticism sought to reconstruct the traditional sense of a national identity in which Spanishness was defined, above all, as that which was untainted by the outside, the foreign. These polarities became the discriminating axis through which the shaping of the novelistic canon took place. In this way, individual writers—many of whom were women—and whole literary movements are singled out, accused, and condemned of non-Spanishness. The canon was being constructed in much the same way that a nation is constructed; where borders are imagined, drawn, and subsequently policed in order to protect national security from outside elements. In 1891 Clarín, clearly weary of the protectionist and isolationist stance of literary criticism, creates a particularly fitting image to describe those contemporary critics involved in forging this critical discourse: 'esos partidarios de la balanza de comercio literaria . . . quieren convertir las aduanas de las letras en fortalezas inexpugnables' [those partisans of a literary trade balance . . . that want to turn the customs houses of letters into inexpugnable fortresses] (Beser 163).

In 1918 Cejador y Frauca published his monumental and multivolumed *Historia de la lengua y literatura castellana*. He structures his discussion of the nineteenth-century novel through the 'castizo'/foreign paradigm. Whereas Cejador merely recirculates what was by this date already an old argument, what is significant about his theory of the Spanish novel is that he finally makes explicit and elaborates the linkage between national identity and literary quality:

Alarcón, Fernán Caballero y Trueba, Pereda y Galdós no tienen pizca de francés. La literatura, en manos de los buenos escritores, se había, pues liberado enteramente del antiguo dominio gálico, era limpiamente española.

There is not the slightest hint of French influence in Alarcón, Fernán Caballero and Trueba, Pereda and Galdós. In the hands of good writers, therefore, literature managed to liberate itself entirely from its old domination by the French; it was purely Spanish. (viii. 24)

For Cejador, the good writers, that is to say the untainted writers, had been the vehicle through which Spanish literature had been able to liberate itself from French domination and be purely and cleanly Spanish. His conception of literature as an idealist abstraction, an entity in itself to be embodied by writers, permits him critically to link literature to another abstract ideal, national identity. On Cejador's idealist terrain, literature and national identity intersect in the good writer. Through his identification of quality and national purity, Cejador finally fully articulates and, in a sense, seals the tautological argument constructing the text of Spanish literary history which, until that moment, had only been intimated sporadically. In it, Spanish purity is seen as the attribute of good writers and these are seen as naturally 'Spanish'. The process through which this argument was elaborated and consolidated required that literary critics, in their search for purity and Spanishness, sift the vast corpus of novelistic production. The resulting text was one in which, as we shall see, not all Spanish writers were considered to be truly and purely 'Spanish'.

Imitation and the feminization of culture

We have seen Menéndez Pelayo suggest that literary mimicry and imitation characterize a people who have lost their national consciousness, the implication being that, once it is regained, imitation will no longer be necessary. Because the discourse of literary criticism created this causal relationship between national literature and consciousness, literary imitation came to symbolize the internal obstacle that impeded the development of the autochthonous. Francisco Giner in 1863 warns his readers that imitation leads to literary impoverishment.

Pretender, pues, modelar nuestra literatura sobre la suya [la francesa] es empobrecernos nosotros, sin enriquecerla a ella. Desgraciadamente, no siempre hemos resistido ese funesto poder de la imitación, de que difícilmente escapan los escritores ligeros e incapaces de ahondar en la esencia de las cosas y expresarla libremente: harto tiempo, llevando por guía a un ciego, ha encaminado nuestra literatura de vacilación en vacilación, de extravío en extravío, y si no se ha perdido para siempre, es porque nuestro pueblo tiene tradiciones y elementos de vida propios.

To try and model our literature on theirs is not to enrich it but to impoverish ourselves. Unfortunately, we have not always resisted that ill-fated capacity for imitation, which spares few of the less serious writers, unable to plumb the depths and express their findings fluently; for too long now, our literature has been led blindly by this fashion, from one uncertainty to another, from one wrong turn to the next, and the only reason our literature has not been lost forever is that the Spanish people have their own traditions and ways of life. (171)

Left unquestioned by the succeeding generation of literary critics, these assessments of the national novelistic production were echoed throughout the rest of the nineteenth century. We find Valera still arguing in 1886–7 in his 'Apuntes sobre el nuevo arte de escribir novelas' that 'en lo que llaman *novela*, hemos sido estériles, imitadores desmañados, y harto infelices hasta hace poco' [in what they call the *novel*, we have been sterile, awkward imitators, and, until very recently, resoundingly unsuccessful] (1949: 624). What is significant about the uncritical reproduction of this argument and its dominance in literary criticism is that it characterizes as imitative most of the novelistic production before 1868–70. What was it about the copious novelistic production of the 1850s and 1860s that permitted the contemporary critics to overlook, marginalize, and, in fact, degrade it by considering it merely as imitative?[4] I would like to suggest, here, that embedded in these arguments are important questions of gender and class marking the critical discourse about the novel of this period.

The novels of the 1850s and 1860s presented two striking characteristics which signalled a departure from those preceding them: a significant number of these novels appeared in serialized form, the *folletín,* and many of them were written by women and specifically addressed to a female audience.[5] These two traits point to a rise in the reading audience, in general, and specifically to the rise of the woman reader, a fact which did not go unnoticed by literary critics. In fact, as we shall see, the class and gender of the reading audience was to become an important consideration in the discourse about the novel. Moreover, the critical move of downgrading the type of writing produced during this period was done by engendering both style and content and deeming it *feminine* writing.

The *folletín* was quickly seen as a degraded form primarily because of its audience. In the first history of nineteenth-century literature published in 1891, P. Blanco García, writing about Fernández y González, the most famous and prolific writer of the *folletín,* marks the relationship of gender and class to this new way of novel writing.

Qué ángel malo tentaría a D. Manuel Fernández y González para hacerle entrar en esta empresa [the *folletín*], donde arrojó por los suelos la modesta reputación de sus primeros días, a cambio de otra formada por artesanos, costureras y demás clases de plebe literaria?

What bad angel can have tempted Don Manuel Fernández y González to go into this business [the *folletín*], in which he has thrown away the modest reputation acquired by his early work, in exchange for a different one made by artisans, seamstresses, and other kinds of literary rabble? (383)

The 'bad angel' that tempted Fernández y González to disgrace himself in the eyes of the literary world was the angel of mass culture who tempted him with an ever expanding popular audience; an audience which was clearly unacceptable for Blanco García given its class and gender composition. That he considers the *folletín* to be a degraded form, given its mass appeal, corroborates Andreas Huyssen's thesis that during the nineteenth century mass culture was associated with the feminine and, moreover, that 'the male fear of woman and the bourgeois fear of the masses become indistinguishable' (52).

The representation of woman as imitator permeated the discourse of literary criticism from its earliest days and would resonate well into the 1920s. Echoing an already pervasive cliché about women circulating during the latter half of the nineteenth century, Menéndez Pelayo marks sexual difference thus: 'Toda gran mujer ha sido grandemente influida. Ellas pueden realzar, abrillantar, difundir con lengua de fuego lo que en torno de ellas se piensa, pero al hombre pertenece la iniciativa' [Every great woman has been greatly influenced. Women can enhance or polish, they are inspiring propagators of intellectual discoveries around them; but the initiative belongs to man] (30). Man creates, woman brilliantly and passionately re-creates, imitates.[6] Yet what is significant about Spanish literary criticism is the way in which this dominant representation comes to be used in its discourse. Rather than proposing that woman passively reflects and imitates male creativity, which in the literary terrain would translate as Spanish women writers imitating Spanish male writers, women writers are cast as the imitators of French writers.

This critical leap is made by ascribing to women not only the characteristic of imitation but also that of being followers of fashion, literary and otherwise. Fashion, a keyword in the literary discourse about the novel of the period, becomes yet another descriptive term used to articulate the perceived cultural dependence between Spain and other European countries. In rare instances fashion is not linked to gender or at least the connection is not explicitly made. In 1870, Galdós, for example, in his analysis of the state of the Spanish novel is cautious about marking the concept of fashion with gender.

El gran defecto de la mayor parte de nuestros novelistas, es el haber utilizado elementos extraños, convencionales, impuestos por la moda, prescindiendo por completo de los que la sociedad nacional y coetánea les ofrece con extraordinaria abundancia. Por eso no tenemos novela; la mayor parte de las obras que con pretensiones de tales alimentan la curiosidad insaciable de un público frívolo en demasía, tienen una vida efímera.

The great defect of the majority of our novelists is having used foreign and conventional elements imposed by fashion, totally laying aside those abundantly offered to them by contemporary national society. This is why we have no novel; the majority of the texts with novelistic pretensions which feed the insatiable curiosity of the audience's extreme frivolity have an ephemeral life. (115)

In this fragment, part of an important article in which Galdós attempts to persuade his fellow novelists to turn to their own society for their novelistic subject-matter instead of looking to the outside, he sets up a hard-hitting and paradoxical argument in which, while acknowledging the presence of Spanish novelists on the literary scene, he denies their literary texts the stature of novels. This refusal, primarily argued from the point of view of content rather than form, stems from his sense that these novelists have followed literary fashion, which he construes, again paradoxically, as an imposition. The novel, then, for Galdós is the literary text which takes from and is mimetic of contemporary national society. Yet his seemingly ungendered discussion of the negative effect of literary fashion on the novel is tainted by and resonates with images of stereotypically female attributes. His use of the adjectives 'frivolous' and 'insatiable' in his description of the would-be novel reader makes this audience gender specific and female.

Cejador, on the other hand, is not so cautious in his linkage of fashion to women in general and, specifically in the terrain of literature, of literary fashion to women writers. In one of his many comments about Emilia Pardo Bazán, a writer and critic who was attacked by many of her contemporary male counterparts for introducing 'foreign' literary ideas such as naturalism into Spain, Cejador writes that '[l]as modas suelen traerlas las señoras y tras las señoras se van las cabezas de los hombres' [women tend to bring in fashions, and men's heads get turned by women] (viii. 314). Not only does Cejador choose to make no distinction between the world of literature and that of clothing, his way of degrading the literature produced by women by equating it with the perceived 'frivolity' of following fashion, but there is an assumption here that men are not and cannot be influenced by fashion unless they come under the spell of fashionable women. It is again women and, using his own logic, women writers whose dizzy presence causes male writers to follow 'literary fashion'.

In this way the text of Spanish literary history and criticism elaborates a signifying and cultural system in which women as reading and writing subjects were conflated with the woman as sign and positioned at the origin of a chain of signifiers all of which denoted non-Spanishness. The end result of this dominant critical discourse would be the textual exclusion of women writers from literary histories and criticism in order to construct a literary history populated by 'Spanish' authors.

'Feminine' writing and the 'Spanish' novel

In the following fragment Blanco García, foreshadowing Montesinos's argument, while including women writers in his history sets forth the argument which links women's writing to imitation and moreover genders their mode of writing as 'feminine':

De intento he reservado para terminar este capítulo la larga y no gloriosa serie de escritoras más o menos consagradas a la imitación y al cultivo de un género [la novela romántica] que tanto se adapta a las fogosidades y los arrebatos del sentimentalismo femenino. La mujer fue la principal causa de que se difundiesen estas lecturas, lo mismo devorándolas con insaciable curiosidad, que produciéndolas en la forma que le permitía la escasez de su cultura literaria. Casi todas las escritoras de que voy a hablar, se contentan con las bellezas superficiales, hijas de la fantasía o de la pasión, no siempre expresada con sinceridad, y desdeñan el estudio del corazón humano y la difícil sencillez de los grandes modelos.

I intentionally delayed mentioning, until the end of this chapter, the long and inglorious series of women writers, each more or less devoted to imitating and to the cultivation of a genre only too well adapted to the fitful passions of feminine sentimentality. Women were largely responsible for the propagation of this type of reading material—both the women who consumed it with insatiable curiosity, and the ones whose production of it was dictated by the scantiness of their literary training. Almost all of the women writers whom I am going to discuss make do with superficial prettiness in their writing, the product of fantasy and of passions often inauthentically expressed, and they fight shy of the study of the human heart and the complex simplicity of the great models. (388)

Clearly, then, with the onset of what is deemed the 'Spanish' novel, imitation is singularly linked to gender. Women are seen as the producers and reproducers of imitation. In this way, writing by women by definition can never be 'creative' and 'original'. And because imitation is constructed as anathema to Spanishness, literary scholarship can, therefore, neatly argue that women writers and readers are the internal agents, so to speak, that impede the development of a national literature. From here to textual erasure there is only one step.

Woven into the woman writer as imitator argument, there existed another underpinning proposition which warranted the exclusion of women writers from the canon. Implicit in Galdós's argument and explicitly expressed in Blanco García's, it relates to the project of the realist novel, the new way of writing the 'Spanish' novel, which was being promoted after 1868. In the preceding fragments by these two literary critics, it is not coincidental that the language used to reject a certain way of novel-writing and reading is similar, if not identical. The use of the same adjectives—'insatiable curiosity' and 'frivolity'—in their description of the reading public, and in Blanco García's case of women writers, signal the ways in which sexual difference was articulated to describe the act of reading and writing by women. Furthermore, this descriptive mode gives way to a normative one in which 'insatiable curiosity' and 'frivolity' are deemed feminine attributes and constructed in opposition to what the subject of the novel should be: Spanish society, for Galdós, and the human heart for Blanco García. Because, according to Blanco García, the sentimental novel does not and cannot address the true novelistic issues, he can justify his placement of women novelists at the end of a chapter. And thus begins the progressive marginalization of women writers in the text of literary history. Although neither Galdós nor Blanco García chooses to be overtly axiomatic and align the new way of novel-writing, Spanishness, and masculinity, by 1918 this paradigm is so firmly in place and naturalized within the discourse about the novel that Cejador can assume it and argue against it in reference to the literature of Martínez Sierra:

Cuando *Oberon*, en la revista *Atenea*, asentó que Martínez Sierra apenas puede ser considerado como escritor español, me sospecho que miraba a la *delicadeza sentimental* de Martínez Sierra, que *Oberon* creerá reñida con el realismo español, como falsamente lo creen otros críticos.

When *Oberon*, in the journal *Atenea*, affirmed that Martínez Sierra can hardly be considered a Spanish writer, I suspect that he was thinking about Martínez Sierra's *sentimental delicateness*, which *Oberon* thinks is at variance with Spanish realism as do other critics who believe this falsehood. (x. 187)

Meaghan Morris in reference to France has noted in *The Pirate's Fiancée* that 'the problem of women reading, women writing, what they read and wrote and how, became the symbolic battleground of a whole series of social, political and moral conflicts and transformations' (66). In Spain the tendency to feminize certain types of literary expression within the discourse of literary criticism served to construct and subsequently to naturalize, through the negative example of feminine writing, a sense of national identity based on what was perceived to be the truth and Spanishness of the realist novel. As I have already noted, paramount to this nationalist novelistic project was the retrieval and recirculation of the traditional idea of 'lo castizo' which came to function in the discourse as the symbolic representation of 'masculinity' in opposition to the 'femininity' of imitation and sentimental writing.

Conclusion

Before concluding, something must be said of those women writers who have not been erased from the canon. Their inclusion in this text, albeit marginally and often with great reluctance, had to be justified and was done so by arguments in which the axiomatic categories of 'Spanishness' or 'masculinity' were brought into play. Clearly, these two culturally constructed categories could not coincide in a female author but on the canonical balance sheet they were weighed against each other, where the lack of one could be compensated by a surplus of the other. Fernán Caballero, for example, was articulated as 'feminine' but nevertheless 'Spanish' because she wrote novels about her native land, Andalusia. The case of Pardo Bazán is perhaps the most interesting and indicative example of how these categories were used in the elaboration and formulation of the canon. Referred to by Cejador as the 'high priestess of literary fashions' (viii. 23), an epithet which, as we have seen, automatically would have excluded her from literary canonization, Pardo Bazán nevertheless could not be excluded because, I believe, she chose to share the male literary terrain by writing 'realist' fiction. Her exaltation of naturalism was not approved by critics given its 'importation' from France and its unladylike 'dirtiness'. Yet they could not deny that this literary tendency was firmly grounded within the much-aspired-to realist mode of writing. Although her contemporaries were very unsympathetic towards her person and her literary production—if not downright nasty—they could not silence her voice given that she shared their project of a Spanish realist novel which, at least in theory, reflected and spoke to the nation as a whole. The case of Pardo Bazán helps confirm Terry

Lovell's tentative conclusion in *Consuming Fiction* that '[a] condition of literary canonization, then, may have been not so much that the author must be male, as that the work must be addressed to men and read by them, and not addressed exclusively to women' (83).

It may seem ironic to some readers that the only women writers that I have named in this essay are precisely the ones included in the canon of the nineteenth-century novel. It could be argued that I too am contributing to the erasure of the countless other women writing in mid-century Spain. Rather than an oversight, it should be read as a conscious strategy on my part to explain a specific discursive and historical juncture. That is to say, the moment when the emergent discourse of literary criticism assumes the project of reconstructing a national identity through its use of symbolic representations of gender to reread nineteenth-century novelistic texts in order to write the history of the nineteenth-century novel. Furthermore, I would argue that this discourse to this day has remained mostly intact. With a few notable exceptions,[7] critics of the nineteenth-century Spanish novel are still blinded by the originating binary formulation of difference in relation to the novelistic production of that century. And, thus, I have sought to problematize the discourse of literary criticism about the novel by, in turn, rereading it through the category of gender with the hope that this repetitious and tautological discourse can become defamiliarized and, finally, denaturalized.

NOTES

1. 'Se usa lo más a menudo el calificativo de *castizo* para designar a la lengua y al estilo. Decir en España que un escritor es castizo, es dar a entender que se le cree más español que a otros' (Unamuno 13). The translations in this essay are only partially mine; I would like to thank Catherine Jagoe for the difficult and tedious task of translating many of the quotations cited here.
2. In 1868 there existed only one history of Spanish literature written by a Spanish author, Amador de los Ríos's *Historia crítica de la literatura española*. For a discussion of the debate surrounding the moral propriety of the novel as it was elaborated before 1868, see Blanco (1993).
3. It is important to note here that these critics confined their criticism only to literature written in the Spanish language. They did not concern themselves with the literature written e.g. in Catalan.
4. Writing about this period Montesinos states that 'las mediocres novelas españolas de entonces sean . . . simples plagios, serviles imitaciones de ficciones

sentimentales extranjeras' [the mediocre Spanish novels of that period were . . . out and out plagiarism, servile imitations of foreign sentimental fictions] (144).
5. There exists a significant novelistic production by women writers in the period between 1850 and 1880. Perhaps the most important writers of this era are Pilar Sinués de Marco, Faustina Sáez de Melgar, and Angela Grassi. See Blanco (1989), Charnon-Deutsch, and Simón Palmer (1983, 1991).
6. Bram Dijkstra has noted in *Idols of Perversity* that '[b]y the mid-1870's, the idea that woman was inherently an imitator, not an originator, had become one of the most pervasive clichés of western culture' (120).
7. See Andreu, Kirkpatrick, and Simón Palmer (1983: 477–90).

WORKS CITED

AMADOR DE LOS RÍOS, JOSÉ (1861–5). *Historia crítica de la literatura española.* Madrid: Imprenta de José Rodríguez.

ANDERSON, BENEDICT (1983). *Imagined Communities.* London: Verso.

ANDREU, ALICIA G (1982). *Galdós y la literatura popular.* Madrid: SGEL.

BAQUERO GOYANES, MARIANO (1956). *La novela española vista por Menéndez Pelayo.* Madrid: Editora Nacional.

BESER, SERGIO (1972). *Leopoldo Alas: teoría y crítica de la novela española.* Barcelona: Laia.

BLANCO, ALDA (1989). 'Domesticity, Education and the Woman Writer: Spain 1850–1880, in Hernán Vidal (ed.), *Cultural and Historical Grounding for Hispanic and Luso-Brazilian Feminist Literary Criticism.* Minneapolis: Institute for the Study of Ideologies and Literature. 371–94.

—— (1993). 'The moral imperative for women writers', *Indiana Journal of Hispanic Literatures* 2/1: 91–110.

BLANCO GARCÍA, P. Francisco (1910). *La literatura española en el siglo XIX.* 3rd edn., vol. ii. Madrid: Sáenz de Jubera Hermanos.

CEJADOR Y FRAUCA, JULIO (1918). *Historia de la lengua y literatura castellana, vols. viii, x.* Madrid: Tip. de la 'Revista de Archivos, Bibl. y Museos'.

CHARNON-DEUTSCH, LOU (1994). *Narratives of Desire: Nineteenth-Century Spanish Fiction by Women.* University Park, Pa.: Pennsylvania State University Press.

DIJKSTRA, BRAM (1986). *Idols of Perversity: Fantasies of Feminine Evil in Fin-de-Siècle Culture.* New York: Oxford University Press.

EAGLETON, TERRY (1985). 'Ideology and Scholarship', in *Historical Studies and Literary Criticism,* ed. and introd. Jerome J. McGann. Madison, Wis.: Wisconsin University Press.

GINER, FRANCISCO (1876). *Estudios de literatura y arte.* Madrid: Victoriano Suárez.

HUYSSEN, ANDREAS (1986). *After the Great Divide.* Bloomington, Ind.: Indiana University Press.

KIRKPATRICK, SUSAN (1989). *Las Románticas: Women Writers and Subjectivity in Spain, 1835–1850.* Berkeley, Calif.: University of California Press.

LAMBROPOULOS, VASSILIS (1988). *Literature as National Institution: Studies in the Politics of Modern Greek Criticism.* Princeton, NJ: Princeton University Press.

LOVELL, TERRY (1987). *Consuming Fiction.* London: Verso.

MENÉNDEZ PELAYO, MARCELINO (1948). *Obras completas de Menéndez Pelayo,* ed. E. Sánchez Reyes, vol. xl. Santander: Aldus.

MONTESINOS, JOSÉ F. (1955). *Introducción a una historia de la novela en España, en el siglo XIX.* Madrid: Castalia.

MORRIS, MEAGAN (1988). *The Pirate's Fiancée: Feminism, Reading, Postmodernism.* London: Verso.

PÉREZ GALDÓS, BENITO (1972). *Ensayos de crítica literaria.* Barcelona: Ediciones Peninsula.

SIMÓN PALMER, MARÍA DEL CARMEN (1983). 'Escritoras españolas del siglo XIX o el miedo a la marginación', *Anales de Literatura Española*, 2: 477–90.

—— (1991). *Escritoras españolas del siglo XIX: manual bio-bibiográfico.* Madrid: Castalia.

UNAMUNO, MIGUEL DE (1952). *En torno al casticismo.* Buenos Aires: Austral.

VALERA, JUAN (1946). 'A Menéndez Pelayo' (20 Oct. 1886), Letter 220 in *Epistolario de Juan Valera y Menéndez Pelayo 1877–1905*, ed. Miguel Artigas and Pedro Saínz Rodríguez. Madrid: Espasa Calpe. 309.

—— (1949). 'Apuntes sobre el nuevo arte de escribir novelas', in *Obras completas*, vol. ii. Madrid: Aguilar. 622–710.

7

Woman as Language in the First Series of Galdós's *Episodios nacionales*

DIANE FAYE UREY

The First Series of Galdós's *Episodios nacionales* marks a new era in Spanish literary history. Written between 1873 and 1875 these ten 'historical novels' helped pave the way for the tremendous rise of the novel in the late nineteenth century. Their immense popularity was a major contribution to the formation of an enthusiastic reading public in Spain. Although they have often been considered thinly fictionalized, more or less patriotic accounts of Spain's exploits between the years 1805 and 1813 (Trafalgar, the War of Independence), they also display an acute awareness of the equivocal relationships between language and world, fiction and history. Galdós's first *Episodios nacionales* constantly reveal paradoxes that question the ability of language to mean. They effectively demonstrate how traditional approaches to historical discourse or the realist novel lead only to the repetition of the same unsatisfactory, if not trite, conclusions about the individual and the world.

One of the *Episodios*' chief devices for exposing the limitations inherent in conventional discursive practices and for overturning established hierarchies in literary, historical, and cultural systems is their portrayal of intriguingly complex women characters. In fully half of Galdós's seventy-eight novels women characters are protagonists, and they serve as central figures in nearly all of them. While the dominant voice in the First Series appears to be the old narrator/young protagonist Gabriel Araceli as he recalls and writes his life and his history of Spain, his identity and his story take shape only through his interactions with numerous women characters, most importantly his beloved Inés, and her mother Amaranta.[1] Inés, in fact, 'embodies' Gabriel's self-image, and is in this way a figure for the discourse of the historical novel. As an emblem of the text, the character 'Inés' provides great insight into how symbols are formed and undermined in the *Episodios*, and into how the narrative both incorporates and demythifies normative literary, social, and historical codes and categories, including male and female, self and Other. 'Inés' is a sign that simultaneously assumes and subverts ideological and psychoanalytical values, and consequently serves to question received modes of reading literature and society.

Most critics have treated Inés de Santorcaz in more or less stereotypical terms, or they have simply ignored her role in the narrative process altogether. She is often seen to be a 'flat' character, devoid of realism, and displaying no evolution in the Series whatsoever (e.g. Paradissis 97–101). An evaluation of this sort makes Inés relatively insignificant in the Series; it also implies a preconceived notion about the *Episodios*, that is, that they are meant to be realistic. Yet such an approach is only one way, and not the most productive way, to read the *Episodios*. Even without verisimilitude Inés plays a number of key parts in the narrative. For Alfred Rodríguez, although she 'remains relatively unchanged' throughout the Series, and 'undergoes no important development whatever', she 'clearly embodies the virtues of a feminine ideal' and 'often overcomes this basic characterizational inflexibility in the very exercise of her virtues', at times gaining 'extraordinary relief' (62). Brian Dendle also sees Inés as a prototype of feminine virtue, and as a highly symbolic character: she 'represents an "ideal" Spain', and, 'like the Spain of 1808', is an 'object of manipulation'; an orphan, she is 'like the nation deprived of its natural leaders' (44). Inés does personify Spain; but even more significant, perhaps, are the multitude of ways in which this model heroine exposes the 'mechanics' of idealism and symbolism, the public face of the novels. Through analogy to the various roles of Inés, the reader can glimpse the 'other side', or 'private face', of the discourse. Moreover, it is not so much that she is an 'object of manipulation', but rather that her apparent perfection, femininity, and virtue are the perfect veils behind which the narrative can manipulate the reader's habitual expectations that Inés, Gabriel, and their story will conform to preconceived images of genre and gender.

Galdós uses the exemplary figure of a woman to undermine the desires of Gabriel, or any reader who seeks to define and delimit Inés or Spain, the Other or the world, through his or her own terms. More than an ideal woman, a symbol of Spain, or the object of desire, Inés is a sign of the text as a set of discursive voices, cultural values, and interactions between the perceiving reader and the world perceived, whether as historical or fictional. As a leading character, Inés represents many things; she is virgin, victim, seamstress, white page, secret origin, mirror, truth, beauty, and much more. 'Inés' also subverts these representations and the other narrative elements that weave her character. Understanding the covert functions and effects of Inés's seemingly orthodox role allows the reader to see how the narrative is a fluctuating series of associations among often very diverse words and images, not a univocal and coherent projection of an individual or a world. On the surface the text appears to offer an uncomplicated and basically faithful reflection or mirror of the self—Gabriel or the reader—and of the world—the novelized history of Spain. However, by comparing other elements of the narrative to the example of Inés, the same text may reveal itself to be a figment, or a figure, of the imagination.

As a metaphor for Spain and the object of Gabriel's continual pursuit to eventual marriage at the end of the Series, Inés is a conventional heroine in a sense. The characters and plots of Gabriel and Inés evolve concurrently with the depiction of historical developments during the War of Independence. As Gabriel's 'Other', Inés is essential to his identity, an identity synonymous with the narrative as memoir, fictional autobiography, historical chronicle, or 'novel history'.[2] Yet she neither accepts nor rejects the traditional literary assignment, neither validating nor opposing it. She is, in fact, relatively silent in many parts of the Series; when she does find her full voice, in *Cádiz*, for example, or in the final *episodio*, *La batalla de los Arapiles*, she writes the script for herself and others, including her mother, her father, and her lover Gabriel. She overturns entrenched sexual and cultural, patriarchal and historical, codes. She then disappears again into the *Episodios*, into the gaps between the words of the narrative. She manifests once more, in the end as she has from the beginning of the Series, her essence as language, the elusive, idealized, projection of the self, Gabriel, or another reader, into the Myth of the Other—the Letter or the Woman. From behind her veiling functions of Ideal, Other, Woman, and Word, Inés upsets and overthrows standard, authoritative, modes of reading and writing about self and others, past and present, and dismantles generic and engendered configurations of the represented world. By exposing the 'inner workings' of the narrative's fabrication of illusion, Inés (like Toto and Dorothy with the wizard of Oz) inspires, enables, and perhaps forces the reader to form new or different perceptions of the individual and of the world, unconstrained by orthodox or prescriptive codes and categories. Gabriel plays a familiar role too, as the male reader, historian, and lover who reads himself through his projections on to the Other/woman. Yet his efforts to dominate his narrative—its language and characters—result in a continual upheaval of hierarchies between creator and creation, reader and text, male and female. This process also demythifies historical traditions, literary norms, and boundaries of gender, class, and genre. In their dual functions as conventional and subversive characters Gabriel and Inés undermine accepted practices of historical and fictional discourse, of forming images of self and others, and of perceiving differences in the world.

Gabriel first describes Inés, in the second *episodio*, *La corte de Carlos IV*, as a 'lección viva de mi existencia, pues la enseñanza que de su conocimiento me provino contribuyó de un modo poderoso a formar mi carácter' [a vital lesson for my life, because what I learnt from knowing her contributed powerfully to forming my character] (264).[3] Like Lazarillo de Tormes, Gabriel learns many lessons as he writes his life history. While writing the narrative of himself he also reads and simultaneously writes Inés; she too stands, like Gabriel, for both the creation and the interpretation of signs. Inés is all that Gabriel desires and feels he lacks, serving both 'supplementary' functions of cumulation and lack. He fashions a sublime figure of Inés to mask his own insignificance, a project which mirrors the representational enterprise that Galdós's historical novels continually thwart.

Gabriel refines his self-image in the process of fabricating that of a seemingly distinct Other. This narcissistic procedure marks the linguistic self-consciousness of the text and the self-conscious evolution of the characters' plots and personalities. Julia Kristeva writes of narcissism:

Might narcissism be a means for protecting emptiness? . . . A protection of emptiness (of 'arbitrariness' [of the Saussurian sign], of the 'gaping hole' [of Lacan's mirror stage]) through the display of a decidedly narcissistic parry, so that emptiness can be maintained, lest chaos prevail and borders dissolve. Narcissism protects emptiness, causes it to exist and thus, as lining of that emptiness, ensures an elementary separation. Without that solidarity between emptiness and narcissism, chaos would sweep away any possibility of distinction, trace and symbolization, which in turn confuse the limits of the body, words, the real and the symbolic. (242)

Gabriel forms Inés, his other self, and writes his autobiography, his youth in Spain, to veil the emptiness of his identity and the lack of reality behind his words. The narcissistic relationship between Gabriel and Inés marks the narrative design and practice of the *Episodios*, texts which continually uncover the precariousness of the boundaries and distinctions through which one perceives traces of the world.

Gabriel casts Inés as a patient, loving, 15-year-old helpmate of the saintly and humble Doña Juana, whom she thinks is her mother. Her portrait is clearly hyperbolic; it demonstrates well the underlying dissolution, characteristic of the entire narrative, of standard usages of symbolism and idealism:

Poseía esta muchacha, además de las gracias de su persona, un buen sentido, cual no he visto jamás en criaturas de su mismo sexo, ni aún del nuestro, amaestrado ya por los años. Inés tenía el don especialísimo de poner todas las cosas en su verdadero lugar, viéndoles con luz singular y muy clara, concedida a su privilegiado entendimiento, sin duda para suplir con ella la inferioridad que le negó la fortuna. No he visto en mi larga vida otra hembra que se le asemeje, y estoy seguro de que a muchos pareciera este tipo invención mía, pues no comprenderán que haya existido, entre las infinitas hijas de Eva, una tan diferente de los demás. Pero créanlo bajo mi palabra honrada.

This young woman possessed, besides her natural graces, more common sense than I have ever seen before in creatures of her sex, nor even in ours, however wise with years. Inés had the very special gift of always putting things in their true perspective, of seeing them with her own unique and clear light of reason; it was a gift granted to her privileged mind, no doubt, in order to make up for the inferior social position that fortune allotted her. In my long life I have never seen another female like her, and I am sure that many will think that this description is sheer invention, but that is only because they cannot understand that there may have existed, among the infinite daughters of Eve, one so different from the others. But believe it, on my word of honour. (264)

Inés's difference from other women is her identity for Gabriel, and implies a subtle disdain for those other 'daughters of Eve', a disdain that takes on larger proportions with each new woman character introduced in the Series. They all somehow fall short of this privileged being; yet by referring to Inés with the rather demeaning term 'hembra', Gabriel seems determined to retain, in spite of his great praise for her, his masculine superiority.[4]

Gabriel goes on to say that Inés always has the ability to put things in their true place. She declares, for example, 'que en el mundo, al fin y al cabo, pasa siempre lo que debe pasar' [that in the world, after all is said and done, whatever should happen always does] (267). She makes similar statements throughout the Series, lending 'authority' to the eventuality that Gabriel, the 'pícaro',[5] will marry the soon-to-be-reinherited aristocrat Inés. The assertions Gabriel attributes to Inés imply a rather static signifying process: according to his portrayal, Inés can stop the play of meaning. As with his one-sided description of her—she is different from all other creatures of her sex—the immature Gabriel would fix his reading of self and Other, write a static text, and mould a 'flat' Inés. Inés, her 'characters', escape such confines, however, just as the multifaceted discourse of the *Episodios* rejects and escapes the confines of labels like history and fiction. Finally, Gabriel's insistence that Inés is not an invention, that she does indeed exist, reminds the reader, instead, that she is as illusory as is the young Gabriel, a fabrication of the aged, though likewise illusory, narrator's mind together with the reader's suspension of disbelief. The 'palabra honrada' of the *pícaro* Gabriel can be no more than a word; nor can that of the old narrator.[6] Gabriel's credibility—when young or old—and the meaning of his words depend upon their association with other terms in the narrative system, whether that be viewed in literary, linguistic, historical, social, psychoanalytical, or in any other terms.

As Gabriel refines the portrait of Inés, it becomes clear that he is highly self-conscious of the power of representation:

Si ustedes hubiesen conocido a Inés y notado la imperturbable serenidad de su semblante, imagen del espíritu más tranquilo, más equilibrado, más claro, más dueño de sí mismo que ha podido animar el corporal barro, no pondrían en duda lo que digo. Todo en ella era sencillez, hasta su hermosura, no a propósito para despertar mundano delirio amoroso, sino semejante a una de esas figuras simbólicas que, sin estar materialmente representadas en ninguna parte, se dejan ver de los ojos del alma cuando las ideas, agitándose en nuestra mente, pugnan por vestirse de formas visibles en la obscura región del cerebro.

If you had known Inés and appreciated the imperturbable serenity of her countenance, an image of the most tranquil, balanced, and clear soul, of a soul more mistress of itself than any which has ever given spirit to weak flesh, you would not doubt what I am telling you. Everything about her is simplicity itself, even her beauty, not designed to awaken worldly lust, but rather a beauty like that of one of those symbolic figures which, without being materially represented anywhere, allow themselves to be glimpsed by the eyes of the soul when ideas, stirring our minds, struggle in a corner of the brain to dress themselves in visible form. (254)

Like most passages describing Inés, this one can be read in both metafictional and fictional modes. Metafictionally, Inés is like a mirror of the reading process; the reader forms pictures of people from 'characters'. As a 'figura simbólica', Inés is a figure for the discourse as process; it only becomes significant through its transformation by the reader. In the fictional mode, the reader knows that Gabriel, unlike Inés, is not yet 'dueño de sí mismo' [master of himself], and his attainment of that state at the end of the Series owes at least as much to Inés, and to her mother Amaranta, as to his own efforts. Thus it is that Inés, the ideal Other, symbolizes and will eventually supply what Gabriel lacks, in common sense, in self-respect, and ultimately in spiritual and social equilibrium.

Gabriel achieves a momentary state of serenity at the end of *La corte de Carlos IV*. His 'corporal barro' receives an 'ánima' in the presence of Inés's peaceful demeanour at the side of the deceased Doña Juana. He says her attitude is 'para mi espíritu como una aura serena, como un templado y regenerador ambiente que equilibra la atmósfera' [like a serene aura for my spirit, like a temperate and regenerating climate that stabilizes the atmosphere] (353–4). Germán Gullón writes of these 'narcisistas observaciones del narrador' [the narrator's narcissistic observations] that they represent 'la nueva conciencia narrativa, que constata la necesidad del equilibrio en el empeño creador' [the new narrative conscience, that makes manifest the need for balance in the creative endeavour] (52). Gabriel sees in Inés both what he desires in himself and the incarnation of his narrative objective. His narcissistic reverie continues when he imagines his soul as a lake: 'Jamás he podido comparar con más propiedad mi alma con la imagen de un terso lago, de igual y no alterada superficie, ni jamás he distinguido con tanta claridad el lejano fondo' [Never have I been able to compare my soul more appropriately to the image of a shining lake, with a smooth and unruffled surface, nor have I ever before seen so clearly the extent of its profound depths] (353–4). The Myth of Narcissus is a frequent intertext in the Series, which is no surprise in novels so replete with the manifestations of subject/object desire as are these. Ovid is one of the first literary texts mentioned in *La corte de Carlos IV*, the *episodio* in which Inés is introduced. Like *Don Quijote*, it is woven through the Series in specific mythological references and in the general attitudes and situations of characters. Ovid is preferred to Aristotle by the love-sick and jealous actress Pepita, Gabriel's newest employer (257). Pepita in fact becomes an Echo to another of the novel's Narcissus figures, the actor Isidoro Maíquez. Maíquez's narcissism parallels Gabriel's own in one of the Series' many self-reflexive interpolated stories within stories (see pp. 334–54). Earlier (286) a narcissistic Gabriel, who is 16 here (the age of Narcissus at the outset of his Ovidian figuration; Graves 286), sees himself in Inés; she is essential to and inseparable from the identity that he writes for himself. And Gabriel's admiration for Inés is a paradigm for the admiration he desires from a reader reflecting on his character in the *Episodios nacionales*.

Inés is a quintessentially poetic figure in passages like those cited above. There is no attempt to make her conform to 'reality', to seem realistic. The contrast between terms like 'symbolic', 'eyes of the soul', or 'ideal', on the one hand, and 'material', 'represented', 'clothed', and 'visible', on the other, emphasizes the evocative ephemerality of her character. This 'untouchable' aspect of Inés also suggests a possessive ploy by Gabriel. She is only a simple beauty who will not awaken the 'worldly and delirious sexual desire' of other men; in this way she is different from Rosita, the object of Gabriel's unrequited childhood love. Rosita was won by a suitor who did not even see Gabriel as a rival. Gabriel ultimately succeeds in dispensing with rivals for Inés, a feat he was unable to accomplish with Rosita. Inés is hidden away, behind her seeming perfection, different from everyone else, inaccessible. The many incidents in the Series where she is locked behind closed doors, windows, or bars serve as projections, just like her 'flatness', of Gabriel's jealous possession of her, even if the illusion of that possession cannot always be maintained in the narrative. Their marriage, too, takes place behind the scenes, outside the pages of the First Series, secreted away in Gabriel's soul, or the obscure regions of his mind, as a

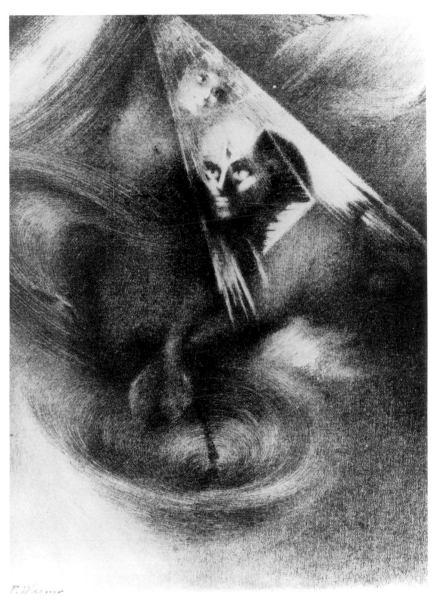

Plate 1. J. F. Wagner. *The Dream*

Plate 2. Gustave Moreau. *Oedipus and the Sphinx*

Plate 3. Fernand Khnopff. *The Supreme Vice*

Plate 4. Jan Toorop. *The Sphinx*

Plate 5. M. Gómez. *Galería árabe de un harém* [Arab Gallery in a Harem]

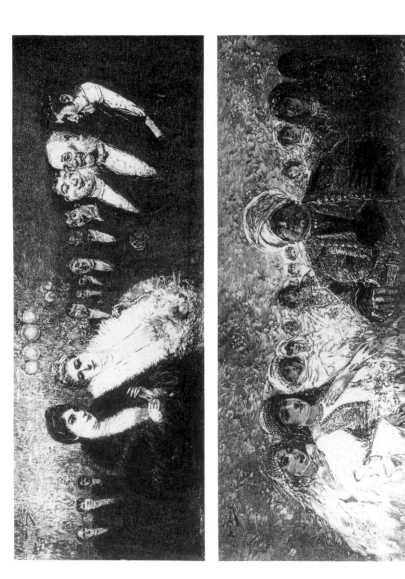

Plate 6. Mariano Barbasán. From *La Ilustración Artística*

Plate 7. Cesare Biseo.
Patio marroquí [Moroccan
Patio]

Plate 8. Francis Simm.
La mujer en Oriente
[The Oriental Woman]

Plate 9. Franciso Masriera. *En presencia de su senōr* [In the Presence of her Lord]

Plate 10. Nathaniel Sichel. *La favorita* [The Favourite]

Plate 11. Maximino Peña y Muñoz. *Una odalisca* [An Odalisque]

Plate 12. Bouchard. *En el harém: cumplimiento de una sentencia* [In the Harem: The Sentence is Carried Out]

Plate 13. José García y Ramos. From *Álbum Salón*

Plate 14. Wally Moes. *La cartomancera* [The Fortune-Teller]

Plate 15. Émile Bayard. From *La Ilustración Artística*

poetic figuration. Inés thus functions as a Pygmalion-like object of love and of art, as well as an ideal or truth to be apprehended. It is Inés's singing and speaking that most poignantly mark her as an art object. Like Narcissus with Echo, Gabriel is drawn to her voice:

Su lenguaje era también la misma sencillez; jamás decía cosa alguna que no me sorprendiese como la más clara y expresiva verdad. Sus razones . . . daban a mi entendimiento un descanso, un aplomo, de que carecía obrando por sí mismo. Puedo decir, comparando mi espíritu con él de Inés y escrudiñando la radical diferencia entre uno y otro, que él de ella tenía un centro y el mío no. El mío divagaba llevado y traído por impresiones diversas, por sentimientos contradictorios y repentinos; mis facultades eran como meteoros errantes . . . mientras las suyas eran un completo y armónico sistema planetario, atraído, puesto en movimiento y calentado por el gran sol de su pura conciencia.

Her speech was also simplicity itself; I never heard her say anything that did not strike me as the clearest and most eloquent truth. The things she said . . . soothed my mind, giving it a serenity and self-assurance that it lacked on its own. I can confidently say, in comparing my spirit with that of Inés and scrutinizing the radical difference between the two, that hers had a centre and mine did not. My spirit came and went, pushed and pulled by diverse impresssions, by contradictory and sudden emotions; my reasoning faculties were like errant meteors . . . while hers were a complete and harmonious planetary system, attracted, placed in movement, and heated by the great sun of her pure conscience. (264–5)

If Inés's simple (spoken?, natural?) language is truth, then it is the ultimate meaning of a 'classic' text and of a conventional reading. Yet the voice of truth, the ideal woman, and the harmonious system of language that Gabriel sees now in Inés escape the boundaries he would lay for her, as does his entire discourse. Like all the words of the *Episodios*, Inés suggests multiple and contradictory readings, no end to the play of meaning, no final truth. To conform to Gabriel's desire, Inés would be an icon, always remaining behind figures, words, and images of art. She would be different and apart from others, static, harmonious, and homogeneous, like the ideals of the mother, the origin, and of pre-symbolic consciousness, where others, like Gabriel, a figure for written language (ironically cultured? supplementary?), are heterogeneous, discordant, de-centred, and without fixed direction. As Gabriel leaves Inés's house he hears her sing, 'y su armoniosa voz se mezclaba en extraña disonancia con los ecos de la flauta' [and her harmonious voice mixed in strange dissonance with the echoes of the flute] of her uncle, Don Celestino (268). The discord that surrounds Inés makes her appear more harmonious, as though inviting Gabriel to enter into a state of equilibrium that she seems to possess and that he lacks. But her harmony and equilibrium, like the ostensible meaning of the *Episodios* as 'historical fiction', is only superficial; like all appearances, Inés's are deceiving, even for Gabriel.

Inés's voice also suggests the mythological temptations of the sirens. Like Odysseus, Gabriel will return to her after his own odyssey—his epic journey to social honour and identity through his military exploits in the War of Independence. The analogy between Penelope and Inés is present in her introduction; Gabriel knows Inés because she and Doña Juana are Pepita's seamstresses. They are 'siempre cosiendo, cosiendo con aguja una tela sin fin' [always sewing, sewing with a needle an endless piece of cloth] (265). Their cloth is like the weave of the narrative, a parallel which is reinforced in the next sentence where the reader is told that Don Celestino continually writes Latin verse and letters of petition to Godoy, 'consumiendo tinta y papel en larguísimos memoriales' [using up ink and paper in interminable petitions] (265). Like the text of this long Series that moves from word to word, symbol to symbol, myth to myth, in its interminable intertextuality, Inés's cloth awaits Gabriel's return to her for its figurative completion. In Gabriel's desire, Inés beckons seductively to him, a representation of beauty, truth, and harmony. Yet as an art object, Inés reflects only herself; she is her own centre, like the sun. And like the sun, she is the centre of a solar system seeking other centres in the galaxy and in the universe; she is a centre concealing other centres in an infinite and ungrounded series that leads to the chaos hidden by the narcissistic enterprise. Kristeva writes:

the loving subject does not have access to that Other as to an object, but as to the very possibility of the perception, distinction and differentiation that allows one to see. That ideal is nevertheless a blinding, non-representable power—sun or ghost. Romeo says, '. . . Juliet is the sun', and that loving metaphor transfers on to Juliet the glare Romeo experiences in the state of love, dedicating his body to death. . . .

The ideal identification with the symbolic upheld by the Other thus activates speech more than image. Doesn't the signifying voice, in the final analysis, shape the visible, hence fantasy? (253)

The sun, the complete sign, the truth, and the woman are always out of reach, deferred and displaced, even if they appear
obtainable to Gabriel. Through her analogy to the sun, one can
see how Inés reinscribes the signifying process of the *Episodios*.
Their representations, their words and associations, are removed
from the reality they appear to describe, masking their emptiness through the illusion of a stable ground—a centre—at the
origin and the end of their discourse.

The recurrent metaphor of Inés as the sun suggests that she
will guide Gabriel's course with her illuminating truth. Yet her
truth is a mirage; truth and Inés are 'out of bounds', unreachable
by Gabriel. 'Her voice of truth', like the narrative voice, always
says something other than what appears at face value. Inés's
simplicity and modesty seem to personify truth, but the truth
and the woman are equally elusive. In *Spurs*, Jacques Derrida
writes of how Nietzsche equates 'woman' with 'truth':

There is no such thing as the truth of woman, but it is because of that
abyssal divergence of the truth, because that untruth is 'truth'. Woman
is but one name for that untruth of truth.
   On the one hand . . . Nietzsche revives that barely allegorical figure
(of woman) in his own interest. For him, truth is like a woman. It
resembles the veiled movement of feminine modesty. (51)

Just as words do not contain meaning, but barely gesture to its
fleeting presence, so the truth of Inés or the *Episodios* is always
deferred. Gabriel is irresistibly attracted to Inés as the sign of
truth and the self-identical: 'Desde que conocí a Inés la amé del
modo más extraño que puede imaginarse. Una viva inclinación
arrastraba mi corazón hacia ella' [From the moment I met Inés
I loved her in the strangest way that you can imagine. A fervent
attraction drew my heart toward her] (265). He attempts to
become one with her, but, like that of Icarus, his effort is futile,
even deadly. What lies behind Inés's image, as centre, sun, truth,
voice, or woman, is the absence of the object of desire. Gabriel
'revives that barely allegorical figure (of woman)' as truth 'in his
own interest'; he sees in Inés all that he lacks (a mother, social
class, desire satisfied), but in doing so fashions only another
figure of what can never be self-identical, beyond language, however simply, clearly, or desirably true.

Gabriel concludes his description of the peerless Inés in a way
that virtually undermines all he has just said, making its 'truth'
as dubious as his 'resurrection' at the beginning of the Series:

'Alguien se burlará de estas indicaciones psicológicas, que yo quisiera fuesen tan exactas como las concibe mi obscura inteligencia; alguien encontrará digna de risa la presentación de semejante heroína . . . ; pero estas burlas no me importan, y sigo' [Someone may make fun of these psychological observations, which I would have be as exact as my humble intellect conceives them; someone may consider my introduction of such a heroine laughable . . . ; but these scoffing remarks do not matter to me, so I will continue] (265). Gabriel now offers an alternative reading of the heroine he created to reflect his own image. His inclination towards her is like a 'cult', like 'la fe que sublima lo más noble de nuestro ser' [the faith that makes the most noble part of our being sublime]. But he also remains free to experience other passions, for other women, 'dejando siempre libre una parte de él para las pasiones del mundo' [always leaving a part of oneself free for worldly passions] (265). Gabriel's espoused reverence for Inés functions in the same way that supposedly inviolate historical and cultural values, like honour and patriotism, do in the Series.[7] The *Episodios* overturn canonized moral and social rules, established hierarchies of gender and class, and prescribed practices in religion and society. Each ideal presented, like Inés, the legend of Spain's past glory, the cult of the Virgin Mary, or of the Spanish god Honour, is held up for admiration only to be demystified and literally dearticulated so that new modes of reading discourse and viewing the world become possible. Gabriel seems to describe all of the equivocal ideals and values of the Series—patriotism, love, heroism, etc.—when he says of Inés: 'He observado que los que se consagran a un ideal, casi nunca lo hacen por entero; dejan una parte de sí mismos para el mundo a que están unidos' [I have observed that those who dedicate themselves to an ideal, almost never do so completely; they keep a part of themselves for the world to which they are tied] (265). His words change from the former, sometimes awestruck, tone when describing Inés, to a more light-hearted, playful, almost burlesque attitude toward the passions of life and love. In the same way, the Series constantly shifts from 'veras' to 'burlas', glorious legends to demythifying versions. Gabriel first sketches his total love for Inés, the paragon of women, and then demonstrates to the reader how to read his emotions, his Other, and consequently himself, 'upside down' or in reverse, a performance he repeats on numerous other occasions in the narrative.

Because of the dynamics between the various facets of Inés—idealistic, realistic, and multiple combinations of the two—she is never static (or 'flat'). Moreover, her function as Gabriel's 'Other' offers him access to his own identity and entrance into the Symbolic itself. David Carroll writes that

for Lacan, Oedipus still determines the truth which informs literature—one which is the ground for differentiating between the Imaginary and the Symbolic, between the sterile, dualistic relation of the ego with its mirror image in the Imaginary, and the 'true' and overdetermined relation with a third term (with the place of the father as the law, with the Other or, basically, with language) in the Symbolic. Oedipus makes evident the opening or lack in existence, where desire, the unconscious, and the 'true, full word' are found, a lack which structures language and determines the place and function of the signifier. To isolate the signifying chain and the place of the 'subject' on this chain . . . is for him, as it was for Freud, 'to interpret the deepest layer' of the text, its origin and truth. But Lacan's 'deepest layer' is not located in the 'impulses in the mind of the creative writer,' as it was for Freud, but in a radical exteriority, in the Other (the Symbolic), which defines both the truth and the letter, the truth in the form of the circulation of the letter. Lacan's version of the truth is complex and even contradictory, 'originating' in a lack rather than a plenitude. (31)

Gabriel's relationship with Inés has evolved to a degree beyond the mirror stage depicted in *Trafalgar* with his mother and Rosita. Yet it is still narcissistic and idealistic, as demonstrated not only by his portrayal of Inés, but also by his ridiculous ambitions in *La corte de Carlos IV* to rise to a position like that of Napoleon or Godoy: 'tener desvergüenza para meterse en todas partes, buscar la amistad de personas poderosas; en fin, hacer lo que han hecho otros para subir a esos puestos en que son la admiración del mundo' [shamelessly to put oneself forward everywhere, to seek friendships among powerful people; in other words, to do what others have done in order to rise to those positions in which they are admired by everyone] (266). Inés's efforts to dissuade Gabriel from pursuing his foolish goals ultimately take hold. He does come to see through the deceptive and manipulating permutations of desire and representation that underlie conventional modes of perceiving the individual and society. For Gabriel, ultimately, all that Inés says is true, because she is truth herself. But that truth, as Lacan asserts and as Nietzsche claimed, is complex, contradictory, originating in a lack, the absence of reality. Gabriel's truth—his identity and his text—do not come from the confused memories of an old man, nor, as he avers above, from his own 'obscura inteligencia' [confused mind] (265). Still less can the 'true meaning' of these volumes be located in the 'impulses in the mind of the creative writer', as some critics might claim for Galdós just as Freud claimed for others. Rather, the only truth of the *Episodios*, Gabriel's truth, will be found in the Symbolic, in Inés as 'figura simbólica', the Other, language.

Inés is a projection of Rosita, Penelope, a utopian Spain, and truth itself, just as *La corte de Carlos IV* is a projection of other literary constructs, like *El sí de las niñas*, *Othello*, Ovid, the *Odyssey*, and *Oedipus* in their universal significance and triangular structures. As Gabriel's love object, Inés also becomes a Dulcinea in the same way that Don Quijote fabricates his unblemished Lady, along with himself and his world, from his imagination. The pervasive Cervantine subtext of the Series is often explicitly linked to Inés. Inés's advice to Gabriel to curb his ambitions to rise to position and power like Napoleon or Godoy (a narcissistic endeavour of a pride as dangerous as that of Icarus, Amaranta specifically warns (313)) comes from *Don Quijote*: 'no he leído más libros fuera de los de devoción, que *Don Quijote de la Mancha*. ¿Ves? A ti te va a pasar algo de lo de aquel buen señor; sólo que aquél tenía alas para volar' [The only book I have read, apart from devotional ones, is *Don Quijote de la Mancha*. Don't you see? Something like what happened to that good gentleman is going to happen to you; only he had wings to fly] (268). Inés's wisdom and truth arise from another book, just as all figures and signs, all discourse, originate elsewhere; they never begin in their apparent centres. The stories that Inés tells Gabriel to make him see the folly of his dreams of miraculously rising above his station on the hand of a 'dama poderosa' (Amaranta) (267) prefigure the other stories that he will witness, overhear, and ultimately tell himself as he learns to write his own (his)story, his memoirs of what he witnessed and was told, the narrative of the First Series of *Episodios nacionales*. But Inés's stories, which Gabriel believes and by which he is guided in the end, are based on the epic that describes, not objective truth, but the workings of subjective desires like Gabriel's, and the impossibility of ever making those desires reality.[8]

The conclusion to *La corte de Carlos IV* leaves Inés an orphan whose true, absent and hidden, origin is now the prime motivating element of the story, and with Gabriel seemingly in control of his discourse, in harmony with Inés, and having claimed for himself a certain measure of personal, if not social, honour. The opening of the next *episodio*, *El 19 de marzo y el 2 de mayo*, finds Gabriel working as a typesetter for the *Diario de Madrid* in March 1808. He exists for Sundays when he can visit Inés, living with her 'uncle', a parish priest in Aranjuez, following the death of Doña Juana. Although Gabriel has more independence now in the third *episodio* than in his role of page to various mistresses and masters in the first two, the nature of his job suggests that it offers fewer possibilities for social mobility and for attaining his yearned-for socially acceptable identity:

No me parecía . . . de gran porvenir la carrera tipográfica; pues aunque toda ella estriba en el manejo de las letras, más tiene de embrutecedora que de instructiva. Así es que, sin dejar el trabajo . . . buscaba con el pensamiento horizontes más lejanos y esfera más honorosa que aquella de nuestra limitada, obscura y sofocante imprenta.

A typographical career did not seem to me . . . to have a great future; even though every aspect of the job has to do with the manipulation of letters, it is more stupefying than instructive. Thus it is that, without leaving my job . . . I searched in my mind for more distant horizons and for a more honourable sphere than that offered by our limited, humble, and stifling press. (357)

Gabriel's mechanical, repetitive job as a typesetter is a 'dead end' in itself; yet the activity inspires him to even greater flights of fancy than before, and serves as a further commentary on Inés and the narrative process. Gabriel sets type in isolation, far from Inés and invisible to the reading public. There is no Other to reflect his gaze, give spirit to his letters, perceive his style. Style, like spirit, woman, or truth, appears to lend individuality, beauty, or significance to what would otherwise be a meaningless and uninteresting copy; but it is also a technique of deceit, a veiling strategy. If the effective difference between two types of writing—mechanical and significant—resides with style alone, both forms are imitations that hide the absence of the centre, truth, origin, and the woman. Style only lends the illusion of difference between versions, copies, representations of the same.

The 'demeaning', unstyled, and artless activity of the copysetter suggests the arbitrary relationship among letters. They at first appear to have order, and to form distinct signs, through their interpretation by the perceiving subject—writer or reader—who manipulates them so as to compose a unique and privileged reading. In the absence of that arbitrary and illusory, yet rhetorically functional, connection between the word and the interpreter, in the absence of imagination and style, there is no spirit to the letters, no image of the Other, no meaning. Gabriel must manipulate not only the letters in the box, but the ones he imagines, in order to write a new text that he controls, styles:

Mi vida al principio era tan triste y tan uniforme como aquel oficio, que en sus rudimentos esclaviza la inteligencia sin entretenerla; pero cuando había adquirido alguna práctica en tan fastidiosa manipulación, mi espíritu aprendió a quedarse libre, mientras las letras, escapándose por entre mis dedos, pasaban de la caja al molde.

At first my life was as sad and as monotonous as that job, which is so elementary that it enslaves one's mind without entertaining it; but when I had acquired a bit of practice at such a bothersome and boring manœuvre, my spirit learned to remain free, while the letters, escaping from between my fingers, moved from the box to the mould. (357)

The separation of the spirit and the letter suggests one way of interpreting or reading language. The letters on the pages of these volumes may seem to disappear as words, and instead take on the proportions of worlds and people, just as Inés and Gabriel seem to come to life. There is no difference, however, between the 'spirit' and the 'letter', since both terms, and the contrast perceived between them, signify only through the manipulation, the interpretation, of words.[9]

Gabriel reiterates his 'centred' view of Inés, where she is again like the sun: 'Yo pensaba en la huérfana Inés, y todos los organismos de mi vida espiritual describían sus amplias órbitas alrededor de la imagen de mi discreta amiga, como los mundos subalternos que voltean sin cesar en torno del astro que es base del sistema' [I thought about the orphan Inés, and all the elements of my spiritual life traced their curves in ample orbits around the image of my discreet friend, like planetary satellites that revolve unceasingly around the star that is the base of the system] (357). For Gabriel there are two kinds of signs here: the written, a tedious manipulation of letters, and the imagined, around which life ceaselessly revolves. Gabriel's account of his work emphasizes the contrast between the deadly written text and the lively imagined one. It is an 'esclavitud' [enslavement] carried out in a 'sótano' [cellar] under the iron hand of the 'regente, un negro y tiznado cíclope' [the boss, a black, tattooed

Cyclops] (357). The bleak, black, depiction of Gabriel's job in Madrid is a counterpart to the description of Inés's beauty and wisdom that he eagerly gives his companions in the print shop: 'Yo, necesitando comunicarme con alguien, les contaba todo sin hacerme de rogar' [I needed to communicate with someone, so I told them everything without them even having to urge me to it] (357). He requires an audience, the gaze or echo of others, to make his ideal real; he then styles a figure of Inés so perfect, wise, and pure as to remove her completely from the domain of realism. This passage is one of many examples of Gabriel's procedure of constructing and then dismantling realist narrative techniques and strategies. This subversion of representationality encompasses every element in the first chapter of the *episodio*; like Gabriel's figuration of Inés, the references to the typesetting letters, the impressionistic techniques of description, the scenes of Aranjuez, and Gabriel's portrait of his own emotions all employ hyperbole. His exorbitant style undermines the validity of his observations, and uncovers the absence of truth, or woman, behind the veil of words. In addition, the juxtaposition of the hyperbolically bleak to the hyperbolically rosy imagery, and the contrasting responses they elicit in Gabriel, prefigures the two directions of the plot in *El 19 de marzo y el 2 de mayo*: toward the love and union of Gabriel and Inés, and toward the revolution of 2 May 1808, separation of the lovers, and ultimately 'death'. Gabriel lives in his illusions now in Madrid; he visualizes Inés while his fingers manipulate the letters, ignoring surrounding reality, as if he did not exist in it. His figurative death to the world here foreshadows the many instances throughout the Series when Gabriel is so self-absorbed and consumed with his desire for Inés that he is oblivious to even the most violent external phenomena. Within the fictional mode of the novel Gabriel's activity specifically foretells his 'death' by firing squad at the conclusion to the third *episodio*; metafictionally it expresses the emptiness behind the image of the Other, the lack of reality beyond words.

The letters in the typesetter's box seem to come alive, contain a spirit, at the same time that they reveal their lack of sense. Gabriel narrates:

Cuando no me ocupaba en estas alabanzas [de Inés], departía mentalmente con ella. En tanto, las letras pasaban por mi mano, trocándose de brutal y muda materia en elocuente lenguaje escrito.

¡Cuánta animación en aquella masa caótica! En la caja, cada signo parecía representar los elementos de la creación, arrojados aquí y allí, antes de empezar la grande obra. Poníalos yo en movimiento, y de aquellos pedazos de plomo surgían sílabas, voces, ideas, juicios, frases, oraciones, períodos, párrafos, capítulos, discursos, la palabra humana en toda su majestad; y después, cuando el molde había hecho su papel mecánico, mis dedos lo descomponían, distribuyendo las letras; cada cual se iba a su casilla, como los simples que el químico guarda después de separados; los caracteres perdían su sentido, es decir, su alma, y tornando a ser plomo puro, caían mudos e insignificantes en la caja.

When I was not occupied with singing the praises [of Inés], I engaged in mental conversations with her. Meanwhile, the letters passed through my hand, transforming themselves from deaf and dumb matter into eloquent written language. There was so much animation in that chaotic mass! In the box, each sign seemed to represent the different elements of creation, thrown here and there, as they were before beginning the great work. I started them moving, and from those pieces of lead arose syllables, voices, ideas, judgements, sentences, prayers, periods, paragraphs, chapters, speeches, human language in all its majesty; and then, when the mould had done its mechanical job, my fingers took apart and distributed the letters; each one went back to its little compartment, like the elements a chemist keeps after he has separated the compound material; the characters lost their meaning, that is to say, their soul, and returning to their leaden state, they would fall, mute and insignificant, into the typesetter's box. (357)

This passage describes the immense potential of writing. Each letter seems crude and mute, part of a chaotic jumble of nonsense which at the same time offers boundless possibilities for interpretation. The extravagant style of Gabriel's reflections exalts the eloquence of language which, on the one hand, appears to create syllables, ideas, discourse, by mechanically, automatically, engendering itself out of lead as the letters merely pass through Gabriel's hands. It is as though he were simply a senseless part of the procedure, not a controlling subject, author, or reader. Discourse generates itself as its terms combine and recombine into the majesty of human speech. Yet, on the other hand, the spirit of these letters, their significance, and Gabriel's visions of and imagined conversations with Inés depend upon their ordering and interpretation by the subject—in this case the reader and copyist Gabriel. Whereas at first the letters seemed totally meaningless to him, in a different frame of mind now, they are profound. The sense that any reader makes of letters, static, black, mute as they are in themselves, depends on how he or she gives them voice, movement, a 'spirit'—'su sentido, es decir, su alma' [their meaning, that is to say, their soul]—just as Gabriel reads Inés as the centre, the soul, and the reflection of his life. The relationship between the letter and the spirit is a function of perspective and interpretation, where each term can substitute for the other in a reciprocal movement as easily articulated— made into syllables, names, paragraphs, etc.—as dearticulated— distributed randomly in a box that offers nothing but darkness and chaos. The ordering movements of Gabriel's hand, together with his disassembling fingers, literally trace the articulation and dearticulation of language.

Gabriel's dark, mechanical job contrasts vividly with the spirit and light of his thoughts about Inés. When he washes off 'las últimas huellas de la aborrecida tinta' [the last traces of the hateful ink], preparing for his trip to Aranjuez, the narrative comments, with chiaroscuro imagery, on the illusions of memory, the ostensible source and origin of this historical novel:

Permitid a mi ancianidad que se extasíe con tales recuerdos; permitid a esta negra nube que se alboroce y se ilumine traspasada por un rayo de sol. Los sábados eran para mí de una belleza incomparable; su luz me parecía más clara. . . .

Pero la alegría no estaba sino en mi alma. El sábado es el precursor del domingo, . . . de aquel viaje al Cielo que mi imaginación renueva hoy, sesenta y cinco años después.

Permit me to become ecstatic over these memories in my old age; let this dark and gloomy cloud rejoice and be illuminated as a ray of sun passes through it. Saturdays were incomparably beautiful for me; their light seemed lighter. . . .

But the joy was still only in my soul. Saturday is the day before Sunday, . . . the day of that trip to Heaven that my imagination can still renew today, sixty-five years later. (358)

At the beginning of the Series the octogenarian Gabriel warns the reader that the narrative is an illusion, and so it can be seen here that the ensuing love story is an elaborate weave of idealized memories and fondly recollected impressions. This light-hearted discourse is also constituted by the movement and association of leaden letters whose spirit is only an illusion. In another passage filled with chiaroscuro imagery, Gabriel compares Inés to the sun and heaven; she becomes the transcendent sign of life and love that emerges from the darkness of a non-existent past. By attributing to her the status of a virtual divinity, echoed in the numerous religious references in the chapter, Gabriel emphasizes the 'spiritual nature' of his writing of her character, his memoirs, and the text of the First Series. His spirit moves the letter and the letter takes on spiritual significance. Gabriel's creation of Inés is one more myth, like the Myth of Creation, another prominent intertext in the Series.

Gabriel's hyperbolic accounts of his interludes with Inés clearly exhibit the dynamics of the evolving subject. When he arrives in Aranjuez, he enters the church and echoes the chant he hears: 'Yo también canto *gloria* en voz baja. . . . Una alegría solemne y grave, que da idea de la bien aventuranza eterna, llena aquel recinto y se reproduce en mi alma como en un espejo' [I too sing 'gloria' in a low voice. . . . A solemn and profound joy, one that suggests blessed eternal life, fills that place and reproduces itself in my soul as in a mirror] (358). Gabriel reproduces himself in harmonious reflection of his object of desire, Inés. He demonstrates similar self-reflexive transformations in many narcissistic moments of the Series. Scanning the women in the church, he observes that 'entre aquellos centenares de mantillas negras distingo la que cubre la hermosa cabeza de Inés. La conocería entre mil' [among the hundreds of black shawls I distinguish the one covering Inés's lovely head. I would recognize her among a thousand] (358). He seems to see through her black veil, distinguishing the woman herself, as though there were no barriers or differences between them. In the same way that the past merges with the present both in the mind of the character and the present tense of the narrator, so Gabriel seems to merge with Inés, dispensing with the veil of words as well as of cloth: 'Inés y yo charlamos con los ojos o con las palabras; pero no quiero referir ahora nuestros poemas' [Inés and I speak with our eyes as easily as with words; but right now I do not want to share our poetry with you] (359). Finally his spiritual harmony with her finds expression in the union of nature:

en el sitio en que el Tajo y el Jarama, encontrándose de improviso, y cuando seguramente el uno no tenía noticias de la existencia del otro, se abrazan y confunden sus aguas en una sola corriente, haciendo de dos vidas una sola. Tan exacta imagen de nosotros mismos, no puede menos de ocurrírsele a Inés al mismo tiempo que a mí.

at the place where the Tajo and the Jarama suddenly find each other, when surely neither one of them knew about the existence of the other, they embrace and their waters are mixed in a single current, making from two lives, one alone. It is such an exact image of us, that it could only have occurred to Inés at the very same time that it did to me. (359)

Gabriel sees his own thoughts in Inés, who is as much an 'exact image' of him as the rivers are of the young lovers. If all copies imply a difference, their exactness and univocality are impossible, however much Gabriel might yearn for it now in his union with Inés, or in the precise expression of his memories in his memoirs, or in the absolute equivalence of his writing with his 'life'.

The opening chapter of *El 19 de marzo y el 2 de mayo* recalls the concluding one of *La corte de Carlos IV.* It portrays a spiritual harmony and peace between Inés and Gabriel at the same moment that it subverts the effect through its pervasive narcissism. Like Narcissus, Gabriel sees only himself in the waters or in Inés's eyes; like Echo, she does not speak her own mind. The union of the rivers, like Gabriel's desired union with Inés, also implies the undercurrent of death, just as in the Narcissus story. The dark symbols of the chapter—the ink, the leaden letters, the basement workshop, the dark cloud, even Inés's black veil— subtly suggest the mythical threat of death that lies within desire. Yet even as Gabriel and Inés are about to be separated until the tenth *episodio* by the dark forces of greed, jealousy, and war, so Gabriel, now 17, has already outlived Narcissus. And he will find that Inés is not his copy, no matter how much he writes her name.

Gabriel returns melancholically to 'la caja [que] me ofrece sus letras de plomo, que no aguardan más que mis manos para juntarse y hablar; pero mi mano no conoce en los primeros momentos sino cuatro de aquellos negros signos, que al punto se reúnen para formar ese solo nombre: *I-N-E-S* [the box that offers me its leaden letters, letters that wait for nothing but my hands in order to come together and to speak; but my hand only recognizes four of those dark signs at first, which suddenly join to form that unique name: *I-N-E-S*] (359). The letters join like the rivers, but their meaning is of Gabriel's articulation; they are not autonomously, 'naturally', or 'spiritually' significant in themselves. Their union and spirit, or lack of it, depend on the manipulating hand and mind of the writer or reader who associates the letters, or characters, and gives them a name. The letter—character, syllable, word, or name—is the irreducible narrative unit. The letter is the woman and the truth, rather than its veil. Gabriel's articulation of the letters I-N-E-S, like the more elaborate portraits of his symbolic Other, illustrates the simultaneously constitutive and deconstitutive strategies of the narration which always exhibits itself as an ongoing process of writing, rather than a finished work or composition, a past reality, or a real self. The *Episodios nacionales* reinscribe their intrinsic and all-encompassing self-consciousness through the literal articulation of the name INES, which evokes an ostensibly significant figure of a woman. 'Inés' emulates and reproduces the discourse of the First Series by demonstrating how a reader, like Gabriel, through narcissistic representations, fashions his illusions of self and Other, language and world.

Galdós's historical novels continually uncover and demythify their own ideological, cultural, and literary practices. These labels too, for allegedly different modes of reading, are themselves both over-determined and indeterminate. Galdós confronts the reader with the impossibility of establishing fixed boundaries between Gabriel and Inés, feminine and masculine, narration and interpretation, in order to re-evaluate the conventions which seek to maintain inflexible boundaries, codes, and categories. The *Episodios* offer a reassessment of received methods of prioritizing, categorizing, and labelling the terms and values that designate differences between fiction and history, reality and illusion. The First Series of *Episodios nacionales* shows how the effort to create an ideal, whether of self or Other, woman or text, love object, or 'objet d'art', or to assert any ultimate truth or definitive interpretation, always turns on itself, subverting and demythifying the very idealized construct it sought to maintain. Gabriel and 'his' text are emblems of the always elusive object of desire, whether called 'truth' or 'Inés'.

NOTES

1. For a detailed study of Amaranta, see Urey 1988.
2. The term refers to the title of Urey's *The Novel Histories of Galdós* which intends to describe concisely the dilemma encountered when attempting to define or delimit a genre.
3. All quotations are from Pérez Galdós 1979. The translations are my own.
4. The term 'hembra' is usually reserved for female animals. Also, regarding Gabriel's still slightly less than whole-hearted endorsement of Inés's

'superiority', consider that Rosita, in *Trafalgar*, seems to be the only completely idealized female character in the Series. Gabriel does not describe Inés's beauty in terms as admiring as those he uses for Rosita, for example, until near the very end of the Series. In that first *episodio*, the child Gabriel's virtual worship of Rosita is similar to that he feels for the fragmented memory of his deceased mother; by the second *episodio* he has moved on to a new stage in his relationship with the Other/woman Inés, one which includes rivalry as well as admiration.

5. Critics have long noted the picaresque intertexts in the First Series, present from the first paragraph of *Trafalgar*, where Gabriel introduces himself in a manner reminiscent of Don Pablos in the *Buscón*.

6. See Urey 1989*b* for a discussion of the 'miraculous generation' of the First Series from Gabriel's memory, the ramifications of his dual role as narrator and character, and the paradoxical function of key terms, like honour and patriotism, in the text.

7. See Peter Bly's discussion of the self-interested motivation behind sentiments like patriotism in the First Series.

8. By invoking the authority of *Don Quijote*, Inés refers to the text that speaks more clearly than any other of the relationships between history and fiction, reality and illusion, that are fundamental to the *Episodios nacionales*. Lukács writes how Cervantes demonstrated that: 'the purest heroism is bound to become grotesque, the strongest faith is bound to become madness, when the ways leading to the transcendental home have become impassable; reality does not have to correspond to subjective evidence, however genuine and heroic. The profound melancholy of the historical process, of the passing of time, speaks through this work, tells us that even a content and an attitude which are eternal must lose their meaning when their time is past: that time brushes aside even the eternal. *Don Quixote* is the first great battle of interiority against the prosaic vulgarity of outward life, and the only battle in which interiority succeeded, not only to emerge unblemished from the fray, but even to transmit some of the radiance of its triumphant, though admittedly self-ironising, poetry to its victorious opponent' (104). These remarks are relevant to a historical vision redefined in the *Episodios nacionales*. History is depicted no longer as a monumental legend of historical grandeur, but as an often trivial, even melancholy and pessimistic account of the ceaseless and repetitive passage of time. It relates to the obstacles between Gabriel and his identity, between Gabriel and Inés, between Gabriel, honour, and social status. Gabriel, like Don Quijote, continually comes up against the prosaic vulgarity of outward life, and in the process must face his own, not always genuine, sometimes grotesquely humorous, ambitions. His ultimate triumph, at the end of the First Series, is also 'admittedly self-ironising', a blend, just like patriotism or idealism, of the serious and the burlesque.

9. Paul Julian Smith offers an excellent analysis of the connections between language, the letter, woman, and desire in another of Galdós's novels, *La de Bringas*.

WORKS CITED

BLY, PETER (1984). 'For Self or Country? Conflicting Lessons in the First Series of *Episodios Nacionales?*', *Kentucky Romance Quarterly*, 31/2: 143–50.

CARROLL, DAVID (1982). *The Subject in Question: The Languages of Theory and the Strategies of Fiction*. Chicago: University of Chicago Press.

DENDLE, BRIAN (1986). *Galdós: The Early Historical Novels*. Columbia, Mo.: University of Missouri Press.

DERRIDA, JACQUES (1979). *Spurs: Nietzsche's Styles/Éperons: les styles de Nietzsche*, trans. Barbara Harlow. Chicago: University of Chicago Press.

GRAVES, ROBERT (1955). *The Greek Myths*, vol. i. Harmondsworth: Penguin.

GULLÓN, GERMÁN (1984). 'Narravitizando la historia: *La corte de Carlos IV*', *Anales galdosianos*, 19: 45–52.

KRISTEVA, JULIA (1986). *The Kristeva Reader*, ed. Toril Moi. New York: Columbia University Press.

LUKÁCS, GYÖRGY (1971). *The Theory of the Novel: A Historico-Philosophical Essay on the Forms of Great Epic Literature*, trans. Anna Bostock. Cambridge: MIT Press.

PARADISSIS, ARISTIDES G. (1979) 'Observaciones sobre la estructura y el significado de *La corte de Carlos IV*', *Anales Galdosianos*, 14: 97–102.

PERÉZ GALDÓS, BENITO (1979). *Episodios nacionales*, ed. Federico Carlos Sainz de Robles, vol. i. 1st edn., 4th reprint. Madrid: Aguilar.

RODRÍGUEZ, ALFRED (1967). *An Introduction to the 'Episodios nacionales' of Galdós*. New York: Las Américas.

SMITH, PAUL JULIAN (1989). 'Galdós, Valera, Lacan', in *The Body Hispanic: Gender and Sexuality in Spanish and Spanish American Literature*. Oxford: Oxford University Press. 69–104.

UREY, DIANE (1988). 'Engendering Style in the First Series of Galdós's *Episodios nacionales*', *Revista de estudios hispánicos*, 22/2: 25–43.

—— (1989a). *The Novel Histories of Galdós*. Princeton, NJ: Princeton University Press.

—— (1989b). 'A Prologue to a Prologue in Galdós's *Trafalgar*', in *Homenaje a Alberto Porqueras Mayo. Estudios en los Siglos de Oro y la Literatura Moderna*. Kassel: Edition Reichenberger. 339–51.

8

Monstrous Inversions: Decadence and Degeneration in Galdós's *Ángel Guerra*

CATHERINE JAGOE

Dark Angel, with thine aching lust . . .

(Lionel Johnson)

Ángel Guerra is the most turbid and outlandish of the *Novelas contemporáneas*. A sprawling and at times lurid novel of obsession teeming with bizarre characters, it mingles mysticism, eroticism, illness, and death in phantasmagoric sequence. Even Galdós's most devoted contemporary readers found its density and length excessive (Pardo Bazán 1095). The hero, who is plagued by terrifying dreams and hallucinations, is a revolutionary *manqué* who falls hopelessly in love with his daughter's governess, Leré, even though she is set on becoming a nun. He follows her to Toledo and spends the rest of the novel unsuccessfully trying to imitate her asexual spirituality. At her instigation, he trains to be a monk himself. He is organizing the creation of a revolutionary new evangelical centre when he is murdered by the grasping relatives of his former mistress, whom he callously abandoned early in the novel. *Ángel Guerra* was published in 1891, at the beginning of a decade notorious for its social and political turbulence; a decade that precariously straddled the death-throes of one century and the beginning of another.[1] It is appropriate, then, that it should prove a transitional, hybrid novel in more ways than one. It is commonly seen as ushering in a new phase in Galdós's writing, in which the emphasis shifts inward from the multifarious urban social milieux of his earlier novels to the spiritual struggles of particular individuals, as seen in *Nazarín* (1895), *Halma* (1895), and *Misericordia* (1897). Critics have largely

focused on the Tolstoyan religiosity of *Ángel Guerra* and shied
away from exploring its equally prominent but less savoury
decadent characteristics and what they might signify for its representation of sexuality, sexual difference, and power relations. I
view this reluctance to probe the novel's murkier side as part of
the phenomenon recently identified by Noël Valis: Spaniards'
desire to exalt their own country's naturalism as a different,
more spiritual movement than that of France, which they attacked as disgusting and godless, in rhetoric whose virulence
betrays Spanish resentment at being cast as France's cultural
subaltern (Valis 1992: 191). In the arena of gender, *Ángel Guerra*
enacts the reigning European preoccupation with decadence and
degeneration, interests which in Galdós's case lead not to stylis-
tic innovation but to political reaction, since the novel anticipates in a number of significant ways the conservative turn
Galdós's *Novelas contemporáneas* were to take in the 1890s away
from the open-ended, liberatory irony of his urban novels of the
1880s (Jagoe).

   If it is true that *Ángel Guerra* is, as Valis memorably terms it,
a 'monster novel', whose prolix structure displays a plethora of
deformities and incongruities, then Galdós, with his huge and
heterogeneous *œuvre*, is surely the monster novelist. His seventy-
eight novels and twenty-four plays span the turn of the century
like a colossus. Perhaps not surprisingly, given the size of Galdós's
production and the inaccessibility of this particular work, relatively few critics have ventured substantive exegeses of *Ángel
Guerra*. Valis, in a brilliant and innovative reading, interprets
the presence of the many monstrous elements in the novel's
content and form as a metaphor for the monstrosity of the creative imagination itself. The naturalist novel itself is, as she notes,
a hybrid product of biology and imagination (1993: 220). Her
essay opens up an interesting question for feminist scholarship
by noting, but not explicitly relating, the presence of monstrosity and gender inversions in the novel. In another important
recent article, D. J. O'Connor relates the 'eerie strangeness' of
the novel, steeped in eroticism and violence, to the paintings of
Hieronymus Bosch (73). Yet the novel's characteristic strangeness, the gender inversions, and the preoccupation with monstrosity noted by both critics belong also to a period much closer
in time, since they were manifestations of the *fin-de-siècle* decadent
vision found in European art and letters. Galdós transmogrifed

facets of his contemporaries' preoccupation with degeneration and many important motifs of decadent iconography, including but not limited to masks, monsters, doubles, androgynes, and tortured sensuality, into his own ironically Manichaean novelistic idiom, thereby creating the peculiarly disturbing character that is the hallmark of this novel.

The term decadence refers, etymologically, to that sense of a falling off, impotent decline, hopelessness, and impending doom that characterized the Western world-view at the end of the nineteenth century. Elaine Showalter describes it as a 'pejorative label applied by the bourgeoisie to everything that seemed unnatural, artifical, and perverse, from Art Nouveau to homosexuality, a sickness with symptoms associated with cultural degeneration and decay' (169). Scientific interest in degeneration began with the French physician Bénédict Morel, who coined the term in 1857. As the nineteenth century drew on, social commentators in a wide variety of disciplines became increasingly concerned at what they saw as their society's 'polymorphous morbidity' (Perrot 622), manifesting itself in growing rates of crime, alcoholism, cretinism, syphilis, prostitution, neurasthenia, parasitism, mental and sexual disorders such as hysteria, and a weakening of the social fabric due to the growth of anarchism, terrorism, feminism, and socialism. Morel and others, such as the Italian criminal anthropologist Cesare Lombroso (1835–1909) and the English psychiatrist Henry Maudsley (1835–1918), used Lamarckian evolutionary theory in their hypothesis that urban life in the industrial age was leading to the physical, mental, and moral enervation of the race, and that this was being transmitted to and intensified with each succeeding generation of offspring. Debate about the notion of degeneration reached a crescendo in the 1890s (Pick 8). The Austrian Max Nordau, in his famous and highly alarmist work *Degeneration*, first published in 1892, asserted that Europe was undergoing a severe epidemic, 'a sort of black death of degeneration and hysteria' (537).[2] Like others of his time, he contended that the pace and intensity of life had sped up immeasurably under capitalism, and that the human organism was being subjected to an 'enormous increase in organic expenditure' (39). The price of the nineteenth century's much-vaunted progress was inevitable wear and tear on the brain and nervous system, which explained, according to Nordau, the social pathology which he saw as endemic.

The naturalist novel is an important disseminator of such beliefs since, as Seltzer argues, it is predicated on an 'aesthetic of genesis as *de*generation' (quoted in Valis 1992: 192). *Ángel Guerra*, as a realist-naturalist novel, refracts some of the reigning preoccupations about degeneracy. It is peopled with physical and mental defectives who bear the signs of hereditary disease. Both the women with whom Ángel is involved come from degenerate families. Leré's parents have produced a cretinous monster. Her stepfather is parasitic, and horrifically violent. Dulcenombre Babel has a chlorotic complexion, is rachitically thin, and sexually degraded, having been prostituted by her mother before escaping to be Ángel's kept woman. Her mother, Doña Catalina, is the mad and impoverished remnant of a once-proud aristocratic lineage. Dulce herself, her uncle Don Pito, and Leré's father all suffer from alcoholism. Pito is missing a leg and Fausto limps. The Babel sons, who are introduced in list format, like entries in a naturalist's catalogue, are parasites and wastrels, poisoned by urban poverty and smoking,[3] who live in a shadowy criminal underworld of forgery, theft, gambling, and thinly disguised extortion. However, by what the narrator terms a 'sarcasmo etnográfico' [a piece of ethnographic sarcasm] (Pérez Galdós 30), the Babel family are all good looking, even noble in appearance, in ironic contrast to their conduct. This is not, then, a straightforward naturalist work, since, according to Lombroso, one of the leading scientific lights of the day, the criminal tended to reveal his nature in primitive physiognomy. However, the Babel brothers do live in the kind of insalubrious environment and lead the kind of enervating life-style that were believed to breed degeneracy:

El aposento era pequeño, con ventanas a un fétido patio, y de la pared pendían formas extrañas, figuras de guiñol, de estúpida cara, una cabeza de toro disecada, un estantillo con varios frascos de reactivos y barnices; libros viejos y sucios; en el suelo, piedras litográficas, montones de periódicos, herramientas diversas, todo en el mayor desorden, maloliente, pringoso, polvoriento. . . . El uno se restregaba los ojos, encendidos por la fatiga de un largo trabajo con luz artificial.

The room was cramped, and its windows opened onto a reeking courtyard. On the wall hung strange objects: puppet shapes, with idiotic expressions, a stuffed bull's head, a shelf with various flasks of reagents and glazes; old books, covered in dust. On the floor was their lithographic equipment, piles of newspapers, various tools, all in complete disorder, smelly, sticky, and dusty. . . . One of them was rubbing his eyes, which were tired and inflamed from working a long time in artificial light. (38)

Ángel Guerra illustrates two principal motifs of degeneration: morbidity and atavism. The novel begins on a note of febrile unrest and exhaustion that is continued throughout the novel and mutates into numerous other fatal illnesses, such as Doña Sales's heart disease, Ción's fever, Don Tomé's typhoid, and María Antonia's cancer, before ending up with Ángel where he began: wounded and bedridden, but this time about to die. Ángel's hallucinatory ramblings in the opening scene are paralleled by the unbearable droning of the insect in the apartment. He feels a frenzied compulsion to talk, but all he produces is a 'febril y desordenada relación' [feverish and muddled account] (19) of the failed coup. Galdós introduces at this point the spectre of mass hysteria—a subject which was attracting increasing amounts of psycho-sociological commentary thanks to Gustave Le Bon's theories about crowd behaviour—to explain the explosion of blind rage that Ángel experienced the night of the coup, and which resulted in the killing of an officer (Barrows). Throughout the novel, Ángel's continued efforts to transcend his baser instincts are abortive; he is mired in his own carnality and beset by continual regressions to a primitive, animalistic state. Again and again, he finds himself 'ebrio de furor' [drunk with rage], as he was in the incident with which the novel opens. When Ángel assaults Dulce's brother Arístides in Toledo in part ii, the same atavistic mechanism operates:

Ángel obedecía a un ciego instinto de destrucción vengativa que anidaba en su alma, y que en mucho tiempo no había salido al exterior, por lo cual rechinaba más, como espadón enmohecido al despegarse de la vaina roñosa. El temperamento bravo y altanero resurgía en él, llevándose por delante, como huracán impetuoso, las ideas nuevas, desbaratando y haciendo polvo la obra del sentimiento y de la razón en los últimos meses.

Ángel was obeying a blind instinct of vengeful destruction that sheltered in his soul, which was all the more noisy for not having emerged in a long time, like a rusty sword being withdrawn from a mouldering scabbard. His fierceness and arrogance were welling up again, bearing the new ideas before them, like an impetuous hurricane, disrupting and destroying the work of sentiment and reason of recent months. (190)

The representation of this incident, which is repeated in almost identical terms during the culminating scene at the end of the novel when Ángel is robbed by Arístides, Fausto, and Policarpo, is intriguingly ambiguous. On the one hand it appears to valorize conventional, aggressive masculinity, with the phallic image of the sword re-emerging and the use of positive adjectives such as 'bravo y altanero'. On the other hand, aggressiveness is associated with destruction and the primitive—hurricanes, blindness, and the instinctual. The repeated allusions made to Ángel's efforts to 'amarrar la bestia' [restrain the beast] within himself (227, 267, 269) posit the notion of a loathsome but compelling Other lurking within the civilized personality which was remarkably prominent in *fin de siècle* works, to judge by the popularity of R. L. Stevenson's *The Strange Case of Dr. Jekyll and Mr Hyde* (1886), in which a man finds himself host to a bestial other self.[4] When Ángel confesses to having contemplated raping Leré, he declares that the experience was an atavistic one, a sort of relapse to an earlier, brutish self: 'Era ya otro hombre, el viejo, el de marras, con mis instintos brutales, animal más o menos inteligente, ciego' [I was another man, the old one, the one I used to be, with the instincts of a brute, a more or less intelligent animal, blind] (266). Don Pito similarly regresses to a more primitive self—the slave-trader—when he loses his temper and beats up Tirso/*Tatabuquenque*, the peasant whom he considers a being of a lower race (192).[5]

The civilized/Other dichotomy is repeated in Leré, for while her effect upon Ángel is like that of Circe (in, for example, Hacker's 1893 portrait)—she reduces him to animalism—she is simultaneously a rapt, untouchable mystic akin to Rossetti's famous *Beata Beatrix*, the Pre-Raphaelite portrait which inspired many imitations on the Continent in the 1890s. She is what Luce Irigaray would term a 'mystérique'.[6] Contemporary readers, such as Ortega Munilla, were torn between labelling Leré a mystical Beatrice or a modern hysteric (Sotelo 117). Yet Leré's mysticism seems genuine enough. It is Ángel's mysticism that is represented as a sublimated form of sexuality; in this as in other aspects Ángel is subtly feminized, a trait that makes him a decadent man.

The notion of inevitable decline or degeneration produced an aesthetic movement that revolved around a group of 'decadent' or Symbolist writers and painters of the late nineteenth century whose subjects and style made considerable impact on European and American literatures. They included the writers Paul Verlaine, Arthur Rimbaud, Joris-Karl Huysmans, Joséphin Péladin, Maurice Maeterlinck, Villiers de l'Isle Adam, 'Rachilde', Gabriele D'Annunzio, Oscar Wilde, Algernon Swinburne, Walter Pater, Leopoldo Alas, Arthur Symons, Ernest Dowson; and the artists Gustave Moreau, Odilon Redon, Fernand Khnopff, Gustav Klimt, Aubrey Beardsley and Franz von Stuck. United in their belief that God, morality, love, and nature were shibboleths of a pre-Darwinian age, the decadents were dedicated to maximizing the sensations of the moment. Using Baudelaire's *Fleurs du mal* as a model, they explored the strange terrain of sexual perversions, exoticism, and the occult. Arthur Symons explained in 1893 that the decadent movement was dedicated to 'the sensations and ideas of the effeminate, over-civilized, deliberately abnormal creature who is the last product of society' (Siegel 207). Decadents espoused a 'love of art for art's sake', unimpeded by any extra-aesthetic considerations (Showalter 170). While their aesthetic theory is clearly alien to Galdós's outlook, which is deeply concerned with morality and very far from the 'art for art's sake' of the aesthetes, some of their subject-matter does find its way into *Ángel Guerra*, in nuanced form. Valis argues that realists and naturalists were just as interested in the idea of decadence as the decadents and the modernists, although literary technique and point of view differ greatly between them (1981: 10). Despite the fact that Galdós is probably the last Hispanic author of his period to be readily associated with decadence—Rubén Darío, Valle Inclán, and Azorín come to mind far more readily—he nevertheless had plenty of opportunities for contact with the new movement. As John Kronik shows, the French Symbolists' work was well known in Spain from the late 1880s on (1976*b*). Indeed, one of its champions and promoters was none other than Galdós's lover Emilia Pardo Bazán, who had become inspired by it in 1889, during a trip to the Exposition Universelle in Paris. According to Pattison, Pardo Bazán went on a trip with Galdós in Germany directly after visiting the Exposition (24).

One of the decadents' themes was sexual obsession, a painful craving for the impossible, fired by what Verlaine called 'carnal spirit and unhappy flesh' (Gilman 5). In male symbolist writing in particular there is a 'constant search for a female Other', who functions as a combination of erotic object and elusive muse (Andrews 31). This obsession was often mixed with mysticism, usually of a sacrilegious variety. Nordau argued in *Degeneration* that mysticism was one of the main features of degeneracy (22). The torture of erotic self-denial undergone by St Anthony was a popular subject for decadent artists and writers, and Flaubert's *The Temptation of Saint Anthony* (1874) was highly influential. There are obvious parallels between the St Anthony legend and Ángel's painful struggle to master his desire for Leré, as well as his many hallucinatory visions of her while he clings to his imposed celibacy. Furthermore, the fact that the focus of erotic obsession in the novel is a nun situates *Ángel Guerra* within the European *fin de siècle* predilection for veiled women, symbols of feminine mystery and inaccessibility for many artists (Showalter 144).

The most widely represented veiled woman of the time was Salome, who performed the dance of the veils for Herod in order to win John the Baptist's head. Mallarmé's version of her in his *Hérodiade*—as a narcissist with a peculiar 'virginité anubile et ravissante'—epitomized the decadent vision of a mesmerizingly beautiful, pure, but destructive woman (Praz 304). Bram Dijkstra has documented the many artistic incarnations of this figure of patriarchal iconography in *Idols of Perversity*. Even though Galdós's heroine, Leré, is relentlessly saintly, she is by no means exempt from the misogyny that attended *fin de siècle* portrayals of the feminine. She is surrounded by images of violence done to women's bodies; Ángel helps his daughter to play in her presence at disembowelling a doll, an incident with a thematic connection to various other allusions in the novel to St Agatha, a martyr who was hung upside down and had her breasts ripped off with tongs by an official unable to consummate his lust for her (O'Connor 77). The connection could be an innocuous coincidence were it not for the fact that Ángel focuses lustfully on Leré's breasts throughout the novel. The protagonist's relationship with the two women in his life is both sadistic (his relationship with Dulce is based on his callous disregard for her) and masochistic (he subjects himself to physical denial and psychological torment in pursuit of the resolutely impassive Leré). Both these concepts had only recently been coined and popularized, by the German neuro-psychiatrist Richard von Krafft-Ebing in his landmark taxonomic work on sexuality and sexual perversions, *Psychopathia sexualis*, first published in 1886. Ángel fantasizes about raping Leré, and early in the novel performs a symbolic rape by boring a hole through her bedroom door and spying on her one night. He is somewhat repelled at what his voyeurism reveals, namely the extent of Leré's ascetic abhorrence of the flesh: 'tanta, tanta virtud, parecíale ya excesiva y antipática' [he found so very much virtue excessive and unpleasant] (80). Don Pito, in a parallel vein, dreams of making Spain a polygamous state, like the Mormon community, in which he can indulge his womanizing without scruple.

Decadence, as Reed has pointed out, is an art of monstrosity, if we define the monstrous as the impossible juxtaposition of opposites such as virtue and vice, beauty and ugliness, human and animal. 'Many of its topoi emphasize ambivalence—sphinxes with their mixed bodies and dangerous mysteries, hermaphrodites, beautiful but evil women' (17). Decadent art is full of the grotesque, the sexually bizarre, and the freakish—monsters, vampires, angels, all in a hallucinatory mystical dream-world where evil is compellingly, hypnotically attractive (Gilman 86). The monster theme so prevalent in *Ángel Guerra* begins in the opening chapter when Ángel perceives the buzzing insect in his apartment as a monstrous animal (14), and the noises from the street 'se desfiguraban y acrecían monstruosamente' [became disfigured and grew monstrously]; he also imagines that his wound has swollen to become as big as his whole body (15). In the most terrifying oneiric sequence in the novel, an anguished Ángel is abandoned by a serenely merciless Leré to the slavering maws of a herd of composite monsters:

animales repugnantes y tremebundos, culebras con cabezas de cerdos voraces, dragones con alas polvorientas y ojos de esmeralda, perros con barbas y escamas de cocodrilo, lo más inmundo, lo más hórrido que caber puede en la delirante fantasía de un condenado. Todos aquellos bichos increíbles le mordían, le desgarraban las carnes, llenándole de babas pestíferas, y uno le sacaba los ojos para ponérselos en el estómago; otro le extraía los intestinos y se los embutía en el cerebro, o de una dentellada le dejaba sin corazón.

fearsome, repugnant creatures, snakes with the heads of greedy swine, dragons with dust-covered wings and emerald eyes, dogs with beards and crocodile skins; all the foulest, most dreadful beasts that could occur to the delirious fantasy of a condemned man. All these incredible creatures were biting him, tearing his flesh, smearing him with their pestilent drooling; one of them snatched out his eyes, and wore them on his belly; another ripped out his intestines and stuffed them in its own brain, or with a single bite left him with no heart. (295)

Leré, for all her saintliness, is strongly linked to monstrosity. Her mother has given birth to four monsters, of which one, Juan, is still alive: boneless from the waist down, with a man's head and a child's body, he grunts like an animal and has the arms of an octopus but a gaze of 'cierto ángel' [a certain charm] (71). Leré's other brother, Sabas, is puny and wizened but a musical prodigy (71). She herself has a strange defect in her eyes, which causes her constantly to blink and roll her pupils so that exchanging glances with her makes people giddy or dizzy. The giddiness of desire that Ángel feels when he looks at her is also the vertigo that draws him to his death; Leré acts like the feminine vortex of Charybdis evoked in Wagner's *The Dream* (Plate 1).[7] Her gaze is hypnotic, like those of the vampires in popular narratives that riveted turn-of-the-century readers, though not because of a fixed intensity but because of incessant mobility, a 'movilidad constitutiva' (44). While Leré's ocular tic is one manifestation of the monstrosity latent in her family, her asexuality is the other. She herself recognizes that 'Soy una excepción, un fenómeno . . . he salido también monstruo como mis hermanos. El casorio no sólo no me hace maldita gracia, sino que la idea me repugna' [I'm an exception, a freak . . . I've turned out just as monstrous as my brothers. Marriage is not the least bit appealing to me; in fact the very idea of it repels me] (94). The narrator constantly stresses the contrast between Leré's natural, fleshy body and her eerie imperviousness to men. 'Nunca he sentido lo que es atracción de ningún hombre' [I have never felt any kind of an attraction to a man], she declares; 'La idea de casarme con un hombre y de que se ponga muy cerca, muy cerca de mí, me repugna' [The idea of marrying one and having him get very, very close to me is repulsive] (106). Leré is one of the 'odd', unmarriageable females that George Gissing made famous in Britain with his novel *The Odd Women*, published in the same year as *Ángel Guerra*. She has certain qualities of the Sphinx, as depicted by Moreau, Khnopff, Toorop, von Stuck, and Séon: the beautiful breasts and face, together with a tradition of inscrutability and impenetrability, although she is entirely devoid of the dangerous, lurking bestiality of the claws and animal hindparts of the Symbolist sphinxes (Plates 2–4).[8] Yet, paradoxically, it is Leré's very inaccessibility and impregnability that draw Ángel like a moth to a candle: 'tu santidad me cautiva, y si tú no fueras como eres, si no tuvieras esa . . . vocación irresistible, se me figura que me gustarías menos' [your saintliness is bewitching, and if you weren't the way you are, if you didn't have that . . . irrevocable vocation, I don't think I would like you so much] (105).

Masks, which were an important theme for the Symbolists, are also central to *Ángel Guerra*, as Kronik and O'Connor show. Ángel has a recurring dream about a terrifying Greek mask with a gaping mouth and hair standing on end (51); he himself imagines at one point that Leré is covering his body with gold leaf: 'sobre los atributos propios de su ser iba claveteando como una lámina de oro que los ahogaba y envolvía. Era como esas imágenes bizantinas forradas de chapa de metal precioso, que no permite ver la escultura interior' [on top of the traits of his own personality she was nailing a sheet of gold that stifled and enveloped them. He was like one of those Byzantine images covered with a sheet of precious metal, which prevent you from seeing the sculpture underneath] (206). In the scene of the robbery, Arístides appears as a grinning mask of falsehood and Jusepa as a grotesque one, with bulging eyes (336). Earlier, in Toledo, Ángel encounters two masked revellers disguised as a monkey and a black man, who speak in falsetto (234). Both the monkey and the black man were frequently used as symbols of decadent sexuality: they both appear with the Queen of Sheba to St Anthony in Flaubert's *Temptation*. The chilling meeting with the carnival celebrants introduces the Carnival/Lent opposition which subtly underpins much that occurs in the novel.[9]

O'Connor's discussion of *Ángel Guerra*'s numerous 'monstrous configurations of misshapen flesh' and its recurrent images of things being 'jammed, stuffed, or poked into or through something else' (75) bears a marked resemblance to Bakhtin's notion of the carnivalesque, developed by Stallybrass and White. Dismemberment, bulges, and orifices are fundamental attributes of the grotesque body, which constantly strains to transcend its own confines and insert itself into or receive others (Bakhtin 317–18; Stallybrass and White 21–2). Leré's disproportionately bulging breasts in her otherwise slim frame represent the hedonistic grotesque, whereas Dulce's anorexic physique is the Lenten body (Ángel perceives her at one point as a clothed skeleton, 91); the famine versus the feast. Of course, there is an ironic inversion at work here, since it is Leré who is angelically chaste and impenetrable and Dulce the kept woman. Leré copies Ángel's mother, Doña Sales, in using a corset to present a closed, smooth, classical silhouette. Doña Sales forces herself determinedly into 'la férrea máquina del corsé, que daba a su busto la rigidez estatuaria' [the iron machinery of the corset, which gave her a rigid, statuesque bust] (47); her language and ideas are similarly in check, and she is violently opposed to free love. Leré is impatient at the bulges on her body: 'le enfadaba que su seno abultase tanto' [the way her bosom stuck out so annoyed her] (80). Intent on the saintly life she has chosen, she sees only 'la derechura luminosa de su camino, sin reparar en los bultos que a un lado u otro pudieran aparecerse en él' [the straight and shining path ahead of her, and paid no attention to the bumps that might appear from time to time in her way] (140–1). Ángel is one of these 'bultos' but so also is her own 'abultado seno' [well-endowed bosom] (75), which she wishes she could cut off like paring nails (107).

The grotesque motifs of exchange of body parts and voracious feeding, most of which have to do with breasts, reappear at various points in the novel. The obsessive focus on breasts in the novel reflects a motif found in the work of Fernand Khnopff and other Symbolist painters: that of Diana of Ephesus, the many-breasted fertility goddess, who represented a patriarchal vision of Woman as 'symbol of the mystery of the cruel impassiveness and wastefulness [of Nature]' (Dijkstra 238). The theme is echoed in the large bare breasts of the popular Symbolist subjects Eve, Salome, and the Sphinx in many paintings and illustrations of this period. In Ángel's key dream, in which he is pursued by a monstrous he-goat (the satyr who represents his own repressed lust), Leré appears to him with her white breasts bare and tears off chunks of her own flesh to feed the monster. The theme of dismemberment and exchange surfaces again in the multiple allusions to mastectomy, which foreshadow the amputation of Tristana's leg in a novel published the following year. Leré wishes she could donate her breasts to Dulcenombre (107). Later in the novel, she has to nurse a woman who has had a mastectomy, while the blind woman, Lucía, has a vision that Leré has magically torn off her own breasts and given them to the amputee María Antonia.[10]

Just as Leré is at once both grotesque and classical body, feast and famine, the narrative engages in a typically Galdosian play on names and opposing identities, making multiple references to angels and monsters. The novel takes the name of the hero, Angel War, which, as Valis has pointed out, is a composite of two usually incompatible nouns, creating a sense of 'contained antagonism' (1993: 222). Leré is a monster who is by her conduct an angel; Ángel is by name an angel who, despite his seraphic protestations, cannot overcome the monster of lust and rage in himself (257). If Leré is an angel, she is not of the cherished household variety, for she is not domestic and does not want to marry. Dulce would be a domestic angel, but she is not chaste and Angel has no interest in marrying her. In a parallel antinomy, while Angel is often likened to a Quijote figure, the Dulcinea of his dreams is not Dulce. The novel seems to pose the impossibility of a man ever being translated into an angel unless he is desexed or a sexless creature, like Don Tomé. Likewise, Leré cannot be translated into a warm, marriageable female. While both the main female characters personify the altruism associated with the ideal woman, neither follows the orthodox 'heroine's text' of eighteenth- and nineteenth-century novels, predicated on marriage to the hero (Miller). Ángel himself is no more successful in terms of conforming to his gender. Like his predecessors in the *Novelas contemporáneas*, León Roch and Máximo Manso, he is luckless in his search for a wife. While León and Máximo prove incapable of forming their chosen women, Ángel is incapable even of forming himself in the pure image Leré has chosen for him, and like them he reneges on the whole attempt.

Ángel's religious foundation at Toledo grows out of misdirected sexual desire, as does his attempt to remake himself as a holy man. The surname of Ángel's tormentors and eventual murderers, Babel, alluding as it does to the tower erected and destroyed in Genesis, stands as a metaphor for Ángel's unconsciously phallic overreaching that is humbled in the novel. Jacques Derrida, in his remarkable discussion of Babel, remarks that the tower's destruction left mankind facing the combined necessity and impossibility of translation (214), an impasse for which he uses James Joyce's term 'he-war'. Translation, etymologically a carrying over to the other side, is impossible in *Ángel Guerra*; it is impossible to attain that unpolluted, bisexual, semi-divine self that Ángel so desires. It is impossible for him to metamorphose into an angel-man because to do so requires giving up too much of his masculinity.[11]

One of the much-remarked features of degeneration was a

process of de-gendering. The last twenty years of the century, in the words of the English novelist George Gissing, were a period of 'sexual anarchy', in which the boundaries of sexual difference seemed to be dissolving (Showalter 3). Decadent artists frequently experimented with gender, attempting to flout the resolutely constructed binariness of the sexes. Effete aesthetes were popularized by Oscar Wilde's *Picture of Dorian Gray*, published in 1891, the same year as *Ángel Guerra*. The themes of transvestism and androgyny were scandalously explored by the French author Rachilde in numerous novels, and in Huysmans's *A rebours* [Against Nature], which appeared in 1884, as well as by Leopoldo Alas in *Su único hijo* (1890). It was the 'era of the Androgyne', proclaimed Albert Samain in an 1893 poem (Paglia 489); but also of amazons, viragos, bisexuals, homosexuals, lesbians, and hermaphrodites. The decadent vision in *Ángel Guerra* consists largely in multiple troubling inversions of sexual characteristics. This aspect of the novel had been foreshadowed in other works from the *Novelas contemporáneas* series, most notably in the characters of Guillermina, Mauricia, Doña Lupe, and Maximiliano in *Fortunata y Jacinta* (1886–7). Yet while in that novel the occasional blurring of gender lines was daring and mysterious, if at times a little frightening for the narrator, in *Ángel Guerra* it is mingled with misogynistic imagery and linked to pain, frustration, and confusion, signalling a much more conservative vision. The gender misfit is now presented as quixotic, beleaguered, and likely to meet a miserable end. In true decadent style, Ángel abdicates his masculinity to Leré, declaring that he is formed by her, since she is the source of ideas and direction and that he is passive and feminine. His 'abdico mi razón' [I abdicate my reason] (233) is only one of many such statements of gender inversion. Dulcenombre, Ángel's mistress in part i, is so thin she also seems masculine to him. He complains inwardly that 'su seno no abultaba más que el de un hombre' [her bosom was no bigger than a man's] (75). Ángel's mother, Doña Sales, is a virago, possessed of a formidable 'temple varonil' [manly character] (27). Don Tomé, the priest, is an angelic soul who is effeminate and retiring, accused of being a woman in disguise (261). Leré symbolically attempts to castrate Ángel, to make them both live as Abélard and Héloïse, and she usurps the masculine role of Abélard, who had to compel a reluctant Héloïse to enter the nunnery. Ángel himself dies at the end of the novel by stabbing:

a symbolic violation of the passive, 'feminine' Ángel that restores him to his masculine senses. He realizes that all his attempts to follow Leré's angelic directions and divorce himself from his instinctual drives were deluded; religion was a chimera, and what he really wanted all along was simply marriage, which Leré will not hear of. There is a clear suggestion that he has invited his own violation by advertising the fact that he will not defend himself if attacked. Ángel undergoes a crisis in masculinity in the novel; he never asserts himself against his mother nor establishes a satisfactory relationship with Leré in which she accepts his domination as her husband.

One of the substrata of *Ángel Guerra* is an anxiety about female independence, both sexual and emotional. By the turn of the century, the classic bourgeois notion of women's innate capacity for sexual continence was on the wane, as the concept of the separate natures and spheres of the sexes began to come under attack. At that very point, however, female passionlessness found a champion in an unexpected quarter: the nascent feminist movements. Some prominent feminist thinkers such as Christabel Pankhurst and Olive Schreiner took to advocating female celibacy as a political response to male corruption (Showalter 22). Their stance led to fears that the New Woman would no longer wish to get married or bear children, an alarming notion that gained further publicity from widely read novels such as Henry James's *The Bostonians* (1886) and Gissing's *The Odd Women* (1891). Gissing's significantly named heroine Rhoda Nunn has taken vows of chastity and service to her feminist ideals. The Dutch Symbolist Jan Toorop depicts his Sphinx in a nun's head-dress (Plate 4). Passionlessness took on disquieting new feminist connotations—if women really had no sexual need for men, why attach themselves to them at all? They could carry out their redemptive mission independent of marriage. Thus the figure of the angel in the house became a site of struggle, that angel war of the novel's title.

The representation of Leré may be seen as analogous to the representations of New Women beginning to appear in novels by other male writers. She is criticized by her uncle, Mancebo, for entering one of 'esas Órdenes modernísimas de hermanas correntonas, que andan de calle en plaza, pidiendo y refistoleando, metiéndose y sacándose por todas partes' [those newfangled Orders of runaround sisters, who are always on the streets and in the squares, soliciting money and scheming, in and out of everything] (136), instead of being 'reclusas y bien trincadas dentro de los hierros' [secluded and properly pinioned behind bars]. After Ángel dies, Leré moves composedly on to her next nursing assignment, apparently not deeply moved by the tragedy she has unwittingly caused, and unperturbed by her uncle's declaration that she is responsible for Ángel's death. Dulce recovers from her abandonment by Ángel and marries. Neither is punished, in stark contrast to Tristana, the openly feminist protagonist of a Galdós novel published the following year, who ends up mutilated and unhappily married. Leré is a *femme fatale* of an unusual ilk. Even an angel, this novel suggests, can be a destructive will-o'-the-wisp luring men to their deaths, when she is not domestic.

But if *Ángel Guerra* betrays anxieties about the New Woman, an even greater source of alarm is the decadent man—a figure 'as terrible as, and in some ways more shocking than, the New Woman', according to an anonymous contributor to the *National Observer* in 1895 (Siegel 209). Ángel concludes, too late, that the inversion of sex roles between them has made him a misshapen, effeminate monster: 'una ley fatal me deformaba, haciéndome a tu imagen y semejanza' [a fatal principle was deforming me, making me in your image and likeness] (340). *Ángel Guerra* makes the contemporary linkage of degeneration and decadence to feminization that was so typical of the turn-of-the-century mentality: the growing feminization of society was equated with decline, and decadence was construed as effeminate, because civilization itself was seen as a result of masculine intelligence and vigour (Siegel 213). For members of the bourgeoisie in the nineteenth century, any confusion of gender was bound to have implications for civilization itself, which they saw as organized into 'separate spheres', a figure which had planetary, cosmic resonance (Siegel 209, 212). If the spheres were not, after all, separate, the whole concept of civilization and progress as they knew it—the whole ascent from barbarism—was threatened. One of the symptoms of a society whose belief-system is under stress, according to Mary Douglas, is the rigour with which it polices its own arbitrary and internally defined cultural boundaries. Hybrids are alarming—and attractive—because they cross boundaries. Galdós demonstrates both the attraction and the alarm by compulsively producing and then destroying gender hybrids in his novels. All his really memorable heroes have manifestly feminine traits, surrendering some of their masculinity to the women they love, and none of them survives intact: Maximiliano Rubín and León Roch wind up insane, Máximo Manso dies disconsolate, and Ángel Guerra is murdered. As Siegel reminds us, implicit in the argument about woman's place—reiterated with increasing force as women began encroaching on the public sphere—was a warning to men not to cross conventional social boundaries either (206).

For Galdós's friend Leopoldo Alas, the anxieties about masculinity that *Ángel Guerra* engenders seem to have spilled over into anxieties about the paternity of literary works of art, the virility of the writer himself. In his review of *Ángel Guerra*, Alas begins with a long and seemingly arbitrary diatribe against the feminization of the novel in advanced western European societies, where he claims that women novelists almost outnumber men. He then qualifies his attack, allowing that an author must be a slightly feminized man—but not too much so:

No hay por qué renegar de lo mucho que tiene el arte de femenino. No está mal sentirse en el alma un *poco hembra*, siempre que en alma y cuerpo haya garantías sólidas de no llegar a un desequilibrio de facultades . . . pero siempre será verdad que el afeminamiento es un peligro. Se cuenta que los romanos de la decadencia se vestían de mujer.

There is no reason to deny the extent to which this is a feminine art. There is nothing wrong in feeling one's soul to be a *touch womanish*, as long as both soul and body show solid guarantees of not coming to an imbalance of faculties . . . but it will always be true that feminization is dangerous. They say the Romans dressed as women when they grew decadent.

The existence of so many novels, Alas continues, is 'un peligro y hasta un síntoma del mal del siglo' [a danger and even a symptom of our century's sickness], as is the excessive expansiveness, the verborrhoea, that novels typically exhibit (213–14).

Clarín is closer to Nordau in this passage than he himself might have supposed; though he ardently opposed many of Nordau's views, he too held that art was irrevocably being taken over by womanish elements. If art represented civilization and the novel was a mirror of society, then it was deeply disturbing that the novel should be feminized ('un afeminamiento'), since it was a symptom of society's pathological decline. Art was supposed to reflect the times. The excess, self-absorption, chaos, and effeminacy that Alas complains of in Galdós's novel—all of which are part of Arthur Symons's list of decadent characteristics in literature—diverge sharply from Alas's ideal of manly, classical restraint and simplicity (Siegel 208). He finds *Ángel Guerra* perturbing because it *contributes* to the decline of society through its prolix, uncontrolled style, even though it purports to be indicting decadence and degeneration.

Galdós does not go so far as Alas himself, Huysmans, or Rachilde, in dissecting sexual and moral depravity in his characters. Leré has none of Emma Valcárcel's morbid lubricity and vampire tendencies, nor is there a Galdosian female incarnation of pure evil here to match Serafina 'Gorgheggi' of *Su único hijo* in her serpent-like malice. Nevertheless, *Ángel Guerra* clearly bears strong decadent characteristics. This is a novel profoundly ambivalent about progress, full of relapses and failures, and pessimistic about the possibility of remaking a character or switching gender roles. If decadence is, as Mario Praz suggests, a hybrid of old and new, the late incarnation of Romanticism, then *Ángel Guerra*'s privileging of male subjectivity can be seen as an extension of the androcentricity of that movement, which constructs Woman as the Other, never the self. *Ángel Guerra* is itself a hybrid of naturalism, realism, and decadentism, a decadent morality tale—and this separates it from decadent work *per se*, which jettisoned ethics in its pursuit of pure sensation. Gender inversions for Galdós in 1891 are monstrous, or associated with morbidity, not the slightly dangerous but attractive free play they were in *Fortunata y Jacinta*. This is a subliminally conservative and misogynistic novel, for all Ángel's compulsive idealizing of Leré.[12] It combines the androcentricity of Romanticism with the misogyny of naturalism, a movement that was inevitably determinist and essentialist because of its debt to scientific theories that were deeply racist and sexist. While *La Regenta* recasts patriarchal misogyny in naturalist form by constructing the text as a feminine body in the throes of decomposition (Valis 1992), *Ángel Guerra* in contrast is a male body—Ángel's tortured erection—being painfully repressed by a woman who is a particularly *fin-de-siècle* combination of Salome, sphinx, and nun.

That antipathy to any confusion of gender roles masked broader social anxieties seems clear from the excessive, nightmarish rhetoric of disease, monstrosity, and violence employed to articulate it, both in this novel and in the wider social context we have examined. But just as the rhetoric condemning French naturalism bespoke envy and a concerted attempt at emulation, so the rhetoric against gender transgression speaks not only of fear but also, covertly, of longing. The Book of Genesis describes an important chapter in human degeneration: the myth of Babel attests to both the dream of oneness and the fact of dividedness. The translation that is necessary but impossible in a post-lapsarian world involves a crossing over, a kind of linguistic cross-dressing, that will always be desired but never satisfactorily attained. Read sex for language and we have a description of Galdós's *Ángel Guerra*, that monument to a man's confused yearning to possess the Other and to be the Other that forbids the very impulses it enacts.

NOTES

1. The novel was, furthermore, written at a crucial juncture in Galdós's private life, as he experienced possibly his most domestic and his most radical relationships with women. Galdós left Madrid to spend the winter of 1890–1 in Santander, where he bought land and began constructing a villa so that he could be close to Lorenza Cobián, a woman from an Asturian peasant family, who was pregnant with his child. Jan. 1891 saw the birth of his daughter María, to Lorenza, whose name and nickname (Leré) Galdós transferred to the heroine of his novel (Pattison 27). At the same time, Galdós was conducting a clandestine affair with the celebrated novelist and feminist Emilia Pardo Bazán.
2. Nordau's work became notorious in Spain with the publication of the French edition in 1894. Pardo Bazán attacked his theories in a series of articles in *Los Lunes de El Imparcial*, the first of which was entitled 'La nueva cuestión palpitante'. A Spanish translation of *Degeneration* by Nicolás Salmerón was published in 1902 (Davis 307–8).
3. Bénédict Morel attributed degeneration, in part, to the effect of nerve-poisons such as tobacco, alcohol, and opium (Pick 50).
4. Both Jekyll and Hyde's names have transparently sinister double meanings: 'I kill' and 'Hide'. A dramatized version of the work played to packed houses in the West End in 1888. Angel has two other selves, one bad, the other good: as well as the beast, there is a *doppelgänger* priest, who appears later in the novel in hallucinatory episodes that occur during Lent, while Angel is fasting.
5. The description of Tirso, who has lived in rustic isolation from 'civilized' society and progress (180–1), reminds Pito of an African he has known during his slave-trading days. The connection being made in European societies between the supposedly lower classes and races, both of which were characterized as 'barbaric', was a product of turn-of-the-century psychoses about the ubiquitousness of barbarism and the embattled nature of progress.

6. Irigaray merges the terms mystic and hysteric, arguing that mysticism is a feminine function, one of the few areas where female desire may be legitimately and publicly articulated (238–52).

7. This lithograph, published in the art nouveau magazine *L'Estampe originale*, is included in Jullian 202.

8. The Sphinx best represents the fusion of opposites for the decadents: they repeatedly represent her as a female creature, with a beautiful woman's head and naked torso, ending in an animal lower body with claws and tail. The sphinxes of Moreau, Khnopff, and Toorop (Plates 2–4) are reproduced and discussed in Dijkstra 325–31.

9. Ángel is obliged to abstain from seeing Leré during Lent, when he also eats very little (251).

10. The theme of female sexual mutilation and dismemberment was a graphic part of *fin de siècle* mentality in Victorian England, where Jack the Ripper terrorized London in 1888, hacking off the breasts and other parts of prostitutes and hanging them from nails on walls.

11. In their insistence on architectural imagery, Galdós's contemporaries—notably Clarín (Alas 156) and Peres (Sotelo 108)—implicate the novel itself in the Babelian enterprise, complaining of its overreaching excess and remarking that it needed cutting down to size, like the overweening tower itself.

12. One of Nordau's disciples in Spain, Ernesto Bark, accused Galdós's neo-spiritualism of being akin to Carlism in an article in *Germinal* in 1897, 'La crítica decadente' (Davis 314).

WORKS CITED

ALAS 'CLARÍN', LEOPOLDO (1991). *Galdós, novelista*, ed. Adolfo Sotelo Vázquez. Barcelona: PPU.

ANDREWS, JEAN (1991). 'Saints and Strumpets: Female Stereotypes in Valle-Inclán', in Lisa P. Condé and Stephen M. Hart (eds.), *Feminist Readings on Spanish and Latin-American Literature*. Lewiston: Edwin Mellen, 27–35.

BAKHTIN, MIKHAIL (1968). *Rabelais and his World*, trans. Helene Iswolsky. Cambridge, Mass.: MIT Press.

BARROWS, SUSANNA (1981). *Distorting Mirrors: Visions of the Crowd in Late Nineteenth-Century France*. New Haven, Conn.: Yale University Press.

DAVIS, LISA (1977). 'Max Nordau, *Degeneración* y la decadencia de España', *Cuadernos Hispanoamericanos*, 326–7: 307–23.

DERRIDA, JACQUES (1985). 'Des Tours de Babel', in *Difference in Translation*, ed. F. Graham. Ithaca, NY: Cornell University Press. 209–48.

DIJKSTRA, BRAM (1986). *Idols of Perversity: Fantasies of Feminine Evil in Fin-de-Siècle Culture*. New York: Oxford University Press.

DOUGLAS, MARY (1976). *Purity and Danger: An Analysis of Concepts of Pollution and Taboo*. London: Routledge & Kegan Paul.

GILMAN, RICHARD (1979). *Decadence: The Strange Life of an Epithet*. New York: Farrar, Straus & Giroux.

IRIGARAY, LUCE (1974). *Spéculum de l'autre femme*. Paris: Éditions de Minuit.

JAGOE, CATHERINE (1994). *Ambiguous Angels: Gender in the Novels of Galdós*. Berkeley, Calif.: University of California Press.

JULLIAN, PHILIPPE (1971). *Dreamers of Decadence: Symbolist Painters of the 1890s*, trans. Robert Baldick. New York: Praeger Publishers.

KRONIK, JOHN W. (1976a). 'Galdós and the Grotesque', *Anales Galdosianos*, Supplement: 39–54.

—— (1976b). 'Rubén Darío y la entrada del simbolismo en España', in Eleanor Krane Paucer (ed.), *Poemas y ensayos para un homenaje a Phyllis B. Turnbull*. Madrid: Tecnos. 95–106.

LAKHDARI, SADI (1987). 'Le sein coupé dans *Ángel Guerra*', *Les Langues Néo-Latines*, 260: 117–31.

MILLER, NANCY K. (1980). *The Heroine's Text: Readings in the French and English Novel, 1722–1782*. New York: Columbia University Press.

NORDAU, MAX (1968). *Degeneration*, trans. George L. Mosse. New York: Howard Fertig.

O'CONNOR, D. J. (1988). 'The Recurrence of Images in *Ángel Guerra*', *Ánales Galdosianos*, 23: 73–82.

PAGLIA, CAMILLE (1990). *Sexual Personae: Art and Decadence from Nefertiti to Emily Dickinson*. New Haven, Conn.: Yale University Press.

PARDO BAZÁN, EMILIA (1973). 'Ángel Guerra', in *Obras completas*, vol. iii. Madrid: Aguilar. 1093–105.

PATTISON, WALTER (1973). 'Two Women in the Life of Galdós', *Anales Galdosianos*, 8: 23–31.

PÉREZ GALDÓS, BENITO (1982). *Ángel Guerra*, in *Obras completas: novelas*, ed. Federico Carlos Sáinz de Robles, vol. iii. Madrid: Aguilar.

PERROT, MICHELE (1990) (ed.). *A History of Private Life*, vol. iv: *From the Fires of Revolution to the Great War*. Cambridge, Mass.: Harvard University Press.

PICK, DANIEL (1989). *Faces of Degeneration: A European Disorder, c.1848–c.1914*. Cambridge: Cambridge University Press.

PRAZ, MARIO (1968). *The Romantic Agony*, trans. Angus Davidson. Cleveland: Meridian.

REED, JOHN R. (1985). *Decadent Style*. Athens, Oh.: Ohio University Press.

SHOWALTER, ELAINE (1990). *Sexual Anarchy: Gender and Culture at the Fin de Siècle*. New York: Viking.

SIEGEL, SANDRA (1985). 'Literature and Degeneration: The Representation of "Decadence" ', in J. Edward Chamberlin and Sander L. Gilman (eds.), *Degeneration: The Dark Side of Progress*. New York: Columbia University Press. 199–219.

SOTELO, MARISA (1990). *Ángel Guerra' de Benito Pérez Galdós y sus críticos (1891)*. Barcelona: PPU.

STALLYBRASS, PETER, and WHITE, ALLON, (1986). *The Politics and Poetics of Transgression*. Ithaca, NY: Cornell University Press.

VALIS, NOËL (1981). *The Decadent Vision in Leopoldo Alas*. Baton Rouge, La.: Louisiana State University Press.

—— (1992). 'On Monstrous Birth: Leopoldo Alas' *La Regenta*', in Brian Nelson (ed.), *Naturalism in the European Novel: New Critical Perspectives*. New York: Berg. 191–209.

—— (1993) '*Ángel Guerra*, or the Monster Novel', in Jo Labanyi (ed.), *Galdós*. London: Longman. 218–34.

9

The Force of Parental Presence in
La Regenta

ALISON SINCLAIR

Protagonists of novels are well known for their facility for losing parents, particularly mothers, *en route to* the opening pages of chapter 1. Ana Ozores is no exception to this, but *La Regenta* as a novel is exceptional in the degree to which it counterpoises against the traditional image of the absent (because dead and lost) mother that of a present and intolerable one. This is made the more dramatic because the intolerable presence is not that of the protagonist's stepmother (stock hate-image of fairy-tales) but that of a real mother, attached to the man who appears to promise spiritual deliverance to the protagonist: namely Fermín's mother, Paula de Pas. Thus the reader (not to mention the protagonist) is deprived of the let-out provided by a stepmother (she is not really ours, there is no fundamental connection between us and her, other than the simply legal one). Paula poses for us the drama that we cannot avoid, that of a close relationship that suffocates and yet cannot be rejected. She is inescapably there, physically and mentally, throughout the novel: ever present for Fermín, and ever present for the reader as a reminder that the mothering Ana desires might not be the idyllic experience she appears to long for, were she able to achieve it. Paula is also at the root of Fermín's relationship with Ana, affecting the reasons for which he is drawn to Ana and the manner of his separation from her. My intention is to examine two central features of Doña Paula's presence in *La Regenta*: her influence on Fermín's style of masculinity, and her effect on the nature of the relationship between Fermín and Ana. I shall argue that, throughout the text, Fermín and his mother remain locked in an infantile, essentially pre-Oedipal relationship, never resolved and unchallenged by an appropriate father-figure.[1] At the same time I shall highlight the gender-associated resonances of the Fermín/Paula dyad when understood in the context of the honour/shame cultures typical of the Mediterranean.

Ana's absent, or lost, mother is the cause of considerable idealization of the maternal state. Mothering is imagined rather than experienced, and, in Ana's case, longed for rather than rejected. Awareness of the piteous state of Ana Ozores as a motherless child, indeed as eventual orphan, permeates the narrative, not least that which Ana fabricates for herself. Her initial recounting of her life undertaken in preparation for a general confession with Fermín de Pas in chapter 3 verges on a rehearsal or performance to herself of her perceived role in which she appears in a state of solitude that has all the appearance of abandonment.[2] Her vision of motherhood, or rather of the mothering of which the child is object, is, despite its literary self-consciousness, simple and unequivocally positive, in that it presents a traditional, idealistic vision of the mother's role, nature, and function. It is an ideal formulated in the absence of the 'reality' of Ana's mother, who is never presented directly in the text, and whose shifting nature is indicated by the way her occupation changes from dressmaking to dancing in the mouth of Vetusta's gossips.

Other images of mothers in the text are less than positive, ranging from Visitación, who neglects her family for the social excitement of the Vegallana circle, to the pious and ineffectual Doña Lucía Carraspique. These mothers, however, pale in significance when compared with the all-too-present, terrible mother of the text, Paula. Her appearance is delayed until a third of the way through the novel, and the dramatic retelling of her shared history with Fermín occurs significantly in chapter 15, at midpoint.

La Regenta is concerned as much with the excesses of the material world as with the insecurity and inadequacy of human fantasy. Paula's first appearance portrays her as an immovable physical obstacle, and signals her symbolic and emotional connotations. Her appearance in chapter 11 is sudden, her physical bulk dominating Fermín's field of vision:

Cuando Petra iba a atravesar el umbral, ocupó la puerta por completo una mujer tan alta casi como el Magistral y que parecía más ancha de hombros; tenía la figura cortada a hachazos, vestía como una percha . . . Era doña Paula, la madre del Provisor.

As Petra was about to step out of the room, the doorway was completely filled by a woman almost as tall as the canon, who seemed even
broader-shouldered than him; her physique was hewn by an axe, her
clothes hung from her . . . It was Doña Paula, the canon's mother.
(i. 412–13)[3]

Her second appearance at the opening of chapter 15 is equally
dramatic:

En lo alto de la escalera, en el descanso del primer piso, doña Paula,
con una palmatoria en una mano y el cordel de la puerta de la calle
en la otra, veía silenciosa, inmóvil, a su hijo subir lentamente con la
cabeza inclinada, oculto el rostro por el sombrero de anchas alas.

At the top of the stairs, on the first-floor landing, Doña Paula, a candlestick in one hand and the cord for opening the street-door in the
other, watched silently and motionlessly as her son, head bowed, his
face hidden beneath the wide brim of his hat, came up towards her.
(i. 541)

The two delineations of Paula, looming, huge, a figure of power,
are of a character who is larger than life. She blocks the doorway
and bars the way up the stairs. In each case it is as though she
is perceived from the perspective of the child, towering above
him, so that Fermín's perception of her is presented not as that
of a man in his mid-thirties with considerable local importance,
but as that of the child under an omnipotent mother's control.
On these two occasions, moreover, she appears just as a misdeed
of some sort has been committed. In the first instance, her arrival clashes with Fermín's preceding thoughts on his lost 'otro
yo' [other self] (i. 410), and those aroused by Petra's visit with
a letter from Ana. In the second instance, Fermín has failed not
only to return home to lunch, but to inform his mother of his
absence. The two instances thus are overlaid with the sense of
guilt and powerlessness a small child might feel in an unmediated
relationship with his mother.

Paula is presented not only as terrible and omnipotent, but as
a symbol of death. Significantly, however, this is conveyed
through her portrayal as an 'amortajada' (shrouded one), an
image which draws on a tradition linking women to the transi-
tions of life, from the threshold of birth to that of death.[4]
Unusually, however, Paula is not so much the death-bringer as
the one who has herself been victim. She is already dead, her
appearance tells us, and her physical image evokes the mortality

that awaits the living. It also prefigures in graphic form the reproach she will consistently make to Fermín that he is bringing death (failure) to their joint enterprise of social elevation, and, on an emotional level, that by his neglect of her he is causing her death. There is about her presence a strange combination of physical indeterminacy (she appears less than her age, she appears similar to Fermín, her gender is ambiguous), and yet awful clarity:

Tenía sesenta años, que parecían poco más de cincuenta ... la frente era estrecha y huesuda, pálida, como todo el rostro; los ojos de un azul muy claro, no tenían más expresión que la semejanza de un contacto frío, eran ojos mudos; por ellos nadie sabría nada de aquella mujer. ... Parecía doña Paula ... una amortajada.

She was sixty, but looked little more than fifty ... her forehead narrow and bony, pale, like the rest of her face; the only expression given out by her light blue eyes was the semblance of a chilly contact; no one would find out anything from them about that woman. ... Doña Paula seemed to be ... a corpse. (i. 413)

On her reappearance on the landing as Fermín mounts the stairs she has become a solid object, blocking his way, but with the aspect of a ghost: 'El hijo subía y la madre no se movía, parecía dispuesta a estorbarle el paso, allí en medio, tiesa, como un fantasma negro, largo y anguloso' [As her son went up the stairs, his mother did not move, seeming to be about to block his way, standing there in his path, stiff, like a tall, black, angular ghost] (i. 541). In both cases, Paula stands at an entrance and bars the way by filling its space. In the first case, the doorway connects Fermín's part of the house to her own. He is in the seclusion of his part of the house, but has no freedom to move beyond that seclusion. Her presence there at that point signals the way in which she will block his attempted move out of the seclusion of the priesthood in which she has placed him and into an alternative relationship with Ana. In the second case, the doorway leads from the outside world (traditionally the domain of the male) to their shared residence. Her presence this time at the top of the stairs signals not only the heights to which she has elevated the two of them, but the power relationship between them in which she is the dominant, he the subjugated partner. The 'palmatoria' in her hand—a candlestick but also carrying the meaning of the 'ferule' traditionally associated with the schoolteacher in the classroom—reinforces the image of the mother who is in control and the mother who will punish, at the same time signalling her 'magisterial' position, the emotional reality of which is set against the publicly imaged relationship in which he is the magisterial one, the Magistral, and she the subordinate female keeper of the house.

Paula's story, placed before us in full in chapter 15, is violent, entangled, a struggle for social betterment via the route of sexual compromise and astute manipulation of the weakness and susceptibility to public opinion of others, particularly priests: an experience that renders her hypersensitive to Fermín's vulnerability to gossip. Noël Valis has indicated the link between Paula, the earth, the activity of the miners, and the symbolic status contained in her surname Raíces (43). Paula, however, embodies these associations in travestied form. Within the social setting where she grows up poverty reigns; the earth may render riches, but rather than being natural ones they take the form of money (for the miners). Moreover, as a girl Paula is disempowered, prevented from participating in these riches: all she can do is to carry earth (i. 548), not profit from its contents. Her way of desiring money is not initially in the form of ambition, but as something which will fill a void: it is desire rooted in 'lack', on a clear material level but with all the resonances of lack of power in a patriarchal society. She learns of the worth of money 'por la gran pena con que los suyos lo lloraban ausente' [from the degree to which those about her mourned its absence] (ii. 548), but she can only fulfil ambition vicariously through her son. Vicarious and dislocated action and feeling are hallmarks of the novel, not least in this mother-figure who dominates emotionally precisely because she is disempowered.

An example of this dislocation is found in Paula's sexuality. She exudes a strong sense of the sexual, but is portrayed as being ambiguous of gender. It is as if her experience of sexuality is a tool employed merely to achieve social betterment and material comfort. Her strong, ungainly form arouses the appetites of the miners (not to mention the priest to whom she becomes housekeeper), but she is as detached and calculating about her use of her capacity for attraction as might be any pimp for his prostitute. The image of sex as brutal and energetic is not, of course, restricted to the evocation of Paula's battles, whether with Francisco de Pas, the priest, or the miners who sup at her tavern. Significantly it is reiterated in the description given by Álvaro in chapter 20 of his battles with Ramona, conducted, as are the struggles of Paula with Francisco, in a 'panera' [granary].[5] The struggles are silent, conducted with kicks and punches, and, in Ramona's case, aggressively oral (the association of orality/sexuality will recur in the cigar motif discussed below). Indeed the textual resonances between the story of Paula and that of Ramona are such as to arouse within the reader the question of whether the secret history of *La Regenta* might conceivably contain an encounter, however incongruous, between Álvaro and Paula.

Paula's history contains those elements which will underlie her relationship with her son: men have access to riches and power, but men are foolish and can be tyrannized. If they are prey to primitive passion, desire for the earth, riches characterized as 'lodo' [mud], then women's route to power is by their connection with earth and 'lodo': if men have appetite, that is, if they suffer hunger and thirst, then women's power lies in their ability to assuage that appetite. The hunger and thirst of the miners is real and physical enough (i. 554), but is also symbolic of the physical longing and appetite of man. Women, at least to Paula's mind (and arguably more generally in this patriarchal novel), do not enjoy an analogous appetite, simply the power to exploit male appetite for their own comfort and freedom from poverty.[6] Not for nothing is Paula aware of the dangers Fermín ran in his relationship with the Brigadiera. Men are also characterized in the narrative as 'fieras' [wild beasts], which it is the woman's role to tame or civilize. Thus woman, somewhat surprisingly, falls on the side of 'Culture' rather than 'Nature'.

By contrast, Fermín is portrayed as unaware of his own sexuality, or as conveniently denying it, or as satisfying its needs in a place distant even from the text, so private a function is it. As a result, his sexuality is not dislocated but ambiguous, intimately linked with the struggle between himself and his mother for the possession of power and the burden of shame.

In Paula's role in society, in her relationship with men, and in her resulting relationship with Fermín, there is the characteristic splitting of gender attributes found in honour/shame cultures. At the same time the habitual distribution of such attributes is periodically redistributed in a way that accounts for, and is explained by, the sexual ambiguity of the two characters. Within honour/shame cultures, honour is that positive quality which can be possessed by men, whereas women are associated with shame or loss of honour. Although there are ways other than sexual misdemeanour in which loss of honour can occur, the real or suspected sexual transgressions of a woman are the prime reasons for a man's loss of honour. As a result, such cultures produce a vigorous splitting off by men of the attributes of sensuality, flexibility, emotion, and the physical life which, carrying the major risk of honour-loss, are deemed to pertain to women.[7]

Fermín and Paula do not constitute the husband/wife pair basic to an honour culture, or even the father/daughter dyad in which honour is traditionally held or won by the former and lost by the latter, but are son and mother. In the first instance Fermín, being the child, is the dependant, and subsequently the object used by his mother for social advancement. Thus, in a sense, where Paula moves into the masculine domain of controlling money and entering into transactions, Fermín occupies the position of the woman whose usefulness and status is that of an object to be used in social barter and gain. He is 'possessed' by his mother as a useful object, rather than being himself a subject with its own volition. In the way that Paula casts the relationship, Fermín has the female part, the shame. Uppermost in her mind is the awareness that he is the instrument through which honour for the two is liable to be lost, and that this will be through his sexual indiscretion. The case of the Brigadiera has been ample proof of this (i. 419). Her suspiciousness about his potential indiscretion with Ana is conveyed in graphic, physical form at the close of chapter 11 as she examines his room, seeming to 'sniff with her eyes' (i. 424). (Underlying this situation there is the parallel with Ana, also an object, mercilessly subjected to the sexual market by her aunts, her value placed in question by the incident with Germán, as Fermín's value is placed in question by the Brigadiera.)

There is effectively a struggle, even competition, between Fermín and Paula over the question of which of them is to be associated with feminine shame, filth, and lack of purity. Initially the two of them occupy traditional places in the honour/shame dyad: Paula associated with secret filth, the physical life, the dubious traffic with the miners; Fermín kept distanced by his mother from all of this. The way he is viewed publicly as an adult, however, suggests a sexual ambiguity rooted in his unclear place in the honour/shame dyad. The opening pages in which he excites the interest and envy of Bismarck and Celedonio on account of a mixture of attributes declare an uncertainty of gender, or of publicly recognized gender. Hence the prurient interest of Celedonio in Fermín's reputed use of make-up (i. 96), and Bismarck's admiration for his 'señorío' [lordliness], which consists in his feminine attribute of spotlessness: '¡Aquello era señorío! ¡Ni una mancha! Los pies parecían los de una dama' [This was real lordliness! Not a single stain! His feet looked like a lady's] (i. 101).

Bismarck's comment about Fermín's lack of any 'mancha' [stain] alludes to the success of his public separation from shame, while the attribute of having a woman's foot (a motif which will acquire its full measure of shame when Vetusta in its entirety turns out to glimpse Ana's naked feet) places him firmly within the feminine realm, as does the narrative's outlining of the high colour in his cheeks, a denotation relating to love and shame (i. 102).

In their shared past, Paula is shown as regarding herself as the one who is stained by contact while her son is to remain pure: 'Allí estaba ella para barrer hacia la calle aquel lodo que entraba todos los días por la puerta de la taberna; a ella la manchaba, pero a él no' [Her place was to be there to sweep into the street the dirt that came in every day through the door of the tavern; she was sullied by it, but not him] (i. 556). But in so far as she takes a masculine part in the dyad, she assumes responsibility for ensuring that he, like a woman, remains pure, and does not cause the pair of them to lose honour and status.

Fermín is thus placed in the strait-jacket of purity, and, more than that, of social respectability. His role as priest, with its requirement of celibacy, prevents him from expressing his masculine sexuality, making him subject to internal splitting. There is a private self, aware of this unrealized masculinity, and a public self invested in the role of purity foisted on him by his mother's ambition and activity, which is inclined to make her the repository of all shame, as a way of disowning his physical appetites.

Though kept separate from the history of his mother's traffic with the miners, he is clearly aware of it (i. 555–6). The combination of commercial enterprise and sexual barter leads to his association of his mother with money, and hence filth.[8] He projects on to her all the shame-associated financial activity. Thus at the end of the fateful day in which he has eaten with the Vegallanas, failed to return home to eat with his mother, and has projected his own guilt over sexual indiscretion on to the priest from Contracayes (i. 460–4), the prospect of going downstairs to be present for the accounts inspires nothing less than 'asco' [disgust]: 'imaginaba que abajo había un gran foco de podredumbre, aguas estancadas' [he imagined that down below there was a great centre of rottenness, of stagnant water] (i. 564). Situating the concerns of money in the lower part of the house is symbolic of the way both Paula and Fermín push financial dealings below a surface that is apparently pure to public eye. Within the space occupied by them for living, Fermín's apartments are kept strictly separate from those of his mother, and the residence and their entire way of life are marked by austerity, orderliness, and astringent cleanliness.[9]

Despite their sharply demarcated separate realms in the house, Fermín is locked in an uncomfortably close dyad with his mother. For him, her history associated with filth is liable to drag them down, whereas for her it is his potential future action which could have this undesired effect. We can see him struggle to separate from what she represents, taking on as he does so the 'honour' part of the honour/shame relationship. He envisages himself as a conqueror,[10] possessed of his own nobility and 'ambición de dominar' [will to dominate], separate from his mother's sins and 'aquellos a que le había arrastrado la codicia de su madre' [the sins his mother's greed had dragged him into] (i. 423). In taking on the guise of conqueror he is also reacting defensively against his own experience of being conquered or dominated by his mother, just as he resorts to her technique of the icy, silent, stare in order to subjugate others to his power. It is a manœuvre of compensation, reminiscent of the surveillance of the panopticon. It is no surprise that the theological issue we find him contemplating in chapter 2 is the doctrine of infallibility, a doctrine described as a desperate and heroic act like that of the Christians thrown to the lions, the images used to describe it reiterating the view of the miners at his mother's tavern as beasts to be tamed: 'un desafío formidable de la fe. . . . Era como estar en el Circo entre fieras' [a formidable challenge made by faith. . . . It was like being in the Circus amid the wild beasts] (i. 402). Yet when it comes to his own sexual needs, he splits for his own convenience and accepts those provisions for his sexual satisfaction made by his mother (and insinuated to the reader), rationalizing his actions on the grounds that Ana is unconcerned with anything other than his spiritual side: '¿qué le importa a mi doña Ana que mi corpachón de cazador montañés viva como quiera cuando me aparto de ella?' [What does it matter to my Doña Ana how my mountain huntsman's body lives when I am away from her?] (ii. 244).

The Paula/Fermín dyad is spectacularly lacking a father, despite Fermín's possession in the past of a real father, Francisco de Pas, and the effective second father found for him by Paula in the person of Camoirán, the Bishop (i. 559).[11] They present elusive and contrasting possibilities for identification. Francisco, the natural father, represents qualities of strength, sexuality, and aggression, proven by his physical conquest of Paula (i. 550–2). A wastrel, a man of fantasy, who escapes the control even of Paula, he is recalled by Fermín in the stereotypically masculine guise of the 'cazador', an image present when Fermín looks at himself in the mirror and sees a strong body capable of physical exertion (to be exercised in the contained and potentially ridiculous episode of the swing in chapter 13), failing to notice the incipient paunch signalled in the following chapter (i. 525), just as he forgets Francisco's less admirable qualities. In the last visit to El Vivero, he appeals dramatically and ridiculously to Víctor as a fellow huntsman: 'Vamos, Quintanar, usted que es cazador . . . y yo que también lo soy . . . ¡al monte! ¡al monte!' [Come on, Quintanar, you're a huntsman . . . just like me! . . . To the woods now!'] (ii. 407). The occasion of what is to be the fateful meal at the Vegallanas in chapter 13 is his father's saint's day: he visits all the Franciscos of Vetusta society, unmindful of the Francisco most closely related to him.

Camoirán, weaker, effeminate, emotional, represents the emasculated form of masculine power open to Fermín within the Church. His example is of failed rather than achieved masculinity, and the two engage in avoidance. While Camoirán refuses to submit to the influence of Fermín in the capricious, frivolous feminity of his salon (i. 439), Fermín differentiates himself by his style of preaching. Camoirán is all effusion and feeling, but Fermín bases his preaching on dogma, closely argued texts, offering an austerity of presentation, a definitiveness of message that reflects the austerity of his life-style, and an attempt at masculine demarcation within the feminine boundaries of the Church. The essential asexuality of his public figure and mode of activity is the nearest he comes to establishing masculine gender.[12]

Nimetz argues that Fermín in the course of the novel undergoes a second adolescence (247). Even adolescence, however, is disowned, lodged in Camoirán, who on being found by Fermín in the company of Visitación and Olvido 'se ruborizó, como un estudiante de latín sorprendido por sus mayores con la primera tagarnina' [blushed, like a schoolboy caught out by his elders with his first cigar] (i. 454–5). The association of active masculine sexuality and smoking, a set piece in European novels of adultery, appears in *La Regenta* in details ranging from Ana's exasperated contemplation of her husband's unfinished cigar (ii. 10), to Álvaro's leisured smoking while others in the Casino talk of their sexual conquests (ii. 172), and Paula's indication of her phallic masculine tendency in her rolling of a cigarette (i. 414). If Fermín shows his adolescence, it is in his exasperation here with an inadequate parental figure, with whom identification is impossible.

It could equally be argued that Fermín is locked into the earlier pre-Oedipal phase, given the markedly infantile manner of his relationship to his mother, which is transferred on to the relationship with Ana. This primary relationship is powerful and dramatic. Chapter 15 reveals the primitive way that Paula uses silence, the enormous 'parches untados con sebo' [lard poultices] on her temples being the visible signs of her anger. The power of this non-verbal anger, familiar to Fermín, is no less strong for its familiarity. When the accusations come (i. 544) they are pitched at his absence. His offence is ingratitude, abandonment of his mother: '¡Si no hay madre que valga! ¿Te has acordado de tu madre en todo el día?' [It's no good 'mothering' me! Have you given one thought to your mother today?] (i. 544). What is produced here is the rage and fear of the child when the mother is absent, the terror of separation before a sense of time has developed. Here Paula reverses roles and the mother adopts the position of the child: it is she who has been left and is defenceless, and she who can now throw a temper-tantrum in response. But she also subjects Fermín to a catechism inviting submission: 'Fermo, ¿te fue bién toda la vida dejándote guiar por tu madre . . . ? ¿Te saqué yo o no de la pobreza?' [Fermo, have you not found it good all your life to be guided by your mother . . . ? Did I or did I not lift you out of poverty?] (i. 546). Later, a simple state of union (or is the narrator's tongue in his cheek?) results from this emotional bullying: 'Los recuerdos evocados, sin intención patética, por doña Paula, habían enternecido a Fermo. Ya había allí un hijo y una madre' [The memories Doña Paula had conjured up, without meaning to soften him, had touched Fermo. Now once again they were mother and son] (i. 547). The restoration of the mother's power is signalled by her familiar use of 'Fermo'.[13]

Early emotional habits resurface in the relationship between Fermín and Ana. Fermín's desire for an ideal mother is partly a rejection of Paula, partly a desire for early non-differentiation, for an escape from the alternatives of solitude and conflict. His desire for a perfect, non-conflictive mother comes, unsurprisingly, at the end of the dramas of chapter 15 when, in his solitude, he resembles Ana in her consciously motherless state. He engages in a mood of self-lamentation: 'Su madre le quería mucho, a ella se lo debía todo, ya se sabe . . . pero él necesitaba amor más blando que el de doña Paula' [His mother loved him dearly, he owed everying to her, it was clear . . . but he needed a more tender love than that of Doña Paula] (i. 561). Ana responds in chapter 22 to his 'palidez interesante' [interesting pallor] and other Romantically accentuated signs of tiredness, speaks to him 'con voz de madre cariñosa' [in the voice of an affectionate mother] (ii. 243), and in chapter 23 shows her responsiveness to his declared 'motherless state' (ii. 288).

Exposed to the turmoil of his feelings for Ana, Fermín displays a variety of features of the paranoid-schizoid position, a term used by Klein to designate an infant state in which all feelings of discomfort are projected out, thus rendering the external world more hostile and terrifying.[14] Characteristic of this are his violent mood swings, within which Ana is given the attributes of the bad mother. Betrayal, which we might equate with absence or a foreshadowing of the Oedipal crisis, is her crime, one he does not impute to his mother. When Fermín hears of Ana's faint in the arms of Álvaro, he remembers his mother: 'su madre no le había hecho nunca traición, su madre era suya, era la misma carne' [his mother had never betrayed him, his mother belonged to him, she was the same flesh]. Ana's fundamental fault, it would appear, consists in not belonging to that original dyad and thus being alien, an indisputable Other: 'Ana, la otra, una desconocida, un cuerpo extraño que se le había atravesado en el corazón' [Ana, the other one, the unknown one, an alien body that had lodged itself in his heart] (ii. 314).[15]

Fermín also places on Ana that same label of ingratitude Paula had given him. After the interpolation of Paula's story in chapter 15 (i. 547–60), there is a doubly oriented passage where Paula's version of her struggles and his ingratitude is presented as a version of reality ('Ella le había hecho hombre' [She had made him a man] (i. 559–60)), and within which the restricted masculinity imposed on Fermín by his mother is expressed with disarming and repeated naïveté: 'ella le había hecho niño mimado de un Obispo, ella le había empujado' [she had made him the favoured son of a Bishop, she had pushed him] (i. 560). The full impact of what Paula has done, and the irony in her understanding of it, is conveyed by the following passage in which Fermín articulates as if his own her version of affairs, and concludes, after the emotional bludgeoning which has occurred, that he is an ingrate. He apparently has no desire to defend against being dominated by his mother's version of events, but it is significant that, when he encounters what he sees as Ana's 'betrayal' of him, he adopts his mother's role in that newly formed dyad and, disowning or forgetting his own 'ingratitude' to his mother, accuses Ana of it with consummate ease in his reproaches to her in chapter 19. Through his eloquence in the confession 'ella comprendió que estaba siendo una ingrata, no sólo con Dios, sino con su apóstol' [she realized that she had been being ungrateful, not just to God, but to his apostle] (ii. 138). Fermín, full of reproach and apparent self-abasement, demonstrates how completely he has taken over his mother's capacity for emotional manipulation: 'yo esperaba que usted fuese lo que aquella historia que llorando me contaba, prometía . . . lo que usted me prometió cien veces después . . . Pero no, usted desconfía de mí, no me cree digno de su dirección espiritual' [I hoped you would be that person promised by the story you told me in tears . . . what you promised me a hundred times afterwards . . . But no, you do not trust me, you do not think me worthy to be your spiritual director] (ii. 139). Accusations of ingratitude are infectious, with the result that Ana competes with Fermín in the matter of who is the victim of ingratitude. Thus in chapter 23, where Ana will fall under Fermín's power, she reproaches him for failing to recognize her motherless state and for his ingratitude, while at the same time turning her own ingratitude into something close to a virtue, and simultaneously recognizing her debt to him: 'No me ha comprendido usted . . . Yo soy la que está sola . . . usted es el ingrato . . . Su madre le querrá más que yo . . . pero no le debe tanto como yo' [You have not understood me . . . I am the one that is alone . . . you are the ungrateful one . . . Your mother may love you more than I do . . . but she does not owe you as much] (ii. 290). In dyads where ingratitude and betrayal are the key emotions, competitiveness about guilt or need for pity abounds, and extremes of reaction and counter-proof ensue.

The major irony of this is that it will eventually spur Ana on to the public submission to Fermín in the Easter procession, which will compound his effective betrayal of his mother in that it adds to those actions which compromise their public position. Contrasting with Paula's effective caricature of the Virgin,[16] Ana's dramatic adoption of the role of the Virgin in the form of the Dolorosa is a final response to his private dramatization of himself as child in chapter 25. It also confirms the closeness of her association with Paula, the original 'self-sacrificing' mother. Ana's appearance in the procession—in Obdulia's words, 'parece de escayola' [she looks as if she's made of stucco] (ii. 368)—echoes Paula's earlier appearance as an 'amortajada' and also the initial description of Fermín in which his skin had 'reflejos del estuco' [looked like stucco] (i. 102). The procession also draws the narrative full-circle in that Ana's abasement of herself is the acting out of Fermín's early fantasy when in chapter 11 he imagines himself declaring his unworthiness to her (i. 422).

With Ana, Fermín passes through the gamut of possible formulations of the mother/son situation: from betrayal, to the feeling that Ana is 'other', to that sense of timelessness in the face of death that betrayal evokes (ii. 316).[17] When, after a final outburst of emotion, he leaves Ana, his action is strongly reminiscent of the child who storms off, expecting fully that its mother will follow it to engage in pity and/or reconciliation: 'Creyó que Ana le seguiría, le llamaría, lloraría . . . Pero pronto se sintió abandonado' [He thought that Ana would follow him, would call, would weep . . . But soon he felt that he had been abandoned] (ii. 321). Ana does not immediately engage in her promise to join in the penitential Easter procession. Curiously, in this novel of absent and inadequate fathers, her reaction on realizing that Fermín's passion for her is human rather than spiritual is to think of her father, in a travesty of deference to the paternal veto over forbidden relationships: 'había que dar la razón en muchas cosas a don Carlos, al que después de todo era su padre' [one had to admit that in many respects Don Carlos, who after all was her father, had been right] (ii. 331). Later her decision to play Mater Dolorosa to the publicly vilified and shamed Fermín (ii. 336) is experienced as a gesture of suicide, an entry into a zone of feeling which will have no demarcations, no boundaries, no sense of judgement, merely passion: 'quería matar dentro de ella la duda, la pena, la frialdad, la influencia del mundo necio, circunspecto, *mirado* . . . quería volver al fuego de la pasión, que era su ambiente' [she wanted to kill the doubt within her, the pain, the cold, the influence of the stupid, careful, circumspect world . . . she wanted to go back to the fire of passion, which was her natural element] (ii. 337). Here Ana arguably wants to return to a pre-Oedipal warmth, or even state of imagined union between mother and child, before the impingement of alienating experience. Again, just as she fantasizes perfect mothering, so her idea of a return to an original warmth is fantasy.

Fermín's repetition with Ana of the infant/mother dyad leaves him as immobilized in his sexual ambiguity as is Ana in her social ambiguity. His lack of public possession of masculinity is brought to painful climax in the closing scenes where he endeavours to make Víctor the instrument of his revenge, unable to play the part he feels is his right.[18] The final gesture in the Cathedral, in which he towers above Ana, replicates for the reader those powerful initial moments in which Paula appears, just as the impotence of the hand raised to strike, but which does not strike, resumes Fermín's imprisonment in the mould cast for him by his mother.

NOTES

1. Paternal absence in *La Regenta* is discussed by Nimetz, but not in the specific psycho-dynamic terms that will be explored here. On Ana's lack of a mother, see Urey 356–60.

2. The sense of solitude evoked here is akin to the desolate loneliness which for Melanie Klein characterized the first sense of the experience of separation from the mother. It contrasts with Winnicott's understanding of solitude as an experience which need not be desolate providing that the child has come to experience solitude within the bounds of the mother's presence.

3. The translations of passages quoted from *La Regenta* are my own.

4. See Jung: 'On the negative side the mother archetype may connote anything secret, hidden, dark; the abyss, the world of the dead, anything that devours, seduces, and poisons, that is terrifying and inescapable like fate' (110).

5. The 'panera', described as 'casa de madera sostenida por cuatro pies de piedra, como las habitaciones palúdicas sustentadas por troncos, y las de algunos pueblos salvajes' [a construction of wood balancing on four stone feet, like rooms in marshlands standing on poles, and those of certain primitive peoples] (ii. 175–6), suggests a fragile, intermediate dwelling place, the temporary and transitional connotations of which relate to the habitual use of intermediate zones for adultery in the novel. See Labanyi.

6. See Mandrell for a discussion of patriarchy and desire in this novel.

7. For a full discussion of honour/shame culture in Spain see Caro Baroja and Pitt-Rivers.

8. The association between money and filth is not, of course, exclusive to Alas. For some of the psychoanalytic theory on the connection between the two, see Ferenczi and Abraham.

9. This emphasis on cleanliness as the domain of woman is characteristic of honour/shame cultures, since the female private domain must always remain irreproachably unstained and open to potential public inspection. See Sánchez Pérez 89–91.

10. See Valis (43) for the underlying negative connotations of this.

11. See Nimetz 244.

12. On the difference between masculine identity and an asexual form of identity traditionally associated with the masculine, see the comments of Keller on the 'masculinity' of scientists (91).

13. See Gullón 158–62.

14. For discussion of this, see Sinclair 6–8.

15. The suggestion that Fermín lacks experience of the Other ignores the experience of the Other that the child has in its intersubjective relation with the mother. That experience is valid, but distinct from the experience of the Other introduced by the Oedipal crisis. See Benjamin ch. 1.

16. See Simon 29.

17. See Klein for the connotations of the initial anguish of the child/mother situation which are resuscitated in adult life in bereavement.

18. For discussion of this see Sinclair 212–17.

WORKS CITED

ABRAHAM, KARL (1979). 'The Spending of Money in Anxiety States' (1917), in *Selected Papers on Psychoanalysis*, trans. D. Bryan and A. Strachey. London: Maresfield Reprints. 299–302.
ALAS 'CLARÍN', LEOPOLDO (1981). *La Regenta* (1884–5), ed. Gonzalo Sobejano, 2 vols. Clásicos Castalia 110, 111. Madrid: Castalia.

BENJAMIN, JESSICA (1990). *The Bonds of Love: Psychoanalysis, Feminism and the Problem of Domination* (1988). London: Virago.

CARO BAROJA, JULIO (1965). 'Honour and Shame: A Historical Account of Several Conflicts', trans. R. Johnson, in J. G. Peristiany (ed.), *Honour and Shame: The Values of Mediterranean Society*. London: Weidenfeld & Nicolson. 81–137.

FERENCZI, SANDOR (1952). 'The Ontogenesis of the Interest in Money' (1914), in *First Contributions to Psychoanalysis*, ed. and trans. E. Jones. International Psychoanalytical Library 45. London: Hogarth Press. 319–31.

GULLÓN, AGNES MONCY (1990). 'Naming in Chapter XI of *La Regenta*', in Noël Valis (ed.), *'Malevolent Insemination' and Other Essays on Clarín*. Michigan Romance Studies 10. Ann Arbor, Mich.: University of Michigan. 155–66.

JUNG, CARL GUSTAV (1982). 'Psychological Aspects of the Mother Archetype' (1938, rev. 1954), in *Aspects of the Feminine*, trans. R. F. C. Hull. London: Routledge & Kegan Paul. 101–40.

KELLER, EVELYN FOX (1985). *Reflections on Gender and Science*. New Haven, Conn.: Yale University Press.

KLEIN, MELANIE (1988). 'On the Sense of Loneliness' (1964), in *Envy and Gratitude and Other Works 1921–1942*, introd. H. Segal. London: Virago. 300–13.

LABANYI, JO (1986). 'City, Country and Adultery in *La Regenta*', *Bulletin of Hispanic Studies*, 63: 53–65.

MANDRELL, JAMES (1990). 'Malevolent Insemination: Don Juan Tenorio in *La Regenta*', in Noël Valis (ed.), *'Malevolent Insemination' and Other Essays on Clarín*. Michigan Romance Studies 10. Ann Arbor, Mich.: University of Michigan. 1–28.

NIMETZ, MICHAEL (1971). '*Eros* and *Ecclesia* in Clarín's Vetusta', *Modern Language Notes*, 86/2: 242–53.

PITT-RIVERS, JULIAN (1965). 'Honour and Social Status', in J. G. Peristiany (ed.), *Honour and Shame: The Values of Mediterranean Society*. London: Weidenfeld & Nicolson. 21–77.

SÁNCHEZ PÉREZ, FRANCISCO (1990). *La liturgia del espacio*. Madrid: Nerea.

SIMON, ELIZABETH (1989). 'La figura de la Madona y del Mesías en *La Regenta*: un estudio a partir del color', *Hispanófila*, 32/3: 21–34.

SINCLAIR, ALISON (1993). *The Deceived Husband: A Kleinian Discussion of the Literature of Infidelity*. Oxford: Oxford University Press.

UREY, DIANE (1987). '"Rumores estridentes": Ana's Resonance in Clarín's *La Regenta*', *Modern Language Review*, 82: 356–60.

VALIS, NOËL (1981). *The Decadent Vision in Leopoldo Alas*. Baton Rouge, La.: Louisiana State University Press.

WINNICOTT, DONALD (1985). 'The Capacity to be Alone' (1958), in *The Maturational Processes and the Facilitating Environment: Studies in the Theory of Emotional Development* (1965), ed. J. D. Sutherland. International Psychoanalytical Library 64. London: Hogarth Press and Institute of Psychoanalysis. 29–36.

Mothers' Voices and Medusas' Eyes: Clarín's Construction of Gender in *Su único hijo*

ABIGAIL LEE SIX

Gender ambiguity is central to *Su único hijo*, as its title demonstrates, with the semantic polyvalence of the possessive adjective *su* ('his', 'her', or 'their'). Indeed, questions are raised throughout the novel about gender identities, conventional and otherwise, about ideals of manhood and womanhood, ridiculed, travestied, and disappointed.[1] As Noël Valis indicates, the characters are depicted 'in near archetypal fashion' (4) and she later asserts that they are decadent types, which include 'the androgyne, the domineering female, or the weakling male counterpart' (16). Despite his heterosexuality, Reyes's masculinity is problematic throughout the novel: even in his desire to become a parent, he vacillates between wishing to be the mother and to be the father of his child. Such gender ambivalence is compounded by equally troubling contradictions in the depictions of the two principal female characters with whom he interacts, namely, Emma Valcárcel, his wife, and Serafina, known as La Gorgheggi, the opera-singer who becomes his mistress. And yet, simply to label Emma domineering or Bonifacio a weakling does not explain how Alas constructs the characters that bring these descriptions to life with a psychological accuracy that speaks to the most contemporary theories.[2]

Valis explains that 'one of the major romantic inversions in decadent typology consists in the reversal of roles in males and females' (136), but there is more to this reversal in *Su único hijo* than meets the eye. Not only is it effected through the proleptic presence of today's theories on gender, applied to the opposite sex, but there is increased complexity arising from the simultaneous

presence of classic features of the feminine and the masculine
attached to characters of the right sex, even if nuanced. For
example, the traditional metaphor for sexual possession of the
woman by the man as his devouring of her is used by Clarín
without reversal of roles, even though the classic topos is miti-
gated by visualizing Serafina as 'manjar muy superior' [a deli-
cacy too rich] for Bonifacio's 'estómago empobrecido por tibias
aguas cocidas' [stomach weakened by lukewarm broth] (76).[3]
This use of classic topoi of masculinity and femininity is also
observed by Valis, but separately from her discussion of the
role-reversal phenomenon, whereas this article will consider how
they coexist in what remains notwithstanding a realist novel. It
will focus on voice and gaze in the text, for these are prominent
in the descriptions of the characters and provide a useful measure of their simultaneous transgression of gender identities and
exploitation of archetypical features of femininity and masculinity.

There is a clear hierarchy of authority and power in the central couple, whereby Emma is indisputably the boss and Bonis
the underdog. This is depicted as attributable to a range of
factors. Adding to Reyes's lack of authority in the household,
due to his own lack of wealth and failure to manage his wife's,
is his class inferiority; he married above himself (17). Wealth
and class are separate issues even if they both have the same
effect of undermining Bonifacio's status; the whole of the Valcárcel
family excepting Emma is impoverished, but none the less more
respected by her than her husband is because of its aristocratic
stock, which he signally lacks. Without wealth of his own or the
ability to manage his wife's, beneath her in class, lastly, Bonis's
weak personality relative to Emma's leaves him in a position of
absolute submissiveness to her (79).[4] The reversal of gender
typing is inflected by a network of socio-cultural factors woven
into the treatment of masculinity and femininity.

A particularly striking example of the novel's reversal of gender roles is Emma's pride in her husband's good looks and her
habit, passively accepted by him, of dressing him up to show him
off: 'Lucía a su marido, a quien compraba buena ropa. . . .
[Bonifacio] se dejaba vestir. Su resolución era . . . callar a todo'
[She showed her husband off, buying him smart clothes. . . .
[Bonifacio] let himself be dressed up. He was determined . . . to
keep quiet no matter what] (8). One of the points commonly
made by feminist critics is that, in patriarchal society, the woman

is reduced to an object of beauty, created and appreciated by the male; here we have the man as passive mannequin and the woman as active (and exploit̥ative) creator of his image. Susan Gubar's comments are applicable in exact gender reversal to the case of Emma and Bonifacio: 'Woman is . . . an art object: an icon or doll'. Gubar goes on to study the 'long tradition identifying the author as male who is primary and the female as his passive creation' (295).[5] In *Su único hijo*, though, it is Bonis who is Emma's artefact. The reversal is strengthened by the depiction of him as a mere appendage to Emma; his good looks serve only to enhance her status: '*Su Bonifacio* no era más que una figura de adorno para ella' [*Her Bonifacio* was no more than a decorative piece for her] (8).

This phenomenon of having a man as object and a woman as creating and desiring subject has an important effect on the question of gaze in the novel. As Paul Julian Smith explains: 'For Lacan . . . the eye is an organ of desire, as well as of perception. . . . The object is . . . deprived of integrity, because it is always already implicated in the look' (16). Thus, Emma's objectification of Bonis sets up a relationship whereby she is the looker and he the looked at. This develops further the gender reversal within the couple, for as E. Ann Kaplan observes: 'To own and activate the gaze, given our language and the structure of the unconscious, is to be in the masculine position' (331).

It is not only theoretical argument which makes Emma the owner of an active, objectifying gaze and Bonifacio the victim of it; this is literally true within the text as well. Emma's gaze is mentioned repeatedly. Sometimes the narrator describes it in isolation, without following the direction in which it is aimed: thus, he alludes to 'un brillo frío y siniestro de la mirada [de Emma], antipático como él sólo' [a cold and sinister gleam in her eye [Emma's] that was uniquely unpleasant] (11). Sometimes, it is Bonifacio's nervous imagination which visualizes his wife's angry look directed at him: ' "Emma saltaba de la cama . . . echando fuego por los ojos y avanzaba en silencio hacia él" ' ['Emma would leap out of bed . . . her eyes blazing and silently go up to him'] (60). But such a fiery stare is not a wild exaggeration on his part, as the narrator, blurring indistinguishably with Bonifacio's train of thought, is careful to establish: 'Por fortuna aquello no era más que un cuadro imaginado. . . . Pero la realidad podría llegar a parecérsele' [Fortunately, that was only an imagined scenario. . . . But real life could resemble it] (60). At other times, the description appears to come in straightforward fashion from the narrator, as when Emma first sees Bonis after discovering, to her horror, that she is pregnant: 'Abrió los ojos, y lo primero que hizo con ellos fue lanzar un rayo de odio y otro de espanto sobre el atribulado esposo' [She opened her eyes and the first thing she did was hurl one thunderbolt of hatred and another of terror at her troubled husband] (203).

Worth noting in these descriptions is the active nature of the verbs describing Emma's gaze: *echar* and *lanzar* (both meaning 'to throw'). This implies control and volition on Emma's part; it suggests that she can deliberately make her stare fiery or venomous. It is not then the cliché found in Golden Age literature and elsewhere, of the eyes being the windows of the soul, with its implication that gaze uncontrollably reveals the innermost character of the person concerned. This is more like the mythological pattern of, for example, the Gorgon Medusa malevolently using her stare on her victims.[6]

Serafina has equal control over the power of her gaze and uses it on Bonifacio just as ruthlessly. If anything, even more than Emma, she can deliberately make her gaze resemble Medusa's: 'Para hacerle la operación peligrosa de la *declaración* . . . tuvo que cloroformizarle con miradas eléctricas' [In order to accomplish the dangerous operation of the *declaration* . . . she had to anaesthetize him with an electric stare] (45, Clarín's italics). However, in the scene of Emma's and Serafina's encounter, a third element comes into play in what then becomes a hierarchy rather than a two-way relationship of subject and object, for no sooner has La Gorgheggi subjugated Bonis with her look, than Emma turns her objectifying gaze on the soprano ('Devoraba con los ojos a la tiple' [She devoured the soprano with her gaze] (173)), turning the tables on Serafina, who had earlier made Emma the object of a non-aggressive, but none the less conquering look; when Serafina 'la miraba con ojos muy abiertos, muy brillantes, que chisporroteaban simpatía' [looked at her with eyes wide open, gleaming very bright, sparkling with kindness] (169), Emma had started to be won over emotionally (the job was finished by La Gorgheggi's feigned amazement at Emma's supposed resemblance to a celebrated opera-singer). The reciprocal nature of the two women's gaze suggests a latent lesbian attraction between them, reinforced by the description of them 'acariciándose con ojos y sonrisas' [caressing each other with their eyes and their smiles] (171). But the chapter ends with a description of how Bonifacio 'paseaba la mirada triste, seria y tiernamente curiosa, del rostro pálido, ajado de su esposa, al vientre que una vez había engañado sus esperanzas' [let his eyes wander sadly, seriously, and with tender curiosity, from the pale, drawn face of his wife to the belly which once had dashed his hopes] (173). His eyes do not have the cannibalistic element attributed to his wife's, nor the spellbinding qualities of those of his mistress, but the pathetic overtone of the harmless voyeur who watches without being seen himself, who can desire but do nothing further. In contrast to the exploitative power-wielding eyes of the two women, Bonifacio's gaze is merely taking a thoughtful stroll, as the Spanish verb *pasear* suggests.

Nevertheless, the equivocal portrayal of Reyes is constructed in part by a dual quality to his gaze; in the bedroom, he adopts the masculine position of desiring looker. When Emma, to his surprise, orders him to stay with her on their return from the opera, this 'le hizo mirar de repente a su esposa con ojos de juez de la hermosura' [made him suddenly look at her with the gaze of one judging her beauty] (132) and it is this contemplation of his wife and, significantly, his interpretation of her gaze and other non-verbal signals that cause him to be suddenly seized by desire for her. It is interesting additionally to note the classical echo of his mode of looking at her, bearing in mind her Gorgon Medusa image, for, like Perseus, he contemplates only her reflection—'la veía retratada por el cristal' [he saw her framed in the mirror] (132)—as if it would be too hazardous to look at her directly. Emma, on the other hand, has no hesitation in feasting her eyes directly on her husband: 'echaba chispas por los ojos, y seria y callada miraba el cuello robusto y de color de leche de su marido' [her eyes were throwing sparks and she seriously, silently contemplated the strong, milk-white neck of her husband] (133). This bold staring by her gives Emma the upper hand in the sexual encounter, so that Bonifacio even here fails to dominate: she looks at him straighter than he at her and she, after all, had instigated the sexual activity by inviting him to stay in the first place.

Thus, we may conclude that, where gaze is concerned, Bonifacio's position relative to both Emma and Serafina follows most strikingly in classical tradition[7]—he has to deal with the women's bewitching stare as best he may—but, at the same time, present-day theories of the possessive, desiring gaze contribute to an understanding of his position, because they reveal one of the ways in which both Emma and Serafina retain their dominance over him, confirming the role-reversal idea of decadent typology.

Throughout *Su único hijo*, the concept of the mother and the nature of maternal and anti-maternal qualities in a woman are recurrently examined, by characters and narrator alike. But what are the implications of the maternal ideal as this is construed by a male protagonist and male narrator, and imposed upon Emma and Serafina?

With its veneration of the Virgin Mary, the Roman Catholic Church (ineluctable backdrop to post-medieval Spanish literature generally) traditionally separates the maternal function from the sexual act which, barring miracles, must precede it. The classic vision of motherhood is thus associated with asexuality and purity and much is made of the uniqueness of mother-love, perceived as altruistic, in contrast to sexual love, which is supposedly tainted by a selfish drive for personal bodily—hence base—satisfaction.[8] Miguel de Unamuno would deal with the paradox of both motherhood and virginity being the desirable goals for women through creating a character like La Tía Tula in the novel of that name, who achieved both simultaneously by adopting the children of others.[9] But one might argue that Alas had prepared the ground for him, with his creation of Bonifacio Reyes and the factors influencing this character's falling in love with Serafina, as well as those determining his feelings for his wife.

An idealization of the maternal is seen by Nancy Chodorow as a consequence of a universal masculine fear of the mother stemming from her total power over the child in infancy.[10] She continues:

Folk legends and beliefs are often attempts to cope with this dread: poems and ballads talk about fears of engulfment by whirlpools and allurement by sirens who entice the unwary and kill whom they catch. Women and symbols of women in these creations and fantasies represent for grown men what the all-powerful mother is for the child. . . . Ways of coping with dread are to glorify and adore women—'There is no need for me to dread a being so wonderful, so beautiful, nay, so saintly'— or to debase and disparage them—'It would be too ridiculous to dread a creature who, if you take her all round, is such a poor thing'. (35)

This psychoanalytic theory accounts for the typically Christian split in the vision of woman between the ideal virginal type and the demoniacal temptress, by tracing it back to a single source, namely, the original experience of the mother by the (male) infant. Indeed, the two female figures are linked in Church tradition by calling Mary the second Eve. And in *Su único hijo* the maternal ideal and the siren-like woman are fused even more strongly, as we shall see, suggesting Bonifacio's fluctuation between these two ways of coping with what Chodorow (34), quoting Karen Horney (351), calls the masculine dread of women.

The main cause of Bonifacio's attraction to La Gorgheggi is that he perceives her singing voice as maternal (31). It is made clear from the outset that this is meant figuratively, for he admits that his own mother never sang (32). What we are considering here, then, is what Chodorow calls the 'powerfully experienced . . . internal mother-image' (184). In other words, one may assume that there is something in the quality of her voice which he associates with an abstract ideal of woman as the perfect mother and, through his meditations on Serafina's voice, the elements of this ideal emerge. We learn that it must be soothing, even soporific; it must comprehend honesty, goodness, and the voice brings to Bonifacio's mind the traditional occupations of the virtuous woman ('así debieran cantar las mujeres hacendosas mientras cosen la ropa o cuidan a un convaleciente' [this must be how industrious women sing while they sew clothes or take care of a convalescent patient] (32)), suggesting that, in his mind at least, a good woman and a mother are indistinguishable concepts. Soon after, more features are added to the maternal ideal, closely allied to its soothing function, for Bonifacio tells Serafina that her 'voz de madre' [mother's voice] consoles him, gives him hope and strength (51). Later, when he has made her his mistress, he dwells upon the contrast between her passionate lovemaking and her reversion to maternal type when she grows tired, adding the notion of holiness to his view of motherhood:

las caricias que ella hacía soñolienta, parecían arrullos inocentes de cariño santo, suave, que une al que engendra con el engendrado. Entonces, *la diabla* se convertía en la mujer de la voz de *madre*, y . . . [a Bonis] se le llenaba el espíritu . . . de nostalgias del regazo materno.

her caresses when she was sleepy resembled the innocent lulling of gentle, holy affection uniting parent and child. Then the *she-devil* turned

into the woman with the *mother's* voice and . . . his [Bonis's] spirit was
filled with nostalgia for the maternal embrace. (77; Clarín's italics)

Near the end of *Su único hijo*, when Bonifacio's son is being
baptized, a further component of the maternal function is added,
namely protectiveness. Bonifacio welcomes the ceremony, despite his lack of orthodox piety, because he feels that the Church
is performing a protective role that he associates with its being
seen metaphorically as a mother to the faithful (265). It is at this
point in the novel, too, that Serafina assumes a final stereotyped
female identity. She has already been a mother and a seductress,
but this last was given a positive weighting because of the pleasure afforded to Bonifacio by her sexuality. Now at the end of the
novel, with their relationship over, the allure of the sensual
woman is transformed to take on the features of the serpent-
loving Eve: cold-bloodedness, duplicity, slyness, venomousness:

Aquella mujer tan hermosa . . . le pareció [a Bonis] de repente una cule-
bra. . . . La vio mirarle con ojos de acero, con miradas puntiagudas . . . le
vio pasar por los labios rojos la punta finísima de una lengua jugosa y
muy aguda . . . y con el presentimiento de una herida envenenada, esperó
las palabras pausadas de la mujer que le había hecho feliz.

That woman, so beautiful . . . suddenly seemed like a serpent [to
Bonis]. . . . He saw her look at him with steely eyes, a piercing gaze . . .
he saw her lick her red lips with the extremely fine tip of a juicy, sharp
tongue . . . and with the presentiment of a poisoned wound, he awaited
the measured words of the woman who had given him happiness. (270)

Feminist theory is well known for having claimed that one of
the most fundamental problems for women in patriarchal society relates to language. It is by now commonplace to perceive
the woman as silenced or gagged, whether on the concrete level
through research that has shown how they are expected to keep
quiet in the company of men and interrupted or ignored when
they do speak, or in more abstract arguments concerning the
failure of man-made language to express the female experience
adequately.[11] It is therefore perhaps surprising that a novel by
a man about a man who falls in love with a woman because she
fits with his clichéd ideal of the maternal should portray this
very maternal quality as embodied in the character's voice and
not her silence. And yet Bonifacio is not treated as a man with
eccentric or perverted tastes in women, nor as someone curiously
insensitive to women's voices; on the contrary, he is particularly
upset by the wrong type of voice, namely his wife's shrill tantrums:

Lo que le daba mayor tormento en las injustas lucubraciones bilioso-
nerviosas de su mujer, era el ruido.
'Si todo eso me lo dijera por escrito ... yo mismo firmaría sin
inconveniente.' Las voces, los gritos, eran los que le llegaban al alma,
no los *conceptos*, como él decía.

What tortured him the most in his wife's unjust, peevish, agitated
lucubrations was the noise.
'If she said all that to me in writing ... I should have no objection
to signing it myself.' It was the shouting, the shrieking, which cut him
to the quick, not the *concepts*, as he used to put it. (22–3; Clarín's
italics)[12]

Some explanation is provided by Cora Kaplan, who links woman's injunction to silence in patriarchal society to the phenomenon of certain tones of voice being perceived as feminine or
unfeminine—hence attractive or unattractive—to men. She refers to the 'abstract identification of woman = silence and the
complementary imaging of women's speech as whispered, sub-
vocal, the mere escape of trapped air ... shhhhhhhh' (Cameron
65). This helps to explain why Emma's strident tones are perceived by Bonis as objectionable but does not obviously contribute to an understanding of his love for Serafina's voice, a leading
soprano whose sublime singing, one may therefore assume, would
be anything but hushed. Kaplan's next sentence, however, seems
to provide a key. Commenting on a picture of a woman called
Silence, she says: 'Her speech seems limited by some function in
which she is wrapped as deeply as in the embryonic mist. Mother
or nurse, the silence she enjoins and enacts is on behalf of some
sleeping other' (Cameron 65). Thus, an alternative to the virtuous woman's silence is posited: using a tone suitably gentle to
recall a mother's speech (or, presumably, song) in the presence
of a baby. Now, whilst it might be fanciful of Bonifacio to find an
opera-singer's voice reminiscent of a lullaby-singing mother's,
the significant point here is that he explicitly defines what is
attractive about Serafina's voice as that very correspondence:
'canta con la coquetería que podría emplear una madre para
dormir a su hijo en sus brazos' [she sings with the affectionate
tone that a mother might use to lull her child to sleep in her
arms] (31–2).
   The composite picture of motherhood formed by all the above-
mentioned ideas is, of course, a man's view and a rather unre-
alistic man at that, a man prone to romanticizing, a man whose
love of opera exemplifies his wish for clear-cut stock characters

in real life too. Alas's narrator, on the other hand, demonstrates a greater understanding of the abyss between these masculine conventions of motherhood and the actual event of becoming a mother. This is illustrated by the depiction of Emma's late and totally unexpected (for her) pregnancy. None of Bonifacio's ideas about motherhood enumerated above is here brought into being. Far from demonstrating a protective instinct towards her future child, for example, Emma hopes and tries for a miscarriage and, once he is born, she has Antonio christened before she considers it safe for him to go out, simply to spite Bonifacio. However, Emma remains a character with a strong negative weighting, both before and after she becomes a mother. Were this behaviour attached to a positively portrayed woman character, it would be a powerful argument in favour of positing a distinction between the protagonist's foolishly dreamy view of motherhood and the reality of the condition for a woman as understood by a more enlightened narrator. However, as the text stands, protagonist and narrator's views are related blurrily, even though we are aware of a gently mocking tone directed by the latter at the former throughout the novel. We cannot know, in the specific instance of Emma's attitude to her pregnancy and later to her baby, more than that she is viewed as a less than ideal mother by both Bonifacio and the narrator. Nevertheless, the narrator's vision differs in certain respects—to an incalculable degree—from his protagonist's.

For instance, we sense mockery from the narrator in his depiction of Emma's fears surrounding the delivery. Whilst it is quite reasonable for a middle-aged and hitherto childless woman in the nineteenth century to be terrified of giving birth, this apprehension is conveyed as typical of Emma's self-centred character:

No, no la halagaba ser madre a tales horas; el terror del peligro, que le parecía supremo, no le dejaba lugar para vanidades de ningún género. 'Yo no podré parir; me lo da el corazón. Yo no paro', pensaba, con escalofríos. . . .
    Emma se encerraba en su alcoba; se miraba en el espejo de cuerpo entero. . . . Y arrojándose desnuda . . . en una butaca, rompía a llorar, furiosa; a llorar sin lágrimas, como los niños mimados, y gritaba: '¡Yo no quiero! ¡Yo no puedo! ¡Yo no sirvo!'
    La muerte era probable, la enfermedad segura, los dolores terribles, insoportables. . . . Y su cólera, como siempre, iba a estrellarse contra Bonis.

No, there was nothing gratifying about becoming a mother at this point; terror at the danger, which seemed enormous to her, left no room for self-congratulation of any kind. 'I shall not be able to give birth; I feel it in my bones; I cannot give birth,' she thought with a shudder. . . .

She would lock herself in her bedroom; she would look at herself in the full-length mirror . . . and throwing herself naked . . . into an arm-chair, she would burst out crying furiously, crying with no tears, as spoilt children do, and she would shout: 'I won't! I can't! I'm not made for it!'

Death was probable, illness a certainty, the pains terrible, intolerable. . . . And her rage, as usual, was taken out on Bonis. (218–19)

The assumption that it is natural for women to be limitlessly self-sacrificing as mothers (and prospective mothers) is surely suggested by the narrator's presentation of this scene.[13] And noticeable in the negative slant put on Emma's attitude is the attention to her gaze. Emma's self-contemplation naked in a full-length mirror smacks of egotistical vanity; it implies that she is wrong to take an interest in the look of her body and almost shocks the reader, even a century later, for the perversity of the self-directed voyeurism. Coupled with this, the narrator utilizes exaggeration: the enormity of the danger and death seen as probable. Thus, Emma is mocked for over-estimating the peril in which her pregnancy places her (although feminist historians of obstetric practices in the nineteenth century might argue that any exaggeration here is only slight). The other technique noticeable in reducing sympathy for a character who, however unpleasant a person, should deserve some compassion, is to make Bonis the victim rather than Emma herself;[14] and this is where voice comes into play, albeit implicitly, for we already know that Emma's rage is expressed by shouting at her husband. Thus, Emma is behaving like the spoilt child that the narrator has told us she is in the very first sentence of the novel, marring her husband's legitimate pleasure at approaching fatherhood: 'Emma ni en broma toleraba que se hablase del peligro que corría como de acontecimiento próspero' [Emma could not stand even jesting talk of the danger in which she found herself expressed as a happy event] (219). Reading against the grain, however, a very different picture emerges. Here is a woman who does not wish to be pregnant, facing nineteenth-century childbirth dangerously late in life, with no sympathy from her husband, her family, her lover, or her friends. Emma contemplates 'el terrible abandono de los demás, de Bonis, del tío, de Minghetti' [the terrible desertion of the others, of Bonis, of her uncle, of Minghetti] (219), but again the presentation is scornful and even her closest woman friend, who might have provided moral support, laughs maliciously on referring to the unborn child (219–20). In this episode, then, the narrator is clearly revealing that, if he is not a dreamy romantic about motherhood like his protagonist, he is nevertheless influenced by the phallocratic idea that a woman who does not automatically rejoice and happily embrace the self-sacrificing role it traditionally entails is censurable. The husband of such a woman is to be pitied, implies the narrator's stance, not the woman herself.[15]

However, voice in *Su único hijo* is not solely a marker of maternal qualities (in the case of Serafina's singing) and of negative feminine qualities (as with Emma throughout and Serafina at the end of the novel). Bonifacio's voice also is described at various moments and sheds some interesting light on how Clarín constructs his protagonist's ambiguous masculinity. For example, when he makes his declaration to Serafina, his voice remains feminine in its submissive and emotional shakiness, but gains in virility with its timbre: 'voz temblona, pero de un timbre metálico, de energía, en él completamente nuevo' [tremulous voice, but with a metallic, forceful timbre that was completely new to him] (51).[16] Research has confirmed that, as logic would suggest, when a person's voice combines contradictory elements, the impression created by each mitigates the other (see Berry). Hence, we may venture that Bonifacio's masterful new tone would lessen the impression of effeminacy made by having a trembling voice. Be that as it may, here again we find Clarín simultaneously playing with role reversal—surely it would conventionally be the woman in a love scene whose voice should tremble—and classic gender typing: it is the man who, as active partner, makes the declaration and also he whose voice can be positively associated with metal, linked with all the classic masculine qualities: steeliness, hardness, coldness, money, and weaponry.[17] For a woman to be described as metallic is insulting to her femininity, as with Serafina at the end of the novel and her steely eyes, quoted above, or indeed Margaret Thatcher's 'Iron Lady' epithet.

In parallel to his uncontrolled gaze, Bonis lacks control over his voice; at the end of the novel, for example, when confronted by Serafina at his son's christening, he speaks 'con voz que procuró hacer cariñosa al par que firme, y que le salió temblona, balbuciente y débil' [with a voice that he tried to make affectionate yet firm and which came out as wobbly, stammering, and weak] (270).

However, perhaps more important than Bonifacio's own voice was, as we saw above, his sensitivity to others' voice quality. This fits with his love of music—as both listener and player— and the contrast established between his artistic sense in this field but his failed attempts to write poetry. Words are of little interest or significance to him and when he tremulously declared his love to Serafina with that new metallic tone there were many ellipses in the punctuation, signalling his pauses while he searched for words to express his feelings. He even said in the course of his speech: 'Temo que usted no me entienda. Yo no sé hablar; no he sabido nunca' [I am afraid that you do not understand me. I am no good at talking; I never have been] (51). According to present-day theories of masculinity, this lack of communicative ability in the sentimental domain is typical for a man, who will have been taught to suppress and deny all emotions except anger from an early age (Middleton 212). However, Bonifacio is a romantic and so aspires to emotional expressivity rather than invulnerable silence. Nevertheless, romanticism is treated in the novel as an outdated eccentricity, as removed from real life as the operas that espouse it, so it remains true that he would not have been educated to be a romantic hero and might indeed lack a verbal language of emotion, having to fall back on wordless music (or opera with its foreign and so incomprehensible libretto) for solace.

The question of women's control is given less prominence with respect to voice tones than to gaze, and what little there is tends to be implicit. For example, one could argue that an opera-singer has learnt how to control her voice and may be able to use this training even when she is merely speaking. Thus, when Serafina adopts a sensual tone to ask Reyes to kiss her— 'murmuraba ella *gritando* con voz baja, apasionada' [she murmured, *shouting* in a passionate whisper] (52; Clarín's italics)—one could read this as a deliberate move, consciously designed to make her all the more seductive. But what could be meant by this characterization of her voice? It would seem to suggest a type of stage whisper, which is to say that the voice adopts a hoarse, breathy quality similar to a real whisper, but remains loud enough to be heard at a distance. Research has shown that such a voice tone is perceived as sensual: 'Changes in voice quality are claimed to occur when people become sexually aroused—a change in mucosal lubrication gives rise to a breathiness or huskiness of tone' and 'Breathiness may be flirtingly suggestive of sexual availability, but socially acceptable in a woman if associated with a high pitch that connotes a lack of sexual experience.'[18] The counteracting effect of high pitch, to offset a lack of feminine purity (perceived from the huskiness) could, in Serafina's case, be achieved by her soprano singing voice, even though we are not told about the pitch of her speaking voice. Indeed, the femininity attributable to her soprano status becomes clear if one considers how different our image of her would be had Clarín made her a contralto. Other qualities of her speaking voice also bolster her femininity, thus minimizing any risk of her sensuality compromising it. She has, for example, a supremely sweet, tremulous voice when she speaks to Bonifacio on one occasion (43), and tremulousness, as we have seen, is like sweetness a positive feminine voice quality.

Emma also appears to be in control of her voice, modulating her tone to produce a particular effect:

Con una tranquilidad fría y perezosa, dijo, en una voz apagada que horrorizaba siempre a Bonis:
—Hueles a polvos de arroz.

In a cold, languorous, calm voice she said, in a muted tone that always horrified Bonis:
'You smell of face-powder.' (92)

The fact that she is calm and also the habitual connotations of the imperfect tense of *horrorizaba* and the *siempre* suggest that this is a tone she can and does adopt at will, rather than one that takes possession of her voice in the heat of a particular mood. Interestingly, Emma also becomes hoarse and guttural when wishing for sex, a signal recognized by her husband (93). However, unlike Serafina's case, this seems spontaneous and not a strategy, since we are told that Emma is embarrassed by her sudden passion for Bonis (163).

Gaze and voice, though noticeably accentuated in the novel, are by no means the only non-verbal signals used by Clarín. An examination of references to touch, to the whole range of facial expressions, and even, in one case, to a way of laughing, all contribute to the author's construction of gender and of power relations in the text, and to his portrayal of Bonifacio's less nuanced perception of these. For example, as well as giving him an unmistakable look when she invites him to stay in her bedroom after the opera, Emma is also described as licking her lips. It is the combination of these two elements which, we are told, makes Bonifacio feel 'apetecido' [fancied] (133).

Furthermore, a study of the minor characters and relationships of *Su único hijo* would yield additional examples of Clarín's utilization of gaze and voice to convey conventional and unconventional gender typing.[19]

To conclude, the treatment of motherhood and maternal qualities is a particularly interesting element of the construction of gender in the novel, for it exemplifies the clichéd attitudes of Bonifacio while at the same time betraying the narrator's subtler but hardly more enlightened views, views that we often glimpse precisely through his portrayal of gaze and voice. Indeed, it is surely he who remains the most puzzlingly ambiguous persona of all in *Su único hijo*. He seems superior to the internal characters inasmuch as he is able to see and mock their foibles. He ingeniously presents the type-casting of the main characters through Bonifacio's romantic and simplistic point of view; and yet, where there are chinks through which we can perceive his own attitudes, these disappoint. We have seen his unjust representation of Emma's fears about childbirth. One more example would be his treatment of Bonifacio's reaction to Serafina's cry for help after she leaves town and finds herself alone and penniless, but refuses to live by prostitution: there is no discernible condemnation from the narrator of his abandonment of her. Furthermore, if Bonis is mocked for loving Serafina's maternal qualities, it would seem probable that this is more for perceiving them in such an unlikely candidate than for regarding them as attractive. The voice behind *Su único hijo*—a voice whose absence of sound qualities insidiously imbues it with superhuman authority—suggests a point of view—a gaze without eyes that blink, squint, and otherwise reveal their fallibility—less romantic, less simplistic, and more intelligent than its protagonist but, one must conclude, no less disappointing to the female reader.

NOTES

1. Charnon-Deutsch refers to the 'very unheroic Bonifacio Reyes heroically confronting female adversaries of patently epic proportions' (62).
2. Rutherford makes a similar point in the introduction to his translation of *La Regenta* (8–9).
3. All translations from *Su único hijo* are my own.
4. It is interesting to note the similarity between Bonis and D. Víctor, Ana's husband in Clarín's earlier masterpiece, *La Regenta*. He seems to have a similar submissive streak in his character, but it is Ana who makes their relationship so different from the Reyes' marriage. Because she is not the demanding character that Emma would be, Víctor is able to maintain his credibility as head of household that much more. Socio-cultural factors also improve Víctor's position since he is the one with the money and the more respectable background. This further bolsters his status, in opposition to Bonis, who is weakened by his inferiority to his wife in these respects. However, in terms of personality taken in isolation, the two husbands have much in common.
5. See also Cameron's synthesis of Tillie Olsen (15).
6. Evil eye superstitions in many cultures depend on similar beliefs in certain people's (often women's) power to inflict harm by looking. For a wide-ranging survey see Dundes.
7. Charnon-Deutsch asserts that in *Su único hijo* 'women are cast as archetypes with terrible but frozen roles' (62).
8. Bonifacio latterly transposes the idea of pure love, untainted by concupiscence, which initially had attracted him to the mother's role as parent, to that of the father (191).
9. For Unamuno's attitude to the maternal, see Jurkevich (esp. 66).
10. Charnon-Deutsch also considers the question of men's dread of women (72–3).
11. Spender forcefully makes these and other points about women's problems with language.
12. Later we learn that he prefers a beating from her to a verbal tirade (91).
13. Chodorow confirms that the most traditional view of the perfect mother is to be 'self-sacrificing and giving' (82).
14. Cameron identifies the same phenomenon in the very different context of present-day newspaper reports of a rape, where sympathy for the woman was deflected to her husband, because he had been forced to witness the assault (16–17).
15. Spender argues: 'Women who do not experience the "joys" of motherhood, as defined by males . . . are the "exceptions" . . . rather than the genuine subject encoding experience' (58). Clearly, Emma is treated as an atypical woman in all respects including her attitude to motherhood, bearing out Spender's claim for the marginalization of the woman's experience that disturbs the male view.
16. To connect shakiness of voice with non-masculinity seems justified, since this connotes emotion, weakness, and vulnerability, all of whose opposite qualities are traditionally associated with masculinity. See Middleton, esp. 33–4 (strength), 120 (invulnerability), and 212 (the suppression of emotions other than anger).
17. For the link between manhood and weaponry, see Middleton 88.
18. Graddol and Swann 17 and 37–8 respectively. They point out (18) that

physiological changes in voice due to sexual arousal may have a folk-wisdom element, but this need not undermine the present argument; for our purposes, the important point is precisely that people think huskiness of voice is connected with sexual arousal, whether or not they are right.
19. e.g. Marta's enslavement of Nepomuceno is attributed to a potent combination of her singing and simultaneous looking at him (155). And Minghetti's seductive qualities are linked explicitly to his gaze control and his breathy baritone voice. 'Empezó a marearla [a Emma] con miradas' [the way he looked at her [Emma] began to make her head spin] (176) and 'A sus queridas les cantaba al oído las óperas enteras, como dándoles besos con el aliento' [he used to sing whole operas in his sweethearts' ears, as if kissing them with his breath] (181). Minghetti's seductive strategies demonstrate that the novel does not make any claims about men universally being the victims of women's wiles; he belongs in a different pattern of gender typing: the Don Juan figure.

WORKS CITED

ALAS 'CLARÍN', LEOPOLDO (1988). *Su único hijo.* Madrid: Alianza.
BERRY, DIANE S. (1992). 'Vocal Types and Stereotypes: Joint Effects of Vocal Attractiveness and Vocal Maturity on Person Perception', *Journal of Nonverbal Behaviour*, 16: 41–54.
CAMERON, DEBORAH (1990) (ed.). *The Feminist Critique of Language: A Reader.* London: Routledge.
CHARNON-DEUTSCH, LOU (1990). *Gender and Representation: Women in Spanish Realist Fiction.* Purdue University Monographs in Romance Languages 32. Amsterdam: John Benjamins.
CHODOROW, NANCY J. (1989). *Feminism and Psychoanalytic Theory.* Cambridge: Polity.
DUNDES, ALAN (1981) (ed.). *The Evil Eye: A Casebook.* New York: Garland.
GRADDOL, DAVID, and SWANN JOAN (1989). *Gender Voices.* Oxford: Blackwell.
GUBAR, SUSAN (1986). ' "The Blank Page" and the Issues of Female Creativity', in Elaine Showalter (ed.), *The New Feminist Criticism: Essays on Women, Literature, and Theory.* London: Virago. 292–313.
HORNEY, KAREN (1932). 'The Dread of Women', *International Journal of Psychoanalysis*, 13: 351.
JURKEVICH, GAYANA (1991). *The Elusive Self: Archetypal Approaches to the Novels of Miguel de Unamuno.* Columbia, Mo.: University of Missouri Press.
KAPLAN, E. ANN (1984). 'Is the Gaze Male?', in Ann Snitow, Christine Stansell, and Sharon Thompson (eds.), *Desire: The Politics of Sexuality.* London: Virago. 321–38.
MIDDLETON, PETER (1992). *The Inward Gaze: Masculinity and Subjectivity in Modern Culture.* London: Routledge.
RUTHERFORD, JOHN (1984). Introduction in Leopoldo Alas, *La Regenta*, trans. John Rutherford. London: Penguin. 7–17.
SMITH, PAUL JULIAN (1988). *Writing in the Margin: Spanish Literature of the Golden Age.* Oxford: Clarendon.
SPENDER, DALE (1985). *Man Made Language.* 2nd edn. London: Pandora.
VALIS, NOËL MAUREEN (1981). *The Decadent Vision in Leopoldo Alas.* Baton Rouge, La.: Louisiana State University Press.

The Gendered Gothic in Pardo Bazán's *Los pazos de Ulloa*

STEPHEN M. HART

The role of the Gothic and that of gender in *Los pazos de Ulloa* (1886) by Emilia Pardo Bazán (1851–1921) has been touched on by other critics; in this essay I intend to explore the connections between the two.[1] At the risk of falling into the trap of disciplinary colonialism—namely, the investment of an ancillary discipline (Hispanic Studies) with an ideology adopted from a mainline discipline (English Studies)—I will investigate convergences between the Gothic as understood in English Studies and what is arguably the most significant novel by a nineteenth-century female Spanish novelist. I take the notion of the Gothic from Eve Kosofsky Sedgwick's *The Coherence of Gothic Conventions*, whose observations on the gender dynamic implicit in the genre underscore my conclusion:

Once you know that a novel is of the Gothic kind (and you can tell that from the title), you can predict its contents with an unnerving certainty. You know important features of its *mise en scène*: an oppressive ruin, a wild landscape, a Catholic or feudal society. You know about the trembling sensibility of the heroine and the impetuosity of her lover. You know about the tyrannical older man with the piercing glance who is going to imprison and try to rape or murder them. You know something about the novel's form: it is likely to be discontinuous and involuted, perhaps incorporating tales within tales, changes of narrators, and such framing devices as found manuscripts of interpolated stories. You also know that, whether with more or less relevance to the main plot, certain preoccupations will be aired. These include the priesthood and monastic institutions; sleeplike and deathlike states; subterranean spaces and live burial; doubles; the discovery of obscured family ties; affinities between narrative and pictorial art; possibilities of incest; unnatural echoes or silences, unintelligible writings, and the unspeakable; garrulous retainers; the poisonous effects of guilt and shame; nocturnal landscapes and dreams; apparitions from the past; Faust- and Wandering-Jew-like figures; civil insurrections and fires; the charnel house and the madhouse. (9–10)

I have quoted this passage at such length to illustrate the high level of coincidence between the Gothic and *Los pazos de Ulloa*. Of the elements mentioned in the mise-en-scène, all seem applicable to Pardo Bazán's novel if, as I shall be arguing, the main plot of the novel, on which all else hangs, is its depiction of a not only failed but also non-delineated love affair between Julián Álvarez and Nucha. Los Pazos is, indeed, an 'oppressive ruin' set within a decaying feudal Catholic society, symbolized by the dusty old patent of nobility Julián stumbles on soon after his arrival (iii; 177).[2] Also applicable is Sedgwick's reference to 'the trembling sensibility of the heroine' (in this case Nucha) and 'the impetuosity of her lover' (in this case Julián). The 'tyrannical older man' is, probably, Pedro Moscoso. I will return later in more detail to the component mentioned above by Sedgwick that the tyrant will attempt to murder or rape the lovers.

With regard to the novel's form, it is only fair to say there are fewer coincidences here than with respect to mise-en-scène, for while there clearly are changes of narrator (chapter xxix is told from the perspective of the small child, for example), and the narrative could be seen as discontinuous, there is in *Los pazos de Ulloa* no example of found manuscripts, although there are interpolated stories (the principal example being the stories told by the hunters in chapter xxi). Of the fifteen preoccupations mentioned by Sedgwick as aired in the Gothic novel, at least eleven are present to some degree in Pardo Bazán's novel. These include sleeplike and deathlike states; subterranean spaces and live burial; doubles (superficially in the naturalist comparison between Pedro and his urban-dwelling cousin, but also see below);[3] the discovery of obscured family ties (see incest below); affinities between narrative and pictorial art (mainly in chapter xxi); possibilities of incest (hinted at in *Los pazos de Ulloa* at the conclusion of the novel in the persons of Sabel's son and Nucha's daughter, and fully present in the novel's sequel, *La madre naturaleza*); the unspeakable; the poisonous effects of guilt and shame (as experienced by Julián); nocturnal landscapes and dreams; apparitions from the past (in the form of the butterfly which alights on Nucha's grave in chapter xxx of the novel and which is to be understood as an embodiment of her spirit); and civil insurrections (mainly in the political débâcle which occurs in chapter xviii). Of those elements in the list above I intend now to concentrate on four, which are: (1) sleeplike and death-like states; (2) subterranean spaces and live burial; (3) the un-speakable; and (4) nocturnal landscapes and dreams. As we shall see, these elements offer the richest material for an analysis of the interplay of gender and the Gothic as portrayed in *Los pazos de Ulloa*. The rest of this essay will map out the subterra-nean space within *Los pazos de Ulloa* in which the unspeakable is located but not revealed, and which intersects with the space of death, sleep, and the dream. But before doing this, I need to allude to Freud's theory of the uncanny, which will provide a more technical vocabulary with which to discuss the four ele-ments mentioned above.

In *The 'Uncanny'* (1919) Freud defines the uncanny as 'that class of the terrifying which leads back to something long known to us, once very familiar' (369–70). This Freud justifies by his subsequent philological research of the meaning of *unheimlich*, which includes comparison with equivalents in the various Euro-pean languages, and his conclusion that there is a grey area in which the lexical meaning of *heimlich* (literally 'homely') coin-cides, paradoxically, with that of *unheimlich* (literally 'unhomely').[4] As was his wont, Freud finds confirmation of his psychoanalytic theories in the most unpromising of territories (philology), discovering the secret operations of repression in its dual forms of the Oedipal and the castration complex within the word *unheimlich* itself; as he triumphantly concludes part ii of his essay, 'the prefix "un" is the token of repression' (399). The second most striking part of Freud's analysis concerns his discussion of the connection between the uncanny and the double which we will find particularly helpful for our purposes. He argues that, whereas during the stage of primary narcissism the double is projected as a comforting image of preservation against extinction, it subsequently becomes 'the ghastly harbinger of death' (387), thereby adopting an opposite meaning. These distinctions are relevant to the portrayal of the uncanny in Pardo Bazán's novel, as we shall see. In what follows I want to concentrate on two events described in *Los pazos de Ulloa*, both of which encapsulate the uncanny.

The first of the two scenes occurs in chapter xix when, alerted by a piercing scream, Julián bursts into Don Pedro's and Nucha's bedroom and sees something that, empirically speaking, is not there:

> Iba a dar la vuelta al pasillo que dividía el archivo del cuarto de don Pedro cuando vio . . . ¡Dios santo! Sí, era la escena misma, tal cual se la había figurado él . . . Nucha en pie, pero arrimada a la pared, con el rostro desencajado de espanto, los ojos, no ya vagos, sino llenos de extravío mortal; enfrente, su marido, blandiendo un arma enorme . . . Julián se arrojó entre los dos.

He was at the point of turning into the corridor which divided the archive from Pedro's room when he saw . . . Good gracious! Yes, it was the very scene just as he had imagined it . . . Nucha standing up, but hugging the wall, her face racked with terror, her eyes, no longer dreamy, but unfocused and mortified; in front of her, her husband, brandishing an enormous weapon . . . Julian threw himself between them. (xix; 240–1)

Our first response is to interpret Julián's reaction as that of a person who imagines a scene of marital violence; but the fact that Pedro is brandishing 'an enormous weapon' is enough to make the most hardened anti-Freudian reader smirk. Likewise, given that Julián is sexually jealous of Pedro and since he is described here as placing his body between Pedro and Nucha, the reader is led to suspect that an Oedipal, or at the least a sexual, drama is being played out in Julián's mind. Indeed, given his sexual *naïveté*, it is appropriate to interpret this scene as a metaphoric transposition of, to use Freud's stage directions, the child who witnesses the primal scene. The incongruity of Julián's misreading is enhanced by the discovery that Nucha is screaming not on account of Pedro's 'enormous weapon' but because of an over-large, hairy spider which, no doubt dismayed at the disturbance it has caused, scampers off hurriedly (241). As if to underscore Julián's underlying psychic trauma, we subsequently learn that the spider undergoes a secondary transformation in a dream he has later on that night (the inspiration for which, as Maurice Hemingway suggests (29–31), was probably the work of the English psychologist James Sully). Julián dreams that St George is killing the dragon/spider ('un dragón que parecía araña' [a dragon which appeared to be a spider] (242)), but, in a surprising role reversal, feels the sword penetrating his own body: 'Lo sorprendente es que el lanzazo lo sentía Julián en su propio costado' [The surprising thing was that Julian could feel the lance pierce his own side] (242). As a result of dreamwork, the spider comes to stand for that (hairy) part of Julián's abject and ejected sexual personality which is unconsciously centred on Nucha, and for which he is punished by don Pedro, here transformed metonymically into St George.[5] This first scene, in which Julián discovers, though in a displaced and veiled manner, the sexual nature of his feelings for Nucha, is the antechamber of the following scene in which both Julián and Nucha visit the lower cloisters of the mind, and discover not only sex but also death.

The second scene from chapter xx contains all the ingredients which Claire Kahane, in her essay 'The Gothic Mirror', takes as central to the Gothic novel and which are worth recording here:

Within an imprisoning structure, a protagonist, typically a young woman whose mother has died, is compelled to seek out the center of a mystery, while vague and usually sexual threats to her person from some powerful male figure hover on the periphery of her consciousness. Following clues that pull her onward and inward—bloodstains, mysterious sounds —she penetrates the obscure recesses of a vast labyrinthean space and discovers a secret room sealed off by its association with death. (334)[6]

This encapsulates the symbolic implications of Nucha's visit with Julián to the castle's lower cloister. The image of death central to Kahane's reading is captured in Pardo Bazán's text by the iron ring which once imprisoned a black slave:

Llegados al patín que cerraba el grave claustro, Nucha señaló a un pilar que tenía incrustada una argolla de hierro, de la cual colgaba un eslabón comido de orín.
  —¿Sabe usted qué era esto?—murmuró con apagada voz.
  —No sé—respondió Julián.
  —Dice Pedro—explicó la señorita—que estuvo ahí la cadena con que tenían sujeto sus abuelos a un negro esclavo... ¿No parece mentira que se hiciesen semejantes crueldades? ¡Qué tiempos tan malos, Julián!

When they reached the small patio which was enclosed within the solemn cloister Nucha pointed at a pillar encrusted with an iron ring from which there hung a single chain link, corroded with rust.
  'Do you know what that was?' she murmured in a hushed voice.
  'No,' Julián answered.
  'Pedro says', she explained, 'that there was once a chain there that was used by his grandparents to imprison a black slave ... Isn't it unbelievable that such cruelty existed? What terrible times they must have been, Julián! (xx; 244)

This scene is problematic since there is little historical evidence that black slaves were retained in Spanish households in the early to mid-nineteenth century; we must assume that Pedro's, or indeed Pardo Bazán's, allusion is more fanciful than empirical.[7] Despite this, it is a crucial moment in the book; shortly afterwards, when Julián and Nucha return to the surface, the latter has a fit: 'se reclinaba lanzando interrumpidas carcajadas histéricas, que sonaban a llanto' [she was lying down, uttering shrieks of hysterical laughter which sounded like sobs] (245). While not lacking an 'objective correlative' as decisively as the protagonist of Shakespeare's *Hamlet*, nevertheless there are grounds to suggest that Nucha's reaction is not justified by what precedes, unless some hitherto hidden psychic trauma is in play.[8] Being buried alive is, after all, as Freud suggests, one of the most uncanny sensations possible.[9] For a number of reasons, I would argue that the image of the black slave is a double of Nucha's submerged personality; this would explain, first, why, as a 'harbinger of death', to follow Freud's reasoning, it brings her to hysteria. But, more specifically, the small patio set in the depths of the castle can be likened to that 'dark, secret center' of the Gothic novel which, according to Claire Kahane, is a 'maternal space' inhabited by 'the spectral presence of a dead-undead mother, archaic and all-encompassing, a ghost signifying the problematics of femininity which the heroine must confront' (336). The slave stands, following Kahane's insight, not only for Nucha's absent mother but, more specifically, for her self-image, elicited through her recent experience of motherhood. The projection backwards to the womb, the secret fount of life, becomes simultaneously a projection forwards to her future tomb. There are a number of points of similarity between Nucha and the black slave which ought to be spelled out at this juncture. Like the slave Nucha is a prisoner in her own home; she is repressed because of her gender, just as the black slave was subservient by virtue of his race; her life is a living death and, as in the prototypical Gothic plot, her experience of marriage is that of an individual buried alive, what might be called the mummy/mommy syndrome.

Some implications: Nucha's life is thus a truncated version of womanhood, one which Gilbert and Gubar would interpret as 'murdered', 'penned', and 'penned-in' by the text (13). But this raises problems with regard to her creator's gender: why, we will ask, does a woman writer put a member of her own gender to death? A universalist reading would argue that Pardo Bazán thereby fulfils the patrocentric law underlying realist-naturalist fiction; the plot is already given to her by the genre which she employs (or which employs her). A personalist reading would suggest that Pardo Bazán is projecting elements of a psychological dilemma in her artistic creation. There are a number of elements which support this second interpretation. The most significant is that Pedro Moscoso's uncle bears the patronymic *Pardo* de la Lage (my emphasis) and authors rarely introduce their name, or part of it, into their artistic works disinterestedly. Manuel Pardo is described as commenting to Pedro that he looks more like a Pardo than a Moscoso or a Cabreira (ix; 198), underlining that family lineage is not a trivial matter for Pardo Bazán's artistic purpose. *Los pazos de Ulloa* could therefore be seen as a projection in the person of Nucha, and also perhaps of Julián, of the unease Pardo Bazán experienced within the limiting confinement of provincial life in Galicia, as embodied by the social set to which her parents and, indeed, her husband, José Quiroga, belonged; Pardo Bazán had, we may recall, separated from her husband in 1883, namely, three years before *Los pazos de Ulloa* was published.[10]

An analysis of the depiction of gender in *Los pazos de Ulloa* reveals, at first glance, a stereotypical world. Thus the women in the novel typically cannot evade the patriarchal code according to which they are portrayed as either madonna or whore (Moi 21–49). Nucha's virginal quality and saintliness, for instance, are frequently alluded to by Julián; in particular, he calls her 'señorita' rather than 'señora', and he canonizes her mentally in the closing pages of the novel: 'la santa, la víctima, la virgencita, siempre cándida y celeste' [the saint, the victim, the sweet virgin, forever pure and angelic] (xxx; 283; see also xvi; 225; xviii; 234; xxvii; 272). Sabel, on the other hand, is deliberately contrasted with Nucha and presented as lascivious, since she cohabits with Pedro and tries on two occasions to seduce Julián, first by wearing her blouse open (v; 183), and second by pretending to faint on his bed (v; 184).[11] The men, with one luminous exception, are virile to the point of excess; Pedro is the Lord of his Manor and does not brook any disagreement, while Primitivo's name leaves us in no doubt about his character.

As Maryellen Bieder points out, however, Julián introduces 'an androgynous tension into a gender-determined narrative'

(134). Since he is referred to as either a child or a woman in the novel, we are likely to see him as characterized by what Judith Butler calls 'gender trouble'; namely, a sexual state 'in which gender does not necessarily follow from sex, and desire, or sexuality generally, does not follow from gender' (336). In the opening chapter, for example, Julián is likened to a child (i; 167). Elsewhere a set of associations are evoked—through the central image of blood or its lack—which place Julián within the bounds of femininity. He suffers from an 'encendimiento propio de personas linfáticas' [a flushing peculiar to lymphatic people] (i; 167); the connection between lymph and womanhood reappears later on in the novel, particularly in the speeches made by the doctor, Maximiliano Juncal, during Nucha's labour. Thus Maximiliano argues that a woman's sedentary life leads to a surplus of lymph and a lack of blood (xvi; 227), and is itself related to the feminine disposition of nervousness as epitomized by the term he uses to describe weak women: 'las linfáticonerviosas' [lymphatic-nervous women] (xvii; 230). So far Pardo Bazán is alluding to standard nineteenth-century medical/psychological knowledge which divided individuals into three categories or combinations thereof: the lymphatic (characterized by pale or pink skin, sluggishness, and physical weakness), the sanguine (characterized by a ruddy countenance and a robust constitution), and the nervous (characterized by flabby muscles, abrupt impulsive reactions, and mobile features) (Hemingway 33). But she genderizes this medical knowledge to produce a consistent association in the novel between man/blood and woman/lymph, which is itself supported by a patrocentric ideology which sees men as the progenitors and women as merely the carriers of the masculine seed.[12] Here, as elsewhere, Julián upsets the apple cart of gender. Thus, when Nucha laments, rather oddly given that those were pre-blood-transfusion times, that she would like to be able to buy blood, having lost so much during childbirth, Julián assumes a male role towards her:

— ... Lástima que la sangre no se compre en la tienda ... ¿No le parece a usted?

—O que ... los sanos no se la podamos regalar a ... los que ... la necesitan ...

Dijo eso el presbítero titubeando, poniéndose encendido hasta la nuca, porque su impulso primero había sido exclamar: 'Señorita Marcelina, aquí está mi sangre a la disposición de usted'.

'Is it not a pity that blood cannot be bought in a shop, don't you think?'

'Or that . . . we healthy people cannot give it to . . . those . . . who need it . . . '

The priest said this hesitatingly, blushing right down to his collar, because his first impulse had been to exclaim: 'Marcelina, here, take my blood which I offer you'. (xx; 243)

The primary reference here is Christological: Julián offers his blood in an act of self-immolation. His words appear convincing since they evoke an ideology which sets the woman in opposition to the man as 'saved' against 'saviour', and 'bloodless' against 'bloodful', an association supported by the social reality of religious rite in the nineteenth century, and to a great extent nowadays as well, when during Mass the (male) priest received the blood of Christ, while all others (including women) received only the host. Julián's comment, however, in retrospect takes on an ironic quality since there is a disjunction between what Julián appears to be (a masculine priest) and what he turns out to be (a feminized Don Juan). His offer to give his blood to Nucha is therefore ambiguous; the description of his 'blushing right down to his collar' hints that his intentions are not entirely innocent.

The association between the institutions of Catholicism and patriarchy delineated above leads also to one of the central images of the Gothic in Pardo Bazán's novel, as focused through the female gender, and particularly through Nucha, who begins to imagine that she sees ghostly apparitions:

La ropa que cuelgo me representa siempre hombres ahorcados, o difuntos que salen del ataúd con la mortaja puesta . . . Hay veces que distingo personas sin cabeza; otras, al contrario, les veo la cara con todas sus facciones, la boca muy abierta y haciendo muecas.

The clothes I hang up always look like hanged men, or dead men who spring out of their coffins wearing their shrouds . . . Sometimes I can see headless people; or else I can see the features on their faces, their mouths are wide open and they are grimacing. (xx; 243)

It is not fortuitous that Nucha begins to have these visions almost immediately after her experience of motherhood and of blood loss caused by child birth. An associative web is thereby created in *Los pazos de Ulloa* which groups together the seemingly different images of motherhood, bloodlessness, and death (the dead are, after all, prototypically bloodless people).

Yet it is when one seeks to investigate the specifically gendered components of the Gothic as we encounter them in *Los pazos de Ulloa* that the uniqueness of Pardo Bazán's use of this trope becomes evident. After all, the only characters who are sensitive to the Gothic plot in the novel are Nucha and Julián. Neither Pedro nor Primitivo, nor Sabel, nor occasional visitors such as the doctor, Maximiliano Juncal, shows any awareness of it; from which we must conclude that the Gothic is a plot played out, like a novel within a novel, in the interpersonal space between Nucha and Julián, and no one else. We have already noted that Julián is of ambiguous gender, since he is sometimes a child and sometimes a woman. Given that Nucha is female and Julián feminine, the Gothic must, therefore, be understood as a plot unravelled within the space of the feminine; it is the black hole within the patrocentric space-time continuum of the realist-naturalist novel. It is this black hole which, I contend, contains the undelineated homosexual relationship between two women, a *femme–femme* relationship which upsets the patrocentric Family Romance of Romantic literature.

My point here is that there are two levels of plot in *Los pazos de Ulloa*, the inner and the outer, the inner being the Gothic proper which concerns the interpersonal space between Julián and Nucha, and the outer being the interpersonal world of Pedro, Primitivo, Sabel, and others. In this dialogue between two spaces we have a conflict between two worlds, the first of which, to use Freud's imaginative terminology, is embodied by the hysteric, and the second by the paranoid. As Sedgwick suggests:

Call, for convenience's sake, the heroine of the Gothic a classic hysteric, its hero a classical paranoid. The immobilizing and costly struggle, in the hysteric, to express graphically through her bodily hieroglyphic what cannot come into existence as narrative, resembles in this the labor of the paranoid subject to forestall being overtaken by the feared/desired other. (p. vi)

Here we have a description of a struggle between the two worlds of Nucha as hysteric and Pedro as paranoid. Chapter xx is the point in the Gothic plot when Nucha's inability to express her narrative comes to the fore, as we have already noted; and Pedro's forestalling of her otherness is accomplished by killing her, or leaving her to die, or having someone else kill her, or whatever happens in those ten years which elapse silently between the end of chapter xxix and the beginning of chapter xxx.

Frankenstein has been read, in the feminist-marked Gothic criticism of the last ten years, as an act of womanly revenge against manhood's procreative pride, with the slogan perhaps of 'See what happens when you do it on your own'.[13] *Los pazos de Ulloa*, as a Gothic novel, certainly contains some of the ingredients which led to the creation of Mary Shelley's masterpiece; but it is better read as a *Frankenstein* in reverse. Rather than revenge against man's pride, Pardo Bazán's novel evokes through the character of Pedro a paranoiac-centred fear of female procreation, or, more specifically, a horror of Nucha giving birth to a girl rather than an heir. This, we may recall, is the point in the novel which seals Nucha's fate, and is the main event which directly precedes the womb scene of the novel which this essay has centred on. For the paranoiac plot the female baby is an image of the monster, the uncanny piece of life which cannot be slotted into the patrocentric loom. For this gender-specific mistake Nucha pays with her life.

As a postscript to this discussion, I wish to conclude with some observations about the historical necessity of the Gothic in *Los pazos de Ulloa*. In a cogent piece R. F. Foster has argued with respect to turn-of-the-century Ireland that the Gothic emerged there as a reaction by members of the Protestant Ascendancy against the changing social fabric, and particularly the emergence of a new successor class—the Catholic bourgeoisie—which displaced their position in society; the Gothic served, thus, as at once a refuge from an increasingly disagreeable social reality, and the symptom of the horror felt by the Protestant Ascendancy at the increase in Catholic social power. It would be inappropriate to apply a theory peculiar to the Irish context *in toto* to turn-of-the-century Spain (quite apart from the risks of disciplinary colonialism mentioned in the opening paragraph of this essay), but a historicized reading does help to clarify the social components of the Gothic as expressed in Pardo Bazán's tale. We have already noted a conflict between the enclosing energy of phallocentric realism and the enclosed feminine Gothic plot; in short, between heterosexual and homosexual textuality. This struggle can also be seen as reflecting the historical tension, in Spain at the end of the nineteenth century, between the *Zeitgeist* of the newly dominant bourgeoisie and the fading ghost of the Spanish nobility, a class to which Pardo Bazán belonged. (In 1890, as a result of her father's death, Pardo Bazán inherited the title of countess, which is a landed hereditary rank of nobility of the third rank, immediately below the marquisate.[14]) Therefore, the site of the uncanny, verbalized in the hieroglyphic of Nucha's hysteria in chapter xx, is the uneasy point of intersection in *Los pazos de Ulloa* between the birthing of the monster of homosexual relations from which the heterosexual text of realism recoils in horror, and the phantom-like presence of the aristocracy which would eventually be buried by the forces of history.

NOTES

1. Colahan and Rodríguez have pointed to the following Gothic elements in *Los pazos de Ulloa*: the castle, the feminine heroine, hostile nature, stormy weather, omens, nightmares, sexual repression, witchcraft, evil doings in the vault, unknown family ties, graveyard scenes, and anxiety (399–401). Feal Deibe discusses the womb scene in the novel as Gothic (217). Maurice Hemingway mentions the similarities between *Los pazos de Ulloa* and Poe's *The Fall of the House of Usher* (18). An excellent study of gender is contained in Bieder's article.
2. All translations into English from *Los pazos de Ulloa* are mine.
3. Brown argues of this episode that Pardo Bazán is making a comparison between the two men based on naturalist-determinist criteria (88–9).
4. For Spanish, and indeed the other Romance languages, Freud finds no direct equivalent for *unheimlich* but only approximations such as *sospechoso*, *de mal agüero*, *lugubre* [*sic*], *siniestro* in Tollhausen's 1899 dictionary; modern dictionaries list *misterioso* and *incomprensible* which likewise seem approximative, as if we were dealing with a peculiarly Germanic notion. English, while having the word *uncanny*, does not duplicate the situation in German since it never coincides semantically with *canny* and, indeed, is not in any sense a reverse semantic image of *canny*.
5. Here I am following Kristeva's notion of the abject which is a rejected element of personal identity which, once ejected, inspires horror: 'To each ego its object, to each superego its abject' (2).
6. Colahan and Rodríguez categorize this episode as an example of 'evil doings in the vault' following Brendan Hennessy's lead (400 n. 19).
7. I say early to mid-19th cent. since, if we assume that the events described in *Los pazos de Ulloa* 'take place over a period spanning a year or so before the Revolution of 1868 to a couple of years after the Septembrina' (Henn 125), then 1820–40 would be about the time that Pedro's grandparents would have possessed a black slave. By this time the African slave-trade was already illegal throughout the Spanish colonial empire, having been prohibited from 1820 onwards according to the terms of the Anglo-Spanish treaty of 1817. There is a further reason to suggest that the reference is fantastic; although the Atlantic slave-trade, despite its illegality, *did* continue after 1820 (being finally stamped out only in the 1860s), nevertheless it normally took the form of direct transportation from the west coast of Africa to the Caribbean via non-Spanish-owned slavers (Murray 14, 50–71, 298–326).

8. T. S. Eliot argues of the protagonist of *Hamlet* that he is 'dominated by an emotion which is inexpressible, because it is in *excess* of the facts as they appear' and therefore without an objective correlative (125). These words might be applied to Nucha when she emerges from the lower cloister.

9. 'To many people the idea of being buried alive while appearing to be dead is the most uncanny thing of all. And yet psycho-analysis has taught us that this terrifying phantasy had originally nothing terrifying about it at all, but was filled with a certain lustful pleasure—the phantasy, I mean, of intra-uterine existence' (Freud 397). Zola's 'La Mort d'Olivier Bécaille' (1879) is an intriguing, Gothic exploration of this idea.

10. For details on the factors which led to the breakdown of Pardo Bazán's marriage and her opinion of Galicia during the early 1880s, see Bravo Villasante (92–5), and the letter to Francisco Giner de los Ríos of 19 Nov. 1881 (González-Arias 24).

11. The implication is that she did this on Primitivo's orders since the latter is extremely annoyed when Julián refuses to take the bait (v; 184), thus differing from Pedro, who did fall into his trap.

12. Pedro's reaction when first seeing Rita aptly summarizes this view: '¡Soberbio vaso, en verdad, para encerrar un Moscoso legítimo, magnífico patrón donde injertar el heredero, el continuador del nombre' [A sturdy vessel, in truth, to contain a legitimate descendant of the Moscosos, a magnificent stock where the heir and bearer of the family name could be grafted] (ix; 200).

13. As Mary Jacobus suggests of *Frankenstein*, the 'monster's tragedy is his confinement to the destructive intensities of a one-to-one relationship with his maker, and his exclusion from other relations—whether familial or with a female counterpart. The most striking absence in *Frankenstein*, after all, is Eve's' (99). See also Johnson.

14. A surviving photograph taken of Pardo Bazán in 1890 when in mourning shows her with an aristocratic, if not regal, air (Bravo Villasante 177). Of course, R. F. Foster's argument about the religious components of the Gothic (i.e. Protestant versus Catholic) is not applicable to *Los pazos de Ulloa*. Pardo Bazán was a staunch Catholic; alarmed by accusations of irreligiosity on account of her *La cuestión palpitante*, she took the book to Rome and was assured by an eminent bishop that it contained nothing which was contrary to Catholic doctrine (Bravo Villasante 94). I am grateful to Jonathan Allison of the Department of English, University of Kentucky, for drawing my attention to the Foster essay.

WORKS CITED

BIEDER, MARYELLEN (1990). 'Between Genre and Gender: Emilia Pardo Bazán and *Los pazos de Ulloa*', in Noël Valis and Carol Maier (eds.), *In the Feminine Mode: Essays on Hispanic Women Writers*. London and Toronto: Associated University Presses. 131–45.

BRAVO VILLASANTE, CARMEN (1973). *Vida y obra de Emilia Pardo Bazán*. Madrid: Editorial Magisterio Español.

BROWN, DONALD F. (1957). *The Catholic Naturalism of Pardo Bazán*. Chapel Hill, NC: University of North Carolina Press.

BUTLER, JUDITH (1990). 'Gender Trouble', in Linda J. Nicholson (ed.), *Feminism/Postmodernism*. New York: Routledge. 324–40.

COLAHAN, CLARK, and RODRÍGUEZ, ALFRED (1985–6). 'Lo "gótico" como fórmula creativa de *Los pazos de Ulloa*', *Modern Philology*, 83: 398–404.

DEIBE, CARLOS FEAL (1987). 'La voz femenina en *Los pazos de Ulloa*', *Hispania*, 70: 214–21.

ELIOT, T. S. (1950). 'Hamlet and his Problem', in *T. S. Eliot: Selected Essays*. New York: Harcourt, Brace & Company. 121–6.

FOSTER, R. F. (1989). 'Protestant Magic: W. B. Yeats and the Spell of Irish History', *Proceedings of the British Academy*, 75: 243–66.

FREUD, SIGMUND (1959). *The 'Uncanny': Collected Papers*, trans. Joan Riviere, vol. iv. New York: Basic Books. 368–407.

GILBERT, SANDRA, and GUBAR, SUSAN (1979). *The Madwoman in the Attic*. New Haven, Conn.: Yale University Press.

GONZÁLEZ-ARIAS, FRANCISCA (1992). *Portrait of a Woman as Artist*. New York: Garland Publishing.

HEMINGWAY, MAURICE (1983). *Emilia Pardo Bazán: The Making of a Novelist*. Cambridge: Cambridge University Press.

HENN, DAVID (1988). *The Early Pardo Bazán: Theme and Narrative Technique in the Novels of 1879–89*. Liverpool: Francis Cairns.

JACOBUS, MARY (1986). *Reading Woman: Essays in Feminist Criticism*. New York: Columbia University Press.

JOHNSON, BARBARA (1982). 'My Monster/my Self', *Diacritics*, 12/2: 2–10.

KAHANE, CLAIRE (1985). 'The Gothic Mirror', in Shirley Nelson Garner, Claire Kahane, and Madelon Sprengnetter (eds.), *The (M)other Tongue: Essays in Feminist Psychoanalytic Interpretation*. Ithaca, NY: Cornell University Press. 334–51.

KRISTEVA, JULIA (1982). *Powers of Horror: An Essay on Abjection*, trans. Leon S. Roudiez. New York: Columbia University Press.

MOI, TORIL (1983). *Sexual/Textual Politics*. London: Methuen.

MURRAY, DAVID R. (1980). *Odious Commerce: Britain, Spain and the Abolition of the Cuban Slave Trade*. Cambridge: Cambridge University Press.

PARDO BAZÁN, EMILIA (1973). *Los pazos de Ulloa*, in *Obras completas*. ed. Federico Carlos Sainz de Robles, vol. i. Madrid: Aguilar. 165–283.

SEDGWICK, EVE KOSOFSKY (1986). *The Coherence of Gothic Conventions*, New York: Methuen.

ZOLA, ÉMILE (1976). 'La Mort d'Olivier Bécaille', in *Contes et nouvelles*, ed. Roger Ripoll. Paris: Gallimard. 803–30.

Gender and Journalism: Pardo Bazán's *Nuevo Teatro Crítico*

GERALDINE M. SCANLON

The *Nuevo Teatro Crítico* (1891–3), the monthly journal financed, edited, and written entirely by Pardo Bazán, is undoubtedly one of her most remarkable achievements.[1] Taking her inspiration from the eighteenth-century predecessors of modern journalism, Pardo Bazán hoped to create a literary journalism which would be both erudite and entertaining and thus fill what she perceived as a gap in the press of her day (1891*k*). The scope of the journal was broad: fiction, literary criticism and biography, social and political subjects, history, travel, religion, and cultural events. This ambitious enterprise, though novel, fitted within the mainstream of journalism and departed from the tradition of female journalism which, as recent studies have shown, was well established by the 1890s (Perinat and Marrades, Segura and Selva). Nevertheless, although Pardo Bazán deliberately eschewed the accepted models of a feminine-interest press directed exclusively at women and situated herself firmly in a tradition of male critics—Feijóo, Capmany, Addison, Nipho, Montalvo—she endeavoured to provide in the NTC a distinct female perspective of the cultural scene and reserved considerable space for women's issues. It was significant that she named her journal after the *Teatro Crítico Universal* of the Enlightenment thinker Padre Benito Feijóo, whose defence of the intellectual and moral equality of women had inspired the essay that had first won her public recognition as a serious critic in 1876. Despite modestly disclaiming in her 'Presentación' any ambition to pursue the broad range of reforms undertaken by Feijóo, Pardo Bazán nevertheless clearly shared his desire to dispel 'errores comunes' [common errors]. For her, the chief of these was undoubtedly the dominant concept of woman's role, an error which, she argued, was of almost the same magnitude in her own day as in that of Feijóo and which was shared by members of all colours of the political and ideological spectrum (1892*p*: 73; also 1893*a*: 273–4). Recent events—her separation from her husband (1883), the failure of her attempt to enter the Real Academia de la Lengua (1889), and the death of her father (1890)—had combined to invest Pardo Bazán's feminism with a new militancy: she herself later described these as the 'tiempos apostólicos' [crusading times] of her interest in the feminist cause (Letter to the editor of the *Voz de Galicia*, 8 July 1913, quoted by Bravo Villasante 285). Her proselytizing zeal found expression in her Biblioteca de la Mujer [The Woman's Library] where she published the feminist studies of John Stuart Mill and August Bebel, her articles on 'The Women of Spain', published originally in the *Fortnightly Review* (1889) and reprinted in 1890 in *La España Moderna* and *La Época* and, most importantly, the *NTC*. It was here that she was to find an outlet for that 'ebullición de ideas' [ferment of ideas] about the condition of women only a twentieth of which, as she had lamented to José Yxart, she had been able to express in her articles on 'The Women of Spain' (Letter 20 July 1890, Torres 409).

Pardo Bazán made her most obvious contribution to the feminist debate of the time in those articles in which she expressly addresses social and political questions relating to women. Since these are well known I shall deal with them briefly.[2] With admirable clear-sightedness and wit she challenges the ruling orthodoxies—the exclusion of women from political, social, and intellectual rights, their subordination to men and circumscription to a domestic and reproductive role, the medicalization of female sexuality, the double standard of morality, etc.—dissects with relish the outworn, sentimental rhetoric in which they were customarily couched, and proposes more progressive alternatives. She demonstrates an acute awareness of the ways in which gender identity is structured and, although she frequently employs the conventional positive/negative associations of terms such as *varonil/femenil* [manly/womanly], she sees no reason why women should not appropriate the virtues traditionally ascribed to men.[3] She is aware of the class-bound character of the anti-feminist discourse which identified 'woman' with the middle-class woman but her own ideological position is that of a bourgeois liberal feminist, a remarkably radical position for late nineteenth-century Spain, which lagged far behind other European countries on this matter. Indeed, Pardo Bazán consistently adopts a European perspective, citing the reactionary views of such men as Urbano González Serrano, 'uno de nuestros contados pensadores' [one of our few thinkers], the Marqués del Busto, the famous gynaecological specialist, or the Spanish male political élite as symptomatic of the backwardness and intellectual poverty of Spanish culture as a whole (1892*d*: 58; 1892*p*: 71–6; 1892*n*: 75–6). Feminist discourse is identified throughout as rational; anti-feminist discourse as vulgar prejudice.

Pardo Bazán denounces not only the dissemination of anti-feminist ideas by respected intellectuals, but also the invisibility of feminist issues on the Spanish cultural scene. She laments for example the scant interest shown by the press in the Congreso Nacional Pedagógico of 1892 in which the special section devoted to women's education had proved to be a forum for the exchange of advanced ideas (1892*a*: 95–7).[4] She herself provided ample coverage, publishing her own conference paper, conclusions, and summary of the debates, in which she singles out for special attention the contributions of the women delegates (1892*h*). Similarly, she complains that not one of the three lectures organized in the Ateneo to honour the memory of Concepción Arenal who had died on 4 February 1893 was devoted to her ideas on women, which were, she asserted, by far the most important aspect of her work. Not only, she observes, do these lectures and the obituaries of Arenal tend to omit any mention of her views on female emancipation, hiding them as if they were a crime, but they actually portray her as devoted to the 'labores de su sexo' [housewifely duties], converting her into a type that she herself described as an erroneous ideal (1893*a*: 269–72).[5] Pardo Bazán believes these deliberate omissions and distortions to be inspired by the well-meaning desire of Arenal's admirers to secure the benevolence and approval of the naturally misoneistic masses. She herself has no intention of pandering to prejudice: by publicizing in the *NTC* the progressive ideas of contemporary thinkers such as Arenal, Stuart Mill, Rafael Labra, Rafael Altamira, or the speakers in the 1892 Congreso Pedagógico, quoting the views of writers of the past such as Feijóo, Ximénez Samaniego, and Alvaro de Luna who had defended women, and naming eminent men who support women's causes such as their right to be members of the Royal Academies, she hopes in some measure to counter the stranglehold of traditionalist ideas over the feminist debate in Spain. She also seizes every opportunity to provide empirical evidence to refute the prevailing theories of women's supposed incapacity by drawing attention to their intellectual and cultural accomplishments. Much of her article on Stuart Mill is devoted to his intellectual debt to Harriet Taylor. She accords fulsome praise to the female participants in the 1892 Congreso Nacional Pedagógico, who have demonstrated, she asserts, that woman 'puede alternar con el hombre para los fines superiores de la cultura, sin detrimento de la dignidad, sin menoscabo del pudor, sin gárrulos desplantes ni descompuestas acciones' [can participate with men to achieve the higher objectives of culture without detriment to her dignity or modesty and without noisy petulance or untoward actions] (1892*h*: 71). She points to the lack of public recognition for female achievement: had Concepción Arenal been a man, she argues, by the age of 40 she would have been a university professor, a parliamentary deputy, a director-general in the Civil Service, a member of various academies, a person of great influence and fame (1893*a*: 290). She criticizes those reviewers of María Guerrero's performance in the title-role of Echegaray's *Mariana* who paid more attention to her charm and her costume than to her remarkable acting (1892*g*: 83). Pardo Bazán's treatment of the literary achievements of women will be discussed below.

Pardo Bazán was under no illusion that Spanish society was ready to revise current gender ideology but her tireless indictment of sexism was inspired by the firm conviction, expressed time and again, that no effort was wasted: that what today was in the minds of the most educated and intelligent would soon be in the minds of people in general and then in custom, art, and law. Victor Hugo, she asserts, merely miscalculated the time scale when he prophesied that the nineteenth century would emancipate woman, as the eighteenth had emancipated man (1892*n*: 72).

Pardo Bazán's concern with gender is not confined to her political and social articles: it also pervades her literary criticism. The latter still awaits comprehensive reassessment: contemporary literary scholarship, whilst acknowledging her contributions to the debates on naturalism, the introduction to the Spanish public of the Russian novel, and modern French literature, has concentrated on her creative fiction. The latter is undeniably more original than her literary criticism, which at times relied heavily on the work of others. Nevertheless, Pardo Bazán was much more than a mere popularizer of current literary fashions: her criticism offers a fresh and vigorous perspective which, as Zuleta suggests, owes much to her exceptional position as a woman in a male-dominated terrain (82).[6] Anticipating in some measure twentieth-century feminist critics who have debunked the notion of a value-free criticism, she insists that the most important requirement for a critic who aspires to exercise influence is the energetic affirmation of a 'criterio' or personal viewpoint (1891*k*: 14). Her own viewpoint is consciously gendered: she reads as a woman and makes a significant contribution to the literary criticism of her day by constantly bringing to her readers' attention issues relating to gender and presenting a feminist critique of texts under consideration.

In dealing with writers from earlier periods Pardo Bazán seeks to place their representations of women within the wider socio-historical and cultural context and to explore the relevance of these representations to contemporary society and literature. Thus, for example, she sees Dante's creation of Beatrice as symptomatic of the traditional separation of the life of the intellect from domestic family life: Beatrice's predecessors were the Greek hetairai who provided the literary and artistic society required by the cultivated male who fulfilled his duty to posterity in the gynaeceum. Dante's own life, she argues, was marked by such a division: for domestic and procreative purposes he had a real wife (Gemma Donati), but for all that implied the higher faculties—art, aesthetics, poetry, metaphysics—he created a phantom, because 'el hombre no puede comunicar tales cosas con mujer nacida de mujer' [man cannot share such things with a woman born of woman] (1893*c*: 207; see also 1892*n*: 59). Like recent feminist critics, Pardo Bazán questions the authority of authorial intention and, by offering a perspective different from that of the poet, she exposes the underlying premises of his portrayal of gender relationships. She perceives Dante's idealized image of Beatrice as fundamentally anti-feminist: how, she asks, can a real woman compete with a figure who is endowed with all possible perfections and untainted by any of the physical defects—grey hair, wrinkles, etc.—and moral weaknesses—lies, inconstancy, forgetfulness—that are the lot of normal women? (1893*c*: 208). Challenging critical tradition, she rejects the view that Dantesque love represents the apotheosis of woman, concluding that in reality it is the distilled expression of the disdain and hatred for women inherited from antiquity and the early Christian era (1893*c*: 206–7). The modern ideal of sexual union, she argues, is to unite what Dante and his age separated: body and soul, nature and spirit, the physiological and the psychological: 'La separación que en Dante era sincera y lógica, es hoy inmoral y reprobable, pero subsiste todavía' [The separation which in Dante was sincere and logical, today is reprehensible and immoral, but it still persists] (1893*c*: 212–13). Pardo Bazán's concern with the continuing prestige of the concept of Dantesque love is evident in her essay on Stuart Mill. Comparing the relationship between Dante and Beatrice with that between Stuart Mill and Harriet Taylor, she concludes that Stuart Mill, and the few who thought and felt as he did, had made real what Dante, Don Quijote, and the troubadours and dreamers of all ages had only imagined (1892*n*: 59–60). She thus rejects, as Bretz points out, 'the patriarchal view that female reality is incompatible with art' and argues 'that true poetry incorporates the feminine not as ideal but real' (83). Pardo Bazán is, however, ready to welcome poetic idealizations of women when their characters and conduct challenge traditional notions of femininity. Thus she is charmed by Tasso's Clorinda, the most noble and enchanting of a long tradition of warrior heroines that populate pagan literature and the novels of chivalry, who unites womanly qualities—sensitivity, compassion, affection—with manly virtues —boldness, loyalty, intelligence, nobility, etc. (1893*h*: 59–76).

Pardo Bazán's study on Quevedo, which was based on a work by E. Mérimée, foreshadows several of the concerns of modern feminist criticism. Correcting the androcentric bias of her source, Pardo Bazán focuses in her second article exclusively on gender, developing and bringing into prominence questions which Mérimée examines only briefly or not at all.[7] Although, as in the case of Dante, Pardo Bazán is curious about the relationship between Quevedo's real experience of women and his literary portrayal of them, like modern feminists she is particularly interested in uncovering for history the silenced voice of women: it is the exploration of the feelings of Quevedo's wife, which would, she fears, remain an eternal enigma, that presents itself to her as a most intriguing and attractive project (1892*e*: ii: 48–9). Pardo Bazán explains Quevedo's misogyny in socio-historical terms: such a satirical presentation of women is, she argues, typical of periods of political, social, and moral decadence and

his invective, directed not against women but against the venal
and corrupt society of his day, is a literary convention rather
than the expression of a positive conviction of woman's inferiority. She acknowledges, however, that, for the 'vulgo' [common
herd] at least, his campaign against women and marriage has
lost none of its comic efficacy: his work is still an inexhaustible
source of negative female stereotypes—*dueñas*, mothers-in-law,
etc.—and anti-female burlesque. Unimpressed by Quevedo's
status as a classic, she attributes his continued popularity as the
national comic poet to a failure to rise above the intellectual and
aesthetic demands of the majority (36–7). Pardo Bazán, however, regards the normative impact of Quevedo's misogynistic
humour as less dangerous than that of 'los serios y doctos tratados'
[the serious and learned treatises] of Vives and Fray Luis de
León (23). The latter continued to be recommended reading for
Spanish women in the nineteenth century and, as Pardo Bazán
insists, the contemporary ideal of womanhood differed very little
from that of the fifteenth and sixteenth centuries (1892*h*: 27).
This ideal comes under attack in Pardo Bazán's sympathetic
account of the life of Juana la Loca, which is based on a study
by Rodríguez Villa. Pardo Bazán, like Rodríguez Villa, presents
Juana as a woman driven mad by unrequited love but, whereas
he sees Juana in purely individual terms, she provides a social
context and portrays her as a victim of ideology as expounded
by Vives, the philosopher who replaces 'el culto de Dios con la
idolatría del marido' [the worship of God with idolatry of the
husband] (1892*q*: 69).[8] She presents her critique by embellishing
the facts with speculation as to Juana's state of mind at crucial
moments. Thus, when Juana goes to meet her future husband,
the Archduke Don Felipe, she comments:

Iba hacia lo desconocido, y lo desconocido era el ser casi divino, rey
absoluto del alma femenil: el esposo: aquel cuyo aliento, aunque fétido,
ha de oler a rosas según Vives, para la mujer cristiana. —Las enseñanzas
de la honesta madre; la doctrina del sabio maestro; los preceptos de la
religión; todas las voces que oye la niña como bajadas del cielo mismo,
se unían para decirla: 'Ama, adora, venera al que va a estrecharte en
sus brazos'.

She was going to the unknown and the unknown was that almost
divine being, the absolute king of the female heart: the husband: the
man whose breath, although fetid, must, according to Vives, smell of
roses for the Christian wife. The teachings of her virtuous mother, the

doctrine of her wise teacher, the precepts of religion; all the voices that the young girl hears as if they come from heaven itself, joined to tell her: 'love, adore, worship the man who will embrace you in his arms'. (1892*q*: 71)

Later, Pardo Bazán adds to Rodríguez Villa's simple account of Juana's despair when Felipe insulted and attacked her for having confronted his mistress the hypothesis that Juana undoubtedly reconsidered the matter and found abundant arguments in the social conscience of the period to excuse his behaviour and blame herself. Vives, Pardo Bazán insists, decrees that a wife must suffer patiently her husband's infidelity and he cites as an example of exceptional virtue, worthy of imitation, the case of a wife who for years humbly acted as a servant to her husband's mistress (1892*q*: 80–1). In contrast to this exemplary tale which implicitly counsels women against subordinating their lives to men, Pardo Bazán offers in the relationship between Juana's parents, Isabel and Fernando, a more modern model of a marriage based on mutual respect and collaboration (1892*f*: 22).

Undoubtedly the most interesting and original criticism in the *NTC* is that of contemporary authors and, indeed, it was in this field that Pardo Bazán hoped to make a special contribution to the cultural progress of her society by providing a criticism 'que alumbre y enseñe' [that enlightens and teaches] (1891*k*: 13). Most of the contemporary literature she reviews was written within the realist aesthetic and a central concern is the accuracy with which art mirrors life, especially in the portrayal of women— the 'peligroso escollo' [dangerous pitfall] of the novelist (1891*l*: 68). Constantly invoking her own personal experience as a woman or her knowledge of women in general, she confidently judges the truth-to-life of the female characters of her contemporaries: Pereda has never depicted a real woman except in *Sotileza*, unlike Padre Coloma who is 'el primer perito en psicología femenil que existe en España' [the chief expert in feminine psychology in Spain] (1891*l*: 68–9); Palacio Valdés's female characters are implausible whereas Galdós's are admirable (1891*ii*: 75–6; 1893*e:* 258), and those of Paul Bourget are inferior to his male characters, probably because he subscribes to the common but mistaken view that feminine psychology, unlike masculine psychology, is full of mysteries (1892*k*: 88)—and so on. She is convinced that as a woman her judgements of female characters have more authority than those of male critics: she hopes that Francisco

Villegas will not take amiss her affirmation that she knows women's nature better than he and, dismissing his criticism that it was incomprehensible that Echegaray's Mariana should devote so much time to studying herself and confiding her state of mind to others, she assures him that women of sensitivity, intelligence, and will-power are indeed tireless self-analysts, absorbed in their feelings, because society closes to them all the routes which provide men with an outlet for their energies (1892*g*: 77–8).

Resolutely hostile to didacticism in art, Pardo Bazán nevertheless believes that literature can indirectly incorporate a social or moral message and she reserves special praise for fictional heroines whose psychology illustrates the social oppression of women: Echegaray's Mariana, for example, or the protagonist of Luis Ansorena's *La fea*, whose despair derives from her awareness of the futility of the ugly woman in a society which circumscribes women to love and procreation (1893*g*: 147). Her enthusiasm is even greater for works which depict positive images of women and progressive relationships between the sexes. The type of woman character that most appeals to her is the one like Caroline Hamelin in Zola's *L'Argent* who combines the positive virtues of both sexes: well-read but not pedantic, Caroline has formed

un criterio amplio, equilibrado y tolerante como el de un sabio varón. Sencilla y franca, mujer en la plena aceptación de la palabra por el santo anhelo de maternidad . . . es hombre por la grandeza de ánimo, el desinterés, la lealtad, la rectitud, la facultad de entusiasmo ante las grandes concepciones y el amor de la vida.

a broad, balanced, and tolerant viewpoint like that of a wise man. Unaffected and candid, a woman in the full sense of the word because of her holy desire for maternity . . . she is a man because of her magnanimity, disinterestedness, loyalty, rectitude, capacity for enthusiasm for lofty ideas and her love of life. (1891*m*: 45–6)

Pardo Bazán found another modern heroine in Henny, the protagonist of Enrique Gaspar's *La huelga de los hijos*, a play she considered particularly deserving of careful review because of its feminist implications and whose author she described as an 'ibseniano español' [Spanish Ibsen] for his daring defence of woman's rights. To a modern reader Gaspar's feminism seems modest but the play did provide a progressive perspective on several issues: women's education, marriage, the double standard of morality, and female self-determination. Pardo Bazán constantly contrasts Henny's character and conduct with those of the typical Spanish woman. Brought up in the USA, and given by her father a solid education, freedom, self-awareness, and a vigorous personality, Henny aspires to a home and family, 'sus legítimos y sagrados derechos de mujer' [her legitimate and sacred rights as a woman] (1893*i*: 245). Lacking the coquettishness and false prudery of Julia, her conventionally educated cousin, Henny, guided by her heart and intelligence, has chosen Salvador, in whom she sees the 'compañero, al que nunca pretenderá ser amo despótico mediante el derecho del más fuerte' [the companion who will never attempt to be the despotic master by virtue of the right of might] (244). Henny's affectionate attitude to her mother, a 'fallen' woman in the eyes of society because she has taken a lover after being abandoned by Henny's father, is not, argues Pardo Bazán, the product of uncultivated and instinctive feelings but of mature judgement: she rejects the double standard of morality and recognizes that a woman who has been abandoned, insulted, deprived of her husband and daughter, would need the strength of a heroine and the virtue of a saint to remain pure. The fact that Henny makes no attempt to persuade her mother to renounce her illegal relationship and remake the matrimonial home is interpreted by Pardo Bazán as evidence that she realizes that marriage cannot be the union of two people who do not love, respect, need, or complement each other (248). Pardo Bazán perceptively points to the most revolutionary aspect of the play in a comparison between Henny and Mariana, the eponymous heroine of Echegaray's play, the portrayal of whose character she had praised in an earlier review for its break with the tradition of abstract female characters lacking in humanity which hitherto had dominated Romantic theatre (1892*g*: 61). Both heroines are the product of a broken marriage and fall in love with a man whom they subsequently discover is the son of their mother's lover, but whereas Mariana renounces her own happiness and in despair marries a man she does not love, Henny resists the pressure to give up her marriage and affirms her right to happiness. Mariana's mistake 'es el error común de la mujer: poner su destino fuera de sí misma: creerse algo referente a alguien, y no creerse alguien nunca' [is the mistake women commonly make of putting their destiny outside themselves, believing that they are something in reference to someone and never that they themselves are someone] (1893*i*: 249). She belongs to a long literary tradition of interesting victims, ever ready to suffer and sacrifice themselves for others. Gaspar's originality and the chief merit of his play was, argues Pardo Bazán, that he had abandoned female self-sacrifice as the mainspring of plot and made a woman who demanded happiness both interesting and sympathetic. Given the scarcity of such 'new women' in the Spanish literary panorama, it is not surprising that Pardo Bazán should have been disappointed with Galdós's *Tristana*, which she believes tantalizingly promises the reader that it will deal with woman's rebellion against social oppression, incarnating in Tristana the frustrations of millions of women, but fails to develop adequately this 'asunto nuevo y muy hermoso' [new and most attractive subject-matter] (1892*o*: 81).

As important as the demand for equal educational and professional rights for women implicit in much of Pardo Bazán's literary criticism is her demand for a revision of the prevailing code of sexual morality. She welcomes Orozco's forgiveness of his wife's adultery in Galdós's *Realidad* as an innovative departure from a literary tradition which endorses a code of honour which, although outdated and unjust, still enjoys prestige not only in literature but also in life (*1892l*: 60–2).[9] Elsewhere, Pardo Bazán consistently shows sympathy for female characters guilty of sexual misdemeanours and calls male writers to account for their implicit support of the double standard of morality. Uncovering the assumptions behind Padre Coloma's proposal that the moral reform of society required that a cordon sanitaire be established between virtuous women and immoral women, she points out that this is both impractical and unjust because it places all the weight of social opprobrium 'sobre un solo pecado, y de un solo sexo' [on one sin only and of one sex only] (1891*l*: 63). She scornfully dismisses the view that Alarcón's *La pródiga* is a condemnation of female emancipation, pointing out that the protagonist, Julia, far from being liberated, is so conventional that it never occurs to her to protest against the double standard since she believes in good faith that her past love affairs prevent her from marrying Guillermo de Loja, a man infinitely inferior to her in character, who 'habría tenido otros tantos amoríos y aventuras como ella, por lo menos' [would have had at least as many affairs and adventures as she] (1891*g*: 64). Here, Pardo Bazán has taken liberties with the text, which provides no evidence at all for Loja's supposed love affairs. In her review of the *Kreutzer Sonata* she applauds the verisimilitude of Tolstoy's portrayal of the breakdown of the marriage between the libertine Posdnicheff and his young, innocent wife, drawing attention to the fundamental immorality of such a union sanctioned and protected by law. However, she pokes fun at Tolstoy's defence of virginity as a superior state:

¡Gracioso desahogo de idealista empeñado en enmendar la plana del Autor de la naturaleza, que le impuso la ley de conservarse y derramó mieles dulcísimas en el cumplimiento de esa ley!

the amusing outburst of an idealist, bent on correcting the dispositions of the Author of nature who imposed on him the law of the preservation of the species and made the fulfilment of that law as sweet as honey! (1891*m*: 65)

This unabashed approval of sex within marriage is in itself an implicit challenge to nineteenth-century gender ideology, which identified the truly feminine with a lack of interest in sex. Equally audacious, especially for a woman, is her favourable analysis of Octavio Picón's defence of free love in his *Dulce y sabrosa*: a novel which, Valis tells us, was condemned as indecent by the ultra-Catholic reaction (142). Picón, argues Pardo Bazán, is a moralist albeit a heterodox and revolutionary one: what he proposes 'va contra la moral social y religiosa, sí, pero sin atropellar la ley moral universal o genérica, que ha elevado al amor desde sensación a sentimiento y desde ley fisiológica a ley afectiva' [goes against social and religious morality but not against universal or generic morality, which has raised love from sensation to feeling and from physiological to emotional law] (1891*g*: 59). She reveals a similar unwillingness to commit herself openly to Catholic orthodoxy in her refusal to take a stand on the controversial issue of divorce in her review of Daudet's *Rosa y Niñeta*, which she judges exclusively on artistic grounds (1892*k*: 58–9).

Pardo Bazán's literary criticism in the *NTC* is devoted predominantly to male texts and the only woman writer who merits a substantial study belongs to the past: Sor María de Jesús de Ágreda. The latter's *Vida de la Virgen* was the first text Pardo Bazán published in her Biblioteca de la Mujer and in her introduction, first printed in the *NTC*, she makes a strong case for the nun's inclusion in both the literary and theological canons:

'merece figurar entre nuestros clásicos por la limpieza, fuerza y elegancia de la dicción; entre nuestros teólogos por la lucidez de la interpretación' [she deserves to be included amongst the classics for the clarity, strength, and elegance of her diction; amongst our theologians for the lucidity of her interpretation] (1892*i*: 47).[10] Sor María clearly interests Pardo Bazán above all for her exemplary value: her character and abilities are 'argumento poderosísimo en favor de su sexo' [a most powerful argument in favour of her sex] (63). Claiming a place for her in history, Pardo Bazán highlights the nun's political role as the correspondent and adviser of Philip IV, so clearly her inferior in character. She points out with glee that it was he who displayed those characteristics (weakness, feeble imagination, uncontrolled appetites and passions, deficient reason, superficial judgement, inconstancy, etc.) generally attributed to women and which Sor María's biographers found so difficult to reconcile with the 'robustez moral, ciencia y enseñanza' [moral strength, knowledge, and teaching] of her work (64).

Although Pardo Bazán expresses admiration for established women writers of her own century—Fernán Caballero, Gertrudis Gómez de la Avellaneda, Carolina Coronado—she alludes to them only briefly. Likewise, she devotes little space to the creative writing of her female contemporaries. When she does review their works in the *NTC*, she strives wherever possible to make an explicit or implicit case for feminism. Discussing the work of three women poets (Mercedes Matamoros, Pastora Echegaray and Antonia Díaz de Lamarque), for example, she dwells on the elegiac and lachrymose tone of most women's poetry, arguing that it reflects the hardships of women's lives in a society which leaves them ill-equipped for the struggle for existence. In the same review she commends the widowed Eva Canel as much for her efforts to give her son an education as for the quality of her writing and attributes the formal flaws of the latter to her lack of time and tranquillity (1893*g*: 137–40, 144–5).[11] Blanca de los Ríos is acclaimed but less for her poetry than for her scholarship and in this she is presented as a welcome exception to the 'malas hierbas y flores cursis' [weeds and common flowers] of contemporary female literary production which, Pardo Bazán asserts, have never been so bereft of culture (1891*a*: 88) As Bieder points out in her illuminating essay, for most of Pardo Bazán's literary sisters 'literary creativity originates in inspiration (the romantic model), not in books and archives (the positivist model), and serves the didactic function of reiterating conventional values in familiar language and traditional genres' (24).

Pardo Bazán, however, is concerned with women's texts which challenge, not confirm, established gender ideology: female erudition is especially deserving of her praise and encouragement because it refutes current assumptions about the intellectual inferiority of women. In this she runs counter to custom, which, as Simón Palmer indicates, tended to extol the ignorance of the woman writer, which was considered to be a guarantee of her morality (42). Pardo Bazán enthusiastically reviews the Duquesa de Berwick y Alba's *Documentos escogidos del Archivo de la casa de Alba*, devoting as much space to the fact that an aristocratic woman should have produced such a work as she does to the work itself and, on the basis of the Duchess's introduction—a mere eighteen pages—expresses her confidence that it would be no difficult task for her to write a full-length historical study (1891c; see also 1892a: 88). Similarly, she emphasizes the solid research on which Blanca de los Ríos's forthcoming biography of Tirso de Molina is based and draws attention to the merit of such a work produced by a lady (1893b: 315–16). Elsewhere, she praises Marietta de Ventemilla for her vivid account of political struggles in Ecuador (1891b: 91–3); Gabriela Cunninghame Graham for her perceptive judgements on Spanish letters and society (1891e: 92–3); Sabina Alvear y Ward for her contribution to Spanish history (1892b: 92–3); Madame Sodar de Vaulx for her ability to say something new and moving about the Holy Land (1892a: 92); and Mercedes Cabello de Carbonera for her rejection of both the idealization of women in positivism and their denigration by the theologists of old (1893g: 152–3). Pardo Bazán also endeavours to demolish the commonplace view that learning robbed women of their femininity by drawing attention to the happy combination of the two: Blanca de los Ríos is timid, frail, placid but she also has vast learning and is tenacious in the pursuit of knowledge (1891a: 87); the Duquesa de Alba is both an elegant queen of fashion and a conscientious historian who has produced a work that is 'viril, seria, útil, cumplida' [manly, serious, useful, polished] (1891c: 75).

The *NTC* reveals Pardo Bazán herself not only as scholarly critic and vigorous polemicist but as affectionate daughter and mother: she pays touching tribute to her father (1892n: 68–70), confides to the reader that her worries for her sick 10-year-old daughter have disrupted her concentration (1892c: 106), and reports that she can confirm her daughters' statement that a play she was unable to see 'era muy bonito' y que 'habían llorado mucho' ['was very nice' and that 'they had cried a lot'] because she had seen their 'pañolitos arrugados y húmedos' [crumpled, wet hankies] (1892m: 96). She also admits to a feminine interest in such subjects as embroidery and millinery but sees these from a feminist perspective. Her discussion of the needlework samples which were to be presented at the Universal Exhibition in Chicago becomes an indictment of the inadequate education of Spanish women and a lament for what such work cost in terms of time, patience, and eyesight (1893b: 314–15; 1893f: 146). Her comparison of the relative merits of the mantilla and hats becomes a plea for women's freedom of choice in fashion and an ironical denunciation of the 'personas oficialmente serias' [officially serious people] who ridicule the study of contemporary female fashion but write dull dissertations on some torque or fibula found in a Roman tomb (1892j: 84).

Pardo Bazán's contribution to placing gender on the cultural agenda of her day lay not only in the individual articles of the *NTC* but in what the enterprise as a whole signified in her career as a woman writer. When Pardo Bazán began to publish the journal she was at the peak of her career: a well-established novelist and critic with numerous contributions to daily newspapers and cultural periodicals, she had played a prominent role in literary polemics and in 1891 began the publication of her complete works. She had, however, been denied official recognition when her candidature to the Royal Academy was rejected because of her sex.[12] The erudition and breadth of culture she displays in the *NTC* as she confidently ranges over disciplines— literature, art, history, theology, politics, sociology, philosophy, science, medicine, education—many of which were by common consent regarded as exclusively masculine, makes the journal in itself proof of the injustice of that rejection. Contemporary reviews of the *NTC*, using the gendered language of the period, emphasize her right to be ranked alongside her illustrious male colleagues: the journal demonstrates, wrote a contemporary biographer, the capabilities of her 'varonil espíritu' [manly spirit] (Anon.); Gómez de Baquero affirms that few contemporary male writers would be equal to the task she has undertaken, and

Mariano de Cavia refers to her as 'La Madre Feijóo' [Mother Feijóo], calling her an 'autor' or author rather than authoress because 'es mucho hombre esta mujer' [this woman is some man]. Even her arch-enemy Alas, in two reviews laced with personal and sexist insult in which he accused her of pedantry, ambition, fashion-conscious criticism, self-promotion, faulty erudition, and linguistic solecisms, was obliged to acknowledge her intelligence and learning, and welcome the contribution she could make to the progress of Spanish culture. Indeed, the *NTC* was to make a considerable impact on the cultural life of the day and impressed not only Pardo Bazán's contemporaries but also a younger literary generation. Many years later Pérez de Ayala recalled with nostalgia how as a young student he had read the journal 'hechizado' [bewitched] (56). The *NTC* consolidated Pardo Bazán's reputation as a serious critic and confirmed her place as a member of the literary élite. None of her male colleagues had successfully attempted such an ambitious enterprise and she may be forgiven for her somewhat smug report of how Valera and Menéndez Pelayo had embarked on a similar project and failed where she, a mere woman, had succeeded (1892*b*: 86–7).[13]

NOTES

1. Thirty numbers of the *Nuevo Teatro Crítico* (henceforth abbreviated to *NTC*) appeared in all: twelve in both 1891 and 1892, six in 1893 (Jan.–Apr., Nov., and Dec.). The average length was 100 pages in 1891; 112 in 1892; and 160 in 1893.

2. Schiavo reprints the principal feminist essays from the *NTC*: 1892*h*; 1892*n*; 1892*d*; 1892*p*; 1893*f*; 1893*a*; 1891*d*. See also Adna Rosa Rodríguez.

3. Compare her confession to Galdós that 'de los dos órdenes de virtudes que se exigen al género humano, elijo los del varón' [of the two orders of virtues demanded of humankind, I choose those of the male] (1978: 90).

4. Pardo Bazán did not deign to comment on Alas's accusation that it was her desire for notoriety which had caused the Congress to devote so much time to women's education, a question that in his view it was premature to raise in Spain (Alas 1893: 90).

5. The lectures on Arenal's ideas on penal reform (Rafael Salillas), her social ideas (Gumersindo de Azcárate), and her literary personality (Antonio Sánchez Moguel) were given on 16 and 23 Feb. and 2 Mar. 1893. Pardo Bazán's criticism, although made on the basis of extracts of the lectures, is substantially correct—only Sánchez Moguel mentions briefly Arenal's views on women (Salillas 44–7). Of the obituaries reproduced by Campo Alange (361–71), only that by Joaquín Sama, published in the *Boletín de la Institución Libre de Enseñanza*, comments at length on Arenal's feminist views.

6. The most original aspects of Pardo Bazán's *San Francisco de Asís* (1882) and her *La revolución y la novela en Rusia* (1887), which were based respectively on works by Frédéric Ozanam and Émile de Vogüé, were her comments on women (Clèmessy i. 26, 140–1).

7. The article heading reads: 'Quevedo's Misogyny; The Idea of Woman in Certain Social States; Woman is Merely a Product of the General State of Society; Venality; Satire against Marriage; Quevedo Marries; His Marriage Turns out Badly; Death of Doña Esperanza de Aragón; Portrait of Quevedo' (1892*e*: ii: 20).

8. Rodríguez Villa refers only once to Vives, citing his laudatory comments on Juana's mastery of Latin (10). It is interesting to note that Pardo Bazán published part i (*Tratado de las vírgenes*) of Vives's *La instrucción de la mujer cristiana* in her Biblioteca de la Mujer.

9. See her alarm at the increasing tendency of judicial tribunals to absolve so-called crimes of passion (1893*d*).

10. Pardo Bazán extracted and edited the *Vida de la Virgen* from Sor María's *Mística ciudad de Dios* (1668) to make it more accessible to modern readers. Another woman writer Pardo Bazán believed worthy of inclusion in the canon was Doña María de Zayas y Sotomayor, a selection of whose novels she published in her Biblioteca de la Mujer.

11. The only other contemporary woman novelist Pardo Bazán mentions is Pilar Sinués, whose *Morir sola* (1890) she records in the 'Books Received' section (1/6 (June 1891): 95) but does not review, nor does she include an obituary on Sinués's death in Nov. 1893.

12. Pardo Bazán, regarding herself as an excessively controversial candidate, abandoned her own claim to membership of the Academy and limited herself to the defence of the right of women in general and to that of Concepción Arenal and the Duquesa de Alba in particular (1891*h*; 1891*f*; see also Hilton).

13. For the journal planned by Valera and Menéndez Pelayo, *El Observador*, which was to have appeared in Oct. 1891, see *Valera and Menéndez Pelayo* 435–40.

WORKS CITED

ALAS, LEOPOLDO (1891*a*). 'Palique', *Madrid Cómico*, 417 (14 Feb.): 3–6. (Review of *Nuevo Teatro Crítico*.)
—— (1891*b*). 'Nuevo Teatro Crítico', *La Correspondencia de España*, Suplemento semanal de ciencias literatura y artes (15 Feb.): 1–2.
—— (1893). 'Congreso pedagógico', in *Paliques*. Madrid: Lib. de Victoriano Suárez. 175–80.
ANON. (1891). 'Emilia Pardo Bazán', *La Ilustración Artística*, 10/476 (9 Feb.): 84.
BERWICK Y ALBA, DUQUESA DE (1891). *Documentos escogidos del Archivo de la casa de Alba*. Madrid: Imp. de Manuel Tello.
BIEDER, MARYELLEN (1993). 'Emilia Pardo Bazán and Literary Women: Women Reading Women's Writing in Late 19th-Century Spain', *Revista Hispánica Moderna*, 46 (June): 19–33.
BRAVO VILLASANTE, CARMEN (1973). *Vida y obra de Emilia Pardo Bazán*. Madrid: Editorial Magisterio Español.

Bretz, Mary Lee (1988). 'Emilia Pardo Bazán on John Stuart Mill: Towards a Redefinition of the Essay', *Hispanic Journal*, 9 (Spring): 81–8.

Campo Alange, María (1973). *Concepción Arenal 1820–1893: estudio biográfico documental*. Madrid: Ediciones de la 'Revista de Occidente'.

Cavia, Mariano de (1891). 'La vida literaria: la Madre Feijóo', *El Liberal* (7 Jan.): 3.

Clèmessy, Nelly (1981). *Emilia Pardo Bazán como novelista (de la teoría a la práctica)*, trans. Irene Gambra, 2 vols. Madrid: Fundación Universitaria Española.

Gómez de Baquero, E. (1892). 'Autores y libros: *Nuevo Teatro Crítico* de Emilia Pardo Bazán', *La Época* (4 Jan.): 2.

Hilton, Ronald (1953). 'Pardo Bazán and Literary Polemics about Feminism', *Romanic Review*, 44: 40–6.

Mérimée, E. (1886). *Essai sur la vie et les œuvres de Francisco de Quevedo, 1580–1645*. Paris: Alphonse Picard Editeur.

Pardo Bazán, Emilia (1890). 'The Women of Spain', *Fortnightly Review*, NS 45: 879–904. Repr. in translation as 'La mujer española', *España Moderna*, 17: 101–13; 18: 5–15; 19: 121–31; 20: 143–54; and, in abbreviated form, in *La Época*, 30 June: 2; 16 July: 2; 3 Aug.: 1.

—— (1891*a*). 'Blanca de los Ríos', *NTC* 1/8 (Aug.): 85–91.

—— (1891*b*). 'Bibliografía hispano-americana', *NTC* 1/1 (Jan.): 91–4.

—— (1891*c*). 'Carta de la Duquesa de Alba con motivo de su libro', *NTC* 1/7 (July): 72–83.

—— (1891*d*). 'Con una alemana', *NTC* 1/2 (Feb.): 54–67.

—— (1893*a*). 'Concepción Arenal y sus ideas acerca de la mujer', *NTC* 3/26 (Feb.): 269–304.

—— (1893*b*). 'Crónica', *NTC* 3/26 (Feb.): 305–16.

—— (1892*a*). 'Crónica del movimiento intelectual en el centenario del Descubrimiento', *NTC* 2/22 (Oct.): 83–111.

—— (1891*e*). 'Crónica literaria', *NTC* 1/3 (Mar.): 89–94.

—— (1891*f*). 'Crónica literaria', *NTC* 1/7 (July): 84–93.

—— (1892*b*). 'Crónica literaria', *NTC* 2/15 (Mar.): 85–97.

—— (1892*c*). 'Crónica literaria y teatral', *NTC* 2/14 (Feb.): 106–10.

—— (1893*c*). 'Dante', *NTC* 3/26 (Feb.): 198–233.

—— (1892*d*). 'Del amor y la amistad (A pretexto de un libro reciente)', *NTC* 2/13 (Jan.): 55–72.

—— (1892*e*). 'Don Francisco de Quevedo con ocasión de un libro reciente', i: *NTC* 2/18 (June): 20–59; ii: *NTC* 2/19 (July): 20–51; iii: *NTC* 2/23 (Nov.): 19–60.

—— (1891*g*). 'Dulce y sabrosa', *NTC* 1/6 (June): 53–65.

—— (1893*d*). 'El caso del Pintor Luna', *NTC* 3/26 (Feb.): 261–8.

—— (1892*f*). 'El descubrimiento de América en las letras españolas: las conferencias del Ateneo', *NTC* 2/21 (Sept.): 1764.

—— (1892*g*). 'El estreno de *Mariana*, de Echegaray, o cuando Lope quiere . . . quiere', *NTC* 2/24 (Dec.): 49–84.

—— (1893*e*). 'El Maestrante', *NTC* 3/26 (Feb.): 249–60.

—— (1891*h*). 'La cuestión académica', *NTC* 1/3 (Mar.): 61–73.

—— (1892*h*). 'La educación del hombre y la de la mujer. Sus relaciones y diferencias. (Memoria leída en el Congreso pedagógico el día 16 de octubre de 1893). Conclusiones de la Memoria, leídas en el Congreso pedagógico el día 17 de octubre de 1892. Resumen de las ponencias y memorias de la Sección V. Leído en el Congreso pedagógico el 19 de octubre de 1892', *NTC* 2/22 (Oct.): 14–59, 60–6, 67–82.

—— (1891*i*). 'La espuma', _NTC_ 1/2 (Feb.): 68–76.

—— (1893*f*). 'La exposición de trabajos de la mujer', _NTC_ 3/27 (Mar.): 142–56.

—— (1892*i*). 'La Venerable de Ágreda', _NTC_ 2/14 (Feb.): 42–66.

—— (1893*g*). 'Libros nuevos', _NTC_ 3/29 (Nov.): 137–58.

—— (1892*j*). 'Mantillas y sombreros', _NTC_ 2/23 (Nov.): 84–95.

—— (1892*k*). 'Ojeada retrospectiva a varias obras francesas de Daudet, Loti, Bourget, Huysmans, Rod y Barrés', _NTC_ 2/19 (July): 52–109.

—— (1891*j*). 'Pedro Antonio de Alarcón', _NTC_ 1/11 (Nov.): 26–67.

—— (1891*k*). 'Presentación', _NTC_ 1/1 (Jan.): 5–20.

—— (1892*l*). '_Realidad_: drama de D. Benito Pérez Galdós', _NTC_ 2/16 (Apr.): 19–69.

—— (1892*m*). 'Revista dramática', _NTC_ 2/18 (June): 75–105.

—— (1892*n*). 'Stuart Mill', _NTC_ 2/17 (May): 41–76.

—— (1893*h*). 'Tasso', _NTC_ 3/29 (Nov.): 48–102.

—— (1892*o*). '_Tristana_: novela de B. Pérez Galdós', _NTC_ 2/17 (May): 77–90.

—— (1892*p*). 'Una opinión sobre la mujer: el discurso del Marqués del Busto en la Academia de la Medicina', _NTC_ 2/15 (Mar.): 71–84.

—— (1892*q*). 'Un drama psicológico en la historia: Doña Juana la Loca, según los últimos documentos', _NTC_ 2/14 (Feb.): 67–105.

—— (1893*i*). 'Un ibseniano español (_La huelga de los hijos_ por Don Enrique Gaspar)', _NTC_ 3/30 (Dec.): 240–55.

—— (1891*l*). 'Un jesuita novelista (El P. Luis Coloma)', _NTC_ 1/4 (Apr.): 31–72.

—— (1891*m*). 'Zola y Tolstoy (_El dinero. La sonata de Kreutzer_)', _NTC_ 1/5 (May): 35–73.

—— (1978). _Cartas a Benito Pérez Galdós (1889–1890)_, ed. Carmen Bravo Villasante. Madrid: Turner.

PÉREZ DE AYALA, RAMÓN (1961). 'Doña Emilia', _ABC_ (7 Sept. 1957); repr. in Ramón Pérez de Ayala, _Amistades y recuerdos_, ed. J. García Mercadal. Barcelona: Aedos. 55–8.

PERINAT, ADOLFO, and MARRADES, Mª ISABEL (1980). _Mujer, prensa y sociedad en España: 1800–1939_. Madrid: Centro de Investigaciones Sociológicas.

RODRÍGUEZ, ADNA ROSA (1991). _La cuestión feminista en los ensayos de Emilia Pardo Bazán_. La Coruña: Ediciós do Castro.

RODRÍGUEZ VILLA, ANTONIO (1892). _La Reina Doña Juana la Loca: estudio histórico_. Madrid: Librería de M. Murillo.

SALILLAS, RAFAEL, AZCÁRATE, GUMERSINDO DE, and SÁNCHEZ MOGUEL, ANTONIO (1894). _Doña Concepción Arenal en la ciencia jurídica, sociológica y en la literatura_. Madrid: Lib. de Victoriano Suárez.

SEGURA, ISABEL, and SELVA, MARTA (1984). _Revistes de Dones, 1846–1935_. Barcelona: Edhasa.

SIMÓN PALMER, MARÍA DEL CARMEN (1989). 'Mil escritoras españolas del siglo XIX', in Aurora López and María Ángeles Pastor (eds.), _Crítica y ficción literaria: mujeres españolas contemporáneas_. Granada: Seminario de Estudios de la Mujer, Universidad de Granada. 39–59.

TORRES, DAVID (1977). 'Cartas inéditas de Pardo Bazán a José Yxart', _Boletín de la Biblioteca de Menéndez Pelayo_, 53: 383–409.

VALERA, JUAN, and MENÉNDEZ PELAYO, MARCELINO (1946). _Epistolario de Juan Valera y Menéndez Pelayo, 1877–1905_, ed. Miguel Artigas and Pedro Saínz Rodríguez. Madrid: Espasa Calpe.

VALIS, NOËL M. (1986). *The Novels of Jacinto Octavio Picón*. London: Associated University Presses.
ZULETA, EMILIA DE (1974). *Historia de la crítica española contemporánea.* 2nd edn. Madrid: Gredos.

13

Exoticism and the Politics of Difference in Late Nineteenth-Century Spanish Periodicals

Lou Charnon-Deutsch

Nineteenth-century Spanish exoticism raises questions regarding both the significance of the representation of women as it relates to male sexuality, and the politics of difference in a Spain whose colonialist star was on the wane. Although the desire for the exotic dates back centuries before the period she studies, Lily Litvak argues that it played a prominent role in European art and culture at the turn of the century for reasons that are cross-cultural: a growing discontent with the 'sordid present' created by the industrial revolution (1986: 14), a metaphysical desire to explore man's origins following from discoveries in evolution and ethnology, and a conviction that such absolutes as perfection, peace, and liberty could no longer be imagined in a decadent Europe given over to material pursuits. Exoticism was a symptom of Europe's loss of faith in reason and its re-evaluation of a previously despised irrationality (1986: 17).

Litvak explores how exotic stereotypes fostered escapism while enriching Spanish culture, contributing to the bourgeois 'sueños de distancia' [dreams of difference] (1986: 250), but also opening Spain to valuable secrets about its own complex past. Her conclusion reflects a nostalgia for the exotic that survives even in an era critical of the cultural enterprises of dominant Western societies. This is because, as Litvak's work demonstrates, the desire for the Other is ultimately the desire that one has to countenance the other in oneself: 'nos acerca al misterio de lo otro y a lo oculto dentro de nosotros mismos' [it brings us in contact with the mystery of the other, as well as that which is hidden within us] (1986: 256). Exoticism, she concludes, helps *us* to find what connects *us all* as human beings (256).

Perhaps because of this uncritical approach to exoticism, with its ill-defined, Eurocentric *us*, Litvak does not explore seriously the harder questions that critics of Orientalism and exoticism have addressed in the wake of Edward Said's *Orientalism* (1979).[1] Some of the social and political issues relevant to a study of Spanish exoticisms include: the similarities between late nineteenth-century exoticisms and earlier representations of the exotic dating from Spain's Golden Age of imperialistic expansion; the relation between representations of the exotic and Spain's notion of itself as a nation in decline; the significance of the fact that many engravings appearing in Spanish periodicals were copies of originals by British, German, French, and Italian artists; the ambiguities of Spain's vision of itself as an exotic object for other Europeans; and the sexual, moral, and social postures that depictions of the exotic woman either reinforced or subverted in Spanish gender ideology.

In order to address these issues, Litvak's notion of the exotic must be broadened to include questions of bourgeois ideology, sexuality, and imperialism. This requires an engagement not only with Said's *Orientalism*, which Litvak dismisses all too summarily, but also with more recent appraisals of Orientalism's relation to European colonialism (Kabbani, Young, Bongie), and with exoticism in general as a product of dominant cultures. Most importantly, we must begin to approach the problem of gender as it relates to the various European exoticisms we study, as Lisa Lowe recommends in her study of exoticism and gender, *Critical Terrains*, and as Malek Alloula made painfully clear in *The Colonial Harem*. Using as examples a few of the hundreds of engravings reproduced in Spanish periodicals between 1880 and 1900, this essay addresses especially the question concerning gender and the exotic, while attempting at the same time to recognize the interstices between gender and the Spanish political order.

Said's definition of Orientalism is broader than the word implies. Strictly speaking, Orientalism is based on the distinction of Oriental from Occidental, but in the political context, according to Said, Orientalism is the general tendency of dominant, Western cultures to elaborate geopolitical distinctions that further Western interests, 'to control, manipulate, even to incorporate, what is a manifestly different (or alternative and novel) world' (12). As such, the term is somewhat of a misnomer, since this definition appies equally to Northern and sub-Saharan

Africa, the Near and Middle East, and much of Asia and South America. The notion that Orientalism has more to do with the realities of the dominant culture in which it manifests itself than the exotic cultures that serve as its object of study (22) can be broadly applied to the relationship between Western dominant cultures and all of the above-named areas of the world. But what is significant here in Said's definition is the suggestion that Europe's relation to its others is always a discourse 'of power, of domination, of varying degrees of complex hegemony' (5). Representing women of other cultures in enticing two-page spreads (see Plate 8) is not an innocent depiction of the beauty of exotic peoples but a kind of 'ethnographic alibi' (Alloula 28) arising from the desire to create a sexual text that can be manipulated, interpreted, and exchanged between artist, exotic subjects, and spectators. In the case of Spain, however, the creators and consumers of these images are sexual more than political colonizers of women and this is one of the things that may distinguish Spanish from other European exoticisms. In common with other exoticisms, however, the Spanish artist acts as an intermediary between his pleasure (sometimes verbalized in inscriptions) and the pleasure he subsequently arouses in the reader/viewer. As such he is at the same time a voyeur and a procurer of men's pleasure, as are all artists of erotica.

The exchange of graphic images does not just occur between males (whether colonizers or would-be colonizers) and the men and women of other nationalities depicted in the engravings. It is also a discourse between artists and the men who comprise the viewing public. Included in the equation, if only indirectly, is the Spanish woman, whose traces are found in the enthusiastic display of the exotic other woman. Although Said perceptively describes the Orient as the female to a male Europe, he is only nominally concerned with the implications of this fact for gender relations within Western cultures because his goal is to study the import of geopolitical expansionism on other cultures, not the sexual colonization that occurs within a given culture as a result of its obsession with the exotic. His insight that Europe collapsed so many cultures into its Orientalist discourse in order correctly to envision its world hegemony should lead to a parallel discussion of the way that Europe (including Spain) collapsed the female half of the world's population—both Western and non-Western—into unequal but equally reductionist texts.

When we apply Said's statement that Orientalism responds more to the culture that produced it than to its apparent object, it becomes clear that Spain's sexual Orientalism is part of a larger text that joined Spanish bourgeois women and exotic *other* women in a complex relation of similarity and difference.

In explaining why Orientalism so gripped the European imagination, Said suggests that 'it is perfectly natural for the human mind to resist the assault on it of untreated strangeness' (67). Extending this, we could say that women in nineteenth-century bourgeois culture formed part of the strangeness that needed to be comprehended and controlled. The overwhelming presence of the exotic woman in popular Spanish fiction and graphic art can be explained as a displacement of a text that engages the *strangeness* of the Spanish woman at the same time as that of her exotic counterpart. This strangeness is often figured into the gaze that penetrates the Oriental harem to its most intimate, sexual core. We cannot divorce this dream space from the closed social spaces of the Arab family that the European artist desired to penetrate, but we need to recognize that this need to penetrate the impenetrable also responds to a desire on the part of consumers of exotica to break down the rigid barriers that bourgeois society had allowed itself to erect between men and women.

Technologically advanced Western societies dream the dream of their own imagined wholeness and naturalness, before they became mechanized, materialistic societies. This collective dream and nostalgia, however, are not only attributable to specific stages in European national development: they are the product of men's obsession with the unresolved or underresolved stages of a psychological past that interacts with political circumstances in very complex ways. Fixation on exoticized women can be understood not only as a strategy to resist the assault of ethnographic strangeness, as Said claims, but as an effect and site of a psychological strategy and struggle to deal with the *sexually* strange.

Alloula argues that, because the artist-photographer never transcends the stereotypical in his depiction of Arab women, he is not important as an individual. Instead, he expresses the voyeurism of colonial society as a whole (131). I agree that the artist represents a collective phantasm, only I argue that, because its representation is ethnically interchangeable (a Moroccan, Turkish, Filipino, or Sevillan woman can be substituted in this dream of the exotic), there is more at stake than political colonization. It is not that the nationality of the exotic woman is irrelevant or that we should treat artists as individuals with unique unresolved psychological sexual complexes, but that we should see European artists as a group of men whose fears and desires derive from a shared historical experience. This, then, is the premiss of this essay: exoticism is a psychological mediation that plays a role both in international identity politics and in national sexual ideologies that determine gender roles at the level of the individual family. The fetishism of the female body not only interacted with the hierarchical positions of masculinity and femininity in bourgeois society: in its simultaneous disavowal and insistence upon difference, it constituted a favoured medium to explore what was both threatening and necessary to male subjectivity.

When we attempt to determine the ideal consumer of the hundreds of illustrations and narratives that presented a sexualized version of the non-European woman, and the ways that this *literature* impacted on Spanish gender ideology, the obvious conclusion to reach is that, as masters of this and nearly every other system of representation, it was primarily men who indulged in the pleasurable reading of exotic sexuality. Recently researchers of the exotic have begun to revise this rather pessimistic view of male systems of representation. For example, the masquerade of the harem, it has been argued, also reveals the uncertainty of the colonizer's proprietorship, undermining his authority even while staging a play of the 'Master's veiled Super-phallus' (Apter 214). However, to conceive of the harem scene with its Sapphic undertones as a utopian 'dream of sexuality minus the Phallus' depends on our willingness to overlook the double presence not only of the sultan whose total possession of the female is celebrated, but of the European interloper whose envy of the sultan's power over women is undisguised. In general the most available way for a Spanish woman to position herself in relation to the images reproduced here was to identify herself masochistically with the other woman as a desirable object of male scopophilia.

The overwhelming evidence of male scopophilia does not altogether cancel the notion of feminine pleasure apparent in some exotic images, but it does frame it in such a way as to make female pleasure completely available for male gratification. Rather than a challenge to the phallocratic order symbolized by the sultan, the European interloper-artist who improbably penetrates the Oriental harem repeats the scopic gesture of the Oriental man, revealing his envy of another man's possessions. The harem scene allegorizes not only the colonialist penetration of the Eastern man's territory, as Bongie argues, but the penetration of the female that the Arab man no longer has at his absolute disposal now that a European gaze has penetrated his pleasure. Placing himself outside the frame of the harem scene, the European spectator uses a surrogate—Arab or artist—to focalize his voyeuristic act. In this the artist paradoxically advertises both his envy of something that belongs to another, and his experience of the exotic woman as a scopic object to be enjoyed by other men.

For example, M. Gómez's engraving *Galería árabe de un harém* [Arab Gallery in a Harem] (Plate 5) depicts six Arab women that the author of the accompanying inscription sportingly offers to share with his readers (*La Correspondencia Ilustrada*, 2/337 (1 October 1881): cover). The writer specifies that his gift is not the women themselves—who belong to their 'dueño' [master]— but an engraving that *we* weary Spanish politicians might enjoy 'a solas con nuestro pensamiento y la media docena de señoras que contemplamos' [alone with our thoughts and the half-dozen women we contemplate]. The Arab *dueño*, however, has been supplanted as possessor of all this beauty because he has abandoned the women to their own devices: 'sin un mancebo que las entretenga' [without a man to entertain them]. Consequently, the tired politician is seeing something that the absent husband is not, and significantly more of the 'bello sexo' [fair sex] than is the custom for Spanish women to reveal.

The commentator promises that hours of tedium and weariness will vanish upon contact with this image. He assures his readers that he is not using it to masturbate 'nuestra severa moral no nos permitía *irregularizarlas* ni nada que pudiera resultar reprensible' [our strict morality would not permit us to *irregularize* them nor do anything else reprehensible], yet he invites men to mimic his pleasurable contemplation, so that they might 'sentir los mismos beneficios y sensaciones' [experience the same benefits and sensations].[2] The inscription specifies that pleasure is to be obtained by looking at, not interacting with, the Arab women. Women are best looked at; they exist as a reminder of the impossibility of any true understanding between man and woman. In fact, male viewers are warned not to gaze too long at the engraving, because looking too long at 'niñas guapas' [beautiful girls] can have a fatal consequence, 'La de tener suegra' [that of acquiring a mother-in-law]. Such misogynistic messages, typical of the periodical literature of the 1880s, propagated the myth that a great gulf existed between a woman's beauty and her character, and that men would be infinitely happier if they could possess the one without having to deal with the other.

One of the sultan's advantages is that in a group of six women one could hope to find at least one who passes for the 'Scheherazade' of the harem. The abundance of women available to a single man was an enviable situation in the mind of the popular artist and occasionally this envy of the Arab's bounty overshadows the harem scenario. Plate 6 by Mariano Barbasán (*La Ilustración Artística*, 14/695 (22 April 1895): 295) depicts stereotyped Western and Oriental gender roles, contrasting the excess of adoring women to whom the Arab sultan has sole sexual access with the adoring men fawning over two elegant European women. The inscription explains that the painting's frivolity masks a profound truth about the 'hondo abismo' [profound abyss] separating Eastern and Western civilizations (295), making no mention of the *abismo*, also implied in the painting's oppositions, that separates men from women in both cultures.

The abundance of women so common in the depiction of exotic scenes comprised a feminine mirage that exposed the sexual fantasies of the European spectatorship more than the sexual practices of its putative subjects. Ignoring any referent in real Arab society, the studio artist imagines women with their veils and sometimes even their clothes stripped away. He locates himself inside the walls of the harem and he dis-covers women whose clothes are dishevelled or transparent and whose movements are licentious and obsequious to the male presence outside the frame. As an *insider*, the voyeur/artist erases the barrier separating him from the secluded woman, who then operates as a symbolic representation of male possession. In the process the artist negates the superiority of the Arab man whose fortune is being laid bare.

For example, Plate 7 by Biseo (*Patio marroquí* [Moroccan Patio], *La Ilustración Ibérica*, 7/355 (19 October 1889): 58) shows a wealthy Moroccan woman being dressed by her servants. One of them, semi-nude and crouching on the floor, lifts her mistress's robe ostensibly to arrange her underskirts. High above and to the rear a man looks intently down from a balcony. His position, however, is not as advantageous as that of the artist who is on the same level with the women: the artist (and his viewers) can best witness the servants adjusting the woman's garment. The accompanying inscription reiterates the artist's privileged position that erotically invades even the harem's most sacred spaces. The commentator expresses an architectural as well as erotic pleasure in viewing this Moroccan patio. Like the architecture the women are graceful in their gestures, immersed in their intimate duties, and oblivious to the fact that they can be viewed not only from all of the open corridors leading into and out of the patio, but from all of the balconies and pillared arches majestically framing the master's position. Everything in this scene is harmonious and pleasing to the eye; from any angle imaginable, there is beauty—skirts lifted—to behold.

Plate 8, *La mujer en Oriente* [The Oriental Woman], a dioramic by Francis[co] Simm (*La Ilustración Artística*, 7/341 (9 July 1888): 'Suplemento artístico'), also employs architecture to situate its voyeurs and voyeuristic objects, although here, as is often the case, the harem resembles a brothel more than a living space. The floor is strewn with objects and the several dozen women who, in their abandon and untidiness, contrast sharply with the magnificence and symmetry of their surroundings. Rather than conjuring a scene of domestic intimacy, the artist dazzles his viewers with what could best be described as women defiling the mosque.

As in modern museum dioramas, there is an abyssal feel to this scene of *Oriental* activity. As our eyes travel from one scene to the next in dioramic succession, we notice that each woman or group of women is engaged in a different but like activity. In exemplary fashion, no one of them stands out from the rest, each contributes to the impression that Oriental women exist only to display to the viewer-artist the ways they are entertained or entertain others as part of the daily regimen of the harem. All the paraphernalia of the Arab harem, trays of *kaoua*, hookah pipes for smoking hashish, Oriental carpets, palm branch fans, tiger skins, boxes and tables of inlaid wood, add to the disorder and unstructuredness of the women's activities.

Most of the women are fully clad but a few are naked to the waist or nude, including the woman being carried into the room, as if to add (or return) her to the dioramic spectacle. This woman, more than any other, symbolizes the disposability of the harem

women. Her bearer, meanwhile, represents the artist embellishing his feminine collection with yet another sample to add to the
pleasing specimen case. To the far left of the patio a seated male
figure enjoys a privileged perspective from which to gaze on the
scene, but not as privileged as that of the artist-viewer, located
at centre stage by the looks of two women, one bearing a vase
and another lounging on the bottom-most step.

The pleasure that the artist imagines women of the harem to
be experiencing is the pretext for describing women as content
to be sexual objects, much as the scenes of happy, dancing black
slaves in the Southern US art idiom helped American society to
justify or adjust to slavery. Life inside the harem perfectly suits
Oriental women's childish, indolent character. Better for them,
as one commentator put it, 'la música instrumental y vocal, la
danza, las pantomimas, los baños, los paseos y las carreras en los
jardines y azoteas, los columpios' [vocal and instrumental music,
dance, pantomimes, baths, walks and races in the gardens and
patios, swings] (*El Periódico Ilustrado* (1865): 40). Contemporary
readers would certainly have recognized the argument recom-
mending feminine frivolity and capriciousness since it was used
repeatedly to promote the domesticity of Spanish middle-class
women. In fact, the description of the harem woman's temperament differs little from the stereotyped descriptions of Spanish
women, whom male authors (even the most gifted such as Galdós
or Valera) assured their public were incapable of sustained study
or abstract ideas.[3]

Often the harem scene emphasizes the generic over the specific, showing a class of women whose importance consists in
their number rather than their individual charms. As harem
scenes proliferated, however, a subgenre evolved depicting the
one woman who stood out from all others, preselected by the
artist as the best choice. The star attraction or 'Scheherazade' of
the harem, as the commentator of Plate 5 calls her, became an
intense focus of interest beginning in the mid-1880s and continuing well into the twentieth century. Some of the odalisques that
appeared in the pages of *La Ilustración Artística*, *La Ilustración
Ibérica*, *La Ilustración Española y Americana*, and *Album Salón* were
engravings of paintings by European artists, among them Conrad
Kiesel, Francis Beda, Gustavo Simoni, Eduardo Tofano, G. Gelli,
F. E. Bertier, and Nathaniel Sichel. Just as many, however, were
by Spaniards whose dedication to the theme of the 'favourite' is

well documented: Antonio Fabrés, Francisco Masriera, José Tapiró, and Maximino Peña y Muñoz.[4] In the dazzling odalisque of Orientalist painting the European gaze stakes its most ardent erotic, as well as aesthetic, claim.[5] Alternatively labelled 'la favorita' [the favourite] or 'odalisca' [odalisque] in Spain, she derived her meaning from her unique physical beauty and sensuality, her exquisite accoutrements, and the favours bestowed upon her by her master, to whom she is always sexually available and submissive. She is always, as the title of Masriera's famous painting suggests, *En presencia de su señor* [In the Presence of her Lord] (Plate 9, *La Ilustración Española y Americana*, 3/28 (30 July 1891): 55), although the identity of this lord is often ambiguous. Surrounded by black slaves and servants, bedecked in jewels and loose-fitting clothes, often with breasts or shoulders bared, she recalls an eroticized version of the Virgins paraded about in Spanish religious ceremonies (Alloula 62). Only she is never holding a child: her hands delicately hold a cigarette, pipe, fan, or musical instrument or seductively fondle her loose garments or hair. The viewer of these gifts is no longer the voyeur on the sidelines of the harem scene: he has completely penetrated and is in possession of the harem's most valuable prize. The odalisque reclines in languid readiness on animal skins, embroidered cushions, and Oriental rugs. The hookah by her side in phallic disposition, she is a drugged, perfumed, coiffed, and well-oiled body. With one tug on the clasp about her waist her *haik* would fall to the floor; no buttons, corsets, *bustiers*, or *European* clothing of any kind stand between this simple gesture and the woman's completely nude body.[6]

The Arab man is sometimes represented as the exalted possessor of the odalisque's ready charms or he may be there only by reference as in Masriera's *En presencia de su señor*. Most often, however, nothing stands between the seductive odalisque and her male European viewer-artist, as in Plate 10, *La favorita* by German artist Nathaniel Sichel (*La Ilustración Española y Americana*, 41/16 (30 April 1897): 264–5), and Plate 11, *Una odalisca* by Maximino Peña y Muñoz (*La Ilustración Española y Americana*, 37/21 (8 June 1892): 373). These pornographic images represent not just the colonial phantasm that Alloula sees behind the odalisque's popularity, but the sexual phantasm that presents the exposed female body as the imaginary evidence of man's powers (as well as his anxiety relating to those powers) of possession.

This power of possession is sometimes graphically depicted as a site of torture, enslavement, or rape of exotic women. In Paul-Louis Bouchard's *En el harém: cumplimiento de una sentencia* [In the Harem: The Sentence is Carried out] (*La Ilustración Artística*, 8/417 (23 December 1889): 'Suplemento artístico'; Plate 12) a group of harem women are being attacked by Numidian men holding ropes and sashes to strangle their victims. The central figure is a very white-skinned woman, whose unconscious face and semi-nude body are turned towards the viewer. Across from her a black executioner lunges toward her to carry out the 'sentencia'. In other engravings, such as Arthur Hacker's *¡Vae victis!* (*La Ilustración Ibérica*, 9/420 (17 January 1891): 36), women are being held captive pursuant to an armed battle in which the victors claim them as their war booty. An engraving of F. Eisenhut's *Botín de guerra* [War Booty] (*La Ilustración Ibérica*, 9/461 (31 October 1891): 696–7) shows a woman being presented to a sultan who lounges indolently on his dais as he inspects his war booty. Altogether, two dozen men of vastly different rank and privilege appraise the value of the booty, who is thus a symbol for what every woman is (at least figuratively) to every man regardless of class and circumstance. The woman highlights her speculative value by thrusting her shoulders back and her bust and mid-section forward. Significantly she is turned slightly away from the sultan, with the result that the viewer has a better perspective from which to judge the captured woman's charms than the man to whom she ostensibly belongs. As an image, she belongs to her European *captor*. Weary Spanish politicians who had not found a way to re-establish their influence in Morocco could at least imagine themselves as the possessors of the sultan's booty.

It was also fashionable to depict the slave market with its grouping of female slaves, either nude or semi-clad, surrounded by their owners or prospective buyers. For example, in Lexener's *Mercado de esclavas* [Slave Market] (*La Ilustración Ibérica*, 10/513 (29 October 1892): 697) a group of Arabs barter the sale of a seated female slave and in Ernest Normand's *Esclavitud* [Slavery] (*La Ilustración Ibérica*, 14/718 (19 September 1896): 605) a woman's robe is being removed by a man in order to present her nude to a reclining male figure. The face and upper portion of the woman's torso are turned towards the painting's viewing point and away from the reclining figure.

Despite the vague references to battle scenes or other events of great significance, the women-as-chattel engravings possess a timeless quality characteristic of the Orientalist art idiom. There is little to situate these scenes in any historical context, and, therefore, less opportunity for the European viewer to be distracted from the object of the illustration. Consequently, the post-battle ritual of possession and rape of women or their punishment for unspecified transgressions is made to appear 'natural', an appropriately remote screen 'onto which strong desires—erotic, sadistic, or both—could be projected with impunity' (Nochlin 41). This does not mean, however, that the popularity of these illustrations is somehow timeless. Because of the years when these sadistic scenes were popular (the 1890s), they could be interpreted both as compensations for Spain's loss of influence in Northern Africa and as inducements for Spaniards once again to exert their influence in the region. They justified increased intervention by depicting Arab or African men as cruel and barbaric, especially towards women.[7] On the other hand, the fullness and limpness of the female torsos, such as that of the nude of Plate 12, translated psychologically into an easily accessible (because it could be enjoyed at home) sexual booty for even the most apolitical viewers of illustrations. Like the men depicted in these scenes, viewers too are being presented with the bodies of captive women, over which they enjoy the 'limitless power' (Nochlin 42) of the scopophiliac.

Why the war booty or slave-girl is often a nude woman can be explained by examining the psychological implications of Western representational systems. The nude has a double psychological function that is seemingly contradictory. According to John Berger, the nude offers evidence of women's banality: nude women dispel men's fears of woman's strangeness because their bodies are not mysterious, they hide nothing (59). On the other hand, Lynda Nead argues that the nude, in her aesthetic symmetry and beauty, fulfils the goal of the 'containment and regulation of the female sexual body' (6) for the purpose of establishing not just sexual difference, but the difference between self and Other. The nude is a guarantor of the boundaries that separate the self from the space of the Other; all of her orifices are sealed and her imperfections smoothed out. In both of these interpretations the female nude offers herself up as evidence of her sexual category (Berger 59), controlling a potential risk either to male subjectivity or sexuality. Comparing Bouchard's *En el harém* or Eisenhut's *Botín* with Normand's *Esclavitud* we are reminded not only of the colonialism implicit in the exoticist's project, but of the need for the European bourgeois artist to make any and all women fully visible to him both as objects for sexual gratification and as a projection of psycho-sexual identity.

Spain's specular pastime of depicting and viewing female bodies participates in a collective psychological enterprise greatly facilitated by artistic conventions such as Orientalism. But its particular exoticisms are nevertheless bound to historical circumstances that must be taken into account as well.[8] Spain's fascination with the exotic is a complex phenomenon. On the one hand its Orientalism was a product of its abiding admiration for European culture as much as its interest in Oriental cultures. This is clear from the large number of engravings it produced both of originals by European artists, and of those by numerous Spanish imitators, some of whom seem more familiar with European artistic idioms than with Oriental cultures.

Towards the end of the century, Spanish illustrated weeklies also reproduced hundreds of travelogues and proto-ethnographic studies of African, Middle, and Far Eastern countries originally published by British and French explorers. Since Spain had no obvious political stake in many of the territories explored by these early geographers and ethnologists, its travel exotica were also a European import that can be attributed to the interests of European countries whose colonial expansionism was extensive in the mid- to late nineteenth century. On the other hand, Spain's geopolitical relation with Northern Africa, especially the Western Sahara region, Morocco, and Algeria, with which historically it held the closest ties, had long played an important role in shaping its cultural and political notions independently of European influence. The use of exotic tales of Moorish life and loves often provided Spain with an avenue to re-explore its own literary and political past that had so fascinated its Romantic and *costumbrista* writers. Tetuán or Melilla were not merely exotic locales in the Spanish imaginary imported via their neighbours to the North. They were cities filled with a mixture of Jewish and Arab peoples of which Spain had desired to cleanse itself for many centuries.[9] Semitic peoples held a grip on the Spanish imagination because they constituted the abhorred and repressed other half of itself. The beautiful Judith or Rebecca, the passionate or tragic Jarilla, Xarifa, or Zoraida featured in so many stories, novellas, and illustrations, formed part of a dialogue Spain carried on with itself about the sacrifices it had made in the name of racial purity. Spanish travellers abroad helped to keep this dialogue alive, and Spanish periodicals played a key role in popularizing the feelings of Spanish men who personified their love and loathing of the Orient in the exotic female figure.

Spain's fascination with the exotic spaces and women of Northern Africa, however, was not only a dialogue with its past. It also participated in the dialogue concerning Spain's ongoing colonialist aspirations and activities in Morocco. From the 1893 uprising in Melilla to the battles in the Rif of 1908–9, 1912, and 1919, and the 'war of pacification' of 1921–7, Spain would agonize over its role in Morocco. One sector of the population railed against costly and ineffective interventions, while the other, eventually identified as the 'africanistas', argued in favour of augmenting military and political influence in the region.[10] The countless images of sensuous Arab beauties served to reinforce what some Spanish journalists were arguing in the political sections of the illustrated weeklies: that through its inaction and bungling Spain was relinquishing a valuable prize to its European neighbours.

A third factor in assessing Spain's Orientalism/exoticism as opposed to that of Europe is the tendency for the rising bourgeois culture of the urban centres, Barcelona and Madrid especially, to *exoticize* the south of Spain. Many writers and artists looked no further than Seville, Granada, and other cities that played key roles during the reign of the Arab caliphs, for their exotic female types. In this they both imitated their European and American models, from Flaubert to Washington Irving, and influenced the way the north interpreted the southern character as indolent, sensuous, and passionate.[11] Increasingly Andalusia was imagined as the female to an industrialized northern Spain, much the way the Orient was the female to a male Europe, as Said has posited.

In Plate 13 (*Álbum Salón*, 4 (1900): 157) by artist José García y Ramos, a Sevillana represents not just the archetypically seductive Andalusian woman, but the city of Seville *herself*, whose beauty is a prize for the northern appetite.[12] The eager male visitor, writes the commentator, must surely surrender himself to Seville in springtime when she is adorned with her sweetest smile. A visit to the woman Seville is, we conclude, an orgasmic experience:

Esa es la Sevilla genial, la graciosa, la pintoresca, la que os seduce con
una sonrisa, la que os enloquece con una copla . . . la que os coge con
su mano redonda, pequeña, tibia, y os lleva a su catedral, a sus palacios,
a sus jardines, a su Guadalquivir, adurmiéndose con sus ojos ardientes
y despertando vuestra sed con sus labios húmedos . . . hasta que os
vence, os rinde, os subyuga, y abrasado el cerebro de tanta luz, pedís
aliento.

that is the delightful Seville, the graceful, picturesque Seville who seduces you with a smile, drives you mad with a ballad . . . who takes
your hand in her small, round, warm hand and leads you to her cathedral, her palaces, her gardens, her Guadalquivir, hypnotizing you with
her ardent eyes and awakening your thirst with her moist lips . . . until
she conquers you, subdues you, subjugates you, and, your brain afire
with so much light, you cry out for air. (157)

In an era when northern provinces were evolving into modern, industrialized societies, the south was stymied by agricul-
tural woes and exploitation by Castilian as well as foreign
interests. This exploitation was founded, in part, upon the premiss
that Andalusians were by nature paralysed by inertia, a feminized
culture ripe for northern intervention. At the same time, Andalusia was admired for what the north was fast shedding in the
eyes of Europe: the image of a sensuous and exotic woman-place
that had for so long comprised Europe's vision of *romantic* Spain.[13]
Thus northern Spain's portrayal of the south as an exotic woman
served both as a reminder of its idealized pre-industrial self, and
a pretext for a politics of neglect or exploitation.

In Spain's self-image as a country with an exotic underside
one would expect to find that the Spanish *gitana* played a key
symbolic role. The gypsy had long been a stock feature in European Romantic representations and by the end of the century
Spain had a relatively large and unruly gypsy population that,
despite the many edicts of the previous centuries, had resisted
full assimilation into local economies and customs.[14] But although
the Spanish gypsy was widely featured in Spain's literature,
especially its folklore and legends, the gypsy woman was not
fetishized in pre-twentieth century graphic art to the same degree that the Sevillan or Granadan woman was. She was not
without her allure as a romantic object—fortune-teller, flamenco
dancer, or example of spirited poverty—but she did not obsess
the Spanish artist in the same way as the Eastern gypsy did
other Europeans. In literature Spanish gypsies were often cast in

the light of unflattering stereotypes (cunning and mendacious vagrants, prone to lying and petty thievery) that only thinly disguised the mistrust and antagonism Spanish dominant culture manifested towards its disenfranchised classes.

Meanwhile, reproductions of German, Italian, and French paintings of seductive gypsy women of southern, central and eastern European origin abounded in Spanish periodicals.[15] The sensuality and allure of these imported figures attests to the power of the gypsy woman in the European imagination in general, as well as to the adaptability of the Spanish sexual ideology to this fetishization of the exotic, vagabond woman associated with dance, music, money, and (implausibly) sexual wantonness. The gypsy women's hair, wrists, and neckline are invariably adorned with coins and beads. Their loose-fitting blouses have trouble staying on their soft shoulders. Often a tear in the sleeve of a blouse reveals a plump forearm or shoulder, such as in *La cartomancera* [The Fortune-Teller] by Wally Moes (*La Ilustración Ibérica*, 5/213 (29 January 1887): 650; Plate 14). The gypsy woman is never bare-breasted like the odalisque, but her plunging bodice often advertises her sexual availability. On many faces there is a melancholic or dreamy look that combines with the dishevelled clothing and hair to produce an aura of orphanism and vulnerability. The 'Oriental' gypsy is a softened version of the 'odalisca' of Plates 10 or 11, but she no doubt appealed to the same fantasies.

As visually appealing as the women of the illustrations discussed here may seem, we should not conclude that European or Spanish women were somehow eclipsed by the exotic Other of the late-century press. To make this concluding point, I will analyse the absent image in an engraving that accompanied a serialized novel by French writer Marc de Chandplaix (*El fondo de un corazón*, *La Ilustración Artística*, 11/543–557 (1892)). The 18 July instalment, including a sketch by Émile Bayard (11/551: 459; Plate 15), contains an entry from the diary of one Pierre Larache during his voyage to Madagascar. Larache and the crew of the *Galatea* have been ordered to produce a map of a small island to the east of Madagascar called Île Sainte-Marie. The hero describes in detail his romance with the natives and the natural products he finds in the French colony. Bayard's three-quarter-page sketch of Larache and his black mistress Kaluvassa provides a remarkable synthesis of colonialist discourse, what

Griselda Pollack calls a 'prostitutional discourse' (25), that so captured the Spanish imagination. It also exemplifies the argument made repeatedly here about the importance of the consumer's point of view in the Orientalist artistic medium because it invites comparisons with European bourgeois women who would be read against, or alongside, the exotic island woman.

The walking figures are surrounded by lush jungle greenery, so thick it seems that they would barely be able to advance another step and leave their jungle paradise. Like a Hollywood love scene, the lovers are turned towards the viewer, the woman's half-naked body is slightly slumped against her European lover, and her rapturous face is turned towards his, but her body is in full frontal position. The caption reads 'Si una de ellas os agrada, podéis decírselo muy naturalmente, tal como lo pensáis' [If one of them pleases you, you may just tell her, very naturally, what you are thinking]. The Sainte-Marie women, exults Larache, are like beautiful animals; it is a pleasure to meet them as you stroll through the lanes of Ambodifototra, with their bared breasts and flowing skirts, always ready to be opened. The women of Ambodifototra will sleep with *you*, a European man, as quickly and easily as they would pick and eat a mango from their orchards. If you asked to go home with one of them, she would consider it a matter of simple hospitality to accept you into her bed. In fact, she can refuse you nothing, because she so loves white men, 'esos seres extraordinarios, esos hechiceros que saben tantas cosas' [those extraordinary creatures, those wizards who know so much] (551). For all of his admiration of the naturalness of his 'negra', however, Larache would not want to regress to the primitive state that Kaluvassa symbolizes. Steeped in the mythology of male progress, he reminds his readers that all return to the primitive is impossible (551).

There are pleasures which Larache can enjoy that the silent Kaluvassa will never know. While Kaluvassa sleeps, happy in her ignorance, Larache meditates about civilization and its pleasures as well as its discontents; he has a past worth recalling, while she lives only for the present. A rose will suddenly evoke a distant memory of his true love—Magdalene Nessey—while for Kaluvassa the flower cannot speak because she is without memories. There are some things that only white men can understand, 'todas esas cosas extrañas, exóticas, a las cuales presto una voz; todas esas armonías de la naturaleza que escucho . . .

pero cuya existencia desconoces' [all of those strange, exotic things, to which I give voice; all of the harmonies of nature that I hear . . . but whose existence you are ignorant of] (551). The heroine of *El fondo de un corazón* is not the silent Kaluvassa, but the inspirational Magdalene Nessey. Descriptions of her intelligence, wit, steadfastness, and especially her unusually white skin adorn nearly every instalment so that, by the time of Larache's encounter with Kaluvassa, it is impossible that any other woman will seem on a par with Magdalene; Kaluvassa is merely a foil for Magdalene's European appeal. The editors of *La Ilustración Artística* gambled reasonably that Magdalene would appeal especially to Spanish readers, with her dark hair and pale skin; she is passionate and devoted, but spiritual and civilized at the same time. She is a more suitable lover than Kaluvassa because she has a memory, a past. When Kaluvassa gives herself she gives nothing, her gift is on a par with a piece of delicious fruit that one eats and forgets while Magdalene's love is eternal, symbolizing a lifetime of sacrifice, waiting, and devotion. As elsewhere in Europe, Spanish periodicals were teaching readers to discriminate between groups of women, to understand the relative value of their female possessions.

NOTES

1. Despite many reservations, Litvak maintains that exoticism was a positive cultural force that destroyed Western ethnocentricity (1984: 19). Although she acknowledges the danger in the clichés it fostered (20), she regrets that it can no longer serve as an antidote to the monotony and featurelessness of modern culture (20).
2. Japanese and other Far Eastern women were often depicted in groups that vaguely resemble the Arab harem. The same discourse and groupings are used to describe or depict them as to describe Arab women. See e.g. *Aficiones japonesas* [Japanese pastimes] (*La Ilustración Ibérica*, 15/749 (8 May 1897): 397); *Japonesas* (*La Ilustración Ibérica*, 15/734 (23 Jan. 1897): 49); and *¡A solas!* [Alone!] (*La Correspondencia Ilustrada*, 2/317 (7 Sept. 1881): cover). This last reminds male readers how lucky they are to be able to 'contemplar indiscretamente' [contemplate indiscreetly] the Japanese women in the absence of the Japanese men.
3. According to Galdós, a woman dedicated to investigations of the 'idea pura' [pure idea] does not exist, at least in Spain (37–8).
4. Antonio Fabrés y Costa was born in Barcelona in 1854. A disciple of the Escuela de Bellas Artes de Barcelona, he also studied in Rome and exhibited his works in several of the *exposiciones nacionales*. Several of his paintings depict female odalisques, slaves, musicians, and servants. Franciso Masriera y Manovens was born in Barcelona in 1842. He gained fame in the 1876

Exposición de Bellas Artes in Madrid for his painting *La esclava* [The Slave] and went on to paint dozens of Orientalist scenes, of which *En presencia de su señor* [In the Presence of her Lord], *La morfina* [Morphine], *La flor preferida* [The Favourite Flower], and *Odalisca perfumándose* [Odalisque Perfuming Herself] were extremely popular. José Tapiró was born in Reus (Tarragona) in 1836 and died in Tangiers in 1913. A disciple of Federico de Madrazo, he spent most of his career in Rome and Tangiers, where he dedicated himself to portraying *tipos y costumbres* of the Arab world. Maximino Peña y Muñoz was born in Salduero (Soria) in 1863. His painting covers a broad range of topics but is dominated by portraits of women, among them gypsies, *chulas*, orphans, odalisques, and seamstresses.

5. The word odalisque appears in French early in the 17th cent. It comes from the Turkish *odaliq*, meaning chambermaid: 'Initially a chambermaid or a slave in the service of the women of the harem, the odalisque was metamorphosed by Orientalist painting ... into the sublimated image of the one enclosed by the harem. This jewel of the prohibited space is endowed by the Western imagination with a strong erotic connotation' (Alloula 130–1 n. 24).

6. Among the many possible examples, see *En el harén* by H. Berger (*La Ilustración Española y Americana*, 34/15 (22 Apr. 1890): 249); *La canción predilecta del sultán* [The Sultan's Favourite Song] by Antonio Fabrés (*La Ilustración Artística*, 17/870 (29 Aug. 1899): 561); *Odalisca* by Nathaniel Sichel (*La Ilustración Ibérica*, 3/119 (11 Apr. 1885): 228); *Una odalisca* by Eduardo Tofano, (*La Ilustración Ibérica*, 7/339 (29 June 1889): 412); *Odalisca* by C. Gelli (*La Ilustración Ibérica*, 7/356 (26 Oct. 1889): 676); *La favorita* by Conrad(o) Kiesel (*La Ilustración Artística*, 6/303 (17 Oct. 1887): 388); *La favorita* by Antonio Fabrés (*La Ilustración Artística*, 7/541 (9 May 1892): 295); *El tocado de la favorita* [The Favourite's Coiffure] (*La Ilustración Artística*, 10/489 (11 May 1891): 289); *En el harém* by J. Echena (*La Ilustración Artística*, 6/283 (30 May 1887): 179); *Mujeres del harén* by F. E. Bertier (*La Ilustración Española y Americana*, 34/29 (8 Aug. 1890): 72); *El harém* by A. de Cramer (*La Ilustración de la Mujer*, 2/17 (4 Feb. 1884): 136); and *En el serrallo* [In the Harem] by Nathaniel Sichel (*La Ilustración Ibérica*, 7/565 (30 Sept. 1893): 616).

7. See also Modesto Faustini's *La prueba judiciaria* [The Judicial Trial] (*La Ilustración Ibérica*, 6/306 (10 Nov. 1888): 716), in which an angry dark-skinned Turk prepares to punish his fair-skinned favourite who lies with her partially clothed body against his. In one hand he clutches a sword, in the other the woman's forearm.

8. e.g. in 1880 Spain convened an international conference to sort out the complicated political interests in Morocco. The conference resulted in an accord that was signed by the sultan of Morocco. But both before and during the time the treaty was in effect, the French and Italians benefited from Spain's lack of political and military intervention by expanding their influence in the region. An accord between France and Spain was reached on the division of zones of interest in Morocco in 1904, but by 1912 yet another accord between France and Spain reduced the Spanish protectorate to the northernmost regions of Morocco (Martínez Cuadrado 48–9, 476–7).

9. Spain's obsession with racial purity has a long and tortuous history beginning even before the Inquisition. Nearly every king before the 18th cent. attempted to Christianize Spain by expelling those who refused to conform in dress and religious customs to the dominant race. Between 1609 and

1614 from 275,000 to 300,000 Moriscos were expelled from Spain (Burshatin 113), completing the expulsion of the Moriscos from Spanish territory. Jews were expelled long before, in 1492, by the Catholic Kings. These expulsions were never *successful*, in the sense that, as Israel Burshatin argues, in certain regions of Spain large numbers of Moriscos flourished after the expulsions. The eradication of Jews was more complete, but Spain's obsession with *pureza de sangre* [racial purity] and its deep anti-Semitism are no doubt vestiges of the long centuries when the *judaizantes* [Judaizers] reminded Spain of its racial impurity.

10. Spain finally resigned her protectorate in 1956, leaving 'a poor infrastructure and an impoverished population, the overwhelming majority illiterate' (Driessen 65).

11. Among the Europeans who spread the notion of Spain's exotic character are Victor Hugo (*Les Orientales*), Byron, François René de Chateaubriand (*Les Aventures du dernier Abencérage*), Heinrich Heine (*Almansor*), Théophile Gautier (*Voyage en Espagne*), and artists Henri Regnault, Giroult de Prongey, John Phillips, and Alfred Dehodencq.

12. For other examples of this identification between cities and Andalusian women, see *Un rinconcito de Sevilla* [A Corner of Seville] (by José García y Ramos, *La Ilustración Española y Americana*, 37/1 (8 Jan. 1893): 8), showing a group of Sevillan women one of whom stares arrogantly and seductively out of the frame; *Por Sevilla* by Manuel de la Rosa (*La Ilustración Española y Americana*, 33/16 (8 Apr. 1889): 249), depicting a seated woman raising a glass of wine in her right hand as she fingers the clothing on her hip and turns in her chair to smile complacently out of the frame; *Sevillana* (*La Ilustración Artística*, 20/1027 (1 Sept. 1901): 576), showing a seductive woman with her head cocked and resting on her left hand while her right hand is posed on her hip; and *La florista granadina* [The Granadan Flowergirl] (*La Ilustración Artística*, 7/337 (11 June 1888): 193), showing an elegantly dressed woman offering a flower to the viewer with her left hand, with her right hand seductively posed on her hip and stomach.

13. See Jullian 115–16 for an account of several European visions of romantic Andalusian cities. Most notable is Henri Regnault's description of the Alhambra which rivals Seville's seductions: 'My divine mistress Alhambra calls me: she has sent me one of her lovers, the sun, to let me know she has finished her preparations and is already beautiful and ready to receive me' (Jullian 115). This attitude towards the south, especially Seville and Granada, was echoed by Spanish writers well into the 20th cent. See e.g. Emilia Pardo Bazán's 1911 novel *Dulce dueño* [Sweet Master], in which the Alhambra exerts a mystical power over the emotions of the heroine.

14. Spain's effort to control or expel its gypsies, although dating back to the same moment in the reign of Ferdinand and Isabel when Jews and peoples of Arab descent were required to assimilate or be expelled from Spain, never resulted in the eradication of the gypsy language, occupations, lifestyle, or communities. Edicts (1633, 1783) proclaiming that there was no such thing as a gypsy, only vagabonds who should be incorporated into *normal* occupations and established in fixed communities, failed to erase gypsy culture.

15. For samples of Spanish gypsies painted by foreign artists, see H. Schlesinger's *Una zíngara* [A Gypsy] (*La Ilustración Ibérica*, 3/125 (23 May 1885): 321) and *Danza gitana* [Gypsy Dance] by A. H. Schram (*La Ilustración Artística*, 16/822 (27 Sept. 1897): 625).

WORKS CITED

ALLOULA, MALEK (1986). *The Colonial Harem*, trans. Myrna Godzich and Wlad Godzich, introd. Barbara Harlow. Minneapolis: University of Minnesota Press.

APTER, EMILY (1992). 'Female Trouble in the Colonial Harem', *Differences*, 4/1 (Spring): 205–24.

BERGER, JOHN (1985). *Ways of Seeing*. Repr. London: Penguin.

BONGIE, CHRIS (1991). *Exotic Memories: Literature, Colonialism, and the Fin de Siècle*. Stanford, Calif.: University of Stanford Press.

BURSHATIN, ISRAEL (1985). 'The Moor in the Text: Metaphor, Emblem, and Silence', *Critical Inquiry*, 12/1 (Autumn): 98–118.

DRIESSEN, HENK (1987). 'Images of Spanish Colonialism in the Rif: An Essay in Historical Anthropology and Photography', *Critique of Anthropology*, 7/1: 53–66.

JULLIAN, PHILIPPE (1977). *The Orientalists: European Painters of Eastern Scenes*. Oxford: Phaidon.

KABBANI, RANA (1987). *Europe's Myths of the Orient*. Bloomington, Ind.: Indiana University Press. (London: Pandora, 1988.)

LITVAK, LILY (1984). *Geografías mágicas: viajeros españoles del siglo XIX por países exóticos (1800–1913)*. Barcelona: Laertes.

—— (1986). *El sendero del tigre: exotismo en la literatura española de finales del siglo XIX, 1880–1913*. Madrid: Taurus.

LOWE, LISA (1991). *Critical Terrains: French and British Orientalisms*. Ithaca, NY: Cornell University Press.

MARTÍNEZ CUADRADO, MIGUEL (1991). *Restauración y crisis de la monarquía, 1874–1931*. vol. vi of Miguel Artola (ed.), *Historia de España*. Madrid: Alianza Editorial.

NEAD, LYNDA (1992). *The Female Nude: Art, Obscenity and Sexuality*. London: Routledge.

NOCHLIN, LINDA (1989). *The Politics of Vision: Essays on Nineteenth-Century Art and Society*. New York: Harper & Row.

PÉREZ GALDÓS, BENITO (1944). 'La mujer del filósofo', in *Mujeres españoles del siglo XIX*, ed. Roberto Robert. Madrid: Atlas. 36–47. (Repr. from *Las españolas pintadas por los españoles*. Madrid: 1871–2.)

SAID, EDWARD (1978). *Orientalism*. New York: Pantheon.

YOUNG, ROBERT (1990). *White Mythologies: Writing History and the West*. New York: Routledge.

Index

WITHDRAWN

Gramley Library
Salem Academy and College
Winston-Salem, N.C. 27108